WARFARE AND SOCIETY
IN THE BARBARIAN WEST,
450–900

Warfare was an integral part of early medieval life. It had a character of its own and was neither a pale shadow of Roman military practice nor an insignificant precursor to the warfare of the central Middle Ages. This book recovers its distinctiveness, looking at warfare in a rounded context in the British Isles and western Europe between the end of the Roman Empire and the break-up of the Carolingian Empire. The era was one of great changes in the practice of war.

Guy Halsall relates warfare to many aspects of medieval life, economy, society and politics. He examines the raising and organisation of early medieval armies and looks at the conduct of campaigns. The survey includes the equipment of warriors and the horrific experience of battle as well as an analysis of medieval fortifications and siege warfare.

Warfare and Society in the Barbarian West uses historical and archaeological evidence in a rigorous and sophisticated fashion. It stresses regional variations but also places Anglo-Saxon England in the mainstream of the military developments in this era.

Guy Halsall is lecturer in medieval history at the University of York. He has published widely on the social history and archaeology of Merovingian Gaul and on violence in early medieval society, including *Settlement and Social Organisation. The Merovingian Region of Metz* (Cambridge, 1995).

WARFARE AND HISTORY
General Editor, Jeremy Black
Professor of History, University of Exeter

WARFARE AND SOCIETY IN THE BARBARIAN WEST, 450–900

Guy Halsall

Routledge
Taylor & Francis Group

LONDON AND NEW YORK

First published 2003
by Routledge
2 Park Square, Milton Park, Abingdon, Oxon, OX14 4RN

Simultaneously published in the USA and Canada
by Routledge
270 Madison Avenue, New York, NY 10016

Routledge is an imprint of the Taylor & Francis Group

© 2003 Guy Halsall

Typeset in Bembo by Keystroke, Jacaranda Lodge, Wolverhampton

British Library Cataloguing in Publication Data
A catalogue record for this book is available from the British Library

Library of Congress Cataloging in Publication Data
Halsall, Guy.
Warfare and society in the barbarian West, 450–900 / Guy Halsall.
p. cm.
Includes bibliographical references and index.
1. Military art and science—Europe, Western—History—To 900.
2. Europe, Western—History, Military—To 1500. I. Title.
U37.H357 2003
355′.0094′0902—dc21

2002013881

0–415–23939–7 (hbk)
0–415–23940–0 (pbk)

FOR MY TEACHERS

CONTENTS

ILLUSTRATIONS

Maps

Figures

ACKNOWLEDGEMENTS

This volume has been a long time in gestation and in many ways has had a difficult birth. I am immensely grateful to my editors at Routledge for their patience! I have accumulated a substantial number of other personal and professional debts in the difficult years during which this book was being written.

My colleagues in the School of History, Classics and Archaeology at Birkbeck College provided a fine environment in which to work and to study history at the highest level. My Birkbeck students, especially on my 'Barbarian Migrations in Archaeology and History' and 'Urbanism in the First Millennium' courses, have inspired, helped and usefully criticised my thinking on the early Middle Ages. They have also borne my digressions into the politics of the raising of armies – often during seminars on completely different subjects – with exemplary forbearance! Steve Neate, a survivor of 'Barbarians', read the entire draft, made many helpful suggestions and spotted innumerable 'typos'. Overall, my students' input into this volume (as one put it, 'a history of violent chancers', which just about sums it up) is much more considerable than they realise.

To write a book covering 450 years of the history of most of western Europe is, if one is honest, to walk into the caverns of one's ignorance. I have been enormously fortunate to have had the assistance of numerous guides and lantern-bearers. Paul Fouracre read the whole book in draft and made many helpful observations, all of which have significantly improved the final version. I hope he has gained as much as I have from our debates on the nature of early medieval societies and politics over the last decade or so. Chris Wickham also read most of the volume, has been a merciless scourge of my woolly thinking and saved me from several factual errors in the process. Any qualities the Carolingian section may have are thanks in large part to thorough and critical reading (of more than one draft) by Simon MacLean. Kate Cooper, Falco Daim, Wendy Davies, Julio Escalona Monge, Mark Handley, Matthew Innes, Charles Insley, Jon Jarrett, Ryan Lavelle, Julia Smith and the late and much missed Tim Reuter have all provided discussions, help, information and references. Charles, Ryan and Tim also read substantial sections of the book and provided invaluable feedback. I have not always followed the advice I have been given, so although all the above have played an important part in giving this volume any merits it may possess, they are not to be blamed for any errors, off-beam ideas and woolly thinking that remain.

Paul Kershaw has taught me an enormous amount about early medieval history, not least by putting his voluminous knowledge of early medieval political thought and ideas of war and peace at my disposal, but also by being a very solid and reliable friend. To use a metaphor from this book, in the great shieldwall of life you could not have a better man at your right shoulder.

I count myself exceptionally lucky to have worked with the other medievalists of the University of London and, as well as benefiting hugely from their friendship, I have learnt immeasurably from the other regulars at the Institute of Historical Research's justly famous 'Earlier Middle Ages' seminar, especially Matthew Bennett, John Gillingham, Janet Nelson, Susan Reynolds, Alan Thacker, Andrew Wareham and Geoff West. There is nowhere better than London to learn the art of being an early medieval historian.

Outside academia, I am grateful to Duncan Macfarlane, editor of *Wargames Illustrated*, who first published my thoughts on early medieval warfare in 1983, and has consistently (and with great patience and support) given me access to a broader non-academic audience ever since. Between the early 1980s and mid 1990s, I also learnt much from participation in the 'Guthrum's Army' discussion group, set up to discuss ninth-century Viking warfare. Peter Bone, in particular, has been a very helpful sounding board for ideas. Mohammed Hamika taught me to wield (however ineptly!) a sword, if a modern fencing foil rather than a pattern-welded broadsword, and has increased my insight into hand-to-hand combat considerably. I thank him and my fellow fencers at the Swash and Buckle Fencing Club. Most of this book about the turmoil and rumblings of war, as Sedulius Scottus might have called them, was written in the tranquil surroundings of Carnhedryn Uchaf near St David's. My thanks to Pat and Hedley Picton for providing such a wonderful environment.

My family has given unstinting support through some difficult times. I owe especial thanks to my father for reading through the early drafts of the book to check their clarity. Emma Campbell has brightened my life considerably during the last phase of this book's completion. My thanks also go to those of my friends who are not listed above who have always been there for me. It would take too long to list them all, and be invidious to single out only a few.

To my thanks to all of the above, who are in a very real sense my teachers, I should like to add my profound gratitude to Michael Hickman, Tom Hardwick, Dave Robson and Heather Weston, who taught me history at King Charles I School, Kidderminster. Teaching is a profession which, especially in the state and even more especially in the state comprehensive sector, is misunderstood, unappreciated and all too often insulted. I offer this book as, in a very small way, proof that the hard work by British state school teachers is appreciated, changes countless lives for the better and does, far more often than we are led to believe, bear important fruit.

Guy Halsall

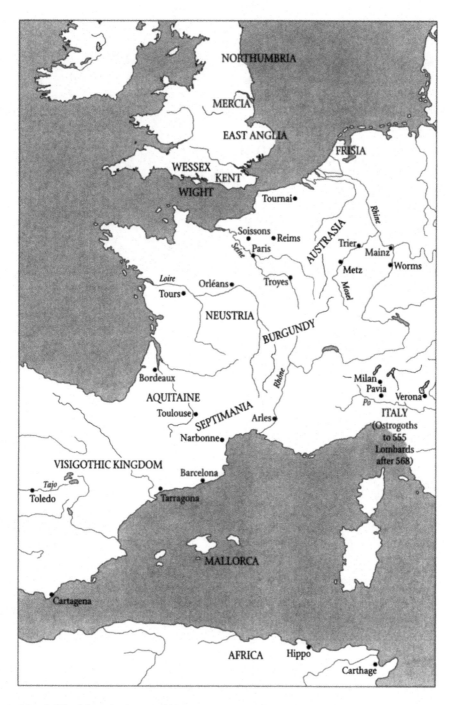

Map 1 The Merovingian world

Map 2 Anglo-Saxon Britain

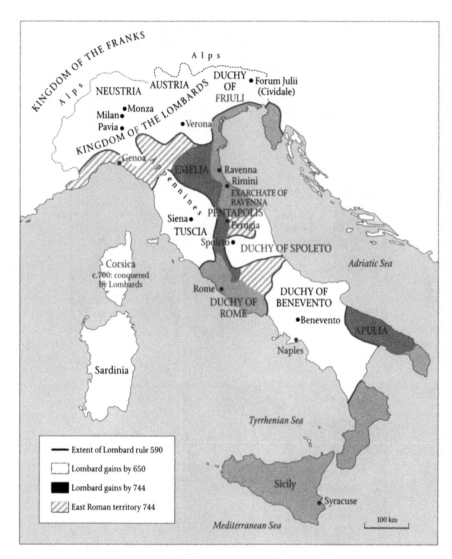

Map 3 Lombard Italy

a)

Slav polities

Louis the
German
(East Francia)

Charles
the Bald
(West Francia)

Lothar
(The 'Middle Kingdom')

Emirate of
Cordoba

Papal
territories

b)

Kingdom
of
Lothar II
(Lotharingia)

Kingdom of
Louis
the German
(East Francia)

Kingdom of
Charles the Bald
(Neustria)

Brittany

Kingdom of
Charles
'the Child'
(Aquitaine)

Kingdom
of Charles
of Provence

Kingdom of
Emperor Louis II
(Italy)

Emirate of
Cordoba

Map 4 The Carolingian Empire

c)

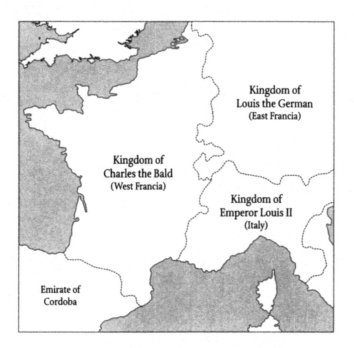

Kingdom of
Louis the German
(East Francia)

Kingdom of
Charles the Bald
(West Francia)

Kingdom of
Emperor Louis II
(Italy)

Emirate of
Cordoba

1

WARFARE AND VIOLENCE IN THE EARLY MIDDLE AGES

Introduction

Early on the morning of Tuesday 18 October 841, Nithard, a Frankish aristocrat, indeed a grandson of the Emperor Charlemagne, sat down to write his account of the events of that year up to the great battle of Fontenoy, which had taken place on 25 June. He tells us the day he wrote because 'while [he] was writing' there was an eclipse of the Sun 'in the first hour' (between about 6.00 and 7.00 a.m.). Nithard had fought at Fontenoy. Presumably he had killed men there; he was engaged in what was apparently the hardest-fought sector of the battle. Battle like this was a bloody, face-to-face affair carried out with what later generations would call 'cold steel', and a nobleman of Nithard's standing would have been stationed in or very close to the front rank. It seems reasonable to suppose that Nithard was by turns frightened and furious, experiencing all the immense and extreme adrenaline-driven emotions which hand-to-hand fighting produces. He had to try his best to kill, and he would have known it: if he did not he would be killed. Almost exactly three years after Fontenoy, on 14 June 844, Nithard was indeed killed in battle in the Angoumois, possibly by some of the same men he had faced at Fontenoy.[1]

Nithard and his account of Fontenoy make a valuable case study of the problems involved in the study of early medieval warfare. Though Nithard is unusual in writing an eyewitness report of an early medieval battle, perhaps even more unusual in that he wrote within four months of its occurrence, and although he tells us much about the negotiations before the battle, his account of the fighting takes barely a paragraph.[2] Even this is more detailed than most early medieval descriptions of battle, but it is nevertheless terse, formulaic and in fact contains less incidental detail than some later ninth- and early tenth-century accounts written by clerics and monks who had not experienced warfare first hand. Nithard wrote stylish, classically influenced Latin and it was by this that he expected to be judged by his audience. To Nithard and his contemporaries, a writer's 'authority' was based upon these things, not on detailed 'factual' knowledge. Autopsy – to be able to say 'I know because I was there' – was rhetorically impressive but, unlike modern historians, neither writer nor reader expected the minutiae of what actually happened to bog down a written account or to take precedence over the display of knowledge of classics, scripture or the writings of the church fathers (patristics). The 'True Law of History' (lex vera historiae)[3] was moral, not empirical. Intellectual weight derived not from factual report but from exegetical understanding and explanation, and thus historical authority rested upon scholarly learning, not the meticulous compilation of accurate records of the lived world. We should not, however, be led into thinking that Nithard's writing, and that of other early medieval authors, was somehow divorced from 'reality'. Theirs was, simply, a different reality from that of post-Enlightenment modern Europe. There was a genuine and pressing need to find meaning and lessons in everyday events in order to understand the workings of God in the world. Thus Nithard saw real relevance in the eclipse which took place as he wrote. The battle of Fontenoy had been a deeply traumatic event, the bloody rupture of a Frankish polity which had (just about) endured for well over a century.[4] How apt, then, that the Lord would mark this dreadful year with an eclipse, the more so that He did so just as Nithard, a participant in the battle, was writing his report for one of the kings who had led the armies there. When Nithard pauses to tell us of the eclipse he illustrates graphically the mental gulf between 'us' and 'them'.

This is underlined by the very brevity of Nithard's account of Fontenoy. As will become apparent throughout this book, during the early Middle Ages people did not write in detail about warfare.[5] This is one of the most intriguing aspects of the study of war in this period. Eric John wrote that Anglo-Saxon society was so violent that fighting and making war were central to its way of life.[6] Kingship was inextricably bound up with warfare. Warfare is best documented in Francia, where rulers like Charles Martel (Frankish mayor of the palace, 717–41) or his grandson Charlemagne went on campaign most years of their lives. The *Royal Frankish Annals* record that in 792 'no military campaign was carried out this year', as though this were in itself newsworthy.[7] Indeed it was, and when the same report was made in 790, a later annalist felt obliged to explain Charlemagne's lack of military activity.[8] However, in 792 the annalists were wrong; an expedition was sent against Benevento in the winter. One of the rank and file, Ripwin, made arrangements in case he did not come back.[9] The Appendix lists all the occasions during one well-documented period of ten years (581–90) when an army was called out or when larger-scale violence broke out in the Merovingian realms.[10] They total thirty-seven incidents. Elsewhere, the records are not as complete, but the picture is still of endemic warfare. Between 600 and 850 fourteen wars are recorded between the Anglo-Saxon kingdoms of Mercia and Wessex; in the same period, Mercia waged eleven wars against the Welsh and fought other opponents on eighteen recorded occasions. This list of forty-two wars almost certainly does not represent a full list of incidents of warfare during this period and possibly consists mostly of the more serious and noteworthy outbreaks of fighting.[11] Yet even on this conservative estimate Mercia found itself at war with one or other of its neighbours every five or six years. In seventh-century England twelve battles were recorded involving the death of at least one king or major royal figure, besides ten other battles and eleven other instances of warfare. That not all warfare was so 'newsworthy', let alone unusual that it would naturally be recorded, is also made clear by a Spanish inscription recording the death of an aristocrat called Oppila on campaign against the Basques – a campaign otherwise completely unknown.[12] Between 791 and 883, the Spanish kingdom of the Asturias was attacked thirty-three times by the Emirs of Cordoba; on at least seven occasions, when not under assault, the Christians took advantage of the respite to attack the Moslems.[13] Warfare was a common and very real feature of early medieval life. The period has, moreover, been described as an 'heroic age'.[14] Why, then, was there so little written in any detail about warfare? Classical Greek writers told all about battle in various genres, taking us from the high-level political and strategic background, through discussion of the tactical course of a battle, to the moral effects of combat and the values of particular formations and weapons and down to the most earthy and human features of battlefield experience: the inexperienced warrior soiling himself with fear as the enemy approached.[15] Roman writers discussed similar things. There is thus a huge difference between the classical Greek and Roman worlds, where we can study strategy, routes and orders of march, orders of battle, battlefield tactics and psychology in detail and try to recover the experience of warfare in all its horror,[16] and the early medieval west, where such things lie largely beyond our purview.

Was warfare too grim to write about or discuss? This is possible but unlikely to be the whole explanation. Early medieval warfare is unlikely to have been more horrific than classical Greek warfare, yet people wrote often and graphically about their experience of the latter. Occasionally we hear of warriors glorying in their exploits. Notker the Stammerer tells us of Eishere, a warrior from his childhood, thus an elder contemporary of Nithard, who would tell of how he fought the Slavs, spitting them on his spear like little birds 'squealing their incomprehensible lingo'.[17] Some epic heroic poetry such as the Frankish epic *Waltharius* may, given that it survives in manuscripts from monastic contexts, represent monkish satire upon secular aristocrats and their silly boasting about fighting.[18]

The explanation for the absence of writing about warfare is, again, to be sought at least partly in contemporary expectations of written sources. The Latin tradition of secular narrative history that emphasised wars and battles, such as epitomised by Sallust, Tacitus and later Ammianus Marcellinus, had largely died out in the Latin west by this period, though the Greek tradition was continued in the east. Thereafter the detailed discussion of matters military ceased to be an accepted part of the narrative historical genres. Nevertheless, early medieval writers were well acquainted with the classics; Nithard used Sallust, for example. Yet only at the very end of our period, from about Nithard's day onwards, do accounts of battles and other military encounters begin to be a little more detailed. What we can learn about past society often depends upon the rules of the genres within which contemporaries wrote, and the genres of historical writing which existed in the early medieval west did not expect the author to discuss warfare in depth. Its existence, the routes of armies, where battles were fought and who won remained an accepted and major part of the subject matter but further detail appears not to have been regarded as appropriate.

Why this should have been the case is unclear. We might wonder if Christianity played a part. Classical historiographical traditions were intricately related to Graeco-Roman religious beliefs and a set of relationships with the divine, which in turn gave rise to particular attitudes towards battlefield prowess and heroism, probably going back to Homer and other early epic poets. Christian attitudes towards killing could be quite different. The western Church had never been particularly easy about the Christian's role in a secular state which might require one to kill.[19] In theory, penance could be required from those who killed in war. Religion might explain a certain reluctance on the part of those who had experienced it to discuss warfare.

This explanation does not seem entirely satisfactory. The Church has usually found sufficient theological elasticity to justify most aspects of human behaviour. In the zealously Christian Eastern Roman or Byzantine Empire, detailed writing about military affairs, both in histories and in military treatises, remained common. A millennium after Nithard, fighting in defence of a fairly inhuman cause, the Confederate commander 'Stonewall' Jackson referred to his troops as the 'Army of the Living God', whilst his colleague, General Leonidas Polk, was Episcopalian bishop of Louisiana. In the early Middle Ages the Church was wedded to militant, martial and often very violent imagery. The fifth-century poet Prudentius was popular in Nithard's day. Prudentius wrote extremely gory accounts of martyrdoms on the one hand, and of the warfare to be waged between virtues and vices on the other.[20] Carolingian manuscript illustrations accompanying Prudentius' work deck out the virtues and vices in contemporary war-gear. Illustrations to Bibles and Psalters are a major source for contemporary depictions of warriors and warfare. In art, the norms of written sources are reversed; although they borrowed models from classical art, early medieval illuminators were quite prepared to bring images from everyday reality into the midst of writing about the remote past. Similarly, Christian poetry in England and on the Continent imported 'heroic' warrior imagery and aspects of contemporary warfare into accounts of biblical or early Christian history.[21] From the seventh century onwards, Old Testament ideas of kingship became increasingly popular; early medieval kings were expected to be warriors and the Book of Kings was an apt source of role models. The Bible, however, says little about *how* battles were won and lost and its explanation of *why* not surprisingly focuses upon the divine. This change in views of agency may bring us closer to explaining the difference between the classical period and the early medieval. Warfare remained part of the established material for historical writing and early medieval writers liked to model their style upon the great Roman practitioners of the genre, yet perhaps the details of human behaviour, weapons and armour on the battlefield remained unnecessary. After all, battles were supposed to be won by divine favour, not human agency.

The fact that most historical writing was carried out by churchmen cannot explain the absence of discussions of warfare. Some of the more detailed accounts of battles were written by clergy or monks. If we look at secular poetry a similarly intriguing picture presents itself; in many ways it is an opposing picture to that provided by prose sources but this serves only to heighten the problem. Much of the surviving poetry from the period concerns warriors, weapons and warfare. This style was projected into vernacular poetry dealing with Biblical or Christian topics. Here Christianity cannot play a decisive role. The same problems, by and large, apply to Scandinavian heroic poetry after the close of our period, poetry which presumably, though to a now unknowable extent, drew upon pre-Christian traditions. This sort of poetry was, we assume (leaving aside the possibility that it is monastic in origin), a staple at the great feasts of the era, and was delivered to audiences comprising people like Nithard, who had fought and knew the business of fighting. Indeed at the very time that Nithard lived, we can trace the earliest written versions of possibly older vernacular tales, especially poems, often concerned with epic battle, as in the Old High German *Hildebrandslied*.[22] This poetry can be called 'heroic'. However, it is standardised and formal, glorifying battle and the role of warriors within it, but saying very little about how it was actually carried out or what happened on the battlefield. It is blunt, triumphalist and in the final analysis, whilst more complex in terms of composition, language and poetic style, in content reasonably to be compared to the more unpleasant, aggressive songs chanted at the opposition every Saturday afternoon at British football grounds. The extent to which poetry like this has much at all to do with actual battlefield reality is debatable (though in chapter 9 an attempt will be made to relate it to action on the battlefield). On the opposite side from Nithard at the Battle of Fontenoy was another Frankish aristocrat, otherwise unknown, called Engilbert. He wrote a poem (in Latin) about the battle, which gives a few fleeting details of the fighting and is infused with a bitter sense of loss.[23] Yet this too eventually retreats into formal clichés about wolves and other carrion beasts feeding on the corpses of the slain. It is interesting to speculate upon how Nithard, Engilbert and others responded to poets. How much did they relish the standard, formulaic phrases telling simply how they or some other heroic army slaughtered their enemies? Did they view them with a certain distaste? Did the bravado serve to mask horrific memories, or provoke more sombre reflection on comrades lost? In the end we shall never know. What seems to confront us again, especially given the warrior Engilbert's own participation in the production of this stylised poetry, is the fact that writers and audiences did not expect everyday 'reality' or lived experience to get in the way of the demands of genre. Again, authority depended upon satisfying those demands, and not upon 'telling it like it was'. Ultimately, the question of why warfare was not written about in detail in the early medieval world remains utterly intractable.

All this illustrates a key problem in studying warfare and society in the 'Barbarian West': the shortage of data. But Nithard and his contemporaries' approach to writing about the recent past also brings us face to face with an even greater problem: the difference in mentalities between twenty-first-century Europeans and their ninth-century precursors. What interests us did not necessarily interest them. Indeed, as we have seen, in the sphere of military history it rarely interested them at all. Trying to create a modern account of how things happened, and why, in post-Roman warfare more often involves a complex confrontation with the early medieval mind than the simple collection and analysis of empirical data. This point is significant because traditions of writing about early medieval warfare have all too often discounted this aspect. Academic historians, like their early medieval subjects, have, with some notable exceptions, usually shied away from the subject of warfare.[24] In quantitative terms, the bulk of writing about 'Dark Age warfare' has been by interested and enthusiastic 'amateur' military historians, retired soldiers, wargamers, or re-enactment enthusiasts.[25] Such authors largely have not been interested in this type of 'history of the mind'. Their work has been guided often by a belief in unchanging human nature and eternal principles of warfare, strategy and tactics. Here, their approach has not differed very much from that of the more 'professional' discipline of military history. Writers in the academic 'war studies' tradition have often sought similar timeless, cross-cultural constants.[26] Examples from other periods are used to explain aspects of the military history of the period. Put rather crudely, if we do not have data on the practice of campaigning in the early Middle Ages, then more plentiful data on this subject from other periods can be used to tell us 'how it was'. The use of analogy should not be rejected entirely; it can be illuminating and suggestive. It cannot, however, be used to decide how things were, or were not, done in the early Middle Ages. Similarly, it has been felt that the course of campaigns can be reconstructed from the few facts available (such as the location of a battle) in accordance with eternal principles of strategic conduct and 'inherent military probability'.[27] One productive academic writer on the subject has argued that the military history of the period be studied using what he terms the 'rational man model'.[28] Because of its insistence on unchanging rules or norms of military history, we might term this the 'normalist' approach.

There might be something in this. Early medieval warriors, like later generals, wished to gain whatever advantage they could over their opponents. They used cunning, surprise attacks, positioned their armies so that their enemies would have the sun in their eyes, and made sensible use of terrain.[29] Yet the normalist method cannot be entirely adequate. As Nithard's example amply demonstrates, the early medieval mind was profoundly different from the modern. This was a world which believed in miracles and that God was active in the world. When commanders had their troops fast, or carry out ordeals before campaigns and battles,[30] this was not mere credulity or something done for show. Nor was it a cynical manipulation of their troops' gullibility; this was a serious matter. How could one possibly hope to win a battle without the Almighty's approval? When, perhaps as we should see it, by sheer coincidence, messengers arrived at King Charles the Bald's camp at Easter, carrying royal liturgical attire, Nithard saw this as a very real sign of God's approval.[31] Thus what an early medieval leader saw as the 'rational' conduct of campaigns was based upon very different ideas of rationality from those of Napoleon I or Alexander of Macedon. Unsurprisingly, similar factors often governed the practice of battle. As the events which Nithard describes before Fontenoy show, ninth-century leaders could see battle itself as a judicial ordeal, in which one placed the outcome of the dispute in the hands of God; if God was on your side, how could you lose? The bishops' absolution of the troops from guilt afterwards made the same point. In 876, Louis the Younger, King of the East Franks, chose men to perform ordeals before he marched against his uncle, the same Charles the Bald who had fought alongside Louis' father, Louis the German, at Fontenoy and who had commissioned Nithard to write his *Histories*.[32] The ordeals were passed successfully. When Louis did this he was stacking the odds in his favour, and increasing his chances of victory, every bit as seriously, and practically, as Field Marshal Montgomery was in 1942 when he made sure he had overwhelming superiority in guns, tanks and airpower before he attacked Rommel at El Alamein. These factors might thus profoundly affect the ways in which a campaign was conducted and battle sought, perhaps in flagrant contradiction of later ideas of strategic 'rationality' or good sense. Furthermore, concepts of honour and shame existed which likewise differed from those of the present day, and these too could govern conduct and battlefield behaviour.

Surely, though, basic emotions like anger and fear are eternal, and these must have played an important role in deciding how wars and battles were waged in detail. Indeed some interesting, important and influential work on military history, though still within the normalist tradition, has been based upon the timelessness of human emotions.[33] Recent work has argued that this too is questionable, and that emotions are social constructs, based upon the ideas and ideals of the day.[34] What exactly 'anger' meant might be entirely dependent upon contemporary values. In a different thought-world, which could believe in battle as a judgement of God, death itself might carry different connotations, and profoundly affect the nature of battlefield fear. So, too, might the deeply ingrained notions of honour and shame already mentioned.[35]

These views would lead us to a quite different approach to early medieval warfare, which we could term 'substantivist'. This would hold that warfare and its conduct can only be understood in terms of the norms, values and mentalities of the society which is practising it. It would link up with the 'social constructionist' approach to the history of emotions to deny that past warfare can be approached through general assumptions about battlefield behaviour. This is closer to the approach which will be adopted in this book. Yet this method presents its own problems. The substantivist approach copes badly with change through time, just as the normalist approach denies it. 'Substantivism' and 'social constructionism' have the merit of making us study societies in the round and try to reconstruct the attitudes of people of the time. This ultimately stems from the 'structuralist' approach pioneered by anthropologists such as Claude Lévi-Strauss. In essence, this analysed the structures according to which worldviews are formed, in particular looking at sets of opposing concepts. Whilst this was, and still is, an important starting point in the study of societies, it has, as stated, huge difficulties in dealing with social change. If people behave (including in their wars) simply in accordance with a set of learned norms and attitudes (structures), entirely dependent upon the society in which they happen to live, how can anything change? After all, as Janet Nelson has convincingly demonstrated,[36] Nithard changed his mind about the wars in which he was involved.

Societies all have their own norms, which govern how people think and behave. These are in a sense the rules by which people, as social actors, play. These 'rules' (the 'structure') do not exist as concrete entities in themselves, however, but as a society's cumulative 'memory bank' of all previous sets of interactions: those which were deemed acceptable and proper and those which were considered 'wrong'. There is therefore a complex, reciprocal relationship between 'structure' and action. The 'structure' governs action, but is itself constituted *by* action. People can play *with* the rules, as well as within them. Whenever anyone manages to get away with an action, or behaviour, hitherto considered inappropriate, wrong or bad, however minor the infraction, then that adds itself to the 'memory bank' and alters the structure (however infinitesimally).[37] Change is then to be expected, and this will be the case in warfare and attitudes towards it, as much as in any other area of human interaction. That change will take place at various rates but there are very few things which can maintain such a structure unaltered for any length of time. There are a number of reasons why the practice of warfare may change more slowly, however. Warfare, though common, was not a permanent state. Especially in the case of major, royally led expeditions, it was waged in a very deliberate and often stylised way. The army, as an important social and political institution, was raised selectively from specified social groups, and campaigning could be hedged about with norms and rituals. This very deliberate nature of the practice of war might have shielded it to some extent from the dynamic change which occurs in the course of constant social interaction. Nevertheless, it cannot have remained static. By adopting this method we can allow early medieval people to strive for their own ends in ways which seem familiar, whilst at the same time recognising that the parameters within which they acted, and the ways in which they thought, were often profoundly alien to those of our own world.

All this is pertinent to early medieval warfare. There were normative rules or codes of conduct, which governed the practice of warfare in various times and places in the post-Roman West. Warfare, after all, is a form of communication, and in some instances a type of diplomacy.[38] When warfare is aimed at making a particular statement to an enemy, or at achieving a specific goal, then it is important that the enemy understands that statement. Thus, as in any other form of communication, both sides need to be aware of what actions or 'statements' mean, and therefore how to respond in a way that the enemy will comprehend. There needs to be a sort of 'grammar' of warfare; codes of conduct, or rules, make these statements easier for the opposition to understand. When, as was often the case in the post-Roman world, warfare was about maintaining a status quo rather than altering it, and was deliberately limited in scope, it was important to know what the appropriate forms of response to actions were, to avoid warfare spiralling out of control and becoming more severe. By the same token, by ignoring the usual codes and norms a statement could be made, and understood, that this was a different, more serious type of war, fought for higher stakes. Yet these rules did not remain unaltered, and participants in warfare could manipulate them to their own advantage. Indeed there were also wars which seem to have paid them no attention at all. Furthermore, substantial and dramatic change could take place as a result of the violent confrontation of societies with different ideas about the acceptable 'rules of engagement'. In particular, it will be stressed that some aspects of warfare in this period, notably those concerned with wars against the Vikings, are to be understood as stemming from clashes of cultures with different mentalities and different attitudes to warfare and its practice.

It is most unlikely, therefore, that warfare, attitudes towards it, and the way in which it was waged remained unaltered for the whole four and a half centuries with which this book is concerned. Early medieval Europe was diverse geographically as well and, though interesting comparisons can be drawn between changes taking place in different areas at the same time, there were numerous differences in detail, at least, between the different regions. Often the study of early medieval warfare, even when not espousing 'inherent military probability' or strategic principles from other periods, has treated the entire period as a uniform whole. If there is insufficient evidence from, for example, sixth-century Francia, then it has been held to be appropriate to take evidence from the seventh century or later and extrapolate it backwards. This of course denies change. Warfare is assumed to be unchanging between the fifth and the ninth, tenth or (especially in the study of Anglo-Saxon England) even the eleventh centuries. Various justifications for this are put forward: a supposedly unifying 'Germanic' ethos, a shared Roman heritage, the common values of a 'heroic society', the apparent lack of technological development in warfare in the period, or even a 'statistical' argument, stemming from the shortage of evidence described above, and endeavouring to put together a 'significant' body of data. None of these justifications is valid. As chapters 3 and 4 will make clear, change in the means of raising the army was dynamic; in the less-well-evidenced areas of battlefield and campaign practice we can also detect variation through time and space. Important transformations seem to have taken place around 600, and again in the ninth century. We must, consequently, contextualise all evidence as far as possible, by date and place. This allows us, on the one hand, to pay attention to the specific worldviews which pertained in particular societies in specific places at a given time; it also allows us to uncover and to explain the processes of change.[39]

This contextual approach necessitates the study of all the available evidence. Hitherto, the study of early medieval warfare has been carried out largely via the study of documents alone. The use of archaeology has in the past been simply to look at the 'hardware' – weaponry and armour. In this volume a multidisciplinary method has been employed.[40] This attempts to use different forms of evidence, written, archaeological and pictorial, on their own terms, studied critically with due account paid to issues of source criticism, to see what they have to say about the subject. Although the nature of the subject is such that most attention will be paid to written sources, as will become clear, archaeology has much to tell us, not simply about those periods and places which are served badly with written records, and not simply about weapons, armour and fortifications. It can shed important light upon mentalities and upon problems such as how armies were raised. This multidisciplinary approach gives the current volume some of its distinctiveness.

This book attempts to put warfare in its broader social and economic context. It does this for two reasons. Firstly, warfare has become something of a neglected area in the academic study of the early Middle Ages.[41] The reasons for this neglect are difficult to pin down. Partly, one suspects, many historians and archaeologists tacitly assume that the study of warfare glorifies the subject. Partly, too, the study of warfare has suffered from the attentions of military historians, who often *do* seem to glorify or sanitise it.[42] Academic military history, with its reliance upon the 'normalist' approach, has not been a theoretically advanced branch of the discipline, and this is only compounded by the parochialism of the subject. Much military history studies strategy, battlefield tactics and weaponry as an end in its own right, with no attempt made to relate this to wider issues. Thus military history has been characterised, not entirely unfairly, as narrow-minded, descriptive antiquarianism.

Yet military history has been no more narrow-minded, descriptive and antiquarian than many another field of early medieval historical endeavour, such as the study of manuscripts, artefacts or art styles. Why it should have been singled out for particular opprobrium is probably related to the modern academic's understandable moral wariness of the study of warfare. It may stem also simply enough from the fact that, as we have seen, there is very little evidence to be had about early medieval warfare in the narrow sense, leading students of the subject all too often to adopt 'eternal military principles' or simplistic approaches to complex and problematic written sources, including acceptance at face value of the 'heroic' ethos[43] or the crude aggregation of evidence from different times and places, none of which increases the subject's academic respectability.

The role of warfare in historical change also has come under scrutiny. Historians and archaeologists no longer seek wars and Great Battles[44] as the primary agents of change. Since the *annaliste* movement of the middle decades of the last century, more holistic approaches to the explanation of historical developments have, rightly, been adduced. Fernand Braudel, one of the great *annalistes*, dismissed high-level politics and such things as warfare as 'surface disturbances', foam on the crests of the great tides of history.[45] Thus trends in academic medieval history have been away from the wars and battles which featured so strongly in histories written in the nineteenth century and the early decades of the twentieth, and into new areas of social history such as the study of gender, which allow us to look at the social relations which made up everyday experience and which lie at the core of processes of change.

As an example of how attitudes have changed, we can cite law 30 of the *Pactus Legis Salicae*, the sixth-century Frankish law-code, 'concerning insults'. Clause 3 of this law concerns accusing a free woman of being a whore, but clauses 1 and 2 are about calling someone (to retain the insulting sense of the original) 'covered in shit' (*cinitum* or *concagatum*). Recent translations of the passage have related this insult to issues of sexuality, making this an accusation of homosexuality, sodomy or pederasty.[46] Yet this seems to rip the sub-clause from its context. The remainder of the law is mostly concerned with insults of cowardice or treachery: to be a hare (i.e., to run like one), to be a fox (an insinuation of treachery),[47] to have cast away one's shield (the classic sign of having 'run for it'). *Cinitum* and *concagatum* are terms which in this context meant that the insulted party was accused of having soiled himself with fear. Again, to retain the sense of the original, '*you* ran away, and *you* shat yourself'. These are terrible insults in a society, like sixth-century Frankish, which was largely constructed around ideas of the 'warrior'. To be sure, there is still a gender issue here; masculinity was constructed around these 'martial' values, as we shall see in chapter 2. Female honour was besmirched by insults about sexual promiscuity, but male by allegations about cowardice.[48] These legal clauses ultimately concern the realities of warfare.

This book seeks to reinstate warfare as a key component of the study of the early Middle Ages. The next few chapters will show that warfare and military service were vitally important to many aspects of early medieval society and politics. This alone ought to make a book on the subject necessary. Warfare does play an important part in bringing about transformations, and we need to reinstate it into this role. If, as outlined above, we see change in this period as dynamic and as being brought about by the interplay of countless identities, then high-level politics play a major role in shaping those identities. We shall see in chapter 3 that ethnic identities were of huge importance in structuring society. This importance derived in part from the means by which armies were raised; ethnic identity was founded upon a military role. The reason why ethnicity should have acquired that role was itself dependent upon high-level political and military change, focused on the end of the Western Roman Empire.

The second reason why warfare should be put in its broader social, economic and political context is not simply because warfare and military matters had an effect on those other issues; it is also because our best way of approaching warfare is through its broader context. We have, as we have seen, very little data on military specifics. We do, however, have substantial evidence for the societies, politics and economies of the early Middle Ages. The safest way to study warfare is to begin from the more securely knowable aspects of its broad background. Some work on the minutiae of early medieval warfare has suffered from being divorced from the mainstream of historical study of the period. The idea, discussed further in chapter 9, that the Anglo-Saxons did not fight on horseback, unlike their British neighbours, is in part derived from an old-fashioned and now unacceptable idea that there was rigid cultural (not to say genetic or racial) division between the 'Germanic' English and the 'Celtic' Welsh. Most work would nowadays stress that these were political groupings, whose members were almost entirely drawn from the same biological stock and drew upon much the same range of Roman and post-Roman cultural traditions. This makes the idea that one group would fight in entirely a different manner from the other most unlikely.

Geographically the present volume spans post-Roman Britain, the Anglo-Saxon and the Welsh kingdoms as well as the Pictish and Scottish polities, Ireland, Visigothic Spain and the Christian states in the north of the Iberian peninsula after the Arab conquest of 711, Merovingian and Carolingian Gaul, Ostrogothic Italy and the Lombard and Carolingian kingdom of Italy (the north of the peninsula) and pre-Carolingian and Carolingian Germany and Scandinavia before and during the Viking age. An attempt has been made to bring all of these regions into the overall picture, though the book concentrates on the areas I know best: northern Europe, especially Frankish Gaul and Anglo-Saxon England. The quantitative and qualitative distribution of evidence ineluctably makes any study of this topic in this period heavily 'Frankocentric', however, and the accusation that the book could have been called 'The Franks and their Enemies' fair but inevitable. The use of archaeology enables us to move away from the usual state of affairs whereby regions of Europe are only brought into the equation as and when they produce documents or come into contact with literate Christian societies. I have not felt confident to discuss Moslem Spain in any detail though, obviously, the armies of the Emirate of Cordoba will impinge on the account.[49] Similarly, though I have drawn upon accounts of the Eastern Roman wars of reconquest in Italy, I have not discussed Byzantine armies. The armies of the East Roman, or Byzantine, Empire are dealt with splendidly in another book in this series, to which the current volume aims to be the companion.[50]

Chronologically, the volume begins with the end of the Western Roman Empire. Here a certain flexibility has been adopted; it makes little sense to start in 476 precisely. Armies in the immediately post-Roman period owed much to the nature of the last Roman armed forces, so these will need some discussion.

More to the point, the end of the Western empire was not a neat process: the existence of 'post-Roman' Visigothic armies in Gaul reaches back to about 418; Burgundians ruled the south-east of Gaul from the 440s; Frankish polities, stemming partly at least from involvement in a Roman field army, can be traced at least to the early 450s; and 'Saxon' forces were operating in Britain at about the same time. Thus *c.*450 has been used as a general shorthand for the book's opening date. I make no attempt to discuss late Roman warfare, however, as that has been thoroughly covered in other publications.[51] The closing date for the volume has been selected as *c.*900. This date makes sense for a number of reasons. In the Frankish world, the Carolingian Empire broke up at this time, following the deposition and death of the Emperor Charles III 'the Fat' (the epithet is apparently not contemporary), and this produced significant effects in France, northern Spain, Italy and Germany; in England, the death of Alfred the Great conveniently stands as marking the end of the first phase of Viking attacks; this phase of Viking activity on the Continent can be closed with the establishment of the Duchy of Normandy in 918. In southern Italy, 900 marked the beginning of a new political phase.[52] Like European history in general, warfare seems to move into a new phase in the tenth century. The evidence begins to take different and more numerous forms; in England we see the start of the West Saxon wars of conquest in the midlands and the north; the political fragmentation of the Carolingian world produces its own effects on the nature of warfare as we move into what is rapidly becoming an age of knights and castles.[53]

There are historiographical reasons, too, for the choice of these parameters. As mentioned, the late Roman army, its wars, equipment and fortifications have been very thoroughly studied in recent decades. Similarly, the tenth century has been the subject of much good work. The period in between, however, has largely been neglected, so that there is no satisfactory study in English of warfare and society in western Europe between the end of the Roman Empire and the break-up of the Carolingian. The classic, useful studies of medieval warfare tend not to discuss this period. Verbruggen's *The Art of Warfare in Western Europe during the Middle Ages* really begins with the Carolingians, about which he makes only a few, though nevertheless useful, points, but he adopts a highly diachronic, normalist approach to warfare, moving back and forth between the ninth and fourteenth centuries via all stops in between. Similarly, Contamine's *War in the Middle Ages* says little about the early Middle Ages. Earlier, Sir Charles Oman's *A History of the Art of War in the Middle Ages* saw the early Middle Ages as a period when armies were simply rampaging barbarous mobs with no strategic or tactical awareness whatsoever. The relevant volume of Hans Delbrück's *History of the Art of War in the Sphere of Political History* was more sophisticated and is still historiographically important and worth reading, but now, needless to say, looks very dated indeed in terms of its historical framework. Similarly useful, but now looking rather old in terms of its explanations, is Beeler's *Warfare in Feudal Europe*. Again, Beeler only dealt with the last century and a half of the period covered by this volume.[54] Beeler's book began in the 730s because, in line with then current views, he saw the battle of Poitiers as of decisive significance. It was felt that Poitiers marked the emergence of heavily armoured shock cavalry as a battle-winning element in western warfare.

Beeler also followed ideas current at the time to propose that it was the combination of technological change, specifically the introduction of the stirrup,[55] and a new military threat in the form of mounted Moslem raiders, which brought about this transformation in battlefield tactics and underlined Poitiers' significance.[56] As with the old idea that Poitiers marked the salvation of Europe from the 'Moslem flood',[57] this view is no longer accepted by scholars, although it survives in more popular views of history. It is therefore an idea to which we shall return in later chapters.

One exception to this rule has been Anglo-Saxon England, where a tradition of the study of military institutions has resulted in some useful work on warfare and society, most notably Richard Abels' excellent *Lordship and Military Obligation in Anglo-Saxon England*.[58] Nevertheless, the study of Anglo-Saxon England has tended to suffer from a certain isolationism, and it is to be hoped that studying England alongside the Continent will provide some fresh insights. Similar points can be made about Viking warfare. Though Viking armies and military techniques have been the subjects of useful scholarly works and will be the subject of a separate volume in the same series as this book, taking Scandinavian warfare beyond our terminal date of *c.*900,[59] the inclusion of the Vikings in a broader context will provide additional perspectives on their effects on European society. Thus this book is aimed to fill a significant gap in the scholarly study of the early Middle Ages. The proliferation of picture books and other non-academic treatments of the subject shows that post-Roman warfare is a far more popular subject outside the groves of academe. These books, though often lavishly produced, rarely treat the subject in sophisticated, up-to-date ways. Another aim of the present volume is therefore to provide more substantial fare for this readership of studies of early medieval warfare. The so-called 'man in the street' with an interest in the subject every bit as serious as any professor deserves better than to be fobbed off with glossily produced but poorly researched, out-of-date and uncritical booklets.

Violence, war and peace in the early Middle Ages

History and social anthropology reveal that many societies have an idea of different scales or levels of violence and the early medieval west was no different. In the modern western world peace is regarded as the default state of affairs and warfare a defined legal concept. When this section was first written, there was considerable debate upon whether the United States and the west were in a state of war in the aftermath of the terrorist assault on New York, an attack which, as far as was known at the time of writing, probably produced more fatalities in a single day than most days of open battle since the First World War.[60] The early medieval west, by contrast, appears to have regarded war and peace as equally formal and extreme states of affairs.[61] Between the two was a broad spectrum of violence.

The lowest levels of violence in the early medieval west were robberies, brawls and fights, which produced injuries, which in turn had to be compensated for. Killing in the heat of anger, though naturally frowned upon by clerics, was regarded as a lesser crime than murder by stealth. In the early Middle Ages, violence carried out in the open was always treated more leniently than that which was concealed. Law also protected an individual's house and courtyard. Violence which involved transgression into that area, or took place against a third party whilst in another man's house, was treated severely. The law worked hard to ensure that violence did not spiral out of control. The law did not tolerate violence perpetrated as an act of revenge unless the initial wrongdoer, and/or his or her family had refused to pay compensation, and in some cases not unless the initially wronged party had sought a judgement from a royal officer. Occasionally attempts were made to outlaw all acts of revenge.[62]

This violence was, for the most part, the business of local communities. Above that level came the violence of bands of armed men, which we might think of as banditry or brigandage, although early medieval people seem not to have thought of this level of violence in such terms.[63] As we shall see, armed bands formed the nuclei of most early medieval armies, and legislation against them was fraught with difficulties. Nevertheless, attempts were made to limit the actions of warriors and their followings, especially when carried out within a kingdom. This type of violence may have been quite common in this period and sometimes the law-codes treat it comparatively leniently. Such bands might not only be composed of an aristocrat and his followers; they might also be gangs of young men of the same age. Such bands would appear to be those referred to as *contubernia* in early Frankish law.[64]

Then we come to larger-scale violence inside a polity. Throughout this period, local or aristocratic factions frequently engaged in violence, probably best thought of as warfare, to secure political ends.[65] This type of violence shaded into rebellion and usurpation. Warfare between kingdoms could take several forms. Most common (doubtless more common than the sources let on) was small-scale border raiding, aimed at the acquisition of booty. That such raiding occurred frequently is best seen in the provisions of various ninth-century Italian peace treaties, which repeatedly outlaw such activity.[66] Other types of war within political systems such as the Merovingian kingdom took on a similarly small-scale and stylised form. However, there were other levels of open warfare, much larger in scale and aimed at the conquest or destruction of an enemy.[67]

Given that many of these types of violence shaded into each other, it is perhaps not surprising that early medieval writers only occasionally attempted to draw distinctions between them. In the early seventh century, Isidore of Seville envisaged that wars could be categorised as internal, external, servile, social or piratical.[68] Another attempt came in the Anglo-Saxon Laws of Ine, which make a distinction between the activities of thieves, bands and 'armies'. However, this law was the result of a specific set of circumstances.[69] Another tripartite conceptualisation of warfare may be found in the eighth-century *Sacramentary of Gellone*, which divides violence into warfare (*bellum*), disputes (*contenciones*) and lesser violence (*invidia* or *latratus hominum*).[70] Again, it seems that this view envisages a division into 'full-scale' warfare, the violence of armed bands (perhaps political struggles within a realm) and violent crime. For the most part, it only seems possible to distinguish between types of warfare on a descriptive level, from accounts of what was done, what the consequences were, what mechanisms were used to limit it, and what (if any) procedures there were for its termination. Theorisation of different scales of warfare was sparse. Such as there was might be reflected in vocabulary. There was occasional reference to 'public war', that waged on the orders of the state. Sometimes, especially later within the period covered, there appears to have been a distinction between *bellum* (warfare waged by the king) and *werra* (other large-scale violent activity within the kingdom, probably equivalent to the *contenciones* of the Gellone Sacramentary).[71]

However, if early medieval writers did not think often about levels of warfare, they did ponder the issue of just war.[72] Here they could draw upon Roman, biblical, patristic and, just possibly, 'Germanic' concepts (though the latter are notoriously difficult to identify, far more so than was once thought).[73] Much warfare seems to have been justified through concepts of revenge; indeed we can detect the mechanisms of 'feud' or vendetta far more readily at this level of violence than at lower levels. Not that many writers on the subject, who, of course, tended to be churchmen, took this view of the justice of warfare. Late Roman church fathers had wrestled with the problem of how a Christian state could administer something as sinful as warfare, but fairly soon seem to have reached a satisfactory compromise, enabling Christian participation in the state and its wars.[74] The general solution, perhaps not surprisingly, appears to have been to take refuge in Old Testament writings rather than the much more pacific Gospels, and to see warfare fought in defence of the Church as just. Similarly, warfare fought to bring Christianity to the unbelievers was justifiable, though not unreservedly so; to use current parlance, a blank cheque was rarely available.[75] In his 'measured but unsystematic',[76] though none the less highly influential thought, Augustine generally believed that some wars at least were a necessary evil, to defend religion and justice. On the whole, he appears to have retreated into the issue of motivation to distinguish between good and evil, just and unjust. A just ruler would only countenance warfare where it was just; what distinguished good from evil in warfare was the motivation behind it:

> The real evils in war are love of violence, revengeful cruelty, fierce and implacable enmity, wild resistance, and the lust of power, and such like; and it is generally to punish these things, when force is required to

inflict the punishment, that, in obedience to God or some lawful authority, good men undertake wars, when they find themselves in such a position as regards the conduct of human affairs, that right conduct requires them to act, or to make others act in this way.[77]

This aspect of Augustine's thinking was particularly influential in the early Middle Ages. Isidore of Seville defined unjust war as one motivated by anger (*furor*),[78] and Augustine's definition also found expression in the penitentials' comments on killing and Carolingian rulings on the matter.[79]

Gregory of Tours does not appear to have approved unreservedly of any kind of offensive warfare, but he clearly thought that warfare against foreign enemies was better than warfare between the various kingdoms of the *Regnum Francorum* (Kingdom of the Franks). If such wars were fought against foreign heretics, such as the Arian Goths, then that could justify conflict to some extent. Though the *Regnum Francorum* was usually split into two or three realms, Gregory always thought of it as a single kingdom. Thus he considered warfare between the *Teilreiche* (partition-kingdoms) as civil war (*bellum civile*). He also considered warfare between the citizens of Tours *bellum civile*, however, which suggests that he was more concerned with the internecine nature of conflict than with its scale.[80]

Some churchmen differentiated formal warfare from other sorts of killing. *The Penitential of Theodore*, drawn up in the seventh century, prescribed the comparatively light penance of forty days for someone who killed in 'a public war'. One imagines that a 'public war', following Roman definitions of public, was that ordered by the king. Theodore differentiated such conflict from slaying 'at the command of one's lord'. The same penance for public warfare was prescribed slightly later in the penitential known as 'Pseudo-Bede I', and in Ireland a very similar penance for killing in battle was set out, providing that the fight was not pursued after the victory was won. At the very end of our period, Regino of Prüm, in his penitential, prescribed exactly the same penance, forty days, for killing in public war. Earlier in the ninth century, the *Roman Penitential* by Halitgar of Cambrai, however, only prescribed penance for someone who killed 'without cause' in the course of a public expedition, though the tariff set was higher: twenty-one weeks. Halitgar left the issue of killing in battle somewhat ill defined. It possibly came under the heading of someone who killed in defence 'of himself or his relatives or his household', in which case no penance was compulsory, though the killer himself might decide to fast. Presumably some leeway was left in the matter.[81] After Fontenoy the bishops accompanying the victorious army of Charles the Bald and Louis the German assembled and, after deliberation, declared that the participants in the army should consider themselves agents of divine will, unless they were conscious of having been motivated by 'wrath or hatred or vainglory or any passion', in which case they were to confess and do appropriate penance.[82] Augustine's influence seems clear.

Over half a century before Fontenoy, the Pope had issued one of the few overt statements on the righteousness or otherwise of a particular war, when he absolved Charlemagne's armies from any sin when they marched against Tassilo of Bavaria, declared to be a rebel and faithless vassal.[83] The Pope's declaration in this matter, which was hardly as straightforward as Charlemagne wished to present it,[84] in some ways represented a continuation of Roman political thought. The Romans had declared opponents in civil wars, and especially defeated adversaries, to be bandits rather than legitimate political opponents. They were thus to be dealt with as perpetrators of the most serious kind of violent crime, rather than given the treatment due to enemies in true warfare.[85]

Another continuation of Roman thinking on the justice of warfare can be found in Ermold the Black's poem on Louis the Pious. Ermold describes the paintings on the walls of the imperial palace at Ingelheim, which included depictions of Charlemagne's campaigns against the Aquitanians and the Saxons; Charlemagne is described as restoring law to the former, and as bringing the latter under his law.[86] Here we are taken back to the world of Roman thought on warfare against barbarians. What distinguished the civilised world from that of the barbarians, so the Romans thought, was freedom, and freedom was defined by the existence of law.[87] Thus warfare against the barbarians, which was usually seen not as true warfare between states but merely the quashing of rebellion, imposed law upon them. By the same token, areas and individuals within the empire who rebelled against the imperial government were described as withdrawing from the rule of law. Warfare in such circumstances was justified by the restoration of law and freedom. In the early Middle Ages, warfare against peoples not regarded as constituting fully-fledged independent kingdoms, such as the Basques or Bretons, was written about in similar terms, which seem to stem from these Roman attitudes.[88] Such campaigns were regarded as punishment for their habitual infidelity and oath-breaking and aimed at restoring them to obedience. Gregory of Tours, for instance, writing of the consequences of a Basque raid on southern Gaul in 587, says 'Duke Austrovald organised several expeditions against them but was unable to inflict any punishment worth talking about.'[89] Similar attitudes towards the Slavs pertained on the Franks' eastern frontier.[90] Doubtless this thinking impinged upon the actual conduct of this type of warfare. One Frankish army which had to traverse Basque territory on its way to Spain began by hanging a leader and then rounded up the women and children of a village to act as hostages.[91] This does not appear to have been usual campaigning behaviour.

All of these views, and the nature of violence within and without a kingdom, led to a particular concept of the peacemaking king.[92] The peaceful king was one who created peace within his realm so that, to use Bede's account of king Edwin of Northumbria, possibly the most famous description of one such king, 'a woman could carry her new-born babe across the island from sea to sea without any fear of harm'.[93] Yet at the same time, a king made 'peace' through warfare, reducing his neighbours to acceptance of his peace. The Roman title *domitor gentium* ('pacifier of the nations') continued to be used to praise a great ruler.[94] Thus there was no contradiction between being a 'peaceful' ruler and waging warfare abroad. Peace was something primarily to be ensured within one's realm. An early medieval head of a household had a responsibility to keep the peace within his or her courtyard or under his or her roof, and other people who violated this peace were, as has been mentioned, punished severely. Similarly, and by extension, the kingdom was the king's domain and he had to maintain peace within it. Ideas of how strong a king thought he was can be judged by the ambition or scale of attempts made in law-codes to enforce this idea. Ine's law-code, referred to above, represents one such attempt.

Consequently the simple absence of 'war' did not constitute peace, even leaving aside the point that cross-border raiding was probably endemic most of the time. Peace between kingdoms was a state of affairs brought about through deliberate rituals and procedures, which we shall briefly consider at the end of the book. In the light of the foregoing discussion it will come as little surprise to find that warfare was a very important element within a wide range of social identities in this period.

2

WARFARE AND SOCIETY

Much of the period with which this book is concerned was an era of large political units. In terms of its geographical expanse, the Roman Empire as a state has never been exceeded in Europe, and its successor kingdoms were also of a geographical extent unsurpassed until the early modern period. In the later seventh century the Frankish kingdom briefly fragmented into semi-autonomous political units but that situation gave rise to the Carolingian state, which eventually encompassed most of western European Christendom. Yet Europe is not an easy place to govern. Physical geography cuts it into myriad small communities, which may not wish to belong to any larger political entity. Subsequent European (and world) history has demonstrated how difficult it is to coerce such communities into incorporation into larger states, even in days of mass conscription, advanced military technology and better communication and travel than existed in the fifth to ninth centuries. How much more serious must the problem have been in the period that concerns us? How large polities were able to exist in the early medieval west is thus a question of profound historical significance, and it is one which the present volume can assist in understanding.

A brief but necessarily superficial digression from the subject of warfare is therefore required.[1] The ties which bound polities together, and with them the dynamics of social and political change in this period (as throughout the Middle Ages), should be sought in the importance of the state in politics at various levels from the local to the supra-regional. Here, following Haldon, I define 'the state' as 'a set of institutions and personnel, concentrated spatially at a single point, and exerting authority over a territorially distinct area'.[2] The 'single point', though not spatially fixed, is the ruler and the central court. Since, as mentioned, it was and is very rarely possible for a state to impose its will simply by force, the key issue is rather the extent to which the state, its patronage and its legitimation of power are necessary within political conflict or competition. Jan Glete's comments on the early modern fiscal-military state apply equally well to the early medieval state:

> [the effectiveness of a state was] based upon [its] ability to penetrate society in order to extract resources and local elites' willingness to

support the state with their social capital: their ability to raise local resources and maintain social control. This willingness was usually greater if the elites found that the state gave them access to its patronage rights and distributed privileges to the elites. Penetration from above and investment of social capital in the state from below might appear in different mixes in different societies, but to some extent both needed to be present if the state was to succeed.[3]

'Penetration from above' and 'investment from below' exist in a dynamic relationship. In some parts (geographical and temporal) of the period covered by this volume the arena for political conflict which the state had to penetrate might be very small indeed: it was the individual rural community, with several local families competing to establish a lasting dominance. Here, investment in the state might be the only means by which a local family could acquire lasting dominance. At other times and places, when families have secured such pre-eminence at a local level, the arena might widen to become more usefully described as regional. Finally, in some circumstances within our period the political arena broadens into the whole polity, kingdom or empire.

The nature of the power of the winners in these political struggles, whom we might term the élite, will vary to some degree with the size of the political arena. We might, for example, distinguish the *de facto* most powerful, who simply possess more land or other resources than their potential rivals for power and whose power might be won or lost, even within a lifetime, from another type of élite – a more narrowly defined group of people, perhaps belonging to particular families and thus having a more hereditary status, and giving indications of a shared idea of cultural superiority over other classes. In an earlier work I used the more general term 'aristocracy' to cover all social élites, however defined, and kept 'nobility' for the latter group.[4] There I also said that a nobility should be legally recognised as well.[5] Here, I have continued to use the distinction between aristocracy and nobility, but have used nobility more sparingly, usually for cases where there are indications that the class shared a cultural identity.[6] Thus, of course, the élite is not to be seen as a single, uniform and unified body. Within a single polity (such as the sixth-century Merovingian kingdom) there may be *de facto* local aristocrats, a service aristocracy (defined by its tenure of posts within the administration) and an hereditary nobility. All might have different relationships with the state and with each other. Where the aristocracy has come to be more established throughout there might still be a distinction between the upper echelons of the nobility and more lowly, locally based families. This emerged, for example, in the ninth-century Frankish kingdoms. There the higher level of 'super-aristocrats' may have related to the state in a different way from lesser families, though the latter may have become more entrenched in their local power bases.[7]

The politics within which the state can intervene might be the simple interplay of identities within local communities through to the peer-group politics of a more powerful and established élite, or more complex situations involving the relationships between different types of élite or between an élite and less powerful classes. It is important not to see this as a 'zero-sum' game between kings and aristocrats, with each gain in power by the aristocracy representing a commensurate loss in power by the kings.[8] Clearly power is not a finite commodity. Furthermore, on the one hand, the élite was, as stated, not a uniform and unified group and, on the other, the personnel of the state are frequently (though not invariably) those very individuals whom we have just identified as the local, regional or supra-regional élite.[9] This is of critical importance in the raising of armies, as will become clear. It might, correctly, be objected that there is no necessary struggle between kings and their élites. A king might be able to draw wealth and power from vast resources without ever needing to worry about whether his writ ran throughout the realm or whether his nobility were in fact more powerful at a local or regional level than he was. Kings and aristocrats might see themselves as sharing a position that exploited the resources of a polity and aristocracies and kings thus benefit mutually from involvement in 'consensual' politics. Even where kings did try to intervene, there were probably, throughout the period, places which were not economically or strategically important enough to merit royal attention.

Yet it is important to note that whatever the theoretical possibilities, aristocrats and kings could and frequently *did* find themselves in competition. The sixth-century Frankish king Chilperic is alleged to have complained that no one had any respect for royal authority, all power having passed to the bishops.[10] Kings tried to undermine the independence of their aristocracies and make them more dependent upon royal patronage.[11] They tried hard to intervene directly in areas of their realms, and they were resisted by local aristocrats. Situations existed where aristocrats resented royal actions to such an extent that they rebelled, tried to seize the throne or sided with rival monarchs, and where kings actively adopted policies to increase their authority or the effectiveness of their rule within their realms. This must surely have been because, to some extent at least, there was, in terms of effective political power, a dialectical relationship between kings and at least some of their aristocrats. Increases in the power of one were perceived as entailing relative decreases in power of the other. Often changes in the power or ideological importance of the state or the élite did in practice affect the power of the other party. One does not have to postulate that power only existed in fixed quantities to argue that.

This dialectical relationship was probably brought about by competition for the basic resources of the kingdom, the produce generated by the land, however those resources were extracted. In order to secure access to those resources through the realm, a king had to ensure effective government. Royal concerns with the rhetoric of justice[12] or with the divinely ordained ministry of kingship were surely brought about by the need to underline the legitimacy of power wielded in the king's name and the illegitimacy of other forms of authority. This would increase the importance and desirability of royal patronage. Where the kings could manage that patronage to prevent the build-up of power bases antithetical to royal interests, they could keep control over the resources of the kingdom and use them in the further dispensation of patronage, in turn further increasing their power.

A static model wherein kings and their élites share in the control of land and combine to increase the possibilities of patronage is a more sophisticated view and represents in almost all ways an advance on the previous 'zero-sum' view of early medieval politics as a bipartite struggle (kings versus aristocrats). However, though this 'consensus' model copes adequately as a description of particular early medieval socio-political formations and practices, it neglects the seeds of change. If politics are simply to be seen as a competition (within the royal and aristocratic élite) for bigger slices in repeated cutting and re-cutting of the cake there would be little incentive for any changes in social structure. Indeed, for this reason, proponents of the view sometimes deny the existence of significant change within the early Middle Ages.[13] However, a long-term view calls this into question. First of all, at the very start of our period, the inheritance of the Roman Empire was not everywhere the same. In some areas there was serious social and economic collapse and in others local and regional nobilities were able to hold on to their positions of social and political dominance. It is clear, too, that there was change through time and, as set out in the previous chapter, this is only to be expected. This is apparent especially when one looks at the material cultural as well as the documentary evidence; because writers throughout the west tended to work within similar genres and from many of the same models the written data can have a tendency to homogenise. Close study reveals, through time, changes in the nature of the élite. The very diversity in the bases and extent of power within the élite produces tensions and com-petition, and the state and the legitimation of power which it provided could be and was used in these struggles. Thus, consensus within early medieval polities usually went hand in hand with conflict, emerging in the course of the resolution of disputes.[14]

To summarise this section, although this book ultimately seeks the dynamics for political change in competition for resources and thus espouses a materialist approach, it nevertheless sees the means whereby surplus was extracted from the primary producers, and its articulation in terms of rent or tax, as of lesser importance in the analysis of socio-political change than the means by which the state maintained its ability to intervene in politics throughout the realm. It shifts the emphasis from the study of the mode of production to the ways in which kings could intervene in the conflict between the private interests of landowners and their public ones,[15] and the means by which the state could maintain consent. This book will not follow any particular grand narrative; the historical conjunctures which produced particular events or situations could have yielded other outcomes, and the historian must discuss and analyse social and political change to reflect that possibility. If, in the end, the story remains the same, this is because we cannot now change those outcomes.

So, to return to our subject of warfare, whether or not a state can maintain an independent coercive force is a key factor in determining the state's ability to intervene in politics, and in the direction and nature of social and political change in the early medieval west. A coercive force could back up the power invested in local officials, increasing the attraction of royally bestowed authority, and protect the interests of the state's supporters. The ability to raise an independent coercive force is in turn closely related to the ways in which surplus is extracted to maintain the state. For example, a state that can raise revenue as tax may use it to raise and pay for a standing army. Providing it can retain the support of the army, the state will probably have a dominant relationship with the élites within its territory, and may reduce their real political power concomitantly. The situation need not always be as clear cut as set out here. The debate on the relationship between standing army and state creation in the early modern period[16] shows how the waters can be muddied when the funds needed to pay armies have to be raised by local or other estates or parliaments representing the interests of local élites. This requires the state to gain the consent of such groups. Trouble for a state equally might be created where local or regional leaders have, or can, gain control of a portion of a standing army. Furthermore, of course, leaders of a standing army have to support the state and its ideology. However, in the period with which this volume is concerned none of these situations ever appears to have pertained, or at least to have been problematic. Nor was there any élite group removed from the usual landownership/military service nexus and able to use its resources to pay for protection in the form of an army.[17] In the fifth to ninth centuries, power was based ultimately upon the control of the surplus from land, however articulated, and the wielders of such power, as we shall see, expressed their élite identity through military idioms.

A state may also raise revenue from its own lands, in the form of rents and so on, and not tax any other landowners. If this enables it to maintain a standing armed force of decisively greater size than those raised by its potential rivals within the polity, then that too will give it a dominant position. If, however, armies have to be raised by calling up the élites of the polity and their followers, in accordance with general systems of obligation, the position of the state is rather weaker. Though foreign wars of plunder and conquest may still be attractive, defensive campaigns in other parts of the polity may not attract the support of aristocrats whose lands were not threatened. Still less popular will be internal campaigns against rebellious aristocrats or those who resist the state's attempts at government. None of these situations need necessarily remain static; all contain possible seeds of change (see chapter 1).

Though this is an issue which will be dealt with in detail in the next three chapters, we can see a number of these possibilities in western Europe in the early Middle Ages. The late Roman Empire raised taxes and supported a standing army, which was thus able to suppress attempts at regional aristocratic revolt; political threat came from those who could claim the support of a significant fraction of the army. Post-Roman kings redistributed various forms of revenue from the landed resources of their realms to their army, thus also giving themselves a sort of independent coercive force. In Spain, the power of King Theudis was based largely upon his creation of a standing personal army of, allegedly, 2,000 men from the estates of his wealthy wife. Whatever the reality of the figure, we can assume that for a while at least (he was assassinated in the end) Theudis was able to raise a bigger force from his estates than any potential rivals, and could thus cow them into submission. Other post-Roman kings, such as the early Merovingians in Gaul, were able to use their patronage to undermine independently powerful local élites and make them dependent upon the state and its offices for their power. Here too, though it was largely comprised of these locally prominent people, the fact that the kings had the 'whip hand' in political relationships meant that the army remained an effective instrument of royal power. Later, as aristocratic power grew in some regions, armies became forces raised from the political community of the realm. This seems to have been the case in later Merovingian and Carolingian Gaul. In this situation the use of the army required a greater degree of consensus. As this book will make clear, a problem which repeatedly arose was the difficulty of raising armies when periods of expansionist warfare ended and a kingdom was more concerned with defending its territories against aggressors. The way in which armies were raised was therefore a key element in social and political change in the early Middle Ages.

With this in mind, it will not be surprising that warfare and the right to control or participate in it was a very important aspect of the construction of various forms of identity in this period. At the very top of society, early medieval kingship was closely bound up with warfare. Traditionally this was seen as an inheritance from ancient Germanic traditions imported into the rest of Europe as Germanic barbarians took over political control of the former Roman provinces. More recently, however, the roots of early medieval warrior kingship have been traced rather differently. In a very important book, Michael McCormick demonstrated a continuous thread of development in ideas which associated good rulership with military victory, from the late Roman Empire into the successor states in 'barbarian' western Europe and the East Roman or Byzantine Empire.[18] Certainly, the third and fourth centuries were periods when Roman emperors were usually soldiers, either by origin (the middle decades of the third century are sometimes referred to as the period of the 'barrack room' emperors and several major fourth-century rulers, notably Constantine the Great, Valentinian I and Theodosius I, rose from the army) or in their actual deeds once they were emperors. A major feature of strong rule in the fourth-century empire was an almost constant imperial presence on, or near to, the frontiers. This was important mainly for internal political reasons, but it was justified by the need to defend the empire from the barbarians. Taxation, largely to pay the army (in turn mainly used to defend against potential internal political threats), was justified by the need for defence.

Emperors spent lavishly upon frontier defences (despite recent theories about 'grand strategic' defence in depth), further justifying this taxation. Thus, not surprisingly, the barbarian threat and the emperor's ever-victorious role in keeping that threat at bay featured heavily in all sorts of imperial propaganda.

Post-Roman kings incorporated this into their ideas of good kingship. Fifth- and sixth-century panegyrics for early medieval western kings habitually stress their martial valour. By the seventh century, the Old Testament had become a key source of ideas about kingship, as it was obviously full of models of the righteous warrior king, such as David and Joshua.[19] In a sense, the characteristics of idealised kingship had not altered, but the idioms through which they were expressed had changed towards a greater relative emphasis upon Old Testament biblical models. Older motifs remained and of course there was considerable overlap between the two, not simply in terms of the array of characteristics regarded as making up a good king,[20] but also because the Western Roman Empire had been Christian for the last century and a half of its existence. It is interesting to speculate about the causes of this shift. In the middle decades of the sixth century the emperor Justinian attempted to reconquer the west, and indeed his armies destroyed the Vandal and Ostrogothic kingdoms and helped plunge the Visigothic realm in Spain into deep crisis. There was considerable ideological output from his court in Constantinople, stressing the 'loss' of the west and the need for its reconquest from the barbarians. It is possible that in the aftermath of this it became more uncomfortable for western kings to use straightforward models of Roman imperial rule to express their legitimacy. Classically derived motifs did not drop out of use; the emphasis merely switched slightly to other available sources of ideas, which could, perhaps, be used with less difficulty and with less apparent deference to a rival, dangerous source of political power.

Another origin for the military function of the post-Roman kings was the Roman army itself. A number of early medieval dynasties, and 'peoples', arose in the context of military service in the Roman Empire. Alaric's Visigoths seem to have originally been a Roman field army,[21] and Theoderic's Ostrogoths, too, took much of their identity and the legitimacy of their power from the facts that they had been in the service of the eastern emperor, Zeno, that their king bore an official Roman title, and that they were sent to Italy (officially) to recover it from the 'tyrant' Odovacar.[22] The king of the Burgundians also bore Roman military titles.[23] Meanwhile it seems that the power of the Merovingian dynasty derived from the fact that they had commanded a Roman field army on the Loire and in the Paris basin.[24] The Saxon kingdoms in southern England, too, may have originated in a fifth-century military command south of the Thames.[25]

Throughout the period, the idea of the warrior king continued to find expression in poetry, sometimes of new forms, and in particular in the vernacular poetry which began to appear during the latter part of our period. Carolingian poetry, for example, celebrates Charlemagne as a great warrior, and his descendants were also celebrated in this way in verse.[26] Similar ideas are found in Old English verse, dealing with biblical, 'heroic' and 'historical' themes, although not all of this can be placed within our period with absolute confidence. Weaponry gained symbolic significance in demonstrating royal power, especially when the weapons in question were regarded as holy relics.[27] In the ninth century, Sedulius Scottus, although promoting the idea that kingship should be viewed as a divinely bestowed ministry, nevertheless recognised that warfare was seen, especially by kings, as a central feature of rulership and that even a good, God-fearing ruler should be 'prudent in war'.[28]

Early medieval rulers had indeed to be war-leaders. Analysis of the evidence from the kingdom of Mercia between the beginning of the seventh and the middle of the ninth century shows that a major campaign of some sort was waged within four years of a change of king (Figure 1); in most cases the interval was much shorter. Mercia, however, is not well served with narrative sources; most of what we know of the kingdom comes from sources written outside Mercia, in hostile territory, and very often rather later than the events described. Had we a full picture of warfare in this period, it is very likely that we would see that Mercian kings led campaigns much more frequently and much sooner after their elevation. This pattern results either from a demonstration of their ability as an active war-leader to neighbouring kings and possible internal challengers for authority, or from attempts by neighbouring kings to 'test' the new king and perhaps create a new set of power relationships between the kingdoms. In Ireland a very similar picture emerges. In some cases it is specified that the king of a particular area was expected to mark the beginning of his reign by leading a raid against a designated enemy kingdom.[29]

The strength of kingship within a realm could affect this picture in practice. Merovingian kings were lauded for their military abilities and liked to present themselves as triumphant rulers.[30] However, the number of occasions when they actually led their troops in the field was at times quite low. The initial phase of Merovingian expansion, between the later fifth century and the 540s, saw repeated military expeditions led by the kings, in particular against foreign peoples. In the next phase of Merovingian history (c.540–c.590), although the kings were adults and engaged in fairly frequent warfare abroad and against each other, they rarely seem to have to led their troops on campaign. Instead, their dukes, counts, and, on occasion, sons, led the armies, as they themselves had done during the reign of their father, Chlothar I. None of this affected their presentation as war-leaders.[31] It seems that their position was so secure that they could collect the credit for any successes their soldiers scored. Nevertheless, there may have been occasions when they positioned themselves formally and publicly at the head of the army. We know that Childebert II of Austrasia held three assemblies in the 590s, at which he passed laws.[32] These assemblies were held on 1 March, the traditional date for the Frankish military muster. At least ceremonially, therefore, for we do not know whether any military activity ensued (though it must be conceded that evidence of warfare on the Franks'

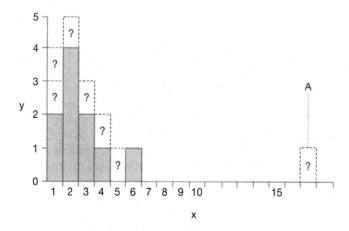

x – Number of years after accession, within which
   first recorded campaign was fought.
y – Number of kings who fought their first recorded
   campaign within x years
A – Average length of reign

Beornred and Ecgfrith of Mercia have not been included
as they only reigned for one year or less.

Figure 1 Incidence of warfare and changes of king in Mercia, 600–850

northern frontiers is extremely scarce at this time), the king had placed himself
at the head of the army. Given the frequency with which armies were raised
in the period, it is likely that his relatives in the preceding half-century had
done the same.

At about the time that Childebert held these assemblies, at the very end of
the sixth century and at the beginning of the seventh, the kings returned to
leading armies themselves, even if often against each other. This may have
been a response to changes taking place within the Merovingian realms, which
centred upon an increase in the power of the aristocracy. War-leadership by
kings such as Theuderic II and Chlothar II may have been needed to demonstrate continuing royal power to a more secure aristocracy, which, as will be
shown in chapter 3, was taking an increasingly important role in raising the
army. Sigibert III may have been the last Merovingian to lead his army on
a campaign outside the Frankish heartlands. Thereafter, the Merovingians
never seem to have gone to war except in the company of their senior palace
official, the mayor of the palace. That the presence of the mayor indicates the
relative impotence of the king is however an assumption drawn from historiographical traditions based ultimately upon the pro-Carolingian historians of the
early ninth century, like Einhard. Even the pro-Carolingian *Earlier Annals of*

Metz give an equal role to Theuderic III in commanding the army defeated by Pippin of Herestal at Tertry, and to Chilperic II in leading the force beaten by Charles Martel at Vinchy.[33] Nevertheless we should remember that the late Merovingians were very often minors, and changes in the nature of politics will also have given pre-eminence to the mayors of the palace.

Conversely, the strength of the Carolingian kingdom in the later eighth century was derived from repeated, intensive royally led campaigning. The Carolingian mayor of the palace, Charles Martel, led frequent campaigns to restore effective Frankish hegemony, which had collapsed after Sigibert III's defeat on the Unstrut (see below). His sons, Pippin and Carloman, and especially his grandson, Charlemagne, continued the tradition until, by 800, Charlemagne had made himself ruler of almost all of Christian western Europe. The Carolingians, however, had inherited a set of political relationships from the later Merovingian period, wherein the local and regional aristocracies were increasingly powerful. The Carolingians themselves were simply the most successful of the aristocratic dynasties which had competed for power in the later seventh and early eighth centuries. The eventual victory of the Carolingians was due in no small part to the military abilities of Charles Martel.[34] That victory was not preordained however, and the assumption of the title of king by Charles' son Pippin in 751 caused much tension and necessitated a great deal of ideological effort aimed at its legitimation. Constant and successful campaigning was also vitally important in binding powerful and potentially rival aristocratic families and factions to the new régime. Thereafter, Carolingian kings always had to be active war-leaders, and most were skilled commanders. Problems, as elsewhere in early medieval Europe, began when expansionist warfare ended.[35] The Visigothic kingdom's problems, with repeated usurpation and civil war, have similarly been associated with the end of the possibility of aggressive warfare against neighbouring realms.

The penalties for failure could be high. One of the best-known vignettes in Fredegar's *Chronicle* depicts the young Merovingian king, Sigibert III, sitting on his horse, weeping at the destruction of his army by the rebellious Thuringians under their duke, Radulf.[36] As a result of this defeat, effective Merovingian hegemony over the peoples beyond the Rhine collapsed, although, as has been very clearly demonstrated, this did not mean that the élites of these areas ceased to be interested or involved in the politics of the Frankish world. On another occasion, the Mercian king, Æthelbald, was defeated by the West Saxons at the battle of Burford (752). This defeat may have temporarily cost Æthelbald his overlordship in southern Britain, although the king of Wessex appears as a witness to one of his last charters, suggesting that hegemony had been restored.[37] It probably, however, cost Æthelbald his life; four years later his own bodyguard did him to death at night. A failure in battle against external enemies could apparently lead to internal rivals attempting to seize power. Kings of the Asturias often went into retirement, voluntary or forced, if unsuccessful or unable to lead the army against the Moslems.

At the end of the ninth century the political crisis which produced the break-up of the Carolingian empire was initiated in no small measure by the perceived failure of Charles III, 'the Fat', to defend his empire effectively against the Vikings. It has been very cogently argued that Charles' military policies were well thought through, and in many ways continued those of his predecessors; in some regards he may actually have been no less successful than other kings.[38] Charles' problem stemmed from the fact that he was unfortunate enough to be seen to fail in campaign against Vikings besieging Paris, the political centre of West Francia, whilst a powerful aristocrat from one of the most politically dangerous West Frankish dynasties, Odo, son of Count Robert the Strong, led a spirited, successful and, to some contemporaries, heroic defence of the city. Charles was seen as failing to help the beleaguered city in its hour of need. Modern analysis of the campaign can show that Charles' campaign was in many respects no different in its methods, and no less successful in its results, than many earlier or later campaigns against the Vikings, who, as will become clear, were very difficult foes. Yet to contemporary writers it was, rightly or wrongly, seen as a dismal failure and therefore the cost to Charles and the Carolingian dynasty was high. These writers, it has been shown, were hostile to Charles largely for their own reasons. Nevertheless, ninth-century politics was not governed by objective strategic analysis. Carolingian kings were expected to win battles, and by failing in a high-profile campaign at just the time when his enemies were winning heroic laurels, Charles presented his enemies with a golden opportunity to denigrate his abilities as king. Within a year or so he had been deposed by his nephew, Arnulf of Carinthia, who took over rule of the East Franks, whilst Odo himself replaced Charles as king in West Francia.

Warfare and the right to participate in it were equally important at lower political levels. Throughout this period, aristocrats were expected to be warriors. The early Roman aristocracy had taken both military and civil service as part of their careers in public life. In the later Roman period, the military and civil branches of the imperial service were separated. Partly this was a response to the civil wars of the late second and third centuries. Henceforth, the governors of territories would not command the troops stationed there, and the military commanders within a region would not control the supply of food and pay to their units. This appears to have ended the possibility of revolt by the high aristocracy. The Roman senatorial nobility seems in any case to have been barred from high military command although, paradoxically, military service could be rewarded with entry into the senatorial ranks. Nevertheless, the Roman aristocracy, at least in the provinces, continued to see military service as important. With the disintegration of the Roman Empire in the course of the fifth century, the provincial aristocracies played a significant military role, both against and for the different barbarian kings. It is therefore a mistake to see the period of political transformation from western empire to barbarian kingdoms as one which saw a straightforward change in the nature of the aristocracy from a civilian bureaucracy to a warrior aristocracy. Even less so can we simply associate developments in this sphere with the settlement of more militarily minded Germanic barbarians. Though often of Germanic descent, the aristocracy of the new kingdoms, like their rulers, derived in no small part from the former Roman army.

In the fifth and sixth centuries, however, even though aristocrats continued at least to make a pretence of interest in the traditional forms of Roman culture, it cannot be denied that the importance of the military role of the aristocracy grew significantly. Civic and military roles came to be merged in the same office, so that counts, for example, held civil jurisdiction over a territory and were also responsible for its defence and the raising of troops there. As we shall see, acquisition of such posts within the administration of the kingdom was often dependent upon performance whilst within the household of such service aristocrats or the king. This involved military and other violent activity. To take part in warfare, to join the army, meant to participate in politics. We shall see repeatedly that the army was the political assembly of a kingdom. Laws were issued with the consent of the army. In Italy the linkage was made especially clear in a document of 864, which listed the obligations placed upon free land-owners as service in the army, maintenance of bridges and attendance at the law courts.[39] Thus, it was the ability to make effective a right to join the army and to go to war, rather than a simple right to carry weapons, which marked aristocrats out from other members of free society. The aristocracy came increasingly to use violent symbols – weapons – as markers of its identity. It is also worthy of note that the exhibition of status through the lavish display of weaponry in burial was most pronounced in areas where local status was most open to competition, especially on the fringes of major political units.[40] This tendency became more marked as the period went on; the raising of armies increasingly became a matter of calling upon aristocrats to bring their retinues and other dependants.[41] The acquisition of a reputation as a warrior might bring status, renown and, in some areas, the chance to make a bid for the throne.

The warlike role of the aristocracy does not find such widespread expression as the king's role as war-leader, which is perhaps not surprising, but the sources do discuss the concept. The *Life of Saint Arnulf*, for example, when it discusses Arnulf's early career as a palatine aristocrat, describes his prowess as a warrior, and how he could single-handedly put entire enemy armies to flight.[42] This seems an odd virtue to find praised in the life of a saint. Indeed it is not a common feature of hagiography, but the author's purpose was to show that Arnulf had been a model secular aristocrat before his career as a model bishop and holy man. An Anglo-Saxon saint's life, the *Life of Guthlac*, also describes how, when he turned fifteen, Guthlac embarked upon a violent career as a warrior, as though this were the normal course for an aristocrat.[43] The *Life of Benedict of Aniane* relates his effective performance of military duties before his conversion to the monastic life (brought about by the drowning of his brother whilst crossing a river on campaign in Italy). The *Life* restricts open eulogy of military prowess to the career of Benedict's father, however.[44] Once again this emphasises how a model ninth-century aristocrat was expected to be a good soldier. Other saints' lives also mention weapons and other military equipment as symbols of aristocratic identity.[45] When a Bavarian aristocrat called Ratolt gave land to Freising Abbey he appeared at the ceremony 'with his sword belted on in virile fashion'.[46] Similarly, on the east wall of the monastery of San Benedetto in the Italian Tyrol, a benefactor was painted holding his sword in front of his body.[47] Some poetry for, or about, members of the aristocracy also demonstrates how the ability to be a good warrior was essential to the construction of the aristocratic image. The Latin eulogy for Duke Eric of Friuli uses many of the same phrases about his military skill against foreign enemies, borrowed from Roman imperial victory ideology, as were used in the praise of kings.[48] The late Anglo-Saxon poem, *Maxims*, states that 'an earl belongs on a charger's back'.[49] At the end of this period the classic central medieval tripartite concept of the division of society appears: *oratores*, *laboratores* and *bellatores*, those who pray, those who work and those who wage war. Note that at this date the word used was *bellatores* – those who wage war – and not simply those who fight (*pugnatores*) or even those who defend (*defensores*).[50] This division of roles is nowhere clearer than in the instance reported by the *Annals of St-Bertin*[51] where the 'common people' between the Loire and the Scheldt formed a sworn association to defend themselves against Viking attack but were attacked and slaughtered by the local aristocrats for presuming to do so.

Ethnic identity was, in the very early part of our period, closely connected with warfare and military service. This stemmed, again, from the nature of the late Roman army. The fourth-century Roman army had recruited heavily from amongst the barbarians. Another consequence of the separation of the military and civil services was that the army appears to have begun to adopt consciously non-Roman identities; what we may call a 'fictive barbarism', but one obviously strengthened by the presence of troops of non-Roman birth within the ranks. As the late Roman period wore on, these identities became more important. Many army commanders were wholly or partly of barbarian origin, and in the chaos of the fifth century some field armies began to adopt their ethnicity. Thus, for example, Alaric's Goths apparently originated as an Illyrian field army, as mentioned above. After the creation of the territorial kingdoms, the troops began to settle on the land (see chapter 3). Military service was thus performed by 'barbarians': Franks, Goths and so on. The Romans paid tax. As we have seen, military service was a path towards social and political power, so this service was a privilege, seemingly much sought after. Ethnic identity thus had a functional dimension, and that function was service in the army. In Italy the military component of Lombard ethnicity was especially clearly expressed; a Lombard freeman was called an *arimannus* (a latinised Germanic term) or an *exercitalis* (its Latin equivalent). Both mean 'army man'. A similar functional difference may have existed in Anglo-Saxon England, where it is possible that burial with weapons was a marker of Anglo-Saxon identity.[52] The barbarian military class formed a higher social stratum and thus this formed one part of the origins of aristocratic military identity. In time these ethnic identities became very widespread, whilst the aristocracy became more powerful. This forced a renegotiation of social structure and a redefinition of the upper social echelons, and was part of the creation of the military aristocracy. To some extent, however, this weakened the military associations of identities such as 'Frankish', 'Gothic' or 'English'.

As will have become clear, an early medieval – like a modern – individual stood at the intersection of a series of social identities: we have just considered social class or rank, and ethnicity. These identities were interconnected, and changes in the definition of one, as noted, brought about changes in the construction of the others. This is a key feature of the processes of social change. Gender and age are other important social identities, and warfare played a part in constructing these too. In the post-Roman period, masculinity was intricately associated with violence. Social politics were bound up with the threat of violence, and the right to defend against such. Dispute settlement involved displays of the right to take violent revenge,[53] and sometimes these rights were translated into action. Thus the male head of a household, with a legal identity and dependants to defend, symbolised this role by carrying weapons. This was certainly violent imagery. It is clear that the social category of 'male' was heavily bound up with the carrying of weapons. The furnished burials of the period show very clearly how weaponry was a male symbol *par excellence*. Cemeteries in northern France, lowland Britain, southern Germany, Scandinavia and northern Italy all reveal the use of weapons to demonstrate masculine identity. This was not the same in all places at all times. The age of the deceased could, furthermore, moderate this picture. None the less, we cannot assume that masculinity was less associated with violence in the areas where weaponry was not buried. The furnished burial ritual was a product of particular social and political circumstances; areas without weapon burials are those areas where these circumstances did not pertain. The custom was by no means uniform in any case. In Visigothic Spain, weapons are used far less commonly in burial deposits, yet it does not seem likely that Spanish society was less warlike, or male identity less bound up with fighting, than elsewhere. As will be seen in chapter 8, numbers and types of weapons do not reflect the scale of violence or the relative level of armament, but the intensity of the competition for local power revealed by the rite.

Nevertheless, important though it was, the type of violence represented by early medieval *faida* is not warfare. Not all masculinities were represented in death by weaponry; not all mature adult males were buried with weapons. Yet the ability to threaten vengeance and to participate in that level of violence was not, at this period, restricted to any segment of the free population. The furnished burial is only one ritual context, and it seems likely that more people carried weapons in life than were accorded the right to be buried with them. Here we begin to see how gender is cross-cut by other social identities. As noted earlier, the presence of weapons in a grave may mark out 'barbarian' identity (Frankish, Anglo-Saxon, Gothic, Lombard, etc.). As we have seen, that identity was associated with warfare and the right to participate in it. Frankish, Anglo-Saxon or Lombard masculinity was symbolised in death ritual with weaponry, and that weaponry symbolised warfare. It is possible, too, that the weaponry which appears in late Roman inhumations of the late fourth and fifth centuries also demonstrates a link with the army.[54]

The carrying of weapons by males clearly brought problems. The Church repeatedly passed regulations banning clerics from carrying arms.[55] By the Carolingian period at least the Church viewed weaponry as characteristic of lay dress and thus the prohibition on clerics carrying weapons was a means of underlining the visible separation of laity from clergy.[56] On the other hand, judging from these canons, it seems that some churchmen felt their masculinity was diminished by not bearing weapons. Perhaps other social groups, such as the 'Romans' of northern Gaul or Britain, felt that theirs was a 'lesser' masculinity and that this also encouraged the widespread adoption of non-Roman ethnic identity. Conversely, we can see why the insults relating to treachery and cowardice on the field of battle and penalised in Frankish and Lombard law were held to be so grievous.[57] They seriously impugned a man's masculinity.

Early medieval battle, as will be discussed in chapter 9, was fought at close quarters in formations which depended upon mutual support for their cohesion. A warrior had to be sure of those who stood to each side of him (especially on his unshielded right-hand side) in the battle-line. This necessity – as we shall see, it was literally a matter of life and death – surely lay behind the communal feasting and drinking which helped to bond the warrior classes. The need to express this martial reliability may have produced the boasting culture apparent in the feasting halls depicted in the late Anglo-Saxon epic *Beowulf* and elsewhere. Conversely, however, this competitive male assertion of martial prowess, this obsession with reputation, honour and saving face, may have led to hot tempers and drunken, hasty, sometimes fatal brawls amongst young warriors. 'From one, an irascible ale-swiller, a man full of wine, a sword's edge will thrust out the life upon the mead bench; previous to that, his words will have been too hasty',[58] as one Anglo-Saxon poet predicted. We might also note the reference to three types of alcoholic drink in this one sentence – a clear indication of the nature of aristocratic feasting!

Women were not expected to take part in warfare. In lower levels of violence it was understood that, however undesirable the situation might be to law-makers, women *did* get involved.[59] Warfare remained the male category of violence *par excellence*, although there are occasional instances of female involvement, especially in sieges.[60] One story in the *Liber Historiae Francorum* depicts the Frankish Queen Fredegund leading the Neustrian army to battle, but the tale is clearly heavily infused with legendary elements. It has the Franks 'carrying' Chlothar II with them, though he would have been twelve or thirteen at the time, and contains a scene reminiscent of Shakespeare's *Macbeth*, where the Neustrians disguise themselves as a forest.[61] Warfare was able to be the most exclusive form of violence because of its scale and the deliberation involved in its practice. Matters may have differed in defensive campaigns, especially in times of emergency, but when an army was raised for an offensive war it was done so selectively, from particular social groups, as we shall see in the following chapters. The army was thus a deliberately exclusive group, and not surprisingly, given that it usually equated with the political assembly of the kingdom. Consequently, participation in the violent activities of the army – warfare – was equally exclusive and involvement in warfare became an important marker of social identity.

Age was also an important social identity. As chapter 3 shows, in some areas of post-Roman Europe age grades were important in the raising of the army. Throughout the period, young warriors were considered as a distinct social category, particularly serving in the households of more powerful freemen. The early medieval terms for retainer, *puer*, *vassus*, even knight (*cniht*), all ultimately mean 'young man', 'boy' or 'lad'. When the count of Bourges sent his retainers to punish some tenants of St Martin's church who had not performed military service on the recent campaigns against the usurper Gundovald,[62] the phrase used by Gregory of Tours, *misit pueros*, can be translated literally as 'he sent the boys round'. It seems that the age at which a boy was expected to begin to perform military service was about fifteen.[63] Yet, in the furnished cemeteries of the period, the age around twenty was symbolised by the acquisition either of new and more numerous types of weaponry or, in some areas, of weaponry of any kind.[64] It would seem that one had to serve some sort of apprenticeship before one was regarded as having the right to be buried with weapons and thus acquire a full social identity (in this case, as we have seen, one based around ethnicity). Later in the period, as social structures were adjusted as the aristocracy became more established and powerful, such age identities continued to be important amongst the élites. The socialisation of a young noble warrior hinged on his acquisition of weapons and the sword belt.[65] As will be discussed in chapter 3, several societies seem to have made an important distinction between the categories of 'young warrior' and 'old warrior'. As we shall also see in the next chapter, the male life-cycle in some social groups was based around military service and the achievements gained whilst performing it.

Military service may often have been the business of rather older men than we might expect in the light of modern experience. Twentieth-century warfare was infamously the business of very young men. In Normandy in 1944, soldiers in their late twenties were regarded by their comrades as 'old' and the average age of the GIs in Vietnam was nineteen. British soldiers in the Falklands in 1982 were even younger: only eighteen on average. However, in the furnished cemeteries of the sixth century full weapon sets typically symbolise mature adult men (between about thirty and fifty, or even sixty). Later, Ripwin, a landowner in the middle Rhine area, first attests charters in 767, suggesting he must have reached legal majority (about fifteen years) by then. Twenty-five years afterwards, in 792/3, he was called out on campaign to Italy and made various dispositions about what was to happen if he did not return. Ripwin's worries were reasonable enough; Italy was a graveyard for armies, if more through disease than battle. Nevertheless, Ripwin did come back – he appears in the documents until 806 – but these charters show that he was still serving in Charlemagne's army until at least his forties.[66] Charlemagne himself continued to campaign actively into his sixties; Liberius led an East Roman army on campaign in Visigothic Spain when he was in his eighties, though whether he did any active fighting is unknown.[67] The ninth-century vernacular poem, the *Hildebrandslied*, describes the two participants in the final tragic combat between father and son (who do not recognise each other) as both being old and experienced fighters. The *Liber Historiae Francorum* also describes Chlothar II, taking the field against the Saxons, as 'white haired'.[68]

Warfare in the early Middle Ages was, as chapter 9 demonstrates, a matter of steel nerves and brute strength, rather than agility. Close fighting with spear and shield requires strength and stamina to be sure, but also, and possibly more importantly, cunning and the knowledge of how to attack and parry – knowing the moves. An experienced warrior can spot the type of attack being launched, parry it and riposte with a minimum of physical effort. He knows where and when to use physical effort, and not to waste it on wild, frenzied attacks. Except possibly against raw, untrained troops, accuracy and blade- or point-control is more important than mere ferocity. Repeated experience of battle made a warrior more likely to survive it. As will be seen, it was this accumulation of experience which made the Vikings such difficult foes to beat. It is very likely that the same factor made eighth-century Frankish armies so successful. Success breeds success. On the other hand, states whose armed forces had had little experience of warfare might find themselves at a distinct disadvantage when attacked by more hardened forces. Thus, it would seem, the easy success over Lombard armies enjoyed by battle-tested Frankish forces in the eighth century. The rapid collapse of the Avar kingdom in the 790s probably owed as much to the Avars' generally peaceful and isolationist existence in the eighth century as to the clever strategies employed by Charlemagne and his commanders.

Warfare was an important factor in early medieval economics as well as social structure. At the level of political economy, it was often vital. Successful wars brought booty. That booty in turn could be distributed amongst the participating warriors who, as we have seen, constituted the political assembly of the kingdom. Such distribution seems to have been carried out according to established custom (see chapter 7). In the gift exchange economy of the early medieval world this was a recognised means of establishing lasting ties of allegiance. Further service would be expected in return for these gifts. Conversely, when, besieged by the Burgundian army in St-Bertrand-de-Comminges, the pretender Gundovald was asked by his general, Mummolus, to return the sword belt that Mummolus had given him, he realised that his supporters were about to desert him.[69] The recipients of these gifts would, in turn, use them to reward their friends and followers and strengthen their own positions of power. In warfare of raid and counter-raid, such as was very common in post-Roman Europe, booty might well be taken back by the other side when they next launched a retaliatory raid. That side would then distribute and redistribute it to maintain its own power structures. As will be seen, however, material booty was not always the most important thing gained from warfare; it also produced gifts of titles, honours and the more intangible benefits of royal or aristocratic patronage. Thus, in the field of political economy, warfare could serve to maintain the status quo rather than alter it. When patronage and political favours were at stake, warfare could often primarily serve the needs of internal politics and mean that the primary relationships involved in this type of violence were not those of aggressor and defender, but the political relationships within the attacking army.[70] On the other hand, the inability to wage such warfare and thus be able to distribute and redistribute these rewards might impose stress upon a kingdom. This surely was one reason for the appearance of internal strife within kingdoms which had (like the Carolingian state in the ninth century) ceased to expand, or (like seventh-century Visigothic Spain) run out of neighbours to attack. These considerations might also explain why Anglo-Saxon kings rarely incorporated the territories of defeated kings into their own, but instead left them as tributary kingdoms.

Warfare could have other effects on the economy, however. On the negative side, repeated Viking attacks, though probably not the primary cause of the decline of the emporia (trading stations) of north-western Europe, doubtless aided their demise. However, the Viking great armies of the later ninth century were paid, or paid off, in large quantities of coin; over 7 million pennies were minted for the purpose in later ninth-century Francia alone.[71] Comparatively little of this coin appears to have made it back to Scandinavia. Instead it would appear to have been spent in the markets of England and Francia. Obviously, the implication of payment in coin is that the troops will then use that coin to buy their own food, drink and other items. This cannot but have stimulated the growth of the markets which had been developing slowly in the hinterlands for the previous century or so. In turn, the injection of large quantities of silver coin into these markets, and into the hands of the people who went there to trade with the Vikings, will have added a considerable impetus to ongoing processes of monetisation. A couple of instances from the *Annals of St-Bertin* may serve as illustrations. In 865 a Viking army against which Charles the Bald was campaigning sent 200 of their number to Paris to get wine (presumably to buy it). In 873, a Scandinavian force besieged in Angers obtained, as part of the peace settlement, the right to hold a market on an island in the Loire until February. Charles the Bald outlawed the selling of arms, armour and horses to the Northmen.[72] Thus the part which the Viking great armies played in bringing about the economic and urban explosion of the tenth century was significant, and should not be neglected.

It may be that much warfare preserved the status quo but warfare also played an important role in bringing about change. The invocation of warfare as a factor in historical change has, as discussed in chapter 1, become unfashionable in recent decades. Warfare *was* important, however. As we have just seen, warfare helped oil the cogs of early medieval political systems and underpin many dimensions of social structure. Consequently, as implied above, an absence of warfare could cause considerable stress within post-Roman kingdoms. The fates of certain kingdoms were themselves governed by warfare. Vandal Africa, Ostrogothic Italy, the Lombard kingdom and Visigothic Spain all had their historical existence terminated by warfare. The kingdom of the Scots went into a period of decline in the middle seventh century as a result of the repeated military defeats suffered by its ruler, Domnall Brec.[73] Later, the final unification of the Pictish and Scottish kingdoms was facilitated by a catastrophic defeat at the hands of the Vikings, which killed off a number of the leading Pictish claimants to the throne.[74] We have noted already that the fates of individual rulers could be determined by their perceived success or failure in war. On the other hand, the Carolingian Empire came into being through the mechanism of conquest.

As is well known, the twenty years of the Gothic wars in Italy were decisive in bringing about the end of the ancient socio-economic order in the peninsula. At about the same time, in Spain a similar period of stress seems to have been occasioned by political weakness within the Gothic kingdom, that weakness itself consequent upon the demise of the royal dynasty which had ruled the Goths since the early fifth century. The demise of the dynasty was brought about by the deaths of Alaric II in battle against the Franks, and of Amalaric, killed during another Frankish invasion by a Frankish warrior called Besso, according to the *Fragmentary Chronicle of Saragossa*.[75] The Gothic kingdom entered a phase of fairly short-lived kings and eventually a civil war sparked by King Agila's defeat by the inhabitants of Cordoba. That civil war in turn produced East Roman intervention and the creation of a Byzantine enclave around the southern coast. From this period onwards we see the end of the old Roman villas and of the production of fine ceramics in the antique tradition within Spain. Furnished burials appear, indicative of local social and political stress, especially around the edges of the kingdom. Conversely, the unified Visigothic kingdom of the late sixth and seventh centuries was created by the conquest by King Leuvigild's Gothic armies of the other, smaller political units within the peninsula.[76]

Although all of these changes took place at a high political level, their effect on society cannot be negated. This is true even where we are not talking of wars as undoubtedly destructive as were the Gothic wars in Italy. Responses to military crises could bring about important change in political structures even at the local level. For example, as will be argued in chapter 4, later ninth-century royal reactions to the Vikings involved attempts to recreate direct links between the royal court and local free landholders, bypassing the usual chains of aristocratic dependence. Royal response in England included the construction of fortified centres, the *burhs*, which aided royal administration and increased the very visibility of the state in the localities, though the full working through of this process lies beyond the scope of the present volume. Other high-level political changes could lead to changes in the relative weight of some of the identities used in local social politics. Much of the social change of the period, as intimated above, was brought about by the interplay of different identities, and we have seen how changes in one dimension of social structure produced changes in the others. Thus the increase in the power and potential independence of the aristocracy, and the gradual adoption of non-Roman ethnicities by the free population, brought about changes in the definition of ethnic identity. That in turn led to the military basis of masculinity and social age, earlier more widespread amongst the free population being confined to particular social strata. In this case especially, we can see just how many of the social identities involved in the processes of change were bound up with the practice of warfare. At the same time as warfare and its role in high politics could bring about change in local social structures, social change could lead to change in the means of raising the army, and it is to that vital subject that we now turn.

3

RAISING AN ARMY (1): POST-ROMAN EUROPE

In terms of wider historical significance, how armies were raised is probably the most important question to confront any examination of early medieval warfare. In this problem lie many of the keys to the dynamics of post-Roman socio-political change. In our period we can chart a development from the last regular standing armies of Roman times to the earliest of the armies of lords and their landed retainers that characterised central medieval military forces. It should not be thought, however, that this development was inevitable or preordained, or that its outlines were everywhere the same. We shall see change dependent upon particular circumstances, and specific attempts to respond to that change. The evidence for the survey is patchy in coverage over both time and place, and never much more than suggestive. We can do no more than sketch its general contours from uneven sources: normative sources that we cannot be sure are descriptive, and descriptive sources that we cannot be sure are typical. It is clear that the development 'on the ground' was much messier than this sketch must inevitably make it appear. Clearly, therefore, to understand how early medieval armies were raised and organised we must break down the four and a half centuries that concern us into sub-periods, and contextualise the evidence as far as possible.

The later fifth and early sixth centuries

The crucial period during and immediately following the final demise of the western Roman Empire is unfortunately badly served by written sources, so much of our discussion must be hypothetical, using the patchy fifth-century evidence and attempting to draw inferences from what appear to be remnants or survivals from this period in the sources of the sixth century. This method is far from satisfactory but a fairly coherent picture seems to emerge.

The Roman Empire had of course maintained a regular army throughout most, if not all, of its existence in western Europe, and continued to do so in the east (the so-called Byzantine Empire) for many centuries afterwards.[1] From the period of the Tetrarchy (the period of reform, c.284–324, when the empire was, notionally at least, ruled by four emperors) military service became separated from the civil bureaucracy; territorial military commands ('the Saxon Shore', for instance) were established which were distinct from civilian administrative units. The army itself was divided into several types of troops, a gradation which came to replace the traditional division into legionaries and auxiliaries. At the core of the empire were the imperial bodyguards and other 'palatine' regiments. Then came the 'praesental' field armies (those 'in the presence' of the emperor) and after them the regional field armies. The troops of the field armies were known as *comitatenses* (companions). The troops on the frontiers were called *limitanei* (borderers) or something similar (*ripenses* – 'river bank troops' – for example). In line with the later Roman Empire's usual workings, those troops further from the Empire's political core (located wherever the emperor was) were more subject to the detrimental results of corruption, such as abuses by their officers. In the later fourth century, however, units of *limitanei* were still called upon and transferred to the field armies (becoming *pseudo-comitatenses*), indicating that they must still have been considered capable of playing some battlefield role, even if only as reserves. The deterioration in the quality of the *limitanei* was, therefore, a slow process.

There are, however, no references to regular armies or regiments in the post-Roman states. What had become of the Roman army? It has been suggested that the reason the Roman Empire fell was that it was unable to keep paying its army and that the army therefore gradually disappeared, leading in turn to an increasing dependence upon barbarian federates and, eventually, to the disappearance of the Roman state itself.[2] As an explanation for the whole problem of 'the End of the Roman Empire' this is unconvincing, for it leaves unanswered the necessary questions, either of why the western Roman state should simply no longer have been *willing* to pay its armed forces or, if it remained willing to pay the armies, of how it lost control of so much tax-producing territory that it was no longer *able* to pay them. Nevertheless, it does appear that, after the increase in size of the Roman armed forces during the Tetrarchy, recruiting within the empire became, unsurprisingly, more difficult, possibly leading to increased enlistment of barbarians. It seems, however, that most barbarians were recruited into the regular units of the army, particularly the field armies and palatine units, which gradually adopted an increasingly barbarian identity, perhaps to differentiate itself from the now more clearly separated civilian population. As the western Empire fell apart, from the end of the fourth century, the barbarian or 'barbarised' units and field armies became the focus for new provincial identities. Generals of barbarian origin, commanding 'barbarised' armies, became kings of peoples, and settled their followers in the territories they governed.[3]

As a result of these processes, the relationships between the army and civilian society in the late Roman Empire formed the model for those between 'barbarians' and 'Romans' in the post-Roman world. The 'barbarians' (Goths, Franks, Lombards and, possibly, Anglo-Saxons) were the army and seem to have been exempt from at least certain forms of taxation, just as the late Roman army had been. In the same way as the army had been subject to its own laws and the jurisdiction of its commanders, the 'barbarians' were often also governed by particular law codes issued by their leaders, now kings. Consequently, as discussed in chapter 2, ethnicity became functional: 'barbarians' fought, Romans paid taxes. Conversely, there was also an ethnic nature to military forces. In northern Gaul, for example, 'the Franks' were the army, just as in Ostrogothic Italy 'the Goths' were the army.

How the barbarians were settled and paid has long been a matter of debate. Legislation and similar governmental material from Visigothic Spain, Ostrogothic Italy and Burgundian south-eastern Gaul, suggests that each 'barbarian' soldier was paid by being allotted a share of a particular estate: a third in Ostrogothic Italy; two-thirds in Visigothic southern Gaul and Spain; and a more complex arrangement, based upon two-thirds of farmland, in Burgundy. Traditionally it has been thought that these 'thirds' were actual shares of an estate's lands. The late Roman army was quartered on the civilian population through what was known as *hospitalitas*, whereby a soldier was assigned to a civilian householder, who in turn handed one-third of his house over to the soldier's use.[4] The similarity in the shares of the house led to the supposition that this system was used to parcel out the estates and, indeed, there were references to barbarian *hospites* (guests) quartered on Roman landlords.[5]

However, in view of the apparent general acquiescence of Roman landlords and, in Ostrogothic Italy, explicit statements that the Goths were funded without the Roman landlords feeling any loss, Goffart suggested[6] that what was in fact divided up was the *tax revenue* of the estates; a barbarian soldier was assigned to a particular estate and the estate holder simply paid to that soldier one third of the taxes which, normally, would have been paid to the government to help pay the army. Goffart also pointed out that the *hospitalitas* system was not concerned at all with the payment or provision of subsistence for a soldier, only with furnishing a roof over his head. Thus it provided no necessary model for the system of paying and provisioning barbarian troops in the later fifth and sixth centuries. In fact none of the references to barbarian 'guests' actually states that the barbarian is any more than simply billeted on the landlord in the old Roman way; there is no suggestion in these references that the barbarian *owned* any of the latter's estate or its produce.[7] Goffart's hypothesis has the advantage of simplicity; the system was streamlined by, to some extent, bypassing the 'middle man' – the tax collector. The soldier simply collected his pay at source. Furthermore, Goffart's proposed system has clear antecedents in Roman legislation about the payment of élite field army troops, precisely the element of the Roman armed forces which included the 'barbarian' units.[8] Ostrogothic Italian evidence seems, on the whole, to support the theory as far as the payment (as opposed to the settlement) of Gothic troops is concerned.[9]

However, not all historians have been convinced by the Goffart hypothesis. It has been pointed out that, to accept Goffart's theory, we would have to accept that the Romans suddenly started using hitherto fairly straightforward words for land and real estate in a completely new way, as shorthand for *the revenue from* land and real estate. Furthermore, a good deal of the evidence, especially that from Visigothic and Burgundian sources, is unambiguous in discussing *terra* – land – and not the revenues from land. It is also clear that the Burgundian situation at least (and probably the others too) was rather untidier than Goffart's attractively neat and simple theory allows for, not least because the details (such as they are) of the settlements are (except in Italy) generally recorded rather late, and probably after several stages, and changes to the original details. References to a serious rebellion involving Roman landowners during the reign of Gundobad of Burgundy also question whether acquiescence in the system was universally the norm.[10]

Another possibility which has been proposed but not expounded in much detail, exploits the difference in Roman law between *ownership (dominium)* and *possession (possessio)*.[11] If the barbarian soldier was granted *possession* of a third (or two-thirds), but the landlord retained *dominium*, then we can see how the barbarian soldiers could have been supported from the yield of the land without the Roman landlords technically losing any of their estates. The landlords would also have their tax bills reduced, providing a further 'sweetener'. In practice, the barbarian soldier would probably exploit his 'third(s)' by simply collecting rents or the old tax revenue, so the general result would be similar to Goffart's system in its day-to-day workings. Overall, however, we should probably not expect a simple, unified and unchanging system, and a single explanation is unlikely to work with complete plausibility in all cases and across the whole period of barbarian settlement. Whatever the exact details, however, for our purposes the main points are, firstly, that an armed force was able to be maintained at (to some extent) the state's expense, providing the latter with an independent coercive force (see chapter 2), and, secondly, that a form of professional, regular (or at least semi-regular, or, as we might today think of it, 'reservist') army existed in many of the states of the post-Roman West.

In Ostrogothic Italy, Theoderic used regular assemblies of the army as a means of displaying royal power and prestige. Such assemblies brought the ordinary Gothic warrior to one of the three main royal centres (Ravenna, Verona and Pavia), where they could be exposed to presentations of royal ideology. By rewarding the faithful and punishing those who neglected their duties he made these assemblies an important means of enhancing the prestige of royal favour, and undermining the authority of such Gothic magnates as were not dependent upon such favour for their social position.[12] Frankish kings appear to have used annual assemblies, which seem to have taken place on 1 March ('the Marchfield') for very similar purposes throughout the sixth century. These gatherings, probably drawing their origin from the post-Roman peoples' beginnings in the Roman army, were very important in maintaining the direct link between rulers and the broad-based rank-and-file of their armies, mediated only by royal officers.

How such an army was organised in detail is difficult to establish. There is no evidence of the survival of any individual regiment of the late Roman army into the post-Roman period anywhere in the west.[13] Any units that did survive the 'fall' of the empire seem rapidly to have become subsumed in the general ethnic nature of the immediately post-Roman armies, that is to say that they *became* Frankish, Gothic or 'Saxon'. This is most likely to be true of the units of the field armies, of which the 'ethnic' armies of the post-Roman period were the direct descendants. What became of the border troops, the *limitanei*, is less easy to establish. Eugippius' *Life of Saint Severinus* contains a famous passage wherein a regiment stationed on the upper Danube in the fifth century realises that it has not been paid for longer than usual, and sends a number of its members to collect their overdue arrears; the latter are, however, killed by the barbarians.[14] The unit deduces that the empire has, to all intents and purposes, come to an end, and disbands. Whether or not this story is apocryphal, its outlines may very well be quite typical of the fate of many border regiments neverthe-less. Others may have transformed into warbands with their old commanders as warlords. Those which did will eventually either have been destroyed or disbanded by rival warbands or armies, or, if they could, joined the successful leaders, those who became kings. If so they too will probably have adopted the ethnicity of their leader.

There may have been occasional exceptions. Gregory of Tours mentions *Taifali* living in Poitou in the late sixth century. The Taifals were a people who had been neighbours and close associates of the Goths north of the Danube in the fourth century,[15] and those who preserved this ethnic identity in Gregory's day were probably the descendants of Taifals settled in the region during the late Roman or Visigothic periods.[16] If so, they may well have been settled in return for military service, retained a military function in later periods, and con-tinued to hold land in return for this, although it must be said that neither of Gregory's references places the Taifals in an explicitly military context (though one refers to an uprising of the Taifals against their bishop). If this speculation is correct, they managed to retain their ethnic identity, rather than being subsumed into the ranks of the Franks. This exceptional survival may have been, firstly, because Taifal identity had previously been subsumed within a more general Gothic identity and surfaced only after the expulsion of the Goths from southern Gaul after 507; secondly, because their settlement was located on what had been the frontier between Goths and Franks in the late fifth century, and such identities tend to be kept longest on frontiers;[17] and, thirdly, because the adoption of Frankish identity by the military and political élite in Poitou never became common. Furthermore, as will become clear, in matters of the raising of armies, post-Roman Aquitaine was rather exceptional.

In some areas, outside Italy, where the Roman aristocracy remained power-ful, most notably in Aquitaine and Spain, it appears to have gained a military role. The 'demilitarisation' of the late Roman aristocracy has been much overstated.[18] In the closing decades of the Western Empire, some aristocrats had indeed raised private armies and attempted to resist the expansion of the 'barbarian' kingdoms. It was not therefore an enormous step for them to take military commands within the post-Roman kingdoms. This was most true in the southern areas of Gaul, where the local nobility were serving in the Visigothic and Burgundian armies and in the Visigothic navy even when the Roman Empire was still in existence, and when other such aristocrats were defending its remnants.[19] In parts of Spain, the local Hispano-Roman aristocracy raised troops from its estates and was able to maintain political independence or semi-independence until the mid sixth century.[20]

It seems most plausible that the dukes and counts of a kingdom were responsible for maintaining and supplying the troops within their areas of jurisdiction, particularly the *civitates* or city-districts which had been the administrative building blocks of the Roman empire and which continued to be so in most of the post-Roman states (Anglo-Saxon England being the most notable probable exception[21]). The troops would need to be parcelled out throughout the kingdom for much of the time to ease the collection of the yield from their *tertiae* ('thirds') in whatever form this took but this was not very different from the late Roman situation, when troops had similarly been billeted throughout the provinces. In times of crisis royal officers would call up the troops in their areas of jurisdiction and then bring them together into larger military commands, armies, usually commanded by *duces* ('dukes', another inheritance from the late Roman situation) if not under royal command.[22]

The bodyguards of individual leaders formed a core element of immediately post-Roman armies. In the last days of the Western Roman Empire individual generals raised their own bodyguards of *bucellarii* ('hardtack eaters', a reference to the double-baked bread which hardened troops took with them on campaign), and post-Roman leaders apparently did the same. *Bucellarii* are mentioned by that name in slightly later Visigothic Spanish sources[23] as the followers of dukes and counts and it seems very likely that they existed earlier. It would be surprising indeed if post-Roman kings and other leaders did not provide themselves with bodyguards. The Ostrogothic king Theoderic is said to have disbanded the old Roman guard units, which had become mere 'show regiments' of little military value,[24] but Procopius mentions bodyguards surrounding the last Ostrogothic kings of Italy in battle.[25] Although he uses the classical Greek word *hypaspistai*, it is likely that these guards were in reality called something like *bucellarii*.[26] Bodyguards are mentioned by Sidonius Apollinaris as in attendance upon the Visigothic king, Theoderic. Some of these units may have been quite large, and formed a cadre of royal officers and other servants. Throughout our period, the royal bodyguard, at the palace, was where warriors, in addition to military training, were taught literacy and other governmental skills.

Thus, in the immediately post-Roman period we can trace transformations in the nature of the army, its methods of recruitment and payment, and its relationships with the state, but these nevertheless remained recognisable descendants of the late Roman system. The most important change would appear to be the end of distinct territorial military jurisdictions. As becomes clear by the later sixth century, the military territorial commands were those of the civil and religious administration, the *civitates*. There are occasional references to ducal commands, with military functions, on the frontiers but, at least by the time we know anything about them in detail, the *duces* in charge appear to have had civic jurisdiction in these areas as well.[27] In Spain the Gothic kings seem to have maintained parallel hierarchies of civil and military offices, and armies were assigned to provinces, but these military areas corresponded with the civil units of province and *civitas*.[28]

The later sixth century

We have rather more detailed evidence to help us by the later sixth century, but it seems clear that things had changed somewhat by the time that authors like Gregory of Tours wrote their works, and this makes it difficult to project their testimony back into the fifth century. The dynamics for change would appear, not surprisingly, to have lain in the ethnic nature of the armies, and in the late and immediately post-Roman system of paying the troops. Gradually, whatever the original details of the settlement, the soldiers paid in 'thirds' began to settle on the land, either converting an earlier right to revenue into one of ownership, or, perhaps, an initial grant of *possessio* into rights of *dominium*. These sorts of conversion, more easily carried out by armed warriors at the expense of civilians, appear to have been the subject of some concern at the court of Theoderic the Great.[29] One might expect this to be particularly common as the soldier in question grew older, married and began to think of settling down. In the late Roman Empire, military service had usually been an hereditary profession. In the early fifth century the empire had enacted that in some cases subsistence payments, made directly from tax-payers, might also be inherited by the sons of senior bodyguards.[30] When military service became associated with an ethnic identity, this was underlined. The sons of Franks or Goths, for example, would be considered Frankish or Gothic too, and thus heirs to their fathers' status, lands, obligations and privileges. Thus troops probably regarded their *tertia* as heritable too.

Soldiers also began to buy or otherwise acquire other lands to live on which they regarded as subject to the same exemptions. The *tertia* granted to barbarians, whether land or revenue, were tax exempt. Roman soldiers had been exempt from the *capita*, the poll-tax, in any case. The 'barbarians' who had become the army in the post-Roman west, regarded these exemptions not only as heritable but also as applicable to all their landed possessions. It would seem that a common political conflict in the sixth century arose between the army (whether it be known as 'Goths', 'Franks' or whatever) who wished to preserve the 'logical' extension of their privileges, and the kings, who attempted to retain the old system in its strict sense, and thus avoid the gradual dissipation of their tax base. This struggle is dimly documented. In Gaul, Gregory of Tours mentions two occasions when 'the Franks' attacked tax collectors who had dared to raise taxes from them.[31] In both cases the hapless tax collectors were assaulted following the death of a king. It would seem that during the reign of an effective adult king such unrest was stifled, but might burst out against royal officers during minorities or periods of confusion in the immediate aftermath of a royal death. The point of these tales is not opposition to taxation in general, but resistance to the taxation of groups who considered themselves exempt. The fact that the attacks took place during periods of weak rule suggests that the taxation had been of assets which were of disputed status: strong kings enforced the levying of taxation on lands which 'Franks' had acquired in addition to those assets which they held in return for their military service and which were exempt from tax. All this would be perfectly legal, but one can see why the 'Franks' themselves, exempt from the poll-tax and unused to paying tax on their other land-based assets, could have seen this as unjust oppression.

Hand in hand with these developments was the gradual adoption of 'barbarian' ethnicities by the free population. The acquisition of Frankish ethnicity in northern Gaul brought, as we have just seen, increasingly thorough exemption from taxation. It also brought legal privilege. Although a Frank would be liable to military service, this was, to all intents and purposes, a privilege, as the army was the political assembly. Good service brought rewards in royal patronage: grants of land or tax revenue, treasures, and offices in royal service. In sixth-century northern Gaulish cemeteries it seems likely that Frankish identity is manifested by the deposition of weapons in burials.[32] By about AD 600, Frankish ethnicity had become more or less universal north of the Loire.[33] Those of the free population who had not managed to acquire this ethnic identity lost their free status as well, so that Romans in seventh-century *Ripuarian Law* are equated with the half-free, and are required to have a free Ripuarian (a Frank) speak for them at law.[34] A similar process seems to have taken place in Visigothic Spain too – by the seventh century, Gothic identity became the norm.[35]

The result of these processes was that by the later sixth century the social group from which the army was raised had become a class of landholders. The nature of service was not defined by landholding, and landholding was often a reward rather than a prerequisite for service, but the members of the army were nevertheless, on the whole, landowners. In some areas they were those who claimed a particular ethnic identity: Frankish in northern Gaul; Gothic in Spain. A similar situation may have pertained in Italy after the Lombard invasion. The period immediately following the initial Lombard attack is very badly documented but it would seem from a rather garbled account in Paul the Deacon's *Historia Langobardorum* that the Lombards adopted the system which had been in widespread use in western Europe up to that point; the Romans seem to have been divided amongst Lombard warriors as *tributarii* (tax-payers).[36] However, this system would appear to have been short lived. There is no very clear indication of it in the earliest Lombard law-code (Rothari's Edict of 643), although the king does describe the political community of the realm as the army (see below).

This situation was not universal, however. A later sixth-century northern Gallic capitulary refers to Roman soldiers[37] and some Romans at least continued to serve in Visigothic armies.[38] In Aquitaine, Roman landholders had, by the sixth century, become subject to military service, this clearly being a development of the situation at the very end of the empire. Gregory of Tours' *Histories* abound with references to the 'men' of particular *civitates* under arms. He refers to king Guntramn of Burgundy calling up those liable for military service, and punishing those who failed to turn up. The implication of his account is that landowners had become liable to military service whereas tenants were exempt.[39] This body of landowners is probably what Gregory of Tours means when he talks of the *populus* of a *civitas*. It also seems that *populus* acquired a military sense in his writing,[40] which is interesting, as the vernacular languages also came to use their words for 'the people' as a synonym for 'the army'. *Minor populus* ('the lesser people') is used on one occasion[41] to mean the rank and file of an army.

The army, as implicit in the foregoing discussion, was still raised by royal officers from old civil administrative units, normally the *civitates* but also its sub-divisions, the *pagi*. Gregory, in his *Life of the Fathers*, seems to refer to a man from the pagi on campaign.[42] In some parts of Gaul, at least by the seventh century, the *pagi* had replaced the *civitates* as the basic units of administration.

As before, bodyguards remained the core of military forces. Sources refer to the personal retainers not only of kings but also of dukes, counts (and their wives) and even bishops. Such troops are, as mentioned, called *bucellarii* in Visigothic Spain, although the term *saiones* is also used.[43] Once granted his weapons, a Gothic *bucellarius* was permitted to keep them for good. Any landed property he received, however, remained ultimately in the *dominium* of his patron.[44] In Lombard Italy, by the seventh century at least, members of the royal retinue were known as *gasindii*. Such royal bodyguards were known as *antrustiones* in Merovingian Francia and as *gardingi* in Visigothic Spain, and are, in all cases, a slightly more complex category than might at first be expected. Although some at least may always have been in attendance on the royal person, by the time anything substantive can be said about them (in the seventh century) they seem to have been high-ranking, probably fairly experienced soldiers, in many cases found not at court but elsewhere in the kingdoms, commanding their own forces.[45] By this time they seem to be a category of service aristocrat. Whether this had always been the case, or whether it was a transformation which had taken place since the sixth century, is difficult to establish. Merovingian evidence suggests the former alternative. In the sixth-century Gallic narrative sources such 'old soldiers', close to the king but only in attendance upon him intermittently, are referred to by a different term, *leudes*, and there are two Frankish references to *spatharii* – one of the terms for late

Roman imperial guardsmen – who are certainly such palatine officers.[46] This last term is also used in an earlier Burgundian source. However, early sixth-century Salic Law refers to two types of royal retainer: the member of the royal *trustis* or retinue (the *antrustio*), and the *puer regis* (king's boy). The former is a powerful figure, with a high *wergild*, as a result of his connection with the king, but seems already to be commonly found away from the court. Often assumed to be a class of unfree or semi-free warriors, the *pueri regis* clearly simply represent a junior, lesser level of the royal bodyguard. One seventh-century saint's life refers to service amongst the *pueri* of the royal court.[47] The word is, furthermore, that most commonly used for the personal retainers of Merovingian dukes, counts and other notables. The general picture would, then, seem to be that young men were sent, or promoted, to serve in the royal bodyguard, where they would, in addition to serving as bodyguards, receive a military and probably administrative education.[48] They would occasionally be sent out to enforce royal orders or administration in the kingdom (Salic Law refers to *pueri regis* who are counts, for example; Burgundian references to such retainers similarly place them in contexts of administrative errands). Gradually, good service would lead to more substantial rewards in land, titles and other valuables and the guardsman would move out from the court either to take up a military/administrative office (as a count or duke, for example) or settle on his lands as an *antrustio* (or *gardingus* or *gasindius*), returning to court for major occasions or for shorter spells of service, perhaps commanding and teaching the junior *pueri*. This pattern, of permanent service at court gradually giving way to a position as a landed aristocrat, remains common throughout the early medieval west. In Spain, King Theudis took the interesting step of raising a personal army of 2,000 slaves from the estates of his wealthy wife.[49] Quite apart from providing him with a handy independent force, this seems to have been the forerunner of the extensive use, in Visigothic Spain, of personal retinues raised from slaves and other lowly inhabitants of one's estates.

Discussion of the *pueri* introduces the point that age and position in the life cycle played a very significant role in the raising of early medieval armed forces.[50] In the immediately post-Roman period it seems to have been particularly important. The process of male socialisation was a long one which began with legal majority between about twelve and fifteen, and did not end until the man married and began a family of his own, perhaps in his late twenties. The Latin term *puer*, as well as meaning 'boy' in the sense in which we would understand it today, could be used to mean any male who had not yet married and settled down. As we have just seen, this is the sense in which it is used in the context of the *pueri regis*. Once he reached legal majority, it seems that a Frankish boy would be sent as an apprentice to an older male from another family, perhaps a royal officer or an ecclesiastical potentate. From there the *puer* might come to the notice of someone more powerful, even the king, and be transferred to their household. Such apprenticeships could clearly be hard on the young apprentice, who was expected to get his master's permission before he could marry, an act which symbolised his change of status and release from the bonds of his apprenticeship.[51] This career path, and military service, was thus an important engine of social mobility and opportunity. Archaeologically, it is revealed by study of furnished cemeteries. Male children are very rarely interred with weapons. Weaponry begins to be acquired at about twenty years of age, and it may be that mature adult males are interred with fuller sets of weapons.[52]

As well as forming the retinues of older and more powerful figures, bound by what might be termed vertical ties to the latter, young warriors might also be bound by 'horizontal' ties into bands of contemporaries. Such warrior bands are probably those called *contubernia* in Salic Law,[53] envisaged as involved in house-breakings and kidnappings, precisely the sort of errand on which *pueri* are often engaged in the narrative sources. The bands of young men within a royal or aristocratic household could be called a *contubernium*.[54] Membership of such a band created long-lasting bonds and a group of young men could be called *contubernales*.[55] Thus it seems likely that in many sixth-century armies, there was a division into older and younger warriors. Whether such warriors were formed into separate units, as in other age-based societies, is perhaps unlikely but far from impossible. This would be more likely in those areas north of the Loire where the social role of age appears to have been more significant. It is possible that such warriors performed different battlefield functions (see chapter 9) though, as with so much discussion of early medieval warfare, this can be no more than speculation.

The development of military service in Britain is even more difficult to establish. Here we must work largely from inferences from the archaeological evidence. Excavated cemeteries provide the primary form of evidence, but, as in Northern Gaul, furnished inhumation with weapons does not become common until the sixth century. In the fifth century, weapon burials seem to represent displays of prestige by the local aristocracy; they are fewer than would be the case in the sixth century.[56] Clearly, military power was an important factor in local leadership. What is perhaps more interesting for our purposes is that in the middle quarters of the fifth century, south of the Thames, a style of metalwork became common which was descended from the official metalwork of the late Roman Empire, and in particular the late Roman army. This 'Quoit Brooch Style' is found on belt buckles, clearly continuing the Late Roman fashion for displaying power and rank through elaborate belt sets, and on some weaponry. This insular development of late Roman military fashions, and its use in burial rituals to demonstrate power, suggests that in Britain we may also be faced with a situation where a late Roman field army gradually evolved into the basis of a post-Roman kingdom, as in Northern Gaul, Aquitaine and Italy.[57]

By the sixth century furnished inhumation had become much more common in lowland Britain. Recent work has shown that weapons, the primary symbols of masculinity, were used as symbols of age.[58] Unlike in Gaul, male children were commonly buried with a spear. However, shields and other weapons tended to be acquired in the late teens and early twenties. Again, this implies that only at this age was it deemed appropriate to symbolise a man's male identity with a full set of weaponry; the symbolic category of 'warrior' seems to have begun at this age, as in Gaul. The overall picture suggests that by the sixth century a system similar to that in Gaul was in place, where armies were levied from broadly defined categories of adult males. The right to symbolise one's status through weapon-bearing seems to have been held quite widely. It seems likely that this weapon-bearing class may have been that which claimed an English identity. The construction of several substantial linear earthworks at this time implies that rulers could levy significant numbers of men through this system.[59] As in Gaul, this may have been modified by service in the household of aristocrats and kings and by the age of the individual in question. Later Anglo-Saxon evidence strengthens the plausibility of this suggestion.

In the west and north of Britain, there is less evidence to help us. Gildas[60] mentions, in connection with the employment of Saxon federates, *hospites* (as mentioned above, the Roman technical term used in billeting) and the payment of *annonae* (food and other supplies raised as a tax), which would indicate a survival of Roman commissariat systems. However, the chronology of Gildas' 'historical section' is notoriously difficult to establish, and he may actually be describing a late fourth-century situation.[61] Though it is difficult to be sure of when Gildas was writing (estimates range from the late fifth to the mid-sixth centuries), we might at least state that when he did write he and his audience were familiar with such institutions. The construction or refortification of numerous hillforts, and the evidence found inside them of craft specialisation and industry suggests that magnates had considerable control of surplus and the ability to mobilise significant amounts of manpower.[62] It would seem that, in the fifth and sixth centuries, the rulers of these areas were rather more powerful than those in the lowland zones. How armies were raised is difficult to know in any detail. From the available evidence we might suggest either that kings raised troops through an intermediary tier of lesser royal officers based in local hillforts, or conversely, that kings mustered armies by calling upon lesser local magnates whose power centred on these fortifications. The two alternatives are equally plausible from the data available, but have rather different implications for the relative strength of the kings; the first suggests powerful, centralised states with effective royal administration of local areas, whereas the second implies a more fragile situation where powerful independent lords would need to be bound into the polity through strategies such as the bestowal of prestigious gifts. Patrick, in his letter to the probably unidentifiable British king, Coroticus, complains of the excesses perpetrated by his soldiers.[63] Contemporary written sources are so few and so unsatisfactory that they allow us to state no more than the barest fact – which we could guess even without any documentary evidence – that kings were able to raise armed forces!

In the former 'Free Germany', similar points may be made from the cemetery evidence as were made for Anglo-Saxon England. In Alamannia, the archaeology suggests change between the fifth and sixth centuries. In the fifth century a number of fortified hilltop centres exist, similar to those in western and northern Britain.[64] These largely appear to have been abandoned around AD 500. At the same time there is a change in the nature of the cemetery evidence. As elsewhere, furnished burial becomes more common within cemeteries. Some sixth-century sites imply that age played an important role in the levying of armies. Children are sometimes buried with arrowheads, and adolescents sometimes have a scramasax or a spear. The full weapon set is reserved for adults above the age of twenty, however.[65] These changes in the archaeological record probably indicate a change in the nature of local authority in Alamannia, from a network of powerful independent local rulers to one wherein power was held by officers appointed by the Merovingian kings and their representatives. This in turn may have meant a change in the way in which armies were raised, but this is difficult to establish.

Further north, it is difficult to say very much. The Saxons and Thuringians proved significant foes for Frankish armies in the fifth and sixth centuries. The Thuringians indeed established a fairly large kingdom and were deemed worthy of alliance by Theoderic of Italy until Clovis' successors eliminated the realm in the earlier sixth century.[66] This may have led to a situation analogous to that in Alamannia, with the removal of earlier power structures and the introduction of a state of affairs in which appeal to Merovingian authority was used as a basis for local power. Archaeologically, the use of weapon burial, increasingly common through this period, implies a social structure wherein local authority was open to competition within a fairly broad weapon-bearing class.

In Scandinavia we have only archaeological data to help us but these have been carefully recovered and studied. The Danish bog finds, which cease to be deposited around AD 500, have been studied and shown to represent armies largely made up of lightly armed infantrymen, led by a smaller number of better-equipped men, who possessed horses as part of their equipment.[67] This suggests some stratification within the armies. However, one must be cautious in using this evidence in too straightforward a fashion. The deposits probably represented the *matériel* taken from the dead and captured members of an opposing force; mounted troops would be more likely to get away, and thus the numbers of such warriors might be significantly under-represented in the bog finds. Throughout Scandinavia at this date, fortifications show an ability to organise significant amounts of manpower. In the west of Norway, a detailed study of large boat-houses[68] has revealed concentrations of such buildings which could house ten or more ships. Such numbers of vessels would need more manpower than the local population could furnish to put to sea. Taken in conjunction with neighbouring high-status settlements and burials, it seems that these clusters of prestigious sites reveal the centres of magnates who could call upon the manpower of more extended areas to raise naval forces. The mechanisms whereby this claim on manpower was articulated are not known; a system of renders paid to a king or kinglet, as elsewhere, or one whereby kinship and gift-exchange networks were used, or some mixture of the two, are all equally possible.

Overall, in much of the west, the sixth century is a period when kings seem to have raised armies by a general levy on certain types of free landowner. In many areas this landowning class was defined by a claimed ethnicity (Frankish, Gothic, Lombard, Anglo-Saxon), which also represented a direct link with the king. Elsewhere the levy may simply have been on all landowners. Such a 'horizontal' levy was carried out by royal officers within the kingdom's administrative districts, and focused on the household retainers of those royal officers. Thus in this situation the king retained a significant amount of power. The army was mobilised according to a general obligation to the king, an obligation complied with because attendance at the muster was one way in which claimed ethnic and other statuses were justified. Furthermore, the officers mobilising and commanding the troops were in many cases service aristocrats whose power and authority over other freemen depended entirely upon their tenure of royally bestowed office, and receipt of other forms of royal patronage. Even where, as for example in Aquitaine, the aristocrats who led the regional contingents came from independently wealthy noble families, they still competed for office, for it was largely their participation in royal administration which cemented and safeguarded their families' local standing. In this context, the king held most of the aces, and could use the army effectively as a royal coercive force. This can be seen very clearly in sixth-century Merovingian Gaul, where the kings frequently called out armies to crush aristocratic dissent.[69]

The seventh century

From the early seventh century the sources available to us are more numerous and more evenly distributed across the west. We have seen how, by this period, the 'ethnic' armies descended from the late Roman field armies had evolved into armies raised from classes of landowners. This evolution continued through the seventh century, and we can begin our survey of this period and of this general development with Frankish Gaul.

In the decades around 600, significant social change had taken place, centring upon a change in the nature of the aristocracy, which increased its local power in a period of royal minorities.[70] *Ripuarian Law*, unlike sixth-century *Salic Law*, mentions free men in the service of others, and that a free man might have what it terms *satellites* (a term which remains one of the most common terms for a Frankish aristocrat's followers), further suggesting the increased importance of ties of dependence between aristocrats and lesser freemen, independent of royal service. Aristocratic family identities were stressed and terms such as 'noble' (absent in sixth-century sources for the north of Gaul) used to describe these people.[71] By the early eighth century in Neustria (north-western France) even the term 'the Franks' could be used to mean only a group of noble lineages.[72] It is clear that the northern Gallic aristocracy was capable of dealing with the kings from a position of much more secure local pre-eminence than had hitherto been the case.

Part and parcel of these changes was the end of old-style taxation.[73] Immunities from royal exactions appear to have increased in number, although these rarely exempted the grantee from military service. At least one extant document, however, expressly states that the king's officers could not exact the *haribannus* (at this date a fine for non-performance of military service, as discussed below) within the estates of the beneficiary,[74] presumably implying that the king's men could not raise troops there either. In other cases, the fact that royal officials could not enter the immunity possibly implied that the estate owner was left to raise troops himself or herself (or, in the case of institutions, itself). In one instance a local *dux* grants land, specifying that his officials may not enter the estate to collect the *haribannus*.[75] This might suggest that the *dux*, Liutfrid, had the right to extract this fine.[76] If so, this would be very interesting, further implying the devolution of the right to raise troops, at least in peripheral areas like Alsace. However, it is also – perhaps equally – possible that the scribe simply borrowed a phrase from a formula referring to royal dues and applied it willy-nilly to an aristocratic donation, regardless of actual rights.

These changes had a bearing on military service. The last reference to a *civitas* levy seems to be the account of the treachery of the men of Mainz, who began the Frankish army's flight in battle against the Thuringians in 639.[77] The same story also refers to a contingent from Saintes campaigning hundreds of miles to the east of their homeland, but a passage in Fredegar's *Chronicle* for 631 points the way to future developments.[78] Here we come across the first reference to *scarae* – bands of chosen warriors. The implication is that military service was now more socially selective, rather than being (theoretically at least) levied upon the whole population of free Franks. This is hardly surprising given the gradual adoption of Frankish identity by almost the whole free population of northern Gaul, noted above. This process may be reflected by the fact that weapon burial seems to become more common in the seventh century. A certain redefinition of social identities, particularly among the élite, was also necessary. It has been argued that, as Frankish identity became universal, the military responsibilities exacted upon the free population were adjusted accordingly.[79] The emergence of a more powerful local aristocracy in the decades around 600 seems to have brought with it the reduction of other members of the free population to dependent (as noted) or even semi-free or unfree status. This might have reduced the numbers of Franks but one imagines that although all Franks continued to be theoretically liable to military service this social group was now too large even if one only counted the heads of families. Military service came to be moderated by wealth, in turn manifested by landholding, as those with real local power used this to secure their place in the army.

However, the power of the Merovingian monarchy after 614 should by no means be underestimated.[80] A document of 694 makes it clear that the obligation to perform military service for the king was still exacted upon landowners. When Theuderic III waged war against the Austrasians in 677 a man called Ibbo refused to go, and was fined a swingeing 600 *solidi*, to pay which he sold his portion of an estate in the Beauvaisis to the Abbot of St-Denis.[81] Clearly the imposition of military service was still taken seriously. *Ripuarian Law* fines all those who do not perform the services due to the king when called upon to do so, imposing the sum of 60 *solidi* on recalcitrants (this sum was later that imposed as the *haribannus*, when that term meant fine for non-attendance at the muster).[82] The law implies that services could be exacted upon all and sundry; the unfree, including 'Romans', who were now subordinate to Ripuarian Franks, have their fine paid by their lord. However, the law makes clear that this is a fine for all types of service: 'if anyone has been lawfully conscripted by order into the king's service, *or into the army*, or into any remaining service' (my italics). It seems likely that service in the army was restricted to free men, especially given that a complete call-up of every able-bodied adult male was impractical and probably undesirable – the military worth of the poor semi-free being at best dubious. This clause cannot support the idea of a more general call-up. Innes has suggested that, although technically a 'fine', *haribannus* might better be understood as a 'royal due', a sort of tax.[83] He collects significant and telling evidence to support this reading and certainly proves the case that the *haribannus* should not automatically be understood to mean a fine for non-attendance at the army. However, the sources showing the *haribannus* as a 'royal due' are almost entirely late eighth or ninth century in date (we shall return to this in more detail in chapter 4), and even in the ninth century it is clear that the *haribannus* could be a fine for non-attendance, and a fairly stringent one at that.[84] Sixty *solidi* was a fair sum (and in Ibbo's case, discussed above, the fine was even heavier). Thus, by the time that we have detailed evidence on the subject, the situation is confused. *Haribannus* could mean two things: a tax for the support of the army raised from those who were not expected to serve in a military context, and a fine for those who were specifically summoned to attend, but who refused.[85] The late Merovingian sources are unambiguous in talking of *haribannus* as a fine, but this does not rule out the existence of an 'army tax' in this early period. It is probably more likely, however, that between *c*.650 and *c*.800 the term broadened in usage from meaning a fine to being used for a due as well.

Nevertheless, it may be that there was a significant change of emphasis. On the whole, it is difficult to see the use of the old administrative units – *civitates* and *pagi* – in the raising of later seventh-century armies. Such levies were perhaps now more selective, although the troops were still called out on the basis of the general obligation of military service. This duty, it would seem, was now laid upon all landowners, rather than upon 'Franks'. The latter identity was now too widespread. As Ibbo's case shows, these were the wealthy landowners, too. Possibly, as in sixth-century Aquitaine, there was a difference between landowners and tenants, with the latter contributing to the cost of the subsistence of the army as an army tax (as was later the case). Even in the absence of evidence, an 'army tax' would be plausible, in a sense maintaining, but simultaneously redefining, the old distinction between military service and the less prestigious payment of dues. That military service was held to be the more dignified alternative is supported by the Saxons' successful renegotiation of their dues to the Merovingian kings; instead of paying an annual tribute in cows, they would defend the Franks' frontier against the Slavs.[86]

Especially given the nature of seventh-century Frankish warfare, it appears that as the seventh century wore on armies were increasingly raised through calling up aristocrats and their dependants, down what one might loosely term a 'vertical' chain of lordship and dependence (this need not necessarily have made the armies themselves any smaller). However, we must see such ties of dependence as forming loose social networks, networks which may have involved gifts of land in exchange for support, and the swearing of oaths of loyalty, but which did not involve formally, let alone legally, established systems of the tenure of land in return for service. Such networks were personal and often informal, and rewards may more often have been in movable goods or even more intangible things such as local backing, support in disputes or intervention in legal cases. As has been seen, an ever messier and more ill-defined situation in the sixth century made it increasingly difficult for post-Roman kings to establish clear-cut relations between landholding and service; it does not seem that aristocrats had as yet created any more clearly defined system. Nevertheless, these factions still fought for control of the royal court for that gave an important degree of legitimacy to the armies which were raised, and to the campaigns that they waged.[87] Such legitimacy probably enabled calling out whatever remained of the old style levy, as we have seen.[88] Possibly, too, acquiring the right to call up the army gave aristocratic factions the ability to penalise and take the lands of those who, like Ibbo, did not support them. This situation contained within it important seeds of change. By the end of the seventh century such changes were already in train, which we shall examine in chapter 4.

The developments of the seventh century did not exclude the continuing importance of age in determining military service. Throughout Gaul, young men still served as *pueri* in royal and aristocratic households, and received education and training in so doing. Such service created other networks of bonds and ties between the young man's family and that of his lord, but these career paths may increasingly have been restricted to members of the emerging nobility and their followers.[89] Thus the political strategy of creating links through these 'apprenticeships' seems to have become limited to a much narrower peer group.

How armies were raised in Aquitaine is difficult to establish.[90] As far as can be seen, the general mechanisms appear to be the same as for the northern regions. The increasingly (in practical terms) independent dukes of Aquitaine may have been able to raise old style city-based levies but this is never specified. What seems clear is the increasing use of troops from the Basque regions (probably lightly equipped horsemen). By the middle quarters of the eighth century Frankish writers even referred to Aquitaine as *Vasconia*. The reasons for this apellation are difficult to determine for sure. It has been suggested that the designation of Aquitanians as *Vascones* (Gascons – Basques) was intended as a slight, to emphasise the Frankish view of their inferior status as a 'rebelling' group, just as in sixth- and early seventh-century accounts. This is not entirely convincing, as Roger Collins has pointed out. Instead it may simply be that the extensive use of Basque troops by the dukes of Aquitaine made it seem to the Franks that that was the identity of their enemies.[91] Another possibility is that the Aquitanian dukes may actually have focused a political identity in opposition to the northern Franks on the Vascones, on the basis of the Basques' military importance. This would be a similar process to that which had happened earlier in other regions. As it was, the Frankish conquest nipped the process in the bud and from 780 an Aquitanian regional identity was promoted.

Military service in Anglo-Saxon England has been a hotly debated subject, and change through time has not commonly been taken into account in arguments which have all too often taken data from all points between our earliest surviving documents, around 600, and the compilation of the great administrative survey of Domesday Book in 1086.[92] The evidence available suggests that the system of raising armies in the seventh-century English kingdoms was not unlike that employed in contemporary *Francia*.

The key element in Anglo-Saxon armies would appear to have been aristocratic followings. Such followings could include men raised from the aristocrat's estates, or the children of clients, as well as men of similar birth. In the later seventh century, Saint Wilfrid, when he reached warrior age, acquired a following of *pueri*; slightly later, Saint Guthlac, at the same age, gathered about him a band of *satellites*.[93] Bede describes the – for its day – huge force raised by Penda of Mercia to attack Oswy of Northumbria, in one of the great showdowns of seventh-century English history, as comprising thirty contingents led by aristocratic leaders. Bede uses the classicising term *legio* but it seems clear that he means the followings of the so-called *duces regii*. Archaeologically, we can also see a change in the nature of the burial rite. Unlike in Gaul, where it might be suggested that more frequent weapon burial relates to the spread of Frankish identity, in Anglo-Saxon England, although English identity was also spreading, weapons became rarer and concentrated in fewer burials.[94] The status denoted by such symbols, whether or not it bore any relationship to actual military experience, seems to have been that of the leading stratum of society: the controllers of military activity.

In King Ine of Wessex's law-code, probably dating to about 694, the king legislated about aristocratic (*gesipcund*) leaders who intercede with their own lords, with the king or with royal officers, on behalf of members of their household, slave or free. It is in this context of the importance of vertical chains of dependence and clientage that we should understand the following, much-discussed clause which sets out fines (*fyrdwite*) for failing to perform service in the *fyrd* (the army): 120 shillings and forfeiture of his estate for a landed *gesip*; 60 shillings for a *gesip* without land, and 30 shillings for a *ceorl* (roughly, a well-to-do free peasant). All such types could be found in an aristocratic retinue.

As with the preceding clause, we appear to be moving down a chain of dependence.[95]

As in Francia, age seems to have played an important role. Anglo-Saxon sources suggest a distinction between the younger warrior, called *geoguþ* in later poetic sources, and apparently usually rendered into Latin as *iuvenis*,[96] and the older warrior, called *duguþ* in Old English and *comes* in Latin.[97] Hagiographic sources make it clear that fourteen or fifteen was the age at which a young male was expected to embark upon a military career.[98] Young warriors would have dwelt with their lord.[99] As in Francia a key point in the life-cycle appears to have been reached when a male married and settled down. This would seem to be confirmed by a celebrated passage in Bede's *Ecclesiastical History*.[100] Having been knocked unconscious during a major battle on the river Trent in 679, a Northumbrian *iuvenis* called Imma was captured by the victorious Mercians. Fearing for his life, Imma denied that he was a soldier (*miles*) and declared that he was a poor, married rustic who had come, with others of his ilk, to bring supplies for the Northumbrian army. The passage has often been discussed, but usually in terms of what it says about the military obligations of peasants (*ceorlas* in Old English). The fact that Imma said that he was a *married* peasant has often been overlooked. It would seem that a poor but married and settled peasant would only be called upon to carry supplies to the army; an unmarried *rusticus* on the other hand might well be serving (as a *puer*) in the military household of his lord, as we have seen.[101] The distinction in age is likely to relate to the landed/landless distinction noted in Ine's laws. Loyal service to a lord would eventually bring its reward in the form of land on which the warrior could settle, thereby enabling him to marry. Thus the *geoguþ* or *iuvenis* became a *duguþ* or *comes*.

The king did not have to rely entirely upon the followings of his aristocrats, having, of course, his own following. Ine's laws refer to a class of king's *geneat* (loosely 'member of a household').[102] Royal followings were almost certainly divided into the young, unmarried household troops and older, married warriors now living on lands granted as a reward for previous service. Such warriors were supposed to turn up with their followings when the king needed them. Ine clearly believed that, as king, he had the right to call up the freemen of his kingdom, and to deprive of their lands those who did not answer his summons. Furthermore, at least by the time of the issuing of his code, there was a category of West Saxon free peasant called the *gafolgelda*: the rent payer.[103] This category could be the equivalent of the Frankish *tributarius*. Thus we would appear to have a similar situation to that which existed in Gaul, with some freemen liable to military service, whilst others paid renders for their upkeep. This may also, in practice, lie behind Imma's claim that, as a married *rusticus*, he and other such men brought supplies to the army. Perhaps the supplies were the tax – *gafol* – exacted upon such men. There seems also to be a similarity between the West Saxon *fyrdwite* and the Frankish *haribannus*. In Ine's Laws, *fyrdwite* is, like the seventh-century *haribannus*, clearly a fine but by the eleventh century it too could also be used to mean a payment for the upkeep of the army.[104] Earlier Anglo-Saxon kings thought of their realms in terms of numbers of assessment units, notionally based upon the household: *hides*.[105] These *hides* could provide warriors or their maintenance, as in Francia probably according to loose networks of patronage and dependence.

The basis upon which land was given to followers, whether or not as outright gift, is unclear. Much work on this problem has employed data, often poetic, which is later in date, and appears to attribute a timeless character to the nature of Old English mentalities, lordship and gift-exchange. By the time of Ine's code, it is clear that the king wished to place restrictions upon the tenure of land, and to make clear the obligations which went with landholding, not least claiming the right to rescind land-grants (or indeed to expropriate his aristocrats) if service was not fulfilled. It seems that Frankish aristocrats had similar concerns at the same time. Moreover, Ine's Laws represent not a passive reflection of Anglo-Saxon social reality which just happened to be written down in 694 but a code issued as an active statement by a king whose father had violently seized the kingdom in 685, who had just terminated a long war with Kent, and who governed a kingdom wherein attempts to seize the kingship, like that made by his own father, were not uncommon.[106] Ine's code represents an attempt, how successful is unknown, to establish royal prerogatives and control, not least of armed force. Thus fines for non-performance of military service are set out.

It is in this context too that we should see the famous clause 13.1: 'We call up to seven men thieves; from seven to thirty-five is a band; above that is an army.' Rather than being a descriptive statement of the normal size of seventh-century armies, as is still all too often assumed,[107] this clause needs to be seen in the context of the whole code. Subsequent clauses (14 and 15) penalise men who take part in attacks carried out by bands and armies, with involvement in the raid of an army being the more severely punished. Clauses 12 and 16 say that a thief caught in the act may be killed with impunity, whilst clause 15.2 says that a thief may not clear himself by oath once he has been captured. Thus members of a band are dealt with more leniently than thieves or members of an army, and thieves are punished more harshly than members of an army. The heavy penalty inflicted on thieves, when viewed in the overall context of the code (especially clauses 43 and 43.1), reflects the condemnation of crime which takes place secretly. As noted, in clause 50 Ine legislates about retinues and followings. In clause 13.1, 14 and 15, he is limiting the size of armed followings. In effect, any magnate with a following of three dozen or more men who commits a breach of the peace will be treated as leading an attacking army and severely dealt with. All members of the 'army' are to pay with their *wergild*.[108]

The evidence upon which a study of military service in Visigothic Spain must be based comes primarily from legal documents: the law-codes issued by the Visigothic kings and the acts of the regular church councils held at Toledo.[109] In addition, we also have one of the most detailed, if highly rhetorical, accounts of an early medieval campaign, that contained in Julian of Toledo's *History of*

King Wamba. Study of these documents reveals some highly distinctive features of the army of the seventh-century Spanish kings, but it also reveals features and concerns which parallel those of the armies and kings of Merovingian Francia and Anglo-Saxon England. The provinces of the Spanish kingdom continued to be used as military districts, with provincial armies commanded by a *dux exercitus provinciae* ('duke of the army of the province').[110] As in the sixth century, the army itself was divided into apparently decimally organised sub-units led by *tiuphadi* (apparently the equivalent of a *millenarius*: 'commander of a thousand'), *quingentenarii* (commanders of 500), *centuriones* and *decuriones*. The army was raised by written summons sent out down the chain of royal officers. Interestingly, in his *Rule for Monks*, Isidore of Seville says that those entering a monastery should be entered into the 'tables' just as military recruits are.[111] This is an intriguing reference and, unless a conscious classicism by Isidore, which is possible though perhaps an unduly sceptical reading, it would suggest that lists were kept of those who did military service. The existence of such lists is clearly implied by other sources in the post-Roman world, such as the reference, already discussed, to Guntramn of Burgundy punishing all those who had not performed their military service – clearly there was some sort of list of who was liable for this duty, just as there were still tax-lists.[112] This reference makes that clear. The late seventh-century *Life of Fructuosus of Braga* refers to lands being used as stipends for warriors,[113] which may hint at a process whereby the army came to be made up of landholders, similar to that in Francia at the same time. On the frontiers royal officials obviously had the authority to call out their armies for local defence.

It has been suggested on the basis of a sixth-century 'commissariat law' that there was a small standing army in Visigothic Spain, based in cities and forts (*castella*).[114] However, the law itself does not provide much support for this interpretation. It discusses the stockpiling of provisions (*annonae*) for the army by city and *castellum* but it does not specify that the troops so fed are permanent garrisons. It seems more likely that the law concerns the supply of the army in general, as it passed through, or was stationed in, the territories of those settlements. That there were permanent cadres of troops available in the royal bodyguard, and those of royal officers, is undoubtedly the case, but it is slightly misleading to describe such as a standing army.[115]

By the later seventh century it would appear that all landowners and royal slaves were liable for military service. Wamba and his successor Ervig both issued laws about military service.[116] That promulgated by King Ervig states that all men, 'whether general, count or *gardingus*, Goth or Roman, freeman or manumitted slave, or any fiscal slave', had to attend the summons.[117] On the face of it, this would seem to mean that military obligation was universal, and sometimes this has been held to be the case. On reflection, however, this would seem to be unlikely. In many ways, the same problem of interpretation arises as with the (almost exactly contemporary) clause about military service in Ine of Wessex's laws. We might read it, in the same way as Ine's, as operating down a chain of lordship and clientship. The provision of Ervig's law, that all such men bring one in ten of their slaves, makes it clear that we are talking about a stratum of reasonably significant landowners. Like Ine's law, Ervig's was also issued at a time of uncertainty in royal succession and this may very well have produced an increased concern to define and enforce the king's claims on military manpower (the last three or four turbulent decades of the Visigothic kingdom produced all of that state's legislation on military obligation to the king).

That we should see this law in terms of aristocrats and their retinues is, as with the Anglo-Saxon case, strengthened by a consideration of the broader context. Visigothic law was very much concerned with ties of lordship and patronage. Legislation repeatedly tried to deal with violence committed by lords' followings, and with the abuse of patronage to protect clients from the workings of the law.[118] Furthermore, from at least the later sixth century, the law had tried to regulate how an aristocrat's *bucellarii* were remunerated; this concern appears to have been stepped up in the later seventh century; as in Francia and England only a few years later, there was a concern to define what exactly a lord could expect from his followers, and what of their property was his if they changed patron.[119] With this in mind it seems that Ervig expected all landlords to perform military service, and to bring all those who were dependent upon them.

Possibly the most interesting aspect of Ervig's military law is the specification that all those who were summoned to the army bring one tenth of their slaves (if they failed to do so, the crown would take those left behind!), and that these slaves be equipped with at least some body armour, shields, swords, spears, bows and arrows and slings. This use of slaves as soldiers is very interesting but seems to be peculiarly Spanish, perhaps going back to King Theudis' recruiting of a slave army, allegedly 2,000 strong. There are no references to slave soldiers from anywhere else in post-Roman Europe, and even mentions of the semi-free and poor free with the army seem on balance to refer to the servants of warriors, or to a supply role rather than a military one.[120] The reasons for the Visigoths' use of slaves may relate to a shortage of manpower for the royal armies. They might also relate to peculiarly Spanish meanings of slavery.[121] How these slave troops were used in battle is sadly unknown; their weapons may imply either a true battlefield function, or simply that they were employed to protect the army's baggage (in much the same way as Byzantine soldiers' slaves and servants were). The latter interpretation is supported by the fact that that paragraph of Ervig's law begins by stating that the king must now turn his attention to how his armies are paid and supplied. On the other hand, a slightly later law of Egica called up all slaves who had been freed by royal intervention, on pain of their return to servile status. This may imply an increasing concern for troops with a direct link to the king himself, to swell the royal bodyguard and thus attempt to bypass the reliance upon aristocrats and their followings. A similar concern may have lain behind Ervig's call-up of *servi fiscales* (fiscal slaves).

The case of Visigothic Spain reveals certain similarities with areas north of the Pyrenees in that the army had become one based upon aristocratic retinues. In the Spanish case this takes on particular importance because of the debate on the nature of the later Visigothic kingdom. Some have argued that the kingdom had entered a destructive spiral of civil war, usurpation and repression.[122] Others have countered that the Visigothic state, on the contrary, was strong and centralised.[123] In the mid-sixth century and again in the first half of the seventh, dynastic instability in Spain was legendary, even amongst contemporaries, as kings were repeatedly faced with revolts by their more powerful magnates. In the central decades of the seventh century Chindasvinth and his son Reccesvinth seem to have maintained a strong hold on the throne, but nevertheless had to deal with repeated rebellions.[124] Reccesvinth's successor Wamba was faced with a rebellion in Septimania, which he soon quelled, but it is noteworthy that his legislation followed this war, and equally significant that, unlike Chindasvinth, Wamba did not feel able or willing to punish his opponents too severely, commuting the death sentence to decalvation.[125] Wamba's own retirement into a monastery may have been involuntary, although it is difficult to be sure as the episode has attracted legendary accretions. Nevertheless, his successor, Ervig, also issued military legislation, as discussed above. Once again, we see that legislation must be viewed in context, rather than seen as passively reflecting age-old situations. There are further hints of instability at the end of the period, just before the Arab conquest[126] but it is nevertheless possible that the instability of the late Visigothic state might have been overplayed.

On the other hand, it seems that significant efforts were made to unify the kingdom ideologically.[127] A fixed capital was established at Toledo, and royal regalia developed from the late sixth century. Periodic councils of the Spanish church were also convened.[128] Archaeologically, the study of artefacts shows the introduction of new, Byzantine styles replacing earlier Gothic forms in the seventh century, again perhaps to underpin Spanish unity.[129] Analysis of funerary customs might also question the real strength of the local and regional aristocrats.[130] Even if one follows the 'downward spiral' view of the Visigothic kingdom, the situation would still have the positive results, firstly, that the current king was almost always, *ipso facto*, the most powerful warrior in the land, and, secondly, that kings and rebels fought for control of the whole kingdom, thus preserving the importance and unity of the Iberian state. The period did see attempts to enforce increasingly repressive legislation against Jews and slaves, which might be viewed as reflecting insecurity, and late Visigothic military legislation might be seen in this context. It might also be that this legislative activity reflected the perceived power of the kingdom.

Pérez Sánchez sees the decline of the Spanish kingdom in terms of a change from a regular royal army in the sixth century to one made up of private magnate retinues in the seventh.[131] It may be going too far to see the sixth-century army as a regular force, but the changes suggested seem to parallel those taking place elsewhere, even if we might not characterise them in quite the same terms. The shift from an army whose mobilisation was carried out by royally appointed officers, and whose rank and file were men claiming a particular identity based around ethnicity and a link to the king, to one where military forces were composed essentially of the followings of greater landholders is similar to that in Francia, and the Frankish parallel shows that it need not automatically have implied a weakening of royal power. However, it does seem, overall, that the Visigothic kings failed to create the independent coercive force to penetrate local society from above and create a situation where local social pre-eminence was dependent upon royal favour. The late seventh-century laws calling up royal slaves and freedmen may be an attempt to create such an army, but it was not to succeed.[132] Instead kings, and successful usurpers, relied upon their factions to maintain them in power. The penalties for failed usurpation were severe; the rewards for success were equally huge: a king could deploy all of his kingdom's resources, in patronage and lands, especially those confiscated from enemies, to pay his followers. Dynastic insecurity led to repeated strengthening of the ideological and theological underpinnings of the royal office, and concomitantly to a hiking up of the penalties for threatening the king's person. At the same time, support for a deposed king could be equally fatal; Fredegar describes the veritable blood-bath which followed Chindasvinth's seizure of the throne in 642.[133] Consequently, it is difficult to avoid the conclusion that, in Visigothic internal politics, the stakes seem to have spiralled. Whether such a spiral was inevitable or irreversible is, of course, a separate matter.

Another point worth discussing concerns the relationship between the perceived problems of the Visigothic kingdom and the end of its military expansion. It has long been pointed out that after the final unification of the Iberian peninsula in 624 the Spanish kings could neither reward their followers with conquered loot and land nor carry out the functions of the war-leader king in the old way. It can be argued that Visigothic politics began to look inwards and armies had to be raised for defence against Basque attacks, or for the quelling of aristocratic unrest. In this situation, as we shall see frequently, the relationship between a king and his magnates, and the difficulties of raising a royal coercive force, were highlighted. These, and the inexperience of Visigothic armies, probably go a long way towards explaining the rapid collapse of the kingdom when faced in 711 by the battle-hardened armies of the Arab caliphate and its Berber subjects. On the other hand, as has been noted above,[134] Basque wars were frequent but are not well documented, and Wamba marked his accession with a campaign in the Pyrenees. Arab sources suggest that the last Visigothic king of Spain, Roderic, did this too after he seized the throne.[135] Other kings may well have done the same, assembling the army and demonstrating their military abilities. Nevertheless, harrying warfare in the Pyrenean valleys, compelling Basque chieftains to submit, was probably not the sort of warfare which would have given the Spanish warriors the sort of experience of pitched battle they needed when faced by the Arab armies.

Such problems did not as yet beset the Lombard rulers of Italy.[136] As mentioned above, the seventh-century Lombard territories appear at first to have raised armies on the model common throughout the west in the sixth century. As far as can be ascertained, though, this system, and taxation with it, seems soon to have withered and there is no evidence for its persistence by the time we have sufficient documentary evidence to examine such issues (in the eighth century). The development of Lombard armies from the ethnic forces of the very early period to Liutprand's armies in the eighth century is difficult to follow. The documentary evidence from Lombard Italy is most uneven in its survival; we have little other than laws for the seventh century, but laws (of a generally different kind from those of the seventh century) and charters in the eighth. The forms of archaeological evidence also change. These differences in evidential nature and survival suggest that there was change between the seventh and eighth centuries, and make it problematic to argue back from the eighth-century situation.[137] Nevertheless, in Rothari's Edict, the political community of the Lombard kingdom is referred to as the army (*exercitus*) and an equation of Lombard ethnicity with military service might be implied. The term *exercitalis* ('army man') is used but only in a context where it could simply mean 'soldier', although it could have a broader meaning as a member of the social group which formed the army.[138] It is not really possible to examine the status of these people in detail until the eighth century.

The Lombard kings were on the offensive for much of the seventh century, engaged in repeated warfare against the East Roman territories in Italy. Serious attacks into Italy by the Franks petered out by the early seventh century and although Avar raids and Byzantine counter-attacks were significant problems, the persistent campaigning provided ample opportunities for the acquisition of booty and land, and to gain prestige and office through good service. This may have helped to strengthen royal power but the extent of royal power over the dukes in the seventh century is difficult to gauge. Seventh-century Lombard royal succession was fairly turbulent. On the other hand, some cemeteries of furnished burials in the kingdom of Italy suggest a competition for local authority, which might have led to the importance of ducal or possibly royal patronage in local society, as in sixth-century Gaul.[139] Certainly it suggests that local authority was expressed through the use of military symbols.

The importance of the retinues of royal officers and of other wealthy aristocrats should not be underestimated. Though it can be argued that this never became too significant in Lombard Italy, on the basis of the eighth-century evidence, it is not impossible that the situation differed in the seventh century. Early in the Lombard period, the settlement of the Lombard newcomers may have been organised, to some extent, by *farae*.[140] The *farae* were once thought to have been large, clan-like, kin-based groupings. The evidence for this is unclear, though, and they may have been smaller military groupings. By the time that we know much about Lombard social and political structures, their importance appears to have waned; the only reference to a *fara* in the laws does imply that it is a family group, if perhaps a small one.[141] As yet, the only members of such followings who concerned the lawmakers were those legally dependent upon a freeman. In Rothari's Edict, freedmen (in other words, men freed from some form of servitude) are referred to in the service (*gasindium*) of dukes or in the *obsequium* of freemen or dukes.[142] Freedmen were, because of their poverty, usually heavily dependent upon the individual who had granted them their freedom. These individuals owned weapons, which were to be inherited, presumably as signs of their legal status. Other gifts from their lords or patrons, if the freedman had not paid back these gifts through his service, were to revert to his lord. Otherwise, any links between members of the broad class of the free were based upon gift and counter-gift, and somewhat informal, as elsewhere at this date.[143] Some Lombard warlords still periodically took service with the Byzantine enemies of the Lombard kingdom and led distinguished military careers with them.[144] They presumably took with them their bands of military followers and dependants.

The organisation of the Lombard kingdom was based upon the *civitas* but in Italy these units were governed by dukes rather than by counts. The city district was thus also the principal unit of military organisation. The duke, assisted by his 'judges' would call up the Lombard freemen within his territory. Lombard law made clear that those liable to military service were obliged to serve when the duke called out the army, as well as when the call-up was on royal initiative.[145] The frontier dukes of the Lombard kingdom were often engaged in warfare and their military successes could make them political rivals of the kings in Pavia. The Lombard kings created the institution of the *gastald* as an officer who reported directly to the king and could, to some extent, act as a counterweight to the duke in local politics. This was an interesting royal response to the problems of ruling an early medieval polity and to the dynamic tension between political core and local society.

Seventh-century military organisation in Germany east of the Rhine is still difficult to examine in much detail. Archaeological evidence suggests the emergence, as in contemporary northern Gaul and Anglo-Saxon England, of more powerful local aristocracies, who demonstrated their power by lavish funerary displays of weaponry and other military equipment. During the century several areas loosened the links which bound them into Merovingian Frankish domination. We have noted the Thuringian defeat of the Frankish army on the river Unstrut in 639, an event of some significance. The military forces of the Alamans, Bavarians, Frisians and Saxons also enjoyed success, but we are ill-informed as to how these forces were raised. In Alamannia and Bavaria we have law-codes to help us. Both law codes repeat the usual post-Roman attempts to limit the deployment of armed force to the dukes or their representatives, and both heavily penalise those who commit acts of violence or theft within the army.[146] Bavarian Law also refers to *minor populi* in the army, once again presenting us with the difficulty of knowing whether this implies a broad-based military obligation or armies raised through lords and their clients and dependants. The phrasing of the law implies the latter. Bavarian Law mentions slaves in the context of the army, as perpetrators of theft, but this probably simply refers to slaves following their masters to fetch and carry.

In Saxony, our evidence comprises chance descriptions in hagiographic sources and later Carolingian law-codes, and it is unclear how much of this is relevant for the seventh century. The Saxons remain distinctive for not having an overall ruler, at least by the eighth century; it is possible, though perhaps unlikely, that they were ruled by a duke earlier in the seventh century but if so this situation had changed by the time that written discussions of Saxon society begin to emerge.[147] If we can project the eighth-century evidence backwards, then the Saxons met at regular assemblies, to which most freemen were invited. There were three principal leaders and an overall war-leader could be elected in times of crisis. Checks and balances existed which served to prevent the emergence of a single ruler.[148] Nevertheless, even a Saxon leader acting on his own could raise sufficient troops to exterminate a village which had defied him.[149] Such forces were raised through fairly loose ties of dependence; Saxon freemen served their noble leaders, but expected rewards. A large Saxon host could present a serious threat. Indeed in the early eighth century the Saxons appear to have been expanding their territory through military conquests towards the Rhine and organising and fortifying their side of the frontier.[150]

As before, Scandinavian military service can only be guessed at through the medium of archaeological evidence. As elsewhere, the period sees significant changes but the extent to which these affected the ability to raise armies, or the organisation of military service, is unclear. In Norway there are some changes in burial custom which are rather similar to those taking place in the Merovingian world and its neighbours at the same time, possibly suggesting an increase in the stability of local power. In this light it is perhaps not surprising that the boathouses mentioned above[151] continue in use. In Denmark, it has been observed that weaponry begins to take on a more distinctively Scandinavian appearance, breaking away in style from the pan-European fashions common in the sixth century.[152] At the same time swords begin to show rings fashioned into their hilts, a practice usually believed to symbolize a client relationship.[153] It is tempting to argue that, as elsewhere, the aristocratic retinue was becoming the key component of military organisation. However, it should be pointed out that such 'ring-swords' are common in the sixth century in the Merovingian world when, as argued above, royal service was the main organising principle of military organisation, but die out by the seventh when, we have argued, aristocratic retinues became more significant. We should, nevertheless, not automatically assume that the same thing should have the same symbolic meaning in all regions at all times. In fact it has been cogently argued that this period saw a steady rise in the power of the Danish rulers.[154] This would fit the idea that the rings on Danish swords might have the same symbolism as those on earlier Frankish swords. In Sweden, the late sixth century saw the earliest of the great mound burials at Vendel and Valsgärde, which contain boats and lavish military equipment, again of distinctively Scandinavian style.[155] These sites remained in use through the Viking period, and seem to denote the acquisition and maintenance of local power by particular aristocratic dynasties, on the fringes of the main settlement areas of the Mälar valley. They appear at about the same time as the abandonment of forts in the region. The construction and symbolism of these burials reveal significant control of manpower and also demonstrate very clearly that power had a clear violent and military component. One imagines that these families could raise significant followings of armed men. The control of surplus by local élites is confirmed by the growth of trading stations in this period, as at Helgö in the Mälar valley. This social change might have been reflected in changes in battlefield tactics. A plausible discussion of the equipment of the Vendel chieftains suggests an increase in specialist military abilities after c.600.[156]

In the western and northern parts of Britain the decades around 600, as in much of the rest of Europe, were a period of change. It was suggested above that in the fifth and sixth centuries the rulers of western and northern Britain were probably rather more powerful than those of the lowland areas (Anglo-Saxon England). This balance of power appears to have shifted around 600. When reliable documentary sources for Britain begin to survive, at about this time, we are in the midst of a burst of aggression by the English kingdoms against their British, Pictish and Scottish neighbours.[157] The reasons for this shift lie beyond the scope of this volume; suffice it to say that economic changes may have produced stresses within the western and northern kingdoms, at the same time as these changes strengthened the Anglo-Saxon realms.[158] Nevertheless, the British, Pictish and Scottish kingdoms were still considerable opponents. The kings of Gwynedd remained powerful rivals of the kings of Northumbria, and probable overlords of at least some Mercian warlords until the middle decades of the seventh century. Although the Northumbrians acquired a hegemony over much of Britain north of the Clyde and Forth in the third quarter of the century, the Pictish victory at Nechtansmere (685) was an event of huge significance, ending not only Northumbrian dominance over the Strathclyde Welsh and Scots as well as the Picts but arguably plunging the northern English kingdom into a long period of decline. This victory is, it is usually thought, depicted on the standing stone at Aberlemno.[159] How the armies of these northern and western British kings were raised and organised is difficult to establish. The most interesting document comes from Scotland: the *Senchus fer nAlban* or Great Census of Alban.[160] This document establishes how many warriors were to be furnished by the different regions of the Scottish kingdom, using the household, grouped into multiples of five, as the basic unit of assessment. It envisages that the armed force raised by this levy was (or at least could be) in the region of 2,000 men. Presumably royal and aristocratic retinues would add to this total. As before, hillforts were occupied and suggest a degree of organisation.[161] Amongst the Picts, we have no such documentary evidence. Archaeological data such as high-status sites and the famous symbol stones, together with inference from later sources and the snippets of information in contemporary Irish and English sources, suggest that the Pictish kingdom was similarly well organised. It has been argued that its army was called out by provincial leaders called *mormaers*. Certainly this was the case by the time that the Pictish kingdom fused with the Scottish in the mid-ninth century.[162]

It is difficult to say very much at all about the raising and organisation of Welsh armies.[163] The heroic poetry attributed to the great bards Aneirin and Taliesin is of uncertain date, though recent work has suggested that it may date to the seventh century.[164] If this conclusion can be accepted it describes armies largely based around the royal bodyguard or *teulu*. The household of a successful king could attract renowned warriors from other kingdoms. Some or all of the members of this royal retinue would have followers of their own. Although it may be that an entire army might be composed of the *teulu* and dependants, larger armies could be raised. Rulers maintained networks of aristocratic clients, who were expected to perform military service in return for gifts and support. These clients would sometimes be in attendance on the king as a member of the *teulu*; sometimes, as youths, they would have been sent there to learn their trade, as elsewhere in Europe. Welsh armed forces would largely have been raised via these clientship networks. There are a few late indications that free peasants had military obligations by the eleventh century at least, while the archaeology of the fifth and sixth centuries also suggests that Welsh leaders could call upon reasonable reserves of manpower. By the eighth century some forms of taxation were being levied by Welsh rulers. It does not seem unlikely that more general obligations existed in the seventh century too, although these could have been restricted to labour services and the payment of dues. A number of the hillforts mentioned earlier were abandoned in this century and trade contacts with the Mediterranean ended. In the documents it becomes clear that the Welsh kingdoms were now often quite small, and it may be that social and political stress had caused the fragmentation of earlier political units. This would obviously affect the size of armed forces raised. The fluid nature of Welsh politics involved the regular taking of tribute through raiding, and the booty so obtained kept the king's *teulu*.[165] When one king had established a relationship of dominance over another it is likely that he required him to perform military service with his *teulu* on the over-king's military expeditions: an extension of clientship to the wider political arena. This not only strengthened the dominant king's forces; it weakened the tributary king by forcing him to divert his own military resources to another king's benefit. This practice seems clearly to have been the case in the tenth century. Cadwallon of Gwynedd's employment of Mercian kings and their troops during his period of domination suggests that it was also the case in the seventh century.[166] The nature of Welsh society and politics argues that all of these mechanisms were fluid, and involved more negotiation than may have been the case elsewhere.

Irish armed forces were certainly raised through similarly fluid clientship networks throughout our period. Irish politics were notoriously violent, centred upon frequent endemic raiding, and involved a fluctuating hierarchy of different types of kings and over-kings. Each king had his own clients, free and 'base', such ties of clientship being mainly defined by gifts of cattle. These links, at least in theory, were contractual and of fixed duration. Although any Irish king would be expected to have at least a couple of spearmen as a permanent body-guard, and the institution of fosterage, as in Wales, would probably add others to his permanent military household, armies would be raised by calling upon the services of one's clients. Kings would also call upon the forces of those kings who were subservient to them. The flexible nature of clientship, intradynastic warfare and challenges by one people (or *túath*) for or against the dominance of another, meant that the outlines of Irish politics were an ever-changing kaleidoscope. Warfare was largely concerned with the taking of tribute because the acquisition of booty, usually in the form of cattle, not only increased one's own ability to reward followers and acquire clients, it also struck directly at one's opponents' ability to do the same.[167]

Conclusion

By the end of the seventh century we can see that the nature of armed forces in the formerly Roman territories had changed considerably since the final days of the Western empire. Certain features, in their general outlines, seem to be common across the former provinces. Paid regular armies had ceased to exist. They were replaced first of all by armies generally raised from people who could claim a particular ethnic identity, usually barbarian: Frankish, Gothic, Lombard or (probably) Saxon. Armies, as far as can be ascertained, were organised by administrative unit and led by royally appointed officers. Service amongst this (potentially) increasingly large group frequently seems to have been moderated by age. Whilst young men might form the households of royal officers, the army called up seems to have been formed of mature males: married heads of house-holds. By the beginning of the seventh century, it seems that social changes had led to a renegotiation of military obligations. As barbarian ethnicities became more common, military service must have been moderated by wealth or ties of dependence. There was as yet, however, no attempt to relate military obligations directly to the amount of land held. Previously more restricted and functional barbarian ethnic identities had become general amongst the free landowning population and it seems that the obligation of these landed free to perform military service remained in force and was, or at least could be, taken very seriously. Nevertheless, it also appears that in practice armies tended to be raised from the more powerful landowners and their dependants and retainers. The facts that these powerful land-owners still generally held titles in theory related to royal service and that the royal legitimation of power remained important makes the change less dramatic than might be supposed but it is significant none the less. The more powerful aristocrats were more established in their local pre-eminence and their tenure of theoretically royally bestowed titles was often more secure too. This made the penetration of state into local politics and into the raising of armies correspondingly more difficult than had been the case, as powerful freemen could intervene in the workings of royal government. This cannot but have changed the relationship between state and élite. By about 700 the aristocratic following seems to have become the principal building block of armed forces throughout the west. These warriors were linked to their leaders by a mixture of formal and informal rewards, and the leaders' position established on the basis of both local social and economic pre-eminence and the tenure of titles. There was no formal system of granting land in return for military service.

Outside the former empire, similar factors may have applied, especially as what had been 'Free Germany' was gradually incorporated within the Frankish polity and its élites came into contact with aristocrats from the previously Roman territories. In some areas, such as Denmark and Sweden, it is possible that the trajectory of development was quite different. In Denmark it would seem that this period was rather one wherein the ability of the kingdom to intervene in local politics was steadily growing (and continued to do so in the eighth century). The appearance of ring swords at a time when they dropped out of use in the Merovingian kingdom might be a graphic indicator of this difference in developmental trajectory. Nevertheless, in some areas, physical geography, ecology and economy made a difference. The importance of cattle in Irish, Welsh and north British warfare has been pointed out. Here, livestock rather than land formed the basis of political power, and the means by which service was retained and rewarded differed accordingly, as, consequently, did the nature of warfare. In other areas, such as Norway, it is likely that lordship and obligations were based upon other forms of resources and that warfare and the raising of armies reflected this.

In the period after 700, further changes took place. One of the most significant developments was the continued reduction in the differences between those areas formerly within the Roman Empire and those outside.

4

RAISING AN ARMY (2): THE CAROLINGIAN WORLD

The eighth century and the supposed creation of 'feudalism'

The eighth century in Francia has often been seen as a crucial point in the development of medieval warfare. From the work of the great late nineteenth-century German legal historian Heinrich Brunner, it was argued that the eighth century, and Charles Martel's wars in particular, saw developments in the means by which aristocratic leaders rewarded their military followings. Martel, it was believed, carried out large-scale confiscations of ecclesiastical land to reward the warriors who followed him. In order to sweeten the pill for the churches, such land was then held by 'precarial tenure': the church retained actual owner-ship of the land, but the secular warrior 'held' it and received the usufruct of the estate. Such rewards in land, it was thought, were necessary to maintain warriors who now needed to be well-armoured horsemen rather than the foot-warriors of old. The Belgian historian F.-L. Ganshof argued that a crucial stage in the development of feudalism occurred around 700, when temporary grants of land (*precaria; beneficia*) began to be made by lords to their retainers in return for the latter's sworn loyalty, known as vassalage. In Ganshof's learned and attractively neat and clear formulation, the union of benefice with vassalage gave birth to feudalism.[1] The idea was elaborated to include military technology. Mounted warriors were, it was argued, necessary because the introduction of the stirrup gave them added battlefield value and because the Arab invasions had also made cavalry more necessary.[2]

All this amounted to a very coherent and persuasive theory, which dominated historiography for a considerable period, determining, for example, the open-ing date of Beeler's *Warfare in Feudal Europe, 730–1200*. Unfortunately, such an overarching and coherent scheme does not really emerge from the actual evidence.[3] Over recent years it has received a barrage of criticism and is no longer held to be valid. We shall return to the military, technological and tactical elements of the theory.[4] Bachrach ably dismantled much of the theory about the development of cavalry,[5] though pushing his counter-argument a little too far. The more complex and much messier issue of land tenure and 'feudalism' concerns us here.[6]

We may begin with *precaria*. Technically, a precarial grant was made in response to a request. The concept was known in Roman law if not in quite the same way as in earlier medieval landholding arrangements. A precarial grant was not permanent. It guaranteed, to use the Roman concepts we encountered when discussing *hospitalitas*, the *dominium* of the grantor and the *possessio* of the grantee, but it could be revoked, or the arrangement could be terminated after a fixed time or with the death of the recipient. This suited the church especially well as holders of ecclesiastical office were not supposed to alienate church land at all. Thus, not surprisingly, the earliest references to precarial grants in post-Roman landholding are to priests and other ecclesiastics receiving land to live on.[7] As the seventh-century northern Gaulish church gained increasingly large estates, it leased out to laymen, as *precaria*, those lands which it could not manage itself.

This type of grant could be very useful to landowners. During the seventh century, aristocratic landowners founded monasteries and endowed them with lands. This was one of several strategies employed to evade the partible inheritance upon which custom insisted, and which dissipated a family's lands every generation by forcing its equal division between the children. By putting a relative in charge of the monastery, a family could retain ultimate control over the resources of large estates, which could not be alienated or divided by inheritance. Other strategies involved the increased use of written legal instruments (including charters) to circumvent custom, including the reintroduction of testamentary disposition (i.e., by will) into seventh-century northern Gaul, probably from Aquitaine. These, however, were less secure than granting estates to a church or, especially, a family monastery and then receiving them back as *precaria*. A relative in control of the abbey could grant the donated estates back to the head of the family and leave large blocks of land in the family's control.

We first hear of such *precaria* in Merovingian charters and other documents in the late seventh century. The practice may go back earlier but it is significant that it does not appear in the charters. At about the same time, the word *beneficium* also appears in relation to landholding. This word had a wide range of meanings and also originated in Roman law. What difference, if any, there was between *precaria* and *beneficia* is unknown; they seem to have been essentially the same thing – the temporary *possessio* of a unit of land, which remained ultimately in another landholder's ownership. *Precaria* simply referred to the way in which the grant had been obtained (through request), and *beneficium* to the way it was granted (as a benefit). Around 700, to judge from the charter evidence,[8] lay landowners as well as the Church began to grant out land as *precaria* and benefice. Support for the idea of a reorganisation of the rural areas of Francia at this time, possibly associated with increased aristocratic control over land, comes from archaeology.[9] Some have termed this archaeologically visible reorganisation 'manorialisation'.[10]

Why these developments should have come about then is probably related to the periods of serious warfare between magnate factions during the very late seventh and early eighth centuries. As we have seen, in the seventh century kings seem to have begun to reward their aristocratic followers with grants of the ownership of land. As far as can be ascertained, these grants were permanent, unlike sixth-century grants of the right to collect royal dues from specified territories. Magnates' gifts to their followers seem to have been equally permanent. Thus rewarding supporters reduced an aristocratic family's estates. One solution to this problem was to receive further grants of land from the court or to obtain them for one's followers. This is one reason (but only one, and perhaps not the most important) why the royal court remained the centre of political action in the seventh century, even though the kings themselves were often minors or under the control of their mayors of the palace.[11]

Another solution was to obtain precarial grants for one's followers from monasteries controlled by one's family. The competing factions appear to have used the lands of allied bishoprics and monasteries for this purpose, although the evidence seems to show that this was done on an *ad hoc* basis, and not on such a widespread scale as later. Ecclesiastical lands thus became increasingly important in these conflicts. This, obviously, carried certain risks. If control of a monastery were lost (and the winners in the aristocratic civil wars were not above removing from office abbots and bishops who backed the losing side), so was control of its land and of any of its tenants' loyalties. Thus a third solution to the problem of dissipating estates through gifts to followers was to make precarial grants from one's own lands. This allowed a family to reward its followers without diminishing its landholdings. The importance of controlling the royal court in seventh-century politics may conversely have made this and the use of church lands preferable in the wars either side of 700. They permitted a faction's supporters to be retained and rewarded, and thus power to be maintained, even in periods of exclusion from the court. The clearest expression of this transformation in the nature of politics came when Theuderic IV died in 737; Charles Martel did not bother to appoint a successor, even as a puppet king.[12]

If, as seems likely, oaths of vassalage (though the term vassal occurs very rarely at this date) became common around this time we might read this, as Fouracre does,[13] as the magnates' appropriation of a hitherto royal (or royally legitimised) military role. We should not assume any neat or legal 'system' of service in return for land; we are not at all well informed as to whether precarial grants were ever made in direct exchange for oaths of support or for specified military service at this time. Such things remained rather loose. Support, and the reciprocal backing of the magnates, could operate in far more fluid and intangible ways. Nevertheless, in the early eighth century, Frankish armies were made up of nobles, their retainers and adherents. The reorganisation of lands seems to have produced greater surplus in the hands of the élites, which may have allowed them to maintain and reward larger followings of mounted warriors, independently of royal control. These warriors were mounted not because of any significant change in tactics; horsemen had always played a role in Frankish warfare, though their numbers might have increased. This in some ways represented the final working through of developments in the nature of Frankish armies which, though never irreversible or inevitable, had started around 600.

All of these developments led to a growth of the power of aristocratic élites and, concurrently, a relative reduction in the royal court's importance. Thus the nature of the Frankish *regnum* changed importantly around 700. We may be closer to the truth if we view this as a loosening of the ties which bound the different regions into one political unit, rather than as political fragmentation. The principal bond, which had held the regions together in the sixth and seventh centuries, was the royal court, and the importance of royally bestowed office and lands in maintaining local power. With the reduction of the court's importance, this bond was significantly loosened. Rather than breaking free from Frankish control, certain regions, such as Aquitaine and Provence, stood back from politics at the core, in Neustria and Austrasia, and took what we might call a semi-detached view. The élites were able to govern their areas, or to compete for regional control, without reference to the kings or their mayors, and to take part in the political struggles in and around the royal courts as and when it suited them. In a sense this resembled what had happened to the areas beyond the Rhine in the mid-seventh century.

Charles Martel's wars against the Frisians, Alamans and Bavarians, and in Aquitaine, Burgundy and Provence, should not be seen necessarily as an aggressive policy deliberately aimed at reuniting the *Regnum Francorum*.[14] The peripheral areas of earlier Frankish hegemony and the regions just described as politically semi-detached had never removed themselves completely from Frankish politics and into independence. The élites in those areas retained all sorts of social and political links with the Frankish core, and Charles' control of Neustria and Austrasia could never be assured until he had either reduced them to subservience or replaced them with his own followers. His wars were fought with mounted armies of his family's and their allies' dependants, retainers and adherents.[15] These armies campaigned with him in return for booty and land taken from the defeated, to be sure, but we need not see loot alone as the primary engine of military service. Such aristocratic warriors also served in return for more nebulous forms of socio-political support and to retain an active involvement at the core of political action, the army. What we can be sure of is that, in their organisation, the way in which they were raised and the political structures behind them, Martel's armies in the 730s were different from the Frankish armies of the 630s, let alone those of the 530s. Brunner, Ganshof and the others had correctly identified a period of important change, and had traced some of its outlines, but their understanding of the precise nature of that change and the factors that produced it was flawed.

The creation of the Merovingian kingdom and its army of *civitas* levies, composed of landowners in the south and 'Franks' in the north, and led by royal officials and their households, had provided the basic template for Frankish armies until the mid-seventh century. The transformations around 700 similarly set in place the template for army organisation for the whole early Carolingian period. The situation, however, did not remain static any more than it had done earlier. By the middle of the century the components of military organisation, which had begun to appear at the end of the seventh century – precarial grants and *beneficia*, and vassalage – became much more important. At the council of Estinnes, Charles Martel's son Carloman set out a more orderly scheme for the use of ecclesiastical lands to provide *precaria* for his warriors. Only such churches as could afford it would be so burdened, and all would receive 1 *solidus* per *cassata* (roughly a tenant farm) granted out in *precaria*, an exceptionally high rent.[16] That change came about in the middle decades of the eighth century is suggested by the fact that precarial grants become much more common in the charters. Smaller landholders begin to give small parcels of land to abbeys and receive them back as *precaria*.[17] This strategy seems to have spread from the higher aristocracy to lesser landowners, to be used for much the same purposes: to maintain their social standing, especially when this was under threat. We shall shortly examine a specific instance of a similar strategy.

Carloman, his brother Pippin (from 751 Pippin I, the first Carolingian king) and Pippin's son Charlemagne also extended the use of the term *vassus*.[18] *Vassi regis* (vassals of the king) became an important social group with many similarities to the *antrustiones* and other forms of bodyguard encountered earlier. Similar classes of people were known as *fideles*. The structure of the Frankish kingdom had changed by the middle of the eighth century and the early Carolingian kings were faced with a quite different situation from that which confronted the early Merovingians. The nature of the relationship between political core and locality, in which the dynamics of early medieval politics were situated, had altered radically. As we have seen, the break-up of the Roman Empire in Gaul had left the Frankish king holding most if not all of the aces in his dealings with local aristocrats and able to deploy an army as a form of coercive force. The Carolingians, who had, after all, originated as only the most successful of a number of powerful aristocratic factions,[19] were faced with regional and local élites who were much more secure in their landed power base than they had been in the sixth century.[20] Their usurpation of the royal title in 751 caused unease, although early ninth-century pro-Carolingian writers tried to cover this up. The exercise of royal power in the localities of the Carolingian world, therefore, of necessity, involved much more negotiation with locally prominent families than had been the case in the sixth century. In response, in addition to promoting oaths of vassalage,[21] the Carolingians developed various strategies to strengthen the ideological basis of their kingship, and not without success. Charlemagne introduced the *missus dominicus*, an officer, usually working as one of a pair, aimed at overseeing the local workings of government and (although often from the local or regional aristocracy) a sort of counterpoint to other local sources of authority, such as the counts, with a direct link to the king. The kings appear to have been very successful in persuading the élite to invest in the Carolingian state and to underpin their local authority with royally bestowed offices.

Throughout the eighth century, ecclesiastical lands were subject to military service.[22] A charter of 775, issued by Charlemagne for Metz cathedral, reserves to the king the 'three duties' of the church's free tenants, specifying these as service in the army when it was called out, watch duty and bridge work.[23] Some immunities exempted the church's estates from military service,[24] but these are remarkably rare. That the king usually did not specify that military service was to be performed suggests that this was taken for granted. The great churches and monasteries of the realm were expected to furnish military contingents from their estates, particularly from those who held *precaria*.[25]

Pippin and Charlemagne continued to make use of *scarae*, such as are attested since the earlier seventh century. As before, these were select bodies of troops, dispatched quickly to trouble spots. Entire campaigns could be waged by *scarae*, or they could operate as lesser formations whilst a major army, or *exercitus*, campaigned elsewhere or along a different line of march. Another term for a small formation, *manus* ('band'), is used in 806.[26] This seems to have been a Latin translation of *scara*, though it may have meant something slightly different. The *manus* sent to ravage Slavic territory in 806 was drawn from Bavaria, Alamannia and Burgundy.

In the later eighth century, Carolingian armies continued to wage successful warfare against foes inside and outside the *Regnum Francorum*. This brought in huge rewards, especially during Charlemagne's long and dramatic reign (768–814). These came in the form of lands taken from defeated foes. We can note the near-total destruction of the Alamannic nobility at Cannstadt, for example,[27] or the introduction of northern Franks into the estates of, for instance, Aquitaine and eventually northern Italy. As well as landed estates, other rewards came in the form of titles (usually with attached lands), referred to as *honores*, and huge quantities of booty, most notably consequent upon the destruction of the Avar kingdom in the 790s. All of these rewards made involvement in the royal armies and adherence to the Carolingian régime very worthwhile, and royal power, as a result, substantial. Charlemagne was able to crush conspiracies against him with some ruthlessness.[28] On the whole, eighth-century armies seem to have been raised from the followings of lay and ecclesiastical aristocrats, linked to the Carolingian kings generally by more or less formal ties. The aristocratic followings were raised down apparently loose networks of dependence.[29] Throughout the eighth century, the rulers of the Franks seem to have been more concerned with the means by which their warriors were rewarded with land than with the technicalities of raising troops. There is little or no discussion of military obligation or the *haribannus*. The armies of Charles Martel, Pippin I and Charlemagne were successful and participation in them attractive.

The Carolingian kings, like their Merovingian precursors, kept a substantial corps of bodyguards in attendance upon them at the palace. This body formed the nucleus of expeditionary armies and could be deployed rapidly to deal with problems which arose. The term *antrustio* was no longer used. *Antrustiones*, as we have seen, were the Merovingians' royal guards, and the name may have been felt to have too many associations with the old dynasty. Thus the Carolingian kings retained the word which had come to be used for aristocrats' household troops, and which they had employed before their seizure of the throne: *vassus*.[30] The nature of these guards was much as before. Young men would serve at the palace and then, if they did well, be rewarded with administrative posts and honours and sent out to the regions, or otherwise given estates and move away from court for most of the year. Like Merovingian *pueri regis* these could be sent out to the regions and given administrative and other responsibilities. When they were older, these warriors received titles, especially that of count, and settled down on the lands received as reward for good service.

An interesting discussion of Carolingian military service has recently been presented in Matthew Innes' book on the middle Rhineland.[31] Innes argues forcefully against formal military obligations based upon legal freedom, social status or landholding, in favour of armies raised through informal local power networks, maintained through gift-exchange and other fluid mechanisms of patronage. Innes argues for a difference between military service and payment of the *haribannus*, which, as noted above,[32] he sees as an army tax. Whether one performed one or other obligation depended upon links of patronage. The state and its offices were important within these networks but in a much less formal way than is often supposed. The relationship between state and local society was much more fluid, dynamic and involved much more negotiation. This is a very attractive and stimulating idea but there are problems. We have already seen that in the seventh century the *haribannus* cannot be read simply as a payment in lieu of military service. In the Merovingian documents it is clearly a fine rather than a support payment, and it retained that sense throughout the Carolingian period, although by then it had acquired other meanings, including being a payment in lieu of service.[33]

As the centrepiece of the other part of his analysis, Innes draws attention to the career of the Rhenish landowner Ripwin, whom we encountered in chapter 2. In 768–9 Ripwin donated land to the monastery of Lorsch in return for a horse.[34] Innes argues plausibly that, given that the horse was the *sine qua non* of the Frankish career soldier, it is likely that this acquisition related to Ripwin's ability to serve in the army and that Ripwin's purchase raised him to the ranks of the Frankish warriors and into the circle of clients and other associates of Lorsch Abbey. He goes on to claim that while Ripwin became a soldier, clearly participating in a campaign in Italy in 792–3, his brother Giselhelm did not perform military service. Ripwin, says Innes, witnessed charters

> mainly in autumn, winter and spring, and never whilst a campaign was going on. That Ripwin's brother did not serve in the army is left beyond doubt by his appearances as a charter witness in the campaigning season; Ripwin's service was not hereditary.[35]

According to Innes, Ripwin's entry into soldiering circles increased his local standing, judged by the frequency of his appearance as a witness to charters, though he never made it into the front rank of local landholders. The purchase of the horse was thus, in this reading, a family strategy to improve its standing in local affairs. This is a very important argument and deserves detailed attention. If proven, the case would show just how fluid military service might be and it would cast real doubt upon traditional ideas about military service relating directly to defined social class (within the free population at least) or a property qualification. It would also show how local relationships of clientage, and the entry into these relationships, could affect the raising of troops and at the same time how being a warrior might improve social status. It is also important because one of the key documents comes at what appears to have been a point of transition in the ways in which armies were raised. Above all, Ripwin's family appears in well over two dozen charters, making it and its circumstances unusually well documented. The comparative rarity of documented cases like this in the early Middle Ages means that (like the far less detailed story of Imma the thegn discussed in chapter 3) these individual instances take on a far greater importance in discussions of the subject than would be the case in later periods, and require close analysis.

There are problems with Innes' argument, which is ultimately based upon Ripwin's statement that he was going to Italy on campaign, when he gave Giselhelm his lands in case he did not return.[36] Giselhelm clearly did not participate in *that* campaign. The argument also rests to some degree upon a claimed difference (quoted above) in the times of year at which the brothers attested charters. However, as Innes admits, the brothers usually attested documents side by side – on fourteen occasions. Ripwin attested alone only three times, and Giselhelm, where definitely identifiable as Ripwin's brother, also on only three occasions, two of which are later than Ripwin's last appearance in the charter record and thus probably after he had died.[37] Giselhelm does make one donation in Ripwin's absence in July (the centre-point of the Carolingian campaigning season), and this could be significant. However, this was in 817, fifty-one years after his first appearance in the Lorsch charters. By this time, Giselhelm must, on a conservative estimate, have been in his late sixties and probably too old to be fighting even by early medieval standards. The occasion when he attested alone in June was also late in his career, and after Ripwin's (presumed) death.

Eight of the fifteen precisely datable occasions when Ripwin witnessed a charter took place in the period from May to August, the usual campaigning season (four times in June).[38] Two of these occasions are not incompatible with Ripwin's (or Giselhelm's) participation in that year's campaigning[39] but it is far from clear that the others did not take place whilst a campaign was being conducted. However, the fact that campaigns could and did begin at most times of year makes any arguments about witnessing charters during the campaign season very insecure.[40] It is thus impossible to argue for any significant difference in the two brothers' patterns of attestation, and thus equally impossible to assume that one of the brothers was consistently a soldier and the other not (though of course this remains a possibility).

We simply have absolutely no way of knowing from the available evidence whether or not Ripwin's military service was hereditary. The purchase of the horse from Lorsch Abbey was not Ripwin and Giselhelm's first appearance in the Lorsch cartulary.[41] Both attested a charter of the previous year (767). Their other brother Stahal (curiously omitted from Innes' analysis) attests six documents (mostly donations) between 766 and 768.[42] Ripwin's family associated itself with Lorsch Abbey, and included itself amongst the monastery's benefactors, more or less from the moment it was founded in 764. Clearly, too, the family was already a reasonably significant landholder in the region (though Innes is doubtless right in not seeing it in the front rank of the local aristocracy). Whether Ripwin's family was rising or falling in local status is impossible to assess. Innes claims a rise in status on the grounds that Ripwin attests charters more often than his father or grandfather.[43] However, given that Ripwin first witnessed a charter only three years after Lorsch's foundation in 764 and continued to do so for the next forty-two years, it is clear that he had rather more opportunity to attest documents than his father, Liutwin (who was dead within two years of Lorsch's foundation and probably before), let alone his grandfather; neither his father nor his grandfather attests any Lorsch charters.[44] In addition to referring to himself as Liutwin's son, Stahal identifies himself as the son of his mother, Massa,[45] which is most unusual and might further suggest that their father had been dead for some time.[46] Association with Lorsch does not seem to have significantly – or lastingly – enhanced the family's status. The three brothers attest eighteen documents between 766 and 779, but only twelve in the thirty-five years between 782 and 817.[47] The association does, however, appear to have kept the family involved in all-important local politics.

Lorsch charter 257 does make it clear that Ripwin and his brother did not *both* go on *every* campaign; in 792–3, only Ripwin went. Military obligations were not therefore levied automatically and equally upon every person of a particular social standing. Ninth-century Carolingian capitularies[48] specified that local counts would have some responsibility for choosing who was to go on campaign and who was to remain. These capitularies, as will become clear below, were also much concerned with those who stayed behind, whether in the case of several brothers who all owed military service or in the case of those who claimed to be needed by local magnates on other business.[49] Though these documents are all somewhat later than Lorsch charter 257, the charter might show in practice the decision over who stayed behind and who went to the army. This would be important in showing that the royal capitularies were not, as is sometimes supposed, entirely symbolic, and divorced from reality. Not very long after Lorsch charter 257 was written, Charlemagne began to be concerned about the problems of recruiting for his army,[50] and this too is potentially interesting.

In the final analysis, the case of Ripwin can be read as easily in support of the traditional views − of Carolingian military service being an obligation related to particular social standing or wealth − as it can in support of a view of Carolingian armies being raised from very loose and fluid networks of clientship. Nevertheless, the latter is perhaps slightly more likely in an eighth-century context. We have seen that the eighth-century Carolingians were more concerned with reward than obligation, and that participation in warfare was attractive. It is probably more important to note, though, that the two views are not mutually incompatible. Military service could be an imposition, an obligation, but at the same time it was also a right and an opportunity. Those who asserted their right to take part in eighth-century warfare were probably the same people as those obliged to perform military service. In the seventh century, as has been shown, military service was expected, probably as an hereditary obligation, from all landowners of a particular status. Certainly, whether or not one had performed the due military service continued to be taken very seriously. This does not rule out strategies for maintaining and enhancing social status, such as gift giving within the élite and association with permanent and powerful institutions like major monasteries. Nor does it imply that armies were raised by the blanket call-up of all those of the relevant status.

Innes clearly succeeds in his primary task of showing that Ripwin was not a member of a distinct class of freemen known to historians by the German term *Königsfreie* (King's Freemen), with a special, direct relationship to the monarch.[51] In detail, however, his own reading does not really emerge from close study of the documents either. Another interpretation is possible, though, which retains key elements of his argument. The family of Liutwin, possibly threatened by the death of the head of the family some time before (as suggested by Stahal's use of a matronymic), rapidly became benefactors of Lorsch Abbey in order to *maintain* their local standing. Divided inheritance also might have caused problems. Liutwin had three sons who had, presumably, shared his estate. Whilst those lands could have supported one warrior comfortably, a third share might not have done. Tensions are perhaps suggested by the fact that whilst Ripwin and Giselhelm often appear together, they appear less often with Stahal, who usually appears on his own, and seems much more closely associated with their mother, Massa. It is possible, therefore, that Ripwin and Giselhelm bought a horse from Lorsch in order to maintain their ability to carry out hereditary military service, at a time when that was called into question.[52] Judging from the relative dates of their first appearance in the charter record, it may be that Ripwin was the youngest of the three brothers and thus most in need of a horse to perform his military service, although this is of course an entirely speculative reading with no explicit support in the evidence. It is also worth remembering that although horses were indeed essential for participation in the army, they were also extremely vulnerable. Campaigns could be very costly in horseflesh (see chapter 7) and Ripwin, like many other landowners recorded in the charter evidence from across Europe, simply may have wanted to acquire an extra (or a new) horse. Therefore the story of Ripwin does show that the role of gift-exchange and informal ties in military service was important, if perhaps not quite in the way that Innes envisages. As Innes does show, very clearly, aristocrats and now, from the mid-eighth century, those of lesser status (Ripwin's is difficult to be sure about) bolstered their position by associating themselves with major abbeys – fixed points in local society, politics and economy.[53] Though the case does not in any way preclude the use of these links to enhance status and enter the warrior classes, in itself Ripwin's story seems rather to show the use of gifts to maintain relationships *within* a social group, and possibly that performing military service was a defining characteristic of membership of this group. There are other instances of this, to which we shall return. Clearly, too, as Innes says, making gifts to an abbey was indeed an effective strategy, sometimes (possibly) in *intra*-family tensions as well as in interfamilial rivalry. However one reads it, the case of Ripwin and his brothers is a very important one for the study of Carolingian military service, probably offering even more scope for discussion and analysis, and deserves rescuing from the relative obscurity of the Lorsch cartulary.

Charlemagne's conquest of the kingdom of Italy in 773–74 was one of his most spectacular successes. The Lombard kingdom in this period[54] represents a useful contrast with the areas north of the Alps and shows that, although it shared many features of social organisation with the northern kingdom, the way in which armies were raised in Italy was quite different. In turn, this suggests that it would have been possible for Frankish armies to be raised along different lines, that is 'horizontally' rather than 'vertically'. The situation which had arisen in Francia by the ninth century was not inevitable. The Lombard kings worked hard to combat the growth of aristocratic followings and to retain an army raised 'horizontally'. By the 770s it would seem that they were facing significant problems but their response to the situation in many ways adumbrates a number of ninth-century Carolingian policies. The Lombard kingdom continued to expand and came close to reunifying the Italian peninsula in the long reign of King Liutprand (712–44), Charles Martel's ally. In some ways the Lombards were victims of their own success. Conquest of the remaining Byzantine enclaves, and incorporation of the southern duchies of Spoleto and Benevento, left only the papal territories around Rome independent of Lombard rule. The subsequent papal isolation, however, brought the alliance of the popes with the Franks and Frankish military intervention. The reign of the last Lombard king, Desiderius, seems to have been fairly peaceful, which may have meant that the Lombard army gradually lost its battle experience and was able to offer less resistance to the more hardened Frankish armies. After the successes of Liutprand's armies, the eighth century in the Lombard kingdom was marked by certain dynastic instability.

Within the Lombard kingdom, local power was achieved largely through the acquisition of royal patronage. Lombard aristocrats were not hugely and independently wealthy landowners, but instead a fairly broad stratum of middling landlords: a 'squirearchy'. Royal authority was constantly referred to in the settlement of disputes, and a pecking order of these 'squires' was established by status in royal service; royally bestowed office legitimised the wielding of local power.[55] The situation was not dissimilar to that in Merovingian Gaul in the sixth century, although Lombard society and politics were more heavily focused on towns and urban life than sixth-century northern Gallic society had been. There are other similarities with the sixth-century Frankish kingdom. The Lombards appear to have introduced the custom of annual assemblies on 1 March in the eighth century.[56] The fourteen dated legal pronouncements made by Liutprand are all issued on 1 March, as are the laws of Ratchis and both codes of Aistulf.

In the eighth century the term *arimannus* (army man, also rendered as *exercitalis*) is used to describe the class of free landowners.[57] As we have seen, the Latin version of the term occurs in the seventh century but in contexts which make its precise meaning unclear. In the eighth century it is more clearly used as a term for a particular social group, outside the confines of the army.[58] Landowners of Roman origin appear to be included in its ranks, and by Liutprand's day the class was divided into strata.[59] Now, possibly following on from the seventh-century usage of *exercitalis*, the status of the *arimannus* was defined by his right to attend the army, and the army was a political assembly presided over by the king's officers. The military basis of social identity extended to regions, the citizens of Siena being collectively referred to as an *exercitus* (army) in a document of 730.[60] Ratchis enacted that everyone should turn out on horseback with shield and spear to support their local judge (seemingly meaning duke or gastald), whether on local business or when summoned to the king.[61] This clause makes clear that such men might be dispatched from the court on military expeditions. Ratchis and his brother Aistulf (see below) seem both to have been attempting to ensure a broad-based attendance at these gatherings, which, as Ratchis' clause makes clear, were also military assemblies. The ideological effort in linking free landowners with the army would also appear to have aimed at making a direct connection between the *arimanni* and the king. All *arimanni* were required to swear an oath to the king.[62] This may have strengthened the importance of royal patronage in local politics, as mentioned above. This system may have been a new development of the eighth century, or it may have existed in the later seventh century. The evidence does not allow us to decide. What does seem fairly clear is the survival, to some extent, of an army raised on the 'horizontal' model discussed in chapter 3.

The law–codes reveal, nevertheless, that military service had become a source of royal concern. As early as 726, Liutprand issued a law restricting the numbers of men that a royal official was allowed to leave behind to work his estates when the army was called up.[63] Most such laws specify the numbers to be brought to the army. Liutprand appears to have been concerned to set out the number which could reasonably be held to manage lands in an officer's absence, and expect such royal agents to turn up with every other available man. This somewhat unusual approach to legislation is also adopted in some later

Carolingian legislation[64] and may have been produced by the same situation: people appear to have obtained from royal officials (probably at a price) exemption from military service on the grounds that the official needed them on other duties at home. The law, like the Carolingian pronouncements, may have aimed to close this loophole and opportunity for 'corruption'.

King Aistulf issued in 750 a law defining the level of military equipment which Lombards should have.[65] As with Ine's Anglo-Saxon code, however, we should think twice before blithely assuming that this was a simple reflection of long-standing reality. Aistulf seized the throne from his brother Ratchis, who in turn had seized it from Liutprand's short-lived nephew and successor Hildeprand. This law was issued in the very year of Aistulf's usurpation. The same code also enacted that royal officers were not to allow powerful men to go home from the army.[66] Aistulf seems to have been very concerned that he might not command the full support of the Lombard military élite. His law on equipment divided those liable to military service into three grades. The top grade was to serve with horse, mail armour, lance and shield, the second grade was to serve with horse, lance and shield, and the third to be equipped with bow and shield. These grades were defined according to the amount of land held or, interestingly, a merchant's wealth. Landowners with seven *casae massariae* fell into the top grade, those with 40 *iugera* of land into the second, and 'lesser men' into the third. Merchants were not so precisely graded, divided simply into 'those who are greater', 'those who come next' and 'lesser men'. The latter gradation is so vague that we can only assume that local dukes and gastalds were left to use their own knowledge of local urban society to determine who fell into which class.

Whether or not Aistulf's laws had any effect is unknown but the scheme he attempted to introduce reveals how military obligation had come to be primarily determined by property rather than by other ethnic or legal identity. It might be assumed that Aistulf was, as in clause 7 of his code, trying to ensure that wealthier landowners performed their military service with full equipment. This might well be the case but we should not neglect the lower classifications. It is at least as likely that the king was encouraging lesser freemen to turn up to the political assembly of the army, even if only with bow and shield, in line with what seem to be the royal policies discussed above. The same may be true of Liutprand's law of 726, mentioned earlier, about how many men a senior official could leave behind when the army assembled.

The Lombard kings worked hard to maintain at least the idea of a 'horizontally' levied army but the personal followings of individual magnates do seem to have become more important, as elsewhere.[67] We encountered the *gasindii*, bodyguards or personal retainers, in the last chapter. In the mid-seventh century, however, we saw that followings were informal. Though not unproblematic the evidence appears to show that, as elsewhere, gifts made between freemen were in perpetuity. The only people who might be expected to return gifts if service was not fulfilled were freedmen. The eighth century is widely supposed to have been a period when individual followings became more important, as else-where. The eighth-century law-codes reveal a concern with lords who protect their adherents from the workings of royal law, such as were encountered in seventh-century Gaul and Spain.[68] Although never as important as north of the Alps, private followings were becoming significant. The Lombard kings' protection of, and preservation of their links with, the less wealthy *arimanni* represented attempts to bypass these lords to some extent or at least to reduce their importance. We saw in the previous chapter how assemblies like this had been important to sixth-century rulers in maintaining their ties to the rank-and-file of their armies, and increasing the importance of royal prestige and royally bestowed office. It seems that the eighth-century Lombard kings were using them to do the same. The upshot was that the transformation from 'horizontal' mechanisms of raising the army (levying military service on a broad social class, via royally appointed officers) to 'vertical' (armies raised down chains of lordship and dependence) never fully took place in Italy until well after the Frankish invasion.

It has been suggested, from the fact that some Lombard landowners made their wills before going off to fight Pippin I's Frankish armies in the 750s, that morale was weakening in Aistulf's armies.[69] This may have been the case. Aistulf does not, as we have seen, seem to have been confident in his subjects' willing-ness to fight for him, and his troops' performance against Pippin will have done little to reassure him. None the less, the conclusion does not necessarily emerge from the evidence of the wills, one of which was made by a bishop (Walprand of Lucca). Ripwin also made provision for what would happen to his property if he failed to return from campaign in Italy, yet that was at the height of Charlemagne's armies' successes.

In Spain, the Visigothic kingdom collapsed in the face of Arab attack in 711.[70] Within a decade Islamic armies had conquered the Iberian peninsula and extinguished a shadowy Visigothic successor kingdom in Septimania.[71] However, a revolt soon sprang up in the Asturias and defeated the local Arab garrisons at Covadonga, a battle which soon became the focus for all sorts of amazing legends.[72] Thus was born the kingdom of the Asturias, which in the tenth century became the kingdom of León and ultimately of Castile. How armies were raised in the Christian north-west of Spain is very difficult to establish.[73] There were doubtless some survivals from Visigothic structures, but it is difficult to know much about this. The extent to which the Visigothic kingdom had wielded power in this part of the peninsula is debatable. It was always governed with difficulty, as the Romans found earlier, but attempts to demonstrate a Visigothic frontier in the area before 711 have not generally been convincing.[74] Documents are sparse before the tenth century and, though it then becomes possible to discuss military organisation, it is dangerous to project these situa-tions back into the ninth, let alone eighth, century in any detail. As we have seen throughout this and the preceding chapter, military organisation did not remain static.

By the mid-tenth century, lands were held in return for military service, termed *fosato* or *fonsado*; exemptions were also being granted from such service. Possibly as early as the ninth century, reference was also made to the duty to perform guard duties. Such obligations could be signs of status, thus perpetuating the old idea that to be liable to fight was the mark of the free. In a kingdom as subject to repeated attack as that of the Asturias it may be that general levies were raised more commonly than elsewhere. In the difficult terrain of the Asturias which, as mentioned, had never been governed easily from the centre of the peninsula, it may be that warfare was not purely the business of the king. Possibly much more negotiation was necessary with local communities. Any more detail than that is difficult to confirm for the eighth and ninth centuries. The army was called out on the royal order, it would seem by royal agents who still bore the old Gothic title of *saio*, suggesting that this may have been a survival from the kingdom of Toledo. Tenth-century charters forbade *saiones* from entering exempted estates. The king seems usually to have commanded the army, though counts could also be deputed to lead expeditions. By the time we know anything much about it, military organisation in the Asturias was not very different from that in the Carolingian Spanish territories in the east.

It was once thought that Alfonso I (739–57) and his son Fruela I (757–68) depopulated the Duero valley frontier with Islamic Spain, moving the Christian population back to the mountainous core of his kingdom, and creating a deserted frontier zone between the Christian and Muslim realms. It was believed that the resettlement of this supposedly deserted area was then done through the granting of land in return for particular services. More recent work, both archaeological and from the charters of the region, has shown that this belief, based, as it is, mainly upon one brief comment in the *Chronicle of Alfonso III*,[75] is mistaken.

The eighth and ninth centuries in England saw a series of developments in the manner in which armies were raised.[76] As in Francia these developments hinged upon the way in which land was held in return for service. The apparent[77] spread of landholding by charter may have altered these relationships, though quite how is still not fully understood. In the 730s Bede wrote, in a long letter to his archbishop Ecgbert about the state of the English Church, that the spread of monasteries of dubious sanctity was posing a threat to the defence of the realm. His argument was that Northumbrian nobles were setting up monasteries and receiving land grants upon which to found them. Thus, complained Bede, the land available to reward warriors was being drastically reduced, forcing such warriors to go abroad. At roughly the same time, Anglo-Saxon charters begin to note that grants to churches are not exempt from the obligation to provide labour for the repair of bridges and fortresses, though they might still be exempt from military service. As Brooks notes, this development took place at different times in different parts of Anglo-Saxon England.[78] By the end of the eighth century, charters in Mercia (the dominant kingdom at this point) and Kent had generally come to reserve to the king the 'three common dues' (*trinoda necessitas*) of fortress work, bridge work and military service, and this remained the case in the ninth, when it spread into other kingdoms like Wessex.

In the most thorough discussion of these changes, Richard Abels[79] argues as follows. In the seventh century, and possibly earlier, land given to retainers was not granted in perpetuity; its tenure, and transmission from father to son, was dependent upon continued good service. Land given to the church appears to have been held in perpetuity and was possibly exempt from military service. This type of tenure became popular amongst lay landholders who wanted their grants from the king 'booked' (held by charter) in the same way as the church, Bede's letter referring to an early stage in this process. Thus the amount of land subject to military duties was gradually reduced. Eventually, the powerful Mercian overlords like Æthelbald and Offa had to specify, when they made a grant, that the lands were not exempt from providing military service. This enabled them to continue to wage successful campaigns and defend their realms from their neighbours, English and Welsh. The Mercian kings also used these dues to create a network of fortresses from which to administer their kingdom.[80] The beginnings of the Viking attacks created a further inducement for local lords to agree to these burdens, and, by the early ninth century, these forms of service were normal. The army was still, nevertheless, formed by the retinues of lords and their men, drawn from their estates, around a nucleus of royal and other magnate bodyguards. This was the background to the reforms of Alfred in the late ninth century, to which we shall return.

This is a sophisticated and convincing reading of the evidence, but other alternatives are possible. As was argued in chapter 3, developments in Anglo-Saxon social and political structures may have had more in common with those in contemporary Francia than is often supposed. As there, it is extremely unlikely that the church was ever completely exempt from military service.[81] At the end of the seventh century, as we have seen, in England as also in Visigothic Spain and Frankish Gaul, there was a concern to define, and perhaps alter, the terms under which land was given to followers, and what did or did not remain in the ultimate possession of the lord. Ine's laws, rather than recording age-old traditions, seem to have been a response to specific circumstances wherein the king was concerned to make sure that landowners performed their military service. Instead of reflecting a traditional system under threat, they may represent an attempt to institute or regularise transformations that were under way. This concern may not have been very different from that which led Æthelbald and later Offa of Mercia to specify that military service was due when they granted lands by charter.

The difference which such grants made from earlier gifts concerned inheritance rather than the perpetuity of the tenure. It is likely that, as in Francia, grants of estates had been permanent throughout the seventh century. As some Anglo-Saxon charters make clear, 'bookland' (land held by charter) could be willed to whomsoever the recipient desired. Thus, exactly as in contemporary

Francia and for exactly the same reasons, the land was removed from the norms of customary partible inheritance. This was important in maintaining a family's landed power base but, although an eldest son might obtain a more secure power base, younger sons could indeed, as Bede feared, find themselves, if not disinherited, at least without sufficient land to raise a family and support their warrior status.[82] In the seventh century it would seem that a fairly broad class of small landowners had been subject to military duties (either of service or of the payment of dues). Even sixty or so years after Bede's letter, the king of Wessex stated that all men of the rank of *comes* were liable to military service.[83] They may have owned land in recognition of that fact. As Brooks puts it: 'Land, therefore, without being the source of military obligation, was the expected reward for loyal military service.'[84] Such a relationship was ongoing and reciprocal. It appears that within the social group bound into these relationships much more land was coming to be held by far fewer individuals. This would indeed reduce the number of warriors able to maintain the cost of service who could be levied by the old means. Furthermore, this right of disposition meant that the land *might* be passed to individuals or institutions not liable to military service, like, *perhaps*, some churches. As in Francia, Anglo-Saxon lords may, as in Ine's Code, have rewarded followers with temporary grants from these landed power bases; a king would have wanted to make sure he still ultimately had a right to the service of these followers.

Many of the old institutions of Anglo-Saxon military service remained in place none the less. The royal household was still the core of any army, and the king maintained links with warriors who had served their time, and earned their rewards in his retinue. The royal bodyguard could be a very important political institution. Æthelbald of Mercia was assassinated by his guards, and Mercia temporarily lost its overall dominance as a result. Similarly, the followings of aristocrats and royal officers remained the building blocks of the army. The story of Cynewulf and Cyneheard shows the importance of sometimes sizeable personal followings.[85] The pattern of service in such military households was still related to age, young warriors serving an apprenticeship before marrying and settling down on their own lands, though these lands may now have been held in a slightly different way.

Before the incorporation of the regions of western Germany (Saxony, Hesse, Thuringia, Alamannia and Bavaria) into the Frankish empire, military organisation east of the Rhine remained much as set out in chapter 3, though this impression may arise from the fact that the comments made there were largely derived from eighth-century sources! Some transformations may have come about during the middle of the eighth century, however. As Bavaria and other trans-Rhenish areas were more thoroughly integrated into the mainstream of Frankish society and politics, changes in landholding seem to have occurred. Charters appear in these regions, and it may be that lordship and landowning took on similar forms to those in contemporary Francia. These similarities included, by the middle of the century in Bavaria, the use of ecclesiastical land to reward followers. Members of the warrior classes, as in Francia, associated themselves with monasteries through donations, sometimes in exchange for military equipment. At some point between 748 and 784, three men called Ratpold, Odalman and Kerperht sold their lands in 'Ursisdorf' to the Abbey of Mondsee.[86] Of the three, Odalman received two horses, a shield and a spear, in addition to five oxen and a cow. This case might be as interesting as that of Ripwin discussed in detail above. Unfortunately, whereas Ripwin's family is well documented, this is the only time that these men feature in history and we are unsure even of the relationship between them. Whether Odalman wanted to enter the warrior class, maintain his ability to fight, or simply increase his equipment, we shall never know. That association with monasteries, and the exchange of military gear, was important is underlined by the fact that between 784 and 788 a man called Adalunc supported an earlier donation of land to Mondsee with a gift of a jewelled saddle and a mail shirt.[87] This would presumably be used by the monastery as a gift in turn, or to help equip its military contingent.

Before its final absorption into the Carolingian polity in 788, the Bavarian duchy enjoyed some military success, defeating the Carinthian Slavs and holding its own against Avar incursions. It has been plausibly suggested that the Bavarian dukes used major religious foundations as strategic points on the frontier, not only as defended and defensible outposts, controlling major routes, but also as means of ensuring the provisioning of armed forces passing through those routes.[88]

Indeed, the eighth century saw an increasing use of fortifications in Germany east of the Rhine. Some of the hilltop forts abandoned around 500 were reoccupied in the eighth century.[89] This may indicate a transformation in the forms of lordship and, consequently, military organisation. It is possible that they are manifestations of the increased concentration of surplus in the hands of local magnates, which other types of evidence confirm was taking place at this time. This in turn might suggest the capacity for larger and better-equipped retinues. The Alamannic nobility, as mentioned, was destroyed at Cannstadt in 744, leading to a large-scale change of personnel, and the introduction of Frankish lords into the region. By the 780s at least, if not much earlier, it would seem that there was very little to distinguish trans-Rhenan 'German' armies from Frankish ones in matters of organisation. Culturally, as has been observed, the Frankish core had spread its norms out to the periphery. This would make the incorporation of these areas into the Carolingian polity much easier and more secure than had been the case during sixth-century Merovingian hegemony. Saxony was possibly an exception to this rule, though again there must have been many similarities; a Saxon army was able to infiltrate its way into a Frankish camp in the 770s,[90] suggesting that the two sides must have looked like each other to some degree. The Saxons were also able to mobilise significant manpower. Their side of the frontier with the Franks was well organised with religious centres and fortifications.[91]

Eighth-century Scandinavian military organisation can only really be approached via archaeological data. The rulers of Denmark appear to have been powerful enough to raise manpower to construct major public works, notably the great Danevirke, a large defensive bank and ditch structure running across the Jutland peninsula. The first phase of this system is dated by dendro-chronology (tree-ring dating) to 737. Another important work, dated to 726 (and possibly ordered by the same ruler, or at least the ruler of the same territory), was the 1 km long Kanhave canal on the island of Samsø, which permitted ships to sail directly across from the island's sheltered harbour to intercept vessels on the west side of the island. Some roads were also repaired in the eighth century, and coin minting began in Ribe in c.720.[92] All these works suggest the wielding of a significant degree of political power. By the end of the eighth century it is clear that the king of Denmark could mobilise significant military forces. King Godfred mobilised a mounted army for a face-off against Charlemagne himself and the Danes established suzerainty over the Obodrite Slavs. Godfred was able to remove the population of a Slavic trading station, Reric, and transfer it to his new foundation of Hedeby (near modern Schleswig). The growth in royal power in Denmark around the end of the eighth century has plausibly been linked to the beginning of Viking attacks, as lesser political leaders and rivals for power were driven to seek fortune and prestige abroad. How Danish armies were raised is unknown, however. Lund has demonstrated clearly that there is no evidence to push back central medieval Scandinavian systems of levying troops – *leidang* – attested from the eleventh or twelfth centuries into the Viking period, let alone before.[93] In other areas, it is difficult to see very much evidence for change between the seventh and eighth centuries in the ways in which armies were raised.

The ninth century

Charlemagne's wars of expansion slowed down after the dramatic conquest of the Avar kingdom, and the final grinding down of Saxon resistance by 802. Significantly, it is at about this time, which also saw the first appearance of the Vikings, that the earliest detailed legislation about military service appears. This fits a pattern that we have already encountered. Periods of successful expansionist warfare do not seem to produce much legal concern with who should or should not perform military service. The rewards in lands, gifts, offices and booty which successful warfare produces appear to have been sufficient to attract aristocrats and their retinues to the royal army. Defensive warfare, especially in areas where an aristocrat did not, himself, hold land, or warfare to punish recalcitrant members of the same aristocratic class, were much less popular. By 811, the ageing emperor heard, in response to an inquiry as to why people were neglecting their military service, the somewhat depressing counsel that 'above all' the majority of the people were becoming ever more disobedient to their counts, and constantly appealing to the *missi*.[94] Thus, not surprisingly, it is from the 790s, but especially the first decade of the ninth century, that Charlemagne began to specify who was to perform military service, and with what sort of equipment.

Since the important work of Reuter,[95] it has been understood that one should see the increasing concern with military obligations as a reflection of a change from expansionist warfare to defensive warfare against, for example, the Vikings. It seems to have been more difficult to persuade the warrior aristocracy to take part in this type of warfare, as noted above, and it is possibly also the case that such defensive warfare meant raising troops from social groups who, whatever their theoretical right to participate in warfare, had in practice largely not previously been involved. This is important as it allows us to see the legislation of Charlemagne's last years in other and less traditional terms than those of a gradual loss of purpose and direction.

Reuter also argued that the end of the possibility to take loot on the frontiers produced tensions within Frankish society, and was a major factor in producing the civil wars of the ninth century. It seems mistaken, however, to see the Franks as having simply run out of room for further conquests, or run up against opponents whom they could not beat. Charlemagne's sons, Charles, Pippin and Louis, all appear to have inherited their father's military abilities. Charles the Younger led very-well-executed campaigns on the Slavic frontier, and Louis, for all that he was long dismissed by historians as the great father's lesser son, conducted skilful and imaginative campaigns on the Spanish frontier.[96] From accounts of these wars, it seems that new territories could still have been acquired, especially in Spain. What is more, some of Charlemagne's legislation from these years is clearly concerned with raising forces for warfare on the frontiers, far from home, and not exclusively for local defence.[97] Thus, even finding troops for aggressive campaigns on the frontiers was proving to be a matter of some concern. Possibly the empire had simply become too large. It was ever more expensive and time-consuming for warriors and their followers to move out from the Frankish political heartlands to the frontiers where wars were fought. Furthermore, the rewards from any territorial expansion on the Slavic frontier were much smaller. The profit margin from warfare was declining. Rewards from fighting on the Spanish March, for example, seem largely to have accrued to local inhabitants rather than the great magnates at the heart of the kingdom. It may also be that as Charlemagne grew old and remained at his palace at Aachen a certain direction and coordination was lost. Furthermore, Charlemagne's sons Charles and Pippin predeceased him, leaving Louis as the only royal, or later imperial, focus for military action. These factors could have cumulated in a certain 'running out of steam' after all.

Pursuing the theme of the importance of loot and tribute, Reuter argued that one reason why western Frankish kings had greater difficulties than the kings of East Francia related to warfare. The East Frankish kings could wage aggressive war on their eastern frontier, rewarding their followers with booty, and thus keeping them happy. East Frankish kings like Louis the German were therefore able to remain 'warrior kings', whereas their western relatives, faced with no possibilities of expansive warfare abroad and thus more restless noble dynasties, were not.[98] The western kingdom was also more subject to Viking attacks, which could be damaging to royal prestige. There is probably something in this, though it is unlikely to be the whole story. Warfare *was* important but not just, and possibly not even primarily, for plunder or captured lands with which to reward followers. The size of the kingdoms and the proximity of all the different regions within it to frontier campaigning areas were also important, as was the relative power and strength of identity of regional aristocracies. All of these factors may have given the East Frankish kings advantages over the kings of West Francia, as may Louis the German's apparently greater success in managing his sub-kings, but they still faced problems. The different regions of Carolingian Germany seem to have had significant political identities, as became clear during the eventual downfall and deposition of Charles III 'the Fat'. Carolingian Italy had as few opportunities for offensive warfare as West Francia, and Louis II's military interventions in the south of the peninsula were not especially successful. Yet Italy seems to have remained stable and well governed.

The ways in which the rules of the game had changed, even by the early ninth century, and the fact that loot was no longer the only, and perhaps not even the most important, motor of military activity is shown by the unwillingness of major Carolingian aristocrats to participate even in offensive campaigns. Two leading magnates, Hugh (subsequently nicknamed 'the Timid'[99]) and Matfrid conducted a campaign to the Spanish March in 828 with such lack of enthusiasm (the army arriving too late to do any good) that they were stripped of their *honores* by Louis the Pious, this punishment eventually sparking the major crises of his reign. Nobles as powerful as Hugh and Matfrid had no especial socio-political need for loot. This was not a campaign led by the emperor, so it offered them little political opportunity – quite the opposite. Campaigning was expensive and more importantly they would be removed from the centre of political action at a crucial moment. Both were linked to a faction forming around Louis' son Lothar, and sending them off on campaign far from the court was a somewhat pointed gesture. The problem was only exacerbated when Louis *did* lead a campaign to Brittany in 830, in the company of Hugh and Matfrid's rival, Bernard of Septimania, brought from the periphery to the political core.[100] This shows that loot and booty cannot have been the primary motive for ninth-century Frankish warfare. If it had been, then surely Hugh and Matfrid would have been happy to serve in Spain, and return to court as triumphant warriors with enhanced prestige and political capital. More to the point, there was mass refusal to join Louis' Breton campaign.[101] If anything, the crisis seems to have been sparked by the emperor's call to arms for that invasion. Clearly the opportunity to take part in offensive warfare and acquire booty and loot, or even less tangible advantages, cannot have been the only consideration. The instance does, however, show the building up of tensions within Louis' empire.

The nature of the political problems facing the Carolingians were, in many ways, the same as those that had faced the Merovingians in the later seventh century, but writ large. The successes of the late eighth century had helped to create a class of magnates, known to historians as the *Reichsaristocratie* (Imperial Aristocracy),[102] who held widespread land and *honores* throughout the empire. There is evidence that the idea of the *nobilitas* (nobility) of these families, drawn from their birth, was continuing to gain currency.[103] These families could pose formidable political problems. The fact that they held lands in several of the *regna*, and had support networks of lesser members of their families in other kingdoms made leading members of these families difficult to remove from power. Kings occasionally executed troublesome magnates, and quite frequently stripped others of their *honores*, but these families had a tendency to bounce back and to prove extraordinarily resilient.[104] They could also be significant sources of patronage in local society. With the wide range of their interests, especially, these magnates were able to play different members of the royal family off against each other for their own advantage. The size and awkward physical geography of the empire also posed problems.

The kings had weapons of their own, though. The heavy Carolingian invest-ment in royal ideology seems to have succeeded in demonstrating that they were the only throne-worthy family.[105] As a result, the legitimacy provided by royally bestowed titles and *honores* was very important in shoring up the local pre-eminence even of the more powerful aristocrats. Royal *honores* were worth fighting and dying for.[106] Access to the court, as before, was vitally important in aristocratic politics. The Carolingians adopted other methods of ensuring that their writ ran throughout their realms too, though with mixed success. By making their sons 'sub-kings', they increased the number of royal centres and raised the number of points of access to royal patronage. Unfortunately, these lesser royals could also be used by aristocrats excluded from power elsewhere to provide foci for political dissent. Again following earlier precedents, the Carolingians toured their kingdoms to try to increase the availability of their patronage, though the extent of their mobility varied significantly from king to king and may have related to differences in effective power. However, the relationships between the kings and the major magnates of necessity involved considerable negotiation, far more so than appears to have been the case in some earlier (especially sixth-century) polities. Kings who tried too hard to impose direct rule from the centre could find that their writ ended up running even less effectively.[107] The consensus demonstrated so well in recent studies of Carolingian politics and ritual accompanied, and was perhaps the product of, repeated conflict between rulers and (at least some of) their magnates in the ninth century.

None the less, difficult though the situation was, it should not be assumed that the dissolution of royal authority throughout France was somehow pre-destined. The number of sources of patronage, though it could be a problem for the kings, could also have been an opportunity.

The Carolingians were not, as is usually thought, swept along by the force of events, but confronted these threats in resolute and concerted fashion. These people were self-conscious political actors, eminently capable of improvisation, and clearly not as tightly bound by contemporary political norms as is sometimes implied in modern scholarship: they were not imprisoned by their circumstances, but were able to engage with them.[108]

If the problems eventually proved insurmountable, and they were not helped by Viking and Arab attacks and dynastic accident (genetic and physical!), this was not the kings' fault.

Carolingian legislation on military service reflects the changed nature of the political situation. The first decade of the ninth century saw Charlemagne issue pronouncements on the ways in which armies were to be raised. Types of military service included watch duty (in frontier areas), garrison duty and service in the *scarae*.[109] In 806 and 807, Charlemagne specified that all landed royal vassals were to perform military service.[110] In the latter year, Charles began to specify how military service was to be imposed on the remainder of the free population, introducing a property qualification and a system of *adiutorium* (loosely 'assistance'), whereby freemen too poor to serve on their own clubbed together to send one of their number to the army. Charlemagne expected military service from all freemen who owned 3, 4 or 5 *mansi* (a landed unit of assessment, like the Anglo-Saxon *hide*) or more. Men who held less than this were banded into groups so that one warrior was sent from every 3 *mansi*. Thus the holder of a single *mansus* joined a holder of 2 *mansi*; holders of 1 *mansus* were grouped into threes, and men who held only 0.5 *mansus* were assembled into sets, with five men equipping a sixth.[111] This was a fairly heavy obligation and in the following year Charlemagne appears to have changed his mind about it, instituting 4 *mansi* as the threshold for military service: four holders of a single *mansus* would club together to provide a soldier, two holders of 2 *mansi* would do similarly, a holder of three *mansi* would be helped by a holder of 1 *mansus*, and so on.[112] The emperor also issued commands about what sort of equipment was to be provided. Holders of 12 *mansi*, for example, were to equip themselves with a mail coat.[113] Earlier he had enacted that all warriors were to have shield, spear and bow with two bowstrings and twelve arrows, apparently expecting everyone to have mail and a helmet.[114] In a circular letter, of which we have the one sent to Fulrad, lay abbot of St-Quentin,[115] he specified that all a contingent's *caballarii*[116] were to be armed with a spear, shield, long sword, short sword, bow, quiver and arrows.[117] Charlemagne also stated that the troops were to be accompanied by carts carrying three months' provisions and other items such as whetstones. Charlemagne mentioned such carts on several occasions.[118] Indeed he was increasingly concerned with the provisioning of his armies in these years.[119]

Whether or not any of this was particularly effective is open to doubt. Hand in hand with the increase in the number of detailed pronouncements on military obligations came a rise in the number of enactments about neglect or abuse of such duties: bribery, desertion, refusal to attend, failure to attend with the right equipment, and other scams such as being ordained into the church in order to avoid conscription.[120] Charlemagne repeatedly enacted that the *haribannus*, as a fine of 60 *solidi*, was to be exacted from those who refused to attend the summons, and that anyone who deserted from the army was guilty of *herisliz* and liable to the death penalty.[121] In 808 the emperor ordered an inquiry into those people who had made a mockery of 'the order we issued for a military expedition' in the previous year.[122] By 811 he had sent his *missi* to find out what excuses were being given for non-attendance at the muster, and later that year he had evidently had enough replies to discuss a range of such reasons.[123]

The document in which these replies are discussed is fascinating and gives a vital glimpse of the workings of early medieval government, and of the ways in which the existence of the state could be used in local politics. The reasons given included poverty as a result of despoliation by the great and the good of the realm. Some people claimed, presumably in association with powerful protectors, that their lords, be they abbots, bishops or counts, needed them as officials (to counter this sort of thing Charlemagne prescribed how many men a lord could leave at home[124]), whilst others argued that they had been summoned to other matters by the emperor's sons, Pippin and Louis. Others still insisted that they were not liable to a summons by the count but only by the *missus*, and some people said, reasonably enough, that they saw no reason why they should attend the summons when the lords whom they had sworn to serve were staying at home. Essentially, the *missi* gloomily reported, no one was doing what he was told any more. When a count ordered something, people would immediately appeal to the *missi*. Chapter 3 of the memorandum is especially interesting. Some freemen complained that the local potentates, lay and ecclesiastical, were expecting poorer freemen to hand over their *allod* (family land, not held from anyone else), and thus become their dependants, in return for exemption from duty in the army. Those who refused were sent off to the army every time it was called out, until such service ruined them and they had no choice but to hand over their lands. To summarise, officials were using the royally legitimised authority of their position to increase their local power, and lesser people were playing off the figures of authority against each other: the emperor versus his sons, *missi* versus counts, lords versus officials. Yet, in some way, all of these scams turned upon the very legitimacy which royally bestowed office was seen as having. Whilst Charlemagne may have despaired of the situation and the way it impeded proper implementation of his orders, we can see how involvement with the state could bring considerable advantage in local politics, and thus encourage local élites' involvement in royal government. However we (or Charlemagne) might view it, such 'corruption' was the glue that bonded early medieval polities.

Charlemagne appears to have wanted to raise an army in the old style – levied evenly across the whole landowning class and commanded by royal officers as in the sixth century. He seems also to have wanted to make sure that lesser freemen also performed their military service. Such an army, he envisaged, would be organised by county around a nucleus provided by the count and other royal vassals. Whether or not this type of force was ever raised entirely in the way he wanted is unknown and possibly unlikely. However, the fact that his pronouncements formed the framework for his successors' thinking on the subject suggests that the system was implemented to some extent. The opportunities that it (or rather its abuse) provided for the locally powerful, as just discussed, also imply that Charlemagne's orders were put into practice.

The system set out in Charlemagne's legislation on military affairs formed the template for pronouncements on military service throughout the Carolingian Empire, and beyond, for the rest of the period. There were regional variations, of course. In Italy[125] for example, some factors led to a certain individuality. Some terminology was inherited from the Lombard kingdom.[126] Another specific factor was the need to defend the coast of the kingdom of Italy from maritime raids by the Arabs, especially after the Byzantines lost Sicily.[127] The 'Saracens' provided a local equivalent of the Viking raids then terrorising more northerly regions of Christian Europe. Nevertheless, military service in Carolingian Italy can conveniently be dealt with along with the other imperial territories in Germany and Spain.[128]

In 815, Louis the Pious specified that freemen on the Spanish March should serve in the army with their lords, and perform guard duty and *explorationes* (service as scouts). Louis' son, Charles the Bald, repeated the enactment that freemen on the March were to serve 'like other Franks' in 844.[129] On the Spanish March, lands taken from the Moslems, sometimes declared to be abandoned or unclaimed 'waste', were granted out in return for the usual forms of Carolingian military service. Some may have been granted to previously landless soldiers who had served well in the region. One such seems to have been the *Hispanus* John who, c.795, defeated an Arab force near Barcelona and, after sending the spoils to Charlemagne's son, Louis of Aquitaine (the future Louis the Pious), received a 'waste' estate.[130] These estates, known as *aprisiones*, were then used by these new landowners to reward their own followers.[131]

Louis the Pious was concerned to regularise his father's system. In 829 he issued three documents which instructed his *missi* to make a proper survey, county by county, of the *adiutorium* system. They were to list who could serve on his own, who had to help provide equipment for another freeman, and who had to be grouped with two, three or four others in order to provide a warrior. Ten years previously he had repeated Charlemagne's instructions that the *haribannus* (meaning the 60 *solidus* fine) was to be paid by anyone refusing to do military service, except those who were entitled to be left at home.[132] In 832 Einhard had to write to the imperial *missus* on behalf of his dependants, who had been accused, wrongly he said, of neglecting their watch duty on the coast and were threatened with the *haribannus* (again in the sense of a fine, not a contribution).[133] In 825 Louis' eldest son, Lothar, specified that freemen with the ability to equip and supply themselves on campaign, which in Italy was called *bharigild*, were to go; the rest were to band into groups of two, three, four or more if necessary, and send the most able to the army. He too threatened punishment of those who neglected their duty, specifying the death penalty if the enemy turned out to be victorious.[134] Louis and Lothar enacted that everyone liable to military service should be well equipped, with horses, weapons, clothing, carts and supplies.[135] Discipline and non-attendance still posed problems for the emperor. Between 823 and 825 he pronounced that those who had done wrong in the previous year's campaign in the Marches should accept their punishment.[136] Louis also enacted that all weapons were to be put down within forty days of the end of a military expedition.[137]

However, military activity within the Carolingian territories, especially after 840, increasingly concerned warfare between various members of the royal house, usually condemned as civil (occasionally as 'worse than civil'[138]) war. Whether the legal or quasi-legal royal pronouncements on military service had very much bearing on this sort of fighting is unknown. Though there is no real proof either way, it seems that these wars were, as before, essentially the business of aristocrats and their loosely defined followings of vassals and other clients. Indeed it is likely that Carolingian armies relied more upon the use of royal vassals, benefice holders and ecclesiastical contingents than upon the *adiutorium* levy. A *formula* (a model legal document which scribes could use, simply filling in names, places and other specifics where necessary) surviving from the court of Louis the Pious specifies the supplies which were to be sent to the army to support contingents raised from vassals and benefice holders.[139] Interestingly, this levy of supplies is described as *haribannus*, making clear that the term did not only mean the 60 shilling fine for refusal to serve. In this period (presumably as a result of gradual extension of the eighth-century state of affairs) it does appear that the sorts of service and support expected in return for landed benefices were well understood between donor and grantee (which is not to say that all benefices were held in return for the same services). Such followings were rarely produced by 'land for service' arrangements set out in written contracts but that does not mean that terms and conditions were ill understood. The exchange of gifts, especially of military equipment, was very important.[140] At a gathering of the better born (*maiores natu*) at 'Suarzesmuor' in 827, for example, the abbot of Fulda oiled the wheels of local politics by bestowing gifts, especially of swords (*gladii*) but also in some cases of horses, upon various local leaders.[141] Horses and military equipment frequently feature as gifts and in payments for land.[142] As before, gifts within the warrior classes and linkage to major monasteries remained important. The expectation remained, however, that members of certain social classes should serve if summoned, as documents exempting individuals from military service make clear.[143]

Warfare might still be an avenue to social advancement. Notker the Stammerer relates a story of how two young bastards prospered at the expense of more nobly born warriors, for good service to Charlemagne.[144] It is difficult to place much factual weight on this tale, given the nature of Notker's work, essentially a collection of edifying tales for Charles the Fat, but whether or not the story bears any relation to actual events is less important than the fact that that Notker felt that he should include in such a collection a story about promoting lesser freemen ahead of their superiors on the basis of military merit.

In these circumstances, the Carolingians continued to make use of the lands of the church.[145] In the ninth century, royal charters or donations which exempt churches from military service are rare, and the authenticity of those which do can often be questioned. Some churches and monasteries, Prüm in Lotharingia for example,[146] were repeatedly exempted from military service, but they were very few.[147] Such exemptions as do exist are usually confirmations of earlier grants, but the kings were not entirely in thrall to the actions of their predecessors. Even at the very end of his reign the much maligned Charles III, for example, altered the immunity for the Abbey of Korvei so that the monastery would have to contribute to military service in cases of emergency.[148] Charles, however, did issue some exemptions in Italy, perhaps to buy support there.[149] The formularies (collections of *formulae*) do not include many exemptions from military service for churches;[150] more are for secular groups or individuals.[151] The lands of churches, nevertheless, made excellent sources of logistical support. This can be seen especially from the survey of the lands of the great abbey of St Germain-des-Prés, which shows how the estates of the monastery were expected to furnish supplies and, especially, money to support the army.[152] The Carolingians could and did attempt to control appointments to bishoprics and abbeys. In doing so, they intended to use the military contingents from church lands as a sort of independent coercive force. They also used church resources to ensure that royal, or royally led, forces were better equipped than their enemies, by making some churches pay annual rents in military equipment.[153]

The kings retained, as before, their personal guards of vassals. Hincmar of Reims' *On the Governance of the Palace*, written for a grandson of Charles the Bald, describes the different grades of guardsman that might be encountered at the palace.[154] It confirms that the earlier state of affairs still pertained. Young warriors served their time at court before gradually being sent out to the regions and eventually settling down on their *honores* with vassals of their own and attending court much more rarely.

The raising of large armies, according to property qualifications, from the landed free classes, including the *adiutorium*, appears unlikely in this warfare between royal and aristocratic factions. The emperors, even Charlemagne, had clearly had problems enough raising such armies in times of internal peace; the problem must have been all the greater in times of fractured polities and loyalties. Foreign wars, however, were a different matter. In Italy, the Carolingians issued three documents about expeditions against external enemies. The earliest concerns an expedition to Corsica in 825.[155] Lothar I set out those who were to go and those who were to stay. He appears to be keeping back those warriors at the core of his kingdom. The force, led by counts, is drawn from other benefice holders, especially from the church, backed up by county contingents raised according to wealth, and an *adiutorium* system. There is no very precise specification on the raising of county contingents or the *auditorium*. Lothar leaves much up to his counts and other officials in deciding who is to go and who is to stay behind. Twenty years later, he issued another edict, this time about the expedition led by his son Louis against the Saracens in southern Italy.[156] This document is interesting in that it says very little indeed about how the army is to be raised, although it lists the men who are to lead the different *scarae*. Apart from a couple of clauses relating to the repair of the walls of St-Peter, the capitulary is mostly concerned with religious matters to ensure divine favour during the campaign.

Another twenty years or so pass before the third of the Italian military capitularies, issued by Louis II before he set off on campaign to Benevento.[157] This is the longest and most interesting of the three. It begins with a lengthy discussion of how the expeditionary force is to be raised, summarising earlier Italian legislation on brothers who share an estate, and how many men may be left behind by counts and gastalds. The *adiutorium* envisages at most only two freemen coming together to send the more able. The code repeatedly emphasises that the more able men serve and the less able stay behind. Much is left to the local knowledge of royal officials, and thus presumably to local custom. Anyone too poor to be included in the *adiutorium* (in other words, anyone with less than half of the property required to furnish a warrior) will perform guard duty, but men with less than 2 *solidi* worth of property will be excused altogether. Otherwise no one is to be excused serving in the defence of the *patria* on any account, and anyone refusing the royal order will be dispossessed. The relevant royal officers are named and given their areas of jurisdiction; any counts who fail to cooperate or turn up with the full contingent will be dismissed from their office and lose their lands. Counts and royal vassals who do not turn up, or abbots and abbesses who fail to send all their men, will lose *honores* and the vassals their benefices. Anyone who is ill must let the officials know and swear that they really are kept back by serious illness. The document passes on to a series of titles about keeping peace and discipline within the army, and ends by setting out the expedition's itinerary.

On the whole, the solution to the problems of furnishing a royal military force seems in Carolingian Italy to have been to ensure that the service of the vassals of great lay and ecclesiastical landowners remained ultimately at the disposal of the king. As the ninth century wore on, the rulers of Italy seem to have become less interested than their relatives north of the Alps in the levy of freemen. As we have noted, by 866 Louis II considered that anyone with less than half the *bharigild* should be left at home. Whilst he never exempted any churches from military service, Louis did exempt some ordinary free individuals.[158]

Although, north of the Alps, there are very few references to military service in the later ninth-century capitularies, one king who adopted several approaches to the problem of military service was Charlemagne's grandson, Charles the

Bald. Charles worked tirelessly to increase the effectiveness of royal power. He strove hard to fortify the ideological and religious foundations of his kingship.[159] He also attempted to distribute and redistribute lands held as *honores* to combat the increase in the landed power of the noble families, and he mutilated and executed some recalcitrants, including his own son Carloman. The very difficulty of this project, in the context of ninth-century politics, is however shown by the constant opposition he faced from the lay and ecclesiastical aristocrats of his kingdom, who made use of his brothers, nephews and even sons, as well as the Bretons and the Vikings, to resist these royal initiatives. In many ways, though, that makes Charles the Bald's policies all the more interesting, especially as regards military service. Charles continued the tradition of making good use of the church in raising armies. The *Annals of St-Bertin* say that during his Lotharingian expedition of 866, Charles' army was 'mostly composed of the bishops' contingents'. During his thirty-seven-year reign he appears only to have issued a single exemption from military service, and that was a confirmation of an earlier privilege to a fairly minor house.[160] Furthermore, when asked to confirm the privileges issued by his forebears to the monastery of Prüm, he rather pointedly did not excuse them from military service.[161]

Charles, however, tried other means of raising a royal army. In 847 at Meersen, he enacted that all were to follow their lords to the army, and that in case of invasion the whole people were to come together to repel it.[162] Although often discussed as a traditional Germanic obligation, this seems to be the first time this duty is mentioned, and Nelson has shown that it is based upon late Roman law.[163] Charles' most important promulgation on military service came in 864 with his Edict of Pîtres.[164] Everyone with a horse, or who could get one, was to serve in the army under their count and no one was to oppress or injure them whilst they were with the army or do anything that would stop them serving. In chapter 27 he repeated his insistence that all had a duty to defend the fatherland in times of serious attack. He repeated his father's instruction that the counts and *missi* make a proper survey of the *adiutorium* system. As in Louis II's capitulary for the Beneventan expedition two years later, anyone too poor to serve in the army was to do something. They were to perform watch duty in the cities or on the Marches, and work on 'the new cities, bridges and causeways across bogs' (*civitates novas et pontes ac transitus paludium*), a reference to the fortified bridges and bridgeheads Charles was constructing to deny the Vikings access to the heart of his kingdom.[165] Charles also repeated his father's law about the putting away of all weapons within forty days of an expedition's conclusion.[166]

There was more to Charles' edict, however, than traditional ninth-century Carolingian foot-stamping. The insistence that ordinary freemen who could afford a horse should serve, without hindrance, and the revival of an up-to-date *adiutorium* system hint at an attempt to re-establish direct links between the king and lesser landlords and freemen. This chimes with other clauses in the Edict,[167] which aim to reserve services and obligations to the crown, by-passing other claims of lordship. He was also concerned to ensure that the poor of the kingdom were not oppressed by the more powerful land-owning classes. When Charles issued chapter 26 of the code, about all freemen with horses attending the host without fear of injury, perhaps he had in mind the occasion five years earlier when noble Franks, significantly during a period when he had been driven out of his kingdom by his brother, had apparently butchered poorer freemen for daring to take up arms against the Vikings.[168] Now he was trying to by-pass the usual lines of lordship and dependence. We have already seen that by giving all freemen access to the king, and opportunities to earn rewards from him, a ruler could build up a following of officers dependent entirely upon his support, and use these men to undermine the power of more entrenched noble groups.[169] The fact that (about twenty years later) Notker was still telling Charles the Fat stories about how the mighty Charlemagne promoted the low born above the noble if they served him well, shows that this idea was not alien to late ninth-century political thought.[170] The new fortifications and bridges, if successful, would be a focus for his system of service rendered by all directly to the king, on royal orders alone, and make a clearly visible statement about royal power.

This is in keeping with much of Charles' activity as king. In 866, two years after Pîtres, he raised a general tax on lands and property to pay off the Vikings, again apparently levied evenly across the whole kingdom. All free Franks were, furthermore, to pay the *haribannus*. This cannot mean the 60 *solidus* fine for non-attendance when called up.[171] Sixty *solidi* would be equivalent to that year's tax levied upon an estate of 120 free *mansi* or 240 unfree *mansi* (remember that Charlemagne expected military service from anyone holding four *mansi* or more, and that anyone with twelve *mansi* was to be fully armoured) and, furthermore, at this rate the tax would have paid off the Viking army if levied only on 1333 free Franks, without the other impositions being necessary. This is another clear piece of evidence that the *haribannus* could mean different things: a fine for non-attendance, and a tax to support the army. Charles issued extensive legislation on the coinage, specifying that royal issues only were to be used, and upon taxation. He also appears to have explored the possibility of using Viking troops as a coercive force; it has, for example, been suggested that he at least connived at a Viking attack in 862 on Meaux, the base of supporters of his (at the time) rebellious son Louis.[172] Perhaps it is significant that the efforts of the Edict of Pîtres came just after Weland, the Viking leader whom Charles seems to have wanted to make use of, was killed in a judicial duel with one of his own men. The failure of one attempt to acquire an independent coercive force led to a different approach to the same end being adopted.

Unfortunately for Charles, his plan does not seem to have worked. By 869 he appears to have adopted the approach of his nephew, Louis of Italy. That year, when trying again to construct fortified bridges against the Vikings (again, such fortifications would act as an important focus for the exercise of royal authority), he had an inquiry conducted into the estates of the major landowners. Bishops, abbots and abbesses were to declare their *honores* and how many *mansi* they held; royal vassals were to draw up similar surveys of the benefices of the counts, and counts were to survey the estates of their own benefice holders. Thus Charles was trying to ensure that the services of the more significant landowners were ultimately available to the king, even if using the usual chains of lordship and dependence.[173] Yet it seems that the royal fortifications were largely left unfinished. By 884, following an incredible run of ill luck, the line of this most interesting and imaginative of Carolingian rulers had been temporarily eclipsed.[174] As stated, however, the ultimate failure of Charles' efforts does not detract from their significance. Across the Channel, his contemporaries were to be more successful in their efforts.

The success of Breton armies in resisting Frankish overlordship in the Merovingian and Carolingian periods – and indeed major victories over Charles the Bald at Balon in 845 and at Jengland on the river Vilaine in 851 – make it clear that Breton rulers must have been able to raise armies efficiently, and that those forces were very effective on the battlefield. Their military value is further suggested by the fact that Frankish aristocrats were happy to make use of Breton forces during the civil wars of the ninth century. Part of the Breton success was based upon their way of fighting, striking hard with highly mobile cavalry. It will be argued in chapter 9 that this was a distinctive way of fighting which Frankish armies found difficult to counter. Military organisation in Brittany is largely obscure throughout the early medieval period but in the ninth century more detailed snippets of information begin to appear.[175] Much that can be discerned suggests common features to those found in Francia.

Royal and aristocratic households made up the core of armies. Regino of Prüm records one aristocratic Breton warband as 200 strong.[176] As elsewhere the junior members of retinues were called *pueri*, and it seems that youths acquired their military education in these followings.[177] Aristocrats, as in Francia, cemented their ability to take part in warfare by making gifts in exchange for weapons and, especially, horses. A man called Risweten demanded a horse and a mail shirt in return for dropping his claim to an estate held by Redon Abbey.[178] The monks offered him 20 *solidi* as a cash alternative, which he refused, with fatal results – being killed at Jengland. As in other polities, the Breton rulers seem to have made use of major religious establishments to furnish military contingents, and act as bastions of princely power.[179]

Whether, or rather in what ways, the Breton rulers, the *principes* (princes) had the right to exact military service from their subjects is unclear. There are references to dues exacted upon the free population, including tribute and *census* (tax), *opera* (works) and *angaria* (carriage duties). Davies cogently argues[180] that the latter may, by the ninth century, have been levied as a form of rent rather than actually in labour services, though that might have been the case earlier within our period. Interestingly, the ruler, or other potentate, had the right to pasture his horses upon the land.[181] That horses are often coupled with dogs in references to this imposition[182] suggests that it was primarily concerned with hunting but we should remember not only the apparent centrality of horses to Breton warfare but also the fact that hunting was one of the most important forms of military training (see chapter 5). There may thus have been some duty to perform military service extracted from some of the free population. The *Acts of the Saints of Redon* states that in 851, before his victory over Charles the Bald, the Breton *princeps*, Erispoë, 'ordered his army to be prepared, and commanded that everyone get ready and advance before him across the river Vilaine. At once all the Bretons rose from their homes.'[183] This at least sounds like the calling out of an army according to some sort of understood military obligation. However, exactly what sort of military obligation hinges on the translation of the word *sedes* (literally 'seats'). If, as here, it is translated as 'homes' it sounds like a general levy. *Sedes*, though, also means political bases – seats of power – and if the word is translated in this way the statement might imply that 'all the Bretons' meant the same thing that 'all the Franks' meant when used by some Frankish writers: 'all the *powerful* Bretons'. This would imply an army drawn from aristocrats and their retinues. It seems that machtierns (locally powerful people) might occasionally fight, or at least take part in the army's activities. One, like Ripwin, bought a horse from a priest in return for land,[184] and as with that case it seems likely that this purchase was related to the ability to perform military service. Indeed, horses feature reasonably often in the prices paid for land.[185]

The relationships between the Breton *principes* and their aristocrats were complex. The latter were landowners with access to resources and dues perhaps not very much less than those of the rulers, although how they related to the small, local village communities is difficult to ascertain. The major aristocrats do not emerge very clearly from the best source for Breton social history, the Redon cartulary.[186] The power of the élite combined with the nature of the physical geography of Brittany to make Breton politics complex. Smith's careful analysis suggests that the dynamics of the political relationships between the Breton rulers and the Carolingian kings and emperors on the one hand and their own magnates on the other were not dissimilar to those of the relationships between aristocrats and their rulers within polities. The Breton *principes* drew prestige and legitimacy from association with the Carolingians; the latter could derive kudos in Frankish politics from the claim that the Breton *princeps* had submitted to them. These relationships, and the frequent negotiation and renegotiation of their terms, were not without conflict however. Breton-Frankish and intra-Breton politics frequently involved fighting.

Around 800, as in Francia, Anglo-Saxon kings began to specify the relationship between military service and land, although as yet very rarely. The reasons for this change may, as in Francia, be related to the need for local defence against Viking attacks. A switch from an expanding kingdom to a defensive one cannot entirely be invoked, as it can in the Carolingian realm. Although Offa began to incorporate subject territories, like Sussex, East Anglia and Kent, into Mercia, rather than leaving them as tributary kingdoms, the old situation reappeared in the short-lived confusion following the death of his heir, Ecgfrith. The Viking threat may have led to the adoption of a Frankish response to a more complex problem. Given the near-identical chronology of developments, though, it is equally possible that the Franks might have adopted a Mercian solution to the Viking threat to deal with a wider problem, or that both kingdoms developed analogous solutions independently, because of the similarity of the pre-existing situation. A Mercian charter of 801 specifies that the recipient of an estate of 30 *hides* bring five men to the army.[187] This would imply (if we could generalise from a single charter) a service ratio of one man from every 6 *hides*. Alternatively, the recipient might have been assumed to serve as a matter of course; this would mean the estate owner *plus five men*, producing six warriors or one man from 5 *hides*. This figure is that which seems to emerge from the (much later) Domesday Book as the standard military service requirement for Wessex and southern England.[188] On the other hand, a possibly ninth-century Abingdon charter gives a series of estates in return for the service of twelve *milites*, a much lighter assessment.[189] Whatever the precise requirement, which was doubtless complex, with many local and individual variations, it seems that at this stage a relationship between military obligation and cadastral units emerged in the Anglo-Saxon territories.[190]

According to the *Anglo-Saxon Chronicle* and Asser's *Life of King Alfred*, in 855 King Æthelwulf of Wessex seems to have carried out a 'decimation' of the royal estates of his kingdom whereby he granted a tenth of the royal estates to the church (Æthelwulf was concerned about the wellbeing of his soul and undertook a pilgrimage to Rome). He seems also, however, to have desired to provide lands for his thegns – the backbone of the West Saxon army – who could in turn grant these estates to the church if they so desired. A series of charters survive, relating in fact to two decimations in 844 and 854.[191] Unfortunately, they are of extremely dubious authenticity, to say the least. One probably authentic deed does survive (this time correctly dated to 855), giving land to a thegn called Dunn,[192] and scholarly opinion seems to be in favour of accepting the outlines of at least the 855 reform.[193] Asser[194] says that the lands given to the church were free of all duties, presumably including military service, which is also what the dubious charters in favour of churches say (though not the one to Dunn). Some credence in this unusually generous grant might be given by the fact that in 857–8 Hincmar of Reims wrote that the English church did not have to perform military service for its lands.[195] Instead, Hincmar thought that the resources for those who fought were allocated from public resources. This might make sense if the archbishop's information derived from his knowledge of Æthelwulf's decimation.

In the last decades of our period, Alfred of Wessex introduced important changes in military service and the defence of his kingdom.[196] These in many ways paralleled those undertaken across the Channel in Frankish Gaul, but were much more successful, perhaps because the kingdom which Alfred ruled was more compact, and the magnates he faced less powerful, than Charles the Bald's and the threat to the kingdom's very existence posed by the Vikings rather greater.[197] After he had beaten off the serious Viking attack of 878, which very nearly cost him his throne, Alfred set himself to reorganising Wessex's defences. This reform had two principal elements. The first was the construction of a series of *burhs*, discussed further in chapter 10, organised so that no one lived more than about a day's journey from one. Each *burh* was assigned to an administrative district, which would maintain the walls and furnish its garrison. We know about the system by which this was calculated from an early tenth-century document known as the *Burghal Hidage*.[198] This states that one man from each *hide* of land would be responsible for the maintenance and defence of about 4 feet of wall. If one measures the length of the walls of Alfred's *burhs*, where this is known, and compares them with the size of the area assigned to the *burh*, the former fits very closely with the latter, according to the *Burghal Hidage*'s formula. The document, as we have it, dates from the reign of Alfred's son, Edward I 'the Elder', roughly to 918. Though it may well represent Edward's formalisation and administrative regularisation of a situation created by his father, during Edward and his sister Æthelflæd's expansion of the burghal system into Mercia and the territories conquered from the Danes, it is equally likely that the system described originates with Alfred's reforms forty years previously.

London is not listed within the document, which has often caused some confusion, as London was certainly within the West Saxon kingdom. It may be that London, which did not really have a rural hinterland and which lay on the edges of several earlier kingdoms and later administrative districts, depended for its garrison and maintenance upon its own burghers.[199] The men of London appear, in military contexts, as a distinct entity from the late ninth century.[200] Thus it would lie outside the provisions of the *Burghal Hidage*'s system. Whilst Southwark is listed in the document, it is assigned to Surrey and, to judge from Domesday evidence, was assigned more or less all of the resources of the county.[201]

The second element of Alfred's reforms was the creation of a permanent army. The *Anglo-Saxon Chronicle* states that Alfred split those who were liable to perform military service into shifts, so that 'always half of its men were at home, half on service, apart from the men who guarded the *burhs*'.[202] This is usually interpreted, from the Chronicler's language, as a twofold division, but, given the last clause of the sentence, a tripartite organisation might rather be implied.[203] A man liable for military service would spend one third of the year (or perhaps campaigning season) at home on his estates, one third garrisoning the local *burh* (whence he would still be able to have some contact with his home and manage his estates) and one third with the king's field army. Apart from seeming like a more reasonable demand on a thegn's time, in this system the replacement contingents would move *en bloc* from the *burh* to the field army rather than arriving as a stream of individuals from innumerable different locations. This would make the reinforcements more likely to arrive safe and sound.

The *burhs* would act as assembly points for the field army's replacement contingents and as places where these groups, which it seems acted as units within the army, could train together and forge bonds of solidarity. Further, this view would enable a tidier fulfilment of the 'three common dues'. For one third of the year, the men would carry out their *fyrd* service, and for one third they would, by manning the *burhs*, many of which were located at crossing points, perform fortress and bridge work. Nevertheless, these contingents of troops, clearly mounted from the frequent references to 'riding' and horses in the *Chronicle's* and Asser's accounts of Alfred's campaigns, must have represented a select levy. The 'one man from one *hide*' levy can only have been raised in times of actual attack to augment the *burhs'* garrisons and perhaps as labour services when defences needed construction or repair.

Note, however, that if the *Burghal Hidage's* system does originate with Alfred, the king was, like his near contemporary, Charles the Bald, instigating a system which imposed a 'flat rate' of military service on land. Possibly this built on the one man from 5 *hides* system of military service, which, as we have seen, might date to the early ninth century. It does not seem unlikely that Alfred was attempting to create a system wherein military service was exacted 'horizontally' on a broad class of landowners, rather than down chains of dependence. The *fyrd* units would be brought together in royal fortifications and commanded by royal officers. Local aristocrats and their retinues of dependants would, to some extent, be by-passed. Charles the Bald and earlier Carolingian rulers may have attempted to establish similar systems; Alfred was clearly more successful. In Alfred's system, the rotation of army contingents may, furthermore, have allowed a certain 'power sharing' amongst local landowners as well as enabling a broader range of such landowners access to the king and the important political institution which was the army. It also gave them the opportunity to impress the king with their exploits and to receive rewards in offices, goods and lands as a result. It may be that it was this military organisation, in many ways similar to that of the strong post-Roman kingdoms of the fifth and sixth centuries,[204] together with the successful campaigning and conquest of lands, that gave the later tenth-century kingdom of England its strength.[205] Even by the end of Alfred's reign, the king was able to use his army as a coercive force within the realm[206] in a way that had been difficult for rulers since the seventh century.

Wessex was, of course, a small kingdom, and the threat posed by the Vikings to its existence may have been enough to make most aristocrats throw in their lot with Alfred. However, we should not assume that even in this situation Alfred's task was easy. The sources show that Alfred faced opposition within his kingdom. Although the West Saxon court propaganda tried to hush it up, it is clear that there was a faction which resisted his assumption of the kingship. In the darkest days of the Viking attack of 878, even Asser has to admit that numerous West Saxon lords made peace with the Danes.[207] Given the Viking Great Army's *modus operandi*, it is far from impossible that its very intervention in Wessex was at the behest of a West Saxon faction. Later, the construction of the *burhs* was carried through in spite of the opposition of West Saxon landlords. Alfred was ruthless. His programme of creating a kingdom pleasing to God may not have prevented him from stripping the *minsters* (major churches) of Kent of huge swathes of land, to be put to his own use.[208]

The Vikings who helped to produce these important transformations in Anglo-Saxon and Frankish military structures were themselves organised much more loosely.[209] The Viking raids can be seen as a manifestation of a particular set of political relationships between core and periphery. As some kings became powerful and imposed their will upon broader areas, losing factions were driven abroad. This is a situation reminiscent of that which produced the barbarian migrations in the fourth and fifth centuries.[210] Only occasionally in the period covered by this book does it seem that Viking armies were sent or led by reigning Scandinavian rulers.[211] The nucleus of Viking armies was made up of the personal followings of significant leaders, the figures referred to in contemporary Anglo-Saxon and Frankish sources as kings and *comites* (counts/earls). Around the core provided by such forces (or cores, since multiple leadership appears to have been a feature of Viking armies), other warriors gathered. That Viking armies were made up of such small bands is made clear by the *Annals of St-Bertin's* description of a Viking army breaking up into its constituent *sodalitates* (bands of companions; 'brotherhoods').[212] By the 830s, Scandinavian raiding forces were large enough to be referred to as armies and frequently comprised several dozen shiploads of warriors, or more. From the 850s, these armies seem to have become more permanent, as they started to over-winter in the territories of the Christian rulers, and the careers of such forces and their leaders can be followed through study of the Frankish and English chronicles.

Nevertheless, though an army might remain continuously in the field for many years, its composition in detail appears to have been fluid. Campaigning armies might join forces.[213] At a lower level of organisation, the constituent bands of warriors and the leaders who raised them apparently came and went. New bands joined successful armies; leaders who felt that the time was ripe to return to Scandinavia and make a bid for power, on the basis of the loot and prestige acquired whilst campaigning abroad, might leave and head back north.[214] Age and the life-cycle might also play a part at key stages in the career of an army. At lower social levels than those of the armies' commanders, it may well be that after some years of successful participation in the campaigns of an army, a warrior would return to Scandinavia to acquire land, marry and settle down. In 875, the *Anglo-Saxon Chronicle* records a split in the Great Army (*micel here*) that had ravaged Britain since 865. Some, under Halfdan, apparently one of the leaders of the original force, went north to Northumbria and in 876 shared out the land there. Clearly, however, this did not spell the end of the army itself. The remainder, under three other leaders, continued to campaign. Some returned to Mercia and divided up the land there in 877 but the rest fought on until, after a decisive defeat (in an admittedly 'near run thing') by

Alfred of Wessex, they shared out the land of East Anglia in 880. It does not seem unlikely that in 876–7, after a decade and more of continued campaigning, the warriors who had landed in East Anglia in 865 (or many of them) felt that the time had come to settle down and so followed one of their original leaders to the north. The remainder, who might be broadly commensurate with the *micel sumer lida* (Great Summer Hosting) that joined the original Great Army in the latter part of the 871 campaign, were probably younger warriors with more taste for continuing the hard but exciting and generally profitable life of mobile campaigning.

Whilst some of the component elements of a Viking army might have been held together by social ties and obligations from their Scandinavian homeland, others (the *sodalitates* of the *Annals of St-Bertin*) may have been joined by more temporary bonds. There is no very clear evidence on the subject from the period covered by this book, but it does not seem unlikely that shiploads of warriors were raised on a short-term basis, for individual seasons or possibly just a few years, possibly formed by groups of landless young men of more or less equal status, perhaps brought together by prestigious warriors. These practices are attested from the late tenth and eleventh centuries at least[215] and it is a reasonable assumption that something similar existed in the ninth century. As mentioned, larger groups of warriors formed around successful leaders did join forces, much as, in the seventeenth and eighteenth centuries, pirate leaders often joined forces for a time. The basis of such alliances is unclear. Perhaps the most suggestive evidence concerns the junction of Weland's army with another Viking force in northern France in 861. Weland had been paid 5,000 lb of silver by King Charles the Bald to attack another band of Northmen. Having been joined by a third Viking force, Weland forced his erstwhile opponents to pay him a higher sum (6,000 lb) and join forces with him. Shortly afterwards the combined force split up into its component elements as mentioned. Some of these entered Frankish service. Others made a brief attempt to continue with their career of pillage and extortion but after Charles inflicted a setback upon them at Îles-lès-Villenoy this force too fragmented into smaller units.[216] Though Weland's deal with his rivals took place in the specific circumstances of an attempt to pay one group of Vikings to attack another, nevertheless it perhaps gives us some important clues. Where Viking bands or armies of roughly equal strength encountered each other, the decision to join together may have been arrived at through a stand-off and veiled (or unveiled) threats to fight if no agreement was reached.[217] Viking forces were not above fighting each other, though they joined forces more often. The arrangement probably specified how the booty from the ensuing campaigns was to be divided, and perhaps how command of the army was to be shared. Where smaller groups joined (or offered to join) larger armies, the agreement doubtless simply outlined the share of the loot to be expected, the length of time for which the new group undertook to serve, and what mutual obligations were involved. There were clearly objects upon which such agreements were sworn. The *Anglo-Saxon Chronicle* mentions a great sacred ring, for example.[218] Thus Viking armies seem, significantly, to have been bound together to a large degree by fairly temporary, contractual bonds. This, as will be outlined in chapter 5, was very important in enabling their use as mercenaries, which in turn introduced a new element into early medieval western European politics and warfare.

It is unlikely that military organisation in Scandinavia differed significantly from that of the Viking armies abroad. The ninth century saw, at least to some degree, a breakdown in the organisation of the Danish kingdom, compared with the eighth century. As has been mentioned, this played some part in bringing about the Viking attacks. Civil strife between various branches of competing royal families was the norm until the establishment of the Jellinge dynasty in the tenth century. This break in political continuity should in itself cast doubt on the idea that eleventh- and twelfth-century systems of raising the army could be projected back to the Viking age. Nevertheless, some successful rulers appear to have been able to raise substantial forces, such as for Horik I's major attack on Hamburg in 845. Horik's apparently strong rule from about 827 to 854 was probably a factor in the resurgence of Viking attacks from the 830s.

Elsewhere it does not seem that attempts to form states were much more successful, although, around the end of our period, Harald 'Finehair' had begun to establish a dynasty in Norway. The chronology of these developments is uncertain, however, and although sometimes placed in the last quarter of the ninth century, seems rather to belong to the first half of the tenth.[219] Most of Norway remained difficult to control. Some lords, like the Ohthere who told King Alfred of his travels, appear to have based their standing upon tribute taking (apparently a mixture of trading and shows of force), amongst the Finns to the north as well as in the Christian states.[220]

Military organisation in the Welsh areas of Britain remained, as far as can be told, much as was discussed in chapter 3, though this impression may well arise simply because of the poor quality of the sources. One change was the hiring of Viking mercenaries. The king of Cornwall indeed appears to have been the first Christian ruler to make such an alliance against another Christian realm, when he joined forces with a Viking army to attack Ecgbert of Wessex in 838. The expedition came to grief when Ecgbert defeated the allies at Hingston Down.[221] As will be discussed below, such usage of mercenary forces may have given rulers increased power within their realms.[222] Much the same comment applies to Ireland. Forces continued to be raised according to links of clientship, particularly from 'free clients'. The extent to which military service was expected from lesser social classes is obscure.[223] Again, though, the Vikings introduced a new element into warfare and politics, in the form of large bodies of hardened warriors, able to be hired out. Thus alliances between the Irish and the Scandinavians began to be mentioned from the 840s.

In northern Britain, amongst Picts and Scots, it may also be that military organisation was becoming more sophisticated.[224] We see the appearance of

King David imagery on, for example, the famous St Andrews Sarcophagus –
imagery much used on the Carolingian continent and associated, obviously,
with the idea of a God-fearing king humble in the sight of the Lord but terrible
to his enemies.[225] Pictish overlordship might have been extensive in this period,
implying an effective ability to raise armies. The Durham *Liber Vitae* (a book
listing names of benefactors for whom the monastic community should pray),
for example, includes the names of three Pictish kings, Uoenan, Unust and
Custenin, in its early ninth-century section.[226] This probably implies that in
some way their power reached into Anglian areas. A curious and much debated
reference in the 'Continuation' of Bede describes Cuthred of Wessex rebelling
against Æthelbald of Mercia and Angus (of the Picts).[227] This would imply some
importance for the Pictish king on the wider British political stage, whether as
an ally of the Mercian overlord against the king of Northumbria or as more
of an equal, a powerful ruler with his own sphere of influence. From about the
end of the seventh century, military imagery becomes ever more common on
the standing stones, very often depicting mounted warriors. Such mounted
forces required a certain level of organisation. A groom appears to be depicted
in the hunting scene shown on the Hilton of Cadboll stone, and it is more than
likely that horse-breeding was necessary to provide such mounts.[228] Towards the
end of the period, Sueno's stone apparently shows a large and well organised
army, though this probably belongs to the period after Cináed mac Ailpín's
unification of *Alba* (the term used from about 900 to denote the new united
Scoto-Pictish realm).[229] As well as mounted warriors, the stones show dismounted warriors and archers. As mentioned above, there may have been
territorial organisational units used for the levying of the bulk of the army,
although the retinues of kings and aristocrats probably provided the mounted
core, as elsewhere. Royal officers called *mormaers* were later used to raise the
military levies of the kingdom. It could also be that, especially given its vexed
date (it exists as a tenth-century text), the obligations of the *Senchus fer nAlban*
applied in this period. Other military obligations may have applied elsewhere.

Conclusion

In the period between 700 and 900 whether or not a polity had once formed
part of the Roman Empire ceases to play any part in determining the nature
of its military organisation. The precise nature of the development differs in
different regions but when our period closes around 900 we can see that in most
of western Europe landowning has become the basis of military service. This
is, obviously, a very different situation from the late Roman state of affairs with
which we started, with its regular standing army. In important details it is also
different from the situation which pertained at the start of this chapter, around
700. There are exceptions to this, particularly in Ireland and perhaps parts of
Scandinavia, but everywhere it would seem to be the case that the élites of the
polity form the basis of its army. This placed the state in a rather weaker position

from which to intervene in politics, to penetrate society, than had been the case in the immediately post-Roman period.

Various attempts were made in the course of the ninth century to confront the situation, particularly with the increased need to be able to raise effective armies for local defence against Vikings and Saracens. The precise military service rendered was, in England and Francia, linked to the amount of land owned. Some attempts were made, in Lombard Italy, England and West Francia, to by-pass the great secular aristocrats and to encourage military service by lesser landowners, promoting a direct link between them and the king and opening up to them possibilities of access to royal patronage. Sometimes other services, such as fortress work, were employed to create visible foci of royal authority. These met with varying success but were most effective in England, which at the end of the period emerged as the area in which the state was most able to penetrate society. This success had much to do with the kingdom's size and ability to wage expansionist warfare, as well as the scale of the threat to its existence posed by the Viking armies, a threat which could be and was made good use of in royal ideology.[230] Other responses included, throughout Christian Europe, making use of the Church's estates to furnish a royal coercive force. Elsewhere, as apparently in Carolingian Italy, the state seems to have accepted that effective military forces would have to be formed by the élite and simply set out to make sure it had access to those forces. Another option, available by the end of the period, was to avoid raising military forces from within the polity altogether, and make use of foreign troops: mercenaries.

5

RAISING AN ARMY (3): ALLIES, MERCENARIES AND TRAINING THE TROOPS

Foreign mercenaries and allies

So far, we have been concerned with the raising of troops from within a kingdom. Foreign mercenaries might also be hired, although this does not seem to have been as common between 450 and 900 as it was in the period immediately afterwards.[1] It only appears to have become frequent during the ninth century, with the appearance, in the north, of Viking bands and, in the south, of Saracen forces often willing to hire themselves out.

Before that, the households of successful kings may have attracted warriors from other kingdoms. This seems to have been particularly true in the British kingdoms. Exiles with their retinues might also be counted under this heading; this would seem to be the only real source of troops which might be counted as mercenaries – such as in later centuries would be called Wild Geese. The British warriors employed by seventh-century Irish kings seem to have been exiles from the contemporary situation in Britain.[2] The existence of exiles with their military followers, who would take service with foreign kings, in some ways continued the situation of the Roman world. Many of the so-called barbarian migrations may have been the movement into the Roman world of such 'losing factions' within barbarian politics. A group of Bulgars took service with the Lombards and was given land on the frontier to defend. Eventually they will have become a part of the Lombard military aristocracy.[3] Various Northumbrian princes spent time in exile amongst the Picts, Scots and Britons, and presumably took their military households with them. Other individual warriors may have found service in the retinues of royal officers and other aristocrats.

A sixth-century merchant had a bodyguard of two Saxons, for example. Another Saxon, Childeric, led a somewhat chequered career in (and out of) the service of the Merovingian kings[4] and Saxon troops are also mentioned amongst a Frankish army driven out of Septimania by Wamba in 673.[5] Saxons seem to have been mercenaries throughout the period (see below) and, given that Childeric does not seem to be a particularly Saxon name, it may be that the epithet *saxo* referred to his mercenary status, which could help explain the outlines of his career. With the end of formal regular armies in the late fifth and sixth centuries in the west, however, there was little scope for the permanent hiring of large units of foreign troops, though these opportunities continued to exist in Byzantium and the Caliphates.[6] Most foreign troops employed on a permanent basis by the late Roman Empire were probably, as noted, hired as individuals or small groups and drafted into the regular army. The fluid politics of the post-Roman world meant that individuals and small groups of warriors would adopt, at some level at least, the ethnicity of their employers, making them rather difficult to detect in the sources. There are few references to the hiring of larger bodies of warriors, however.

The economy may have been an important factor. Large areas of the west were effectively non-monetary in the fifth and sixth centuries, and even thereafter it is difficult to see the early medieval economy as truly monetised. The economy was multilayered, with barter at the lowest level and something approaching a commodity, supply-and-demand economy at the highest level of long-distance exchange where items were fed into the economy.[7] Most exchanges were, however, socially embedded, imbuing the transaction with a longer-term, more personal nature than the simple purchase of goods today. We have seen this already in the gift exchange of weaponry, horses and armour to consolidate social relationships. This was particularly true of gift exchange, and artefacts which changed hands frequently gained value from their use in such exchanges.[8] It has been suggested that this situation did not really change until the tenth century and the development of true markets.[9] Even recent work on the *emporia*, the trading stations of the seventh to ninth centuries, suggests that they functioned largely as centres for aristocratic acquisition of prestigious goods.[10]

With this in mind it is perhaps not surprising that mercenary contingents are rare in our period. The true mercenary employs his fighting skills, or those of the soldiers whom he contracts to supply, as a commodity. A paymaster buys these skills for a set amount of time. When the time is up and the payment received, the relationship between mercenary and master is terminated. In the post-Roman period, however, a warrior rewarded by a lord found himself in an enduring social bond. Completion of the term of service and the receipt of the agreed payment did not end the relationship between soldier and paymaster. This creates a long-lasting bond between warrior and lord. Where payment was in land or the revenue from land, as it frequently was in the post-Roman centuries, this would also create a lasting link between the fighting man and the state or polity for which he had performed military service. In these circumstances it was difficult for a professional warrior to change master if he so desired.

Another explanatory factor, related to the economy, is urbanism. Roman urbanism had declined dramatically after the third century. In northern Gaul and especially Britain, towns suffered even more around AD 400 and many ceased to be urban settlements at all. Throughout the west towns shrank, even, by the seventh century, Rome itself.[11] With the absence of significant urban centres of population, there may have been a shortage of footloose under-employed young males. After all, these elements of urban society were frequently those which provided many of the mercenaries of central and later medieval Europe.[12]

With the appearance of the Vikings, the use of mercenaries increased significantly. The aims of expeditions by Viking bands were usually to acquire wealth, and this could be done as easily by serving a foreign king in his wars, receiving payment and a share of any loot taken, as by attacking him and his realm. It is thus impossible to differentiate between an 'alliance' with a Viking army and the hiring of such a force: the 'alliance' was simply on the terms that the Vikings should attack, or help attack, their allies' enemies in return for payment, probably in terms of the loot taken. The structure of Viking armies was also conducive to their use as mercenaries. As noted, Viking forces were fluid, made up of different bands under the leadership of particular warriors, joining forces for the duration of particular campaigns or campaigning seasons, or until they agreed to part company. Given that Viking bands, their compo-sition and their internal relationships were transient, there was no necessary long-term relationship between them and an employer. Viking leaders wanted paying promptly, and in good coin too, and that did not stop them from changing sides if they were offered a higher sum.[13] It cannot have been easy for ninth-century Christian leaders to comprehend this mentality.

The earliest such use of Vikings took place in 838, when the king of Cornwall used a large body of Vikings to help him try to shake free from the dominance of Ecgbert of Wessex.[14] The Irish allied with Scandinavian bands by 842 at least.[15] The laconic data is now understood to show that the Great Army was used by competing parties in English internal disputes.[16] Frankish kings used Vikings to attack other Vikings, though not always with great success. Sometimes, as Charles the Bald did in 860, they paid the Vikings in coin;[17] at other times they granted lands to Scandinavian chieftains to defend their realms against other Viking leaders.[18] Such, of course, was the ultimate origin of Normandy. A grant of land, were the Viking leader interested in one, was a good means of bringing a mercenary within the polity, and thus of being able to deal with him in more 'normal' fashion. Breton leaders hired Vikings, for use against political rivals, and sometimes to attack Francia. By the end of the ninth century, even Frankish nobles had employed Viking forces. In 862, for example, Count Robert the Strong hired a Viking fleet.[19] It seems that non-Scandinavians joined Viking bands, perhaps because the Vikings offered the opportunity of a career as a roving mercenary.

At exactly the same time as the Vikings were making an impact in the north, Saracen forces began to be used in the same way in southern Italy, inserting themselves in the increasingly complex political situation in the south of the peninsula. They established their own bases and became such an accepted feature of politics in the region that some Christian groups were most reluctant to take the field openly against them. Papal and imperial attempts to organise pan-Christian offensives against their bases, such as Bari, met with very limited success.[20]

Other types of mercenary may also have appeared at about the same time. In his Breton campaign, Charles the Bald is described as posting Saxons in the front line of his army.[21] As Charles did not rule Saxony – part of the East Frankish kingdom – it seems logical to suppose that these were hired warriors. The same may be true of the Saxons deployed at Andernach by Charles' nephew, Louis the Younger, though here, of course, the reference may simply be to a regional contingent. It is interesting that, as noted, Saxons appear as mercenaries in earlier sources, and it may be that they furnished a particular type of soldier, or were particularly renowned as warriors, though we cannot now know whether this was so, or what sort of soldiers they were. The fluid, acephalous nature of continental Saxon society is also noteworthy. Perhaps, as with the Vikings, this enabled the creation of freebooting warrior companies, but this would only be true until about 850 and the final incorporation of Saxony into the usual social structures of the Frankish world. The upheaval which that involved may, however, have added further to the numbers of Saxon warriors available for hire as mercenaries. Other mercenary contingents became known in the tenth century; Welsh rulers used English troops, for example. The Vikings may have set an example. It is also possible, however, that tenth-century developments in the economy and urbanism enabled the creation of mercenary bands. In this period, as noted, towns began to flourish again, and the economy became more monetised and commodity- and market-based. The Viking armies may have played a role in this too, as we have seen.

As was mentioned in chapter 3, Basque troops came to form the basis of the armies of the dukes of Aquitaine[22] and an ethnic political identity may have begun to crystallise around them. The exact ways in which these troops were hired is, however, obscure. They may have been granted land and thus been incorporated into the polity, rather than being paid in cash. The economy of later seventh- and eighth-century southern France was relatively simple in this period, as the region had undergone significant economic regression since the sixth century. Whether this was the sort of monetary economy which could support the true mercenary is perhaps unlikely. Nevertheless there can be no doubt of the importance of Basque warriors in the Aquitanian armies of the period. The availability of these troops may, as with the Saxons, have been a result of a fairly fluid and acephalous political organisation. The fact that the Basques apparently did not employ partible inheritance or primogeniture[23] may also have led to a significant number of landless male heirs being available for employment as warriors.

Foreign mercenaries, for all their bad press, could be of considerable utility to an early medieval ruler. In addition to swelling the ranks of his army, a force of mercenaries, without links to the people, factions or particular regions of the state, and loyal to their paymaster, could be a very useful coercive force. As noted, in the tenth century, these types of troops became very common.[24] Welsh rulers came to rely very heavily upon hired bands of Vikings and Englishmen.[25] Such a hired force enabled a ruler to reduce an enemy to tributary status, without creating obligations towards one's own aristocracy. Alternatively, such troops could be employed against rebels or dissident nobles much more easily than would be the case if one had to persuade other noblemen to levy their contingents against one of their own. It may be significant that the use of mercenaries began to become noteworthy at the time when, as revealed by the survey above, it was becoming ever more problematic to raise troops from within a kingdom.[26] As has been mentioned briefly above, Viking forces are much used in the complex politics of late ninth-century Francia, and it is not impossible that Charles the Bald intended to use such forces, at least on occasion, as this sort of independent coercive force.

Much more common throughout the period was the use of foreign contingents provided by allied or tributary kingdoms. Forcing a defeated enemy to provide a contingent for your army was a very useful political strategy. It raised the size of the dominant king's army, at little or no cost to himself, whilst at the same time diverting the subject ruler's military and economic resources away from his own and towards the over-king's interests. In Britain and Ireland this was especially common. Usually the subject contingent was required to attack the enemy on its own, creating a diversion and forcing the attacked realm to divide its forces. Thus in 630 the Franks launched a three-pronged attack on the Slavs; in addition to an Austrasian Frankish army led by Dagobert I, Alamans and Lombards launched separate invasions.[27] It might easily have been regarded as dangerous to engage in battle alongside subject or tributary contingents; their loyalty and enthusiasm might well be suspect, and, as set out in chapter 9, the panic and flight – let alone treachery – of one portion of an army usually led to the defeat of the whole. As an example we can cite the battle of the Winwaed in 655, where Penda of Mercia's defeat was in no small measure brought about by the desertion or refusal to participate in the battle by allied contingents.[28]

Occasionally, military alliances were made between rulers on an equal basis but this usually operated at the strategic rather than the tactical level. Rarely did allied armies join forces on the battlefield, for the same reasons as subject contingents were most often employed to attack an enemy separately. It was clearly difficult to effect a junction between two armies. In 590 the Franks and Byzantines intended to join forces and fight the Lombards. Gregory of Tours records that after the Franks had advanced in Lombard territory and defeated an enemy army the Byzantine forces did not show up at the rendezvous. However, letters from the exarch of Ravenna to King Childebert of Austrasia suggest that the Franks were the party which failed to keep its part of the bargain, and thus negated Byzantine successes![29] As will be discussed in chapter 7, the aim was usually to attack the enemy from several different directions, forcing a division of their forces. One occasion where allies do seem to have combined their armies on the battlefield took place in 743, when the diverse enemies of the Carolingians – Alamans, Bavarians and others – joined forces to try to throw off their overlordship.[30] In 560, Chramn, rebellious son of Chlothar I, fought his father in alliance with a Breton army.[31] In both cases the allied army was defeated. The battle of Fontenoy (841) was fought between two armies of allied contingents. On the whole, though, the record of armies made up of allied contingents is not good in this period. As discussed in chapter 2, and as will become clearer in chapter 9, trust between the troops in the line of battle was essential. It cannot have been easy to create such trust even between contingents from different areas of the same kingdom, let alone between troops from different kingdoms, speaking different languages and with different customs. With that in mind it is not surprising that Louis the German and Charles the Bald engaged their armies in such elaborate and public swearing of oaths of loyalty and allegiance at Strasbourg in 842, nor that their armies, shortly afterwards, at Worms, engaged in joint rituals, made great shows of friendship, and engaged in joint training games and exercises.[32]

Training the troops

Mention of Louis' and Charles' exercises at Worms brings us to the subject of how troops were trained. There is very little explicit evidence for this. In the early sixth century a letter from the court of Theoderic refers to the training of young archers by royal officers.[33] He also instructed the count of Salona to make sure the local inhabitants (presumably those who were liable for military service) were equipped and drilled.[34] Later, Hrabanus Maurus, re-editing Vegetius' *De Rei Militari*, inserted a comment to the effect that nowadays warriors were trained in the households of princes.[35] This seems to have been true in most regions, not just Francia.[36] This must indeed have been the principal mechanism by which warriors received their training in weapon handling. We have noted that even early within the period royal officials such as dukes and counts, and many other leading figures too, kept bands of young warriors within their households;[37] these were young, unmarried men receiving an apprenticeship. Such apprenticeships were, as we have seen, an important mechanism of social mobility. Young men who distinguished themselves might be transferred to the household of a more senior figure and eventually the king.[38] This sort of apprenticeship also created bonds, not only between the young man and his patron but also between his family and the patron's. Consequently, as Innes has rightly pointed out,[39] to secure a 'placement' with a senior figure, and thus a better quality of training, required influence and standing. This may have become especially important in the latter part of our period, when warfare came increasingly to be the business of more clearly defined upper social echelons. It may also have been one of the reasons why membership of the army became more socially exclusive. Otherwise, it would seem reasonable to suppose that a warrior was trained by his father or, along with other young men, a senior figure within the community.

It is difficult to see how else the less wealthy soldiers of the ninth century, for instance, could have received any training, and some training was absolutely necessary, not simply in how to wield the weapons but in how to wield them in a battlefield formation. A densely packed mass of troops who had never been instructed in the rudiments of spear and shield fighting would be more dangerous to itself than to the enemy. The difference in training between the warrior classes and the common people is demonstrated very clearly by a couple of ninth-century sources. The first is the *Annals of St-Bertin's* chilling comment about Frankish magnates killing a crowd of peasants who had presumed to form a sworn band for mutual defence against the Vikings: 'they were easily slain by our more powerful people'.[40] The second is the *Earlier Metz Annals'* account of the battle of Vinchy (717), which attributes the defeat of Chilperic II's Neustrians to the fact that although it was a large army, it was 'mixed with the common people'. The Metz annalist's other explanation of Charles Martel's army's superiority is also worth note; they were few but 'tested for battle'.[41] Experience of warfare itself was the best training, and this was more likely to be acquired by members of the 'warrior classes'.

The social groups who regularly took part in warfare also took part in regular hunting. Hunting remained the aristocratic, and especially royal, pastime *par excellence*. Hunting was a dangerous and often fatal sport, as King Aistulf of the Lombards, King Carloman of West Francia and King Favila of the Asturias found to their cost.[42] Louis the German and Louis II of Italy were both injured in deer-hunting accidents in 864.[43] Apart from learning to confront danger and to wield weapons coolly in moments of extreme peril such as the rush of wild boar, hunting bred cooperation and trust. It was, furthermore, an ideal training ground for leadership skills. For these reasons, Breton landowners maintained the right to pasture their horses and dogs on the land.[44]

Someone who was going to make a career out of fighting, or who was a member of the classes for whom regular participation in warfare was an accepted and expected part of life, would need training in a variety of skills. As we shall see, such a warrior was expected to be able to fight on horseback or on foot, and to be competent with a number of different weapons: sword and shield (use of a shield needs just as much training as that of offensive weapons), throwing and thrusting spears, bow, and so on. Some of these skills could, as noted, be acquired through hunting. Some training in group manoeuvres was necessary, too. At Worms in 842:

> Saxons, Gascons, Austrasians and Bretons in teams of equal numbers first rushed forth from both sides and raced at full speed against each other as if they were going to attack. Then one side would turn back, pretending that they wished to escape from their pursuers to their companions under the protection of their shields. But then they would turn round again and try to pursue those from whom they had been fleeing, until finally both kings [Charles the Bald and Louis the

German] and all the young men with immense clamour rushed forward, swinging their lances and spurring on their horses, pursuing by turns whoever took flight. It was a show worth seeing because of its excellent execution and discipline; not one in such a large crowd and among such different peoples dared to hurt or abuse another, as often happens even when opponents are few and familiar.[45]

This passage is of crucial importance. Note Nithard's closing comments, which surely imply that military training could itself be dangerous. Indeed it could be fatal. Another of the disaster-prone progeny of Charles the Bald, his second son Charles, accidentally suffered an ultimately fatal injury in 864 when on the way back from hunting.[46] Intending only to play some sort of game, presumably the kind of armed exercise used as military training, he ended up having the side of his head hacked open by one of the other young men of his entourage (Charles himself was only seventeen or eighteen). In its own disturbing way, perhaps even more illuminating of this aristocratic culture of violence and honour is Ado of Vienne's comment that young Charles was dishonoured (*dehonestatus*) by having suffered this injury.[47] This episode and Nithard's reference to 'young men' again emphasise the role of age in military organisation. The danger inherent in games such as Nithard describes came not simply through the possibility of accidental injury, but also through creating a charged atmosphere in which 'abuse', and thus arguments and real fights, might occur. We are all familiar with the serious fights which break out on football and rugby pitches, during what are only supposed to be games. Imagine the participants armed with edged weapons! Finally, Nithard's passage shows that manoeuvres such as the 'feigned flight' were the business of small units, breaking away from the main battle line.[48] Training such as this cannot have been in widespread supply, and this factor was one which limited the size of early medieval armies.

6

RAISING AN ARMY (4):
THE SIZE OF ARMIES

In this chapter we address what might be regarded as the $64,000 question: how big was an early medieval army? This is an issue that has attracted much attention historiographically, and so deserves a chapter of its own. Although we must prefix any answer, as commonly throughout this book, with the specification that it depends on context – where, when and above all what sort of war – the only truly honest answer to this crucial question is that we do not know. That has, nevertheless, not prevented a great deal of scholarly – and some not-so-scholarly – debate on the matter. The earliest classic statement is represented by the work of Hans Delbrück, who concluded from careful study that early medieval armies must typically have been quite small.[1] The argument that early medieval armies were to be numbered in the low thousands was espoused by Verbruggen, and followed by F.-L. Ganshof.[2] In 1968 Karl-Ferdinand Werner[3] argued against this position, using Ottonian sources to contend that the potential military manpower available to tenth-century German rulers could be as high as 20,000 armoured cavalry, and that their armies in the field actually, on occasion and with help from allies, reached this order of magnitude. He claimed that the number of warriors potentially available to Charlemagne at the height of his success must have been even greater. At the same time, Claudio Sánchez Albornoz argued that the kings of the Asturias must also have fielded large armies.[4] This he claimed because of the need to raise every available man in defence of the Christian fatherland against the 'Islamic flood', and especially to counter the armies of the emirs and later caliphs of Cordoba, which Moslem sources number in tens of thousands. One such source lists contingents of levied Moslem Spanish cavalry alone adding up to no fewer than 21,613 in a campaign of 865.[5]

Much of the discussion since then has been concerned with the size of Viking armies, and arose from scepticism in the 1960s about early medieval descriptions of the scale of the Viking threat and from reconsideration of the extent of Viking settlement. This in turn led to discussion of the size of the armies which the Vikings' Anglo-Saxon enemies could have mustered. Peter Sawyer famously argued that even a Viking 'Great Army' should instead be numbered in the low hundreds.[6] Representing the orthodoxy in Anglo-Saxon studies, Sir Frank Stenton, on the other hand, envisaged early medieval Anglo-Saxon and Viking armies as numbering thousands, with Viking hosts perhaps around 5,000 men.[7] Given that Stenton regarded Harold II's army at Hastings, which he estimated at about 7,000 men, as representing substantially fewer than an Old English king could have mustered to face an invasion, he clearly envisaged pre-Conquest English forces as potentially numbering over 10,000, perhaps as many as 20,000 men.[8] However, at about the same time as Sawyer critiqued the accepted views of the size of Viking armies, Eric John countered the then popular notion of the Anglo-Saxon 'Nation in Arms' with an argument in favour of military service performed by aristocrats only, thus also postulating small armies.[9] Sawyer's perhaps deliberately extreme position provoked a healthy debate, but his thesis was convincingly refuted by N.P. Brooks, who showed that Viking armies could indeed, on occasion at least, number hundreds of ships and thousands of men, though probably not tens of thousands.[10] In more recent years, Bernard S. Bachrach has argued that early medieval armies could be very large indeed, perhaps even reaching 100,000 men in the field at one time, if not in the same army.[11] Although Bachrach proclaimed his opinion to represent the orthodoxy on the subject in the late 1990s,[12] this is far from the case. Where early medieval historians express a view on the matter, the consensus appears to be in much the same area as Verbruggen and Brooks left it, with armies in the low thousands.[13] Clearly, however, there is much room for debate.

There are two ways of approaching the problem, both of which must be examined. The first is to consider critically what early medieval sources have to say on the subject, both in terms of descriptive and of normative sources. The second approach is to consider the broader social and economic context of warfare, as this will provide some idea of what sort of force was practical. We can begin with contemporary reports of the size of armies, expressed as totals for the army, as casualty figures, occasionally as the number of troops who got away or, in the case of Viking armies, as the number of ships that carried them. Early medieval writers usually give rounded figures, very often in the high thousands. It is difficult to discuss these numbers as a whole. Different writers very often use figures in different numerical ranges; there are also different historical traditions, so that Irish annalistic writers very often speak in terms of lower numbers than the authors of continental narrative histories. Authors writing in, or conscious of, the Graeco-Roman historical tradition were used to large round numbers being cited as army strengths. The figure 80,000 is used repeatedly of barbarian armies, for example, but, as Goffart showed, it results from demands of genre rather than actuality.[14] Classical authors had themselves shown little consistency.[15] Ammianus Marcellinus, for example, thought nothing of describing the Alamannic army at Strasbourg (357) as 35,000 strong, in his set-piece description of his hero Julian's greatest victory, but elsewhere described the huge difficulties the Romans had in coping with 600 Franks, and mentioned campaigns launched to rectify serious political problems, with armies in the region of 2,000 men.[16] It is tempting to reject high numbers such as 30,000, and to retain small and precise-sounding numbers, but this would be mistaken. Numbers very often had biblical significance. The 3,000 warriors baptised with Clovis according to Gregory of Tours,[17] for example, are derived from the *Acts of the Apostles*.[18] Numbers like three, four and twelve have even clearer biblical and christological significance. Other numbers have poetic resonance: 363, for instance, is thrice one hundred, three score and three. Early medieval numerology was complex. In addition to this, some early medieval historical traditions, such as the Islamic, could employ precise numbers quite spuriously, to give a sense of accuracy.[19]

One thing we can be certain of is that no historical writer from this period (and probably no one else either) ever went and counted an army. Very few indeed were eye-witnesses of the events about which they wrote and, as we have seen, those who were were remarkably unconcerned about the sorts of data which interest the modern military historian. It has often been argued that writers must have used figures which their audience would have found credible. This argument is at first sight attractive, but it is unsatisfactory if we consider it closely. First of all it begs a number of questions. Why should the audience of an Irish chronicle have found reports of armies in the high hundreds or low thousands credible, whereas the contemporary audience (perhaps even composed of the *same people*) of a history written in the classical narrative tradition, perhaps about the same army or events, accepted that armies numbered in many tens of thousands were of a believable order of magnitude? Gregory of Tours describes the Frankish army campaigning in Septimania in 589 as losing 5,000 dead and 2,000 prisoners in a catastrophic defeat which few escaped, whereas his younger contemporary, Isidore of Seville, talks of the same Frankish army as 60,000 strong.[20] Did the two writers have audiences that found armies of completely different orders of magnitude credible and, if so, why? Were authors, and was their audience, interested in such things as accuracy in any case? Late antique writers frequently rounded ages to the nearest multiple of ten. Gregory of Tours, for example, has his holy men die either aged 70, 80 or 90, or in their seventieth, eightieth or ninetieth year;[21] clearly this was short-hand for old, very old and extremely old, just as his reference to the villainous Sichar dying aged about twenty is short-hand for 'a young man'.[22] Gregory was not alone. Epitaphs of the fifth to seventh centuries show the same age rounding took place amongst the levels of society which commissioned inscriptions.[23] Clearly, then, even people from the late antique élite did not know their own age or at least thought of it in round, perhaps symbolic, numbers. It seems unlikely that they expected, or were especially interested in recording, precise and accurate numbers in literary genres such as narrative history.

The size of a body of men is extremely difficult to estimate. The quantitative questions which concerned a commander were not absolute but relative: 'Have they got more men or fewer than us?' 'Twice as many, roughly, or half as many?' In a world where most people might spend an entire lifetime in a community numbering, in its widest sense, a couple of hundred souls at most, 1,000 men must indeed have seemed like a countless multitude, especially if they were attacking. In this largely non-urban period, it is not unlikely that armies represented the largest concentrations of men which anyone, from a king down to the lowliest slave, ever encountered. Whether of 1,000 or 80,000 men would not have mattered to an observer; any such figure would have far exceeded the numbers which any early medieval person used on a regular basis. Even the bookish compiler of a large monastery's polyptych, or the scribes of a royal chancery, dealt with totals from individual estates, not with the cumulative tally for all of the monastic or royal lands. It is modern economic historians, not early medieval scribes, who have added up overall totals from such documents. The probably seventh-century Mercian tribute document, the Tribal Hidage, works in multiples of round, apparently symbolic, figures: 300 hides for a small territory; 7,000 for a small kingdom. At the other end of the scale, any early medieval shepherd would have been numerate enough to count his sheep precisely, but few if any shepherds will have been looking after several hundred (let alone a thousand) sheep, and shepherds did not count soldiers in any case. More to the point, people seem not to have transferred their factual knowledge of the 'real world' to assessments of the accuracy or authority of literary works.

Historical writers of this period, if not (as they often were) describing events far off in time and place, could have access to numerous reliable sources. They might know eye-witnesses; they were occasionally eye-witnesses themselves, though this need not have meant they had any idea of exactly how strong an army was, as we have just seen. More usefully, they might have had access to official documents. Yet, as has been argued, none of this seems to have mattered very much. In early medieval writing force of allusion, weight of learning, competence of composition within the accepted structures of the genre in question all counted for more than accuracy of description. For example, it has been demonstrated that Carolingian geographers had access to contemporary reports of travellers who visited far-off places, yet they allowed their access to eye-witness accounts of contemporary reality, or even their own knowledge of that reality, to impinge very little on their scholarly representations of the world.[24] As Natalia Lozovsky has said, these writers must have known that their writings had little to do with the physical world which surrounded them, but their ideas of the authority of a work of geography depended upon quite other factors. We might also consider hagiography. Occasionally, writers of saints' lives knew a great deal about the saint in question, yet still fictionalised the historical background to their lives and deeds.[25] Again, authority within the genre was based upon other considerations. Similarly, a historical writer may have known that his writing did not represent a straight record of actuality, but that would not have been his concern, or that of his audience. Ultimately the audience of a given genre of historical writing knew what to expect, and that was not painstaking archival research and numerical precision.

One case where numbers might, overall, give a realistic impression of the size of forces concerns the development of Viking attacks. Sources from various areas are quite consistent in describing the earliest Viking attacks in terms of a few ships only; they are then similarly consistent in describing Viking forces as becoming much larger from the 830s, and developing into permanent Great Armies from the 850s.[26] This does not, nevertheless, imply that their figures should be taken as more than vaguely indicative. When the sources do discuss fleets in terms of hundreds of ships, as they frequently and in some cases consistently do after 850, it is still difficult to move from this to an order of magnitude for the army transported, as we do not know how many men were carried in a ship. This could vary from a couple of dozen or fewer to sixty or more.[27] If we take thirty as an average we might not be far wrong. A very large fleet of 200 ships would then carry about 6,000 men. It is likely that contemporary accounts of the payments made to these armies are accurate, although these too might be inflated for rhetorical purposes.[28] However, it is impossible to extrapolate army size from the scale of these payments.

We must then abandon the use of numbers, whether high or low, given by early medieval sources, but some sources need a little further attention as they have featured significantly in debates on this subject. The first is clause 13.1 of Ine's Laws, and need not detain us long. As has been argued above, the code's apparent statement that an army could number thirty-six men needs to be taken in the context of the Laws' promulgation, and not as a statement of the actual size of post-Roman armies. In the poem of Cynewulf and Cyneheard embedded in the *Anglo-Saxon Chronicle*'s entry for 757,[29] Cyneheard very nearly managed to seize the West Saxon kingship from Cynewulf with an army of only eighty-four men. A force of eighty-four warriors could cause considerable damage and terror in the early medieval world. Most rural settlements might number fewer than this number of people in total, men and women, children and adults, so a band of this size could overawe a large swathe of the countryside if it kept moving. However, Cyneheard's putsch took place when he and his followers surprised and killed Cynewulf and the few guards attendant upon him as the king was visiting his mistress; it was not a fully-fledged invasion. In any case, royal supporters rapidly assembled an army large enough to spell doom for Cyneheard and his followers. Thus, whilst we may conclude that a raiding force of this size might cause considerable damage and would need to be taken seriously – as noted, many early Viking raiding forces, seem to have been of these sorts of numbers – we cannot accept that it represents the typical size of a field army. A further anecdote dates from after the end of our period but might be suggestive. In 955, when the Slavs slaughtered a contingent of fifty heavy cavalry under Markgraf Dietrich, it was felt that the Ottonian army had suffered an enormous setback.[30] Although it may be that heavy cavalry formed only a component, perhaps only a fraction, of the whole German army – although the tenor of the account of the campaign suggests otherwise – this would still imply an army numbered in the low thousands at most.[31] Finally, we have the account by Sidonius Apollinaris of his brother-in-law Ecdicius breaking through the Gothic siege of Clermont with only eighteen men.[32] A century later, Gregory of Tours, himself a native of Clermont, wrote that Ecdicius accomplished his feat with *ten* men.[33] Although John Morris suggested that the words *et octo* had dropped from the text,[34] this is unlikely. What we have here is yet another clear indication of Gregory's, or his informants', tendency to round numbers to simple multiples of ten. However, as the original source is a letter from Sidonius to Ecdicius himself, we probably ought to take it seriously. Could eighteen men have broken a Gothic blockade? This is not implausible. The Gothic force would have been spread out around Clermont, so, if Ecdicius chose his time and spot carefully, he could have broken through the lines with his supply convoy, caused considerable damage and confusion, and reached the city before the Goths had time to react and assemble a large enough force to intercept him.

To try to establish the numbers of troops which should be supplied through military obligation is a difficult, and probably fruitless, exercise, as, as we have seen, legal documents setting out numbers of men per cadastral or administrative unit tend to come from periods when a kingdom was having difficulty raising troops. Such documents are frequently late within our period. It was also suggested above that attempts to lay down flat rates of troops provided per unit of land represent efforts to recreate a system which linked warriors directly to royal service, rather than having such service moderated by chains of lordship and dependence. We have no way of knowing how successful such attempts were. There were so many exemptions and exceptions that it is now impossible to guess how many troops even a successful levy would raise. We have, *a fortiori*, even less idea how many men might be liable for military service in the fifth to seventh centuries, when the obligation appears to have been exacted on a comparatively broad band of landholders.

Furthermore, we may doubt that it was often intended to raise every trooper theoretically available. On occasion this may have been the case, as will become clear. Certainly, when threatened by the usurper Gundovald, Guntramn of Burgundy wanted everyone to perform their military service, and set in motion attempts to punish those who had not turned up. Even here, therefore, the impression is that evasion of such duties had been common. Indeed, non-attendance of the military muster appears to have been a frequent concern of early medieval legislators.

There are no documents from our period which calculate the overall number of troops theoretically available to a kingdom. Such documents exist for the tenth century, in the English *Burghal Hideage* of *c.*918 and the Ottonian *Indiculus Loricatorum* of 981. The earlier document is more relevant to us, as it is possible that, as we have seen, the system set out there dates to Alfred's reign. The *Burghal Hideage* refers to a system requiring over 27,000 men to man the walls of the *burhs* at a rate of one man per *hide*. However, using the system of one man from 5 *hides* of land, the same area would provide a much smaller field army, of about 5,500 men. Alfred, as we saw, divided his field army into two or perhaps three, which would give him, on this basis, a standing army of between 1,800 and 2,700 men. Adding royal household troops, and those of leading members of the nobility, this ought to have meant that, at any given time, Alfred had a large enough army to hand to cope with most Viking attacks. The *Indiculus*, by contrast, implies a total manpower of about 20,000 armoured cavalry,[35] although given that the German kingdom was much larger than Wessex this is not surprising.

The figures extrapolated from both documents may be misleading, however. As F.-L. Ganshof said during the discussion of Werner's important 1968 paper on ninth- and tenth-century military obligations, the discrepancy between theoretical 'paper strengths' and actual numbers of troops in the field can be considerable; he suggested that the latter were sometimes 40 per cent of the former.[36] Indeed, to take an interesting comparison from the better documented fifteenth century, King Alfonso of Naples could theoretically call upon 20,000 noble cavalry, yet the largest army he fielded numbered only 6,000 horse and 2,000 foot.[37] Here Ganshof's guess would have been more or less correct. The same difference between actual and theoretical may, equally, have applied to Ottonian armies, as the story of the Markgraf Dietrich's cavalry in 955 seems to imply. We have noted that non-attendance of the muster was a perennial problem for early medieval kings. As chapter 7 will show, desertion and attrition added to these difficulties. On one occasion, in 894, Alfred's rotational system let him down when one section of the army, commanded by Alfred's son Edward, finished its term of duty and went home *en masse* before the next group of warriors had arrived to replace it! This nearly allowed the Vikings they were besieging to escape.[38] It may not be unduly pessimistic to suppose that the standing army in late ninth-century Wessex could have been as small as 1,000 men. This need not have mattered too much; if the *burhs* were built and manned, an invading army shadowed by a mobile force, even one of only 1,000 men, would have had great difficulty finding supplies or making much of an inroad into the kingdom, and this is indeed what happened in the attack of the second Viking Great Army in 893–6.[39]

So we come to the second part of our methodology: to look at the broader socio-economic context. Here we are on firmer footings, as far more is known in detail about the social structures and economy of the early medieval world than about its armies and campaigns. It is important that we work from the (however vaguely) known to the unknown; one flaw of some work on early medieval logistics has been that it started with premises about the size of armies, which, as we have just seen, can never be based upon very solid data, calculated how much food and other supplies would be needed to keep such a force in the field, and then drawn conclusions from that about the nature of early medieval government, economy and society.[40] Clearly this ends up distorting not only our view of the early medieval world, broadly defined, but also that of post-Roman warfare.

The social and economic conditions north of the river Loire differed, some-times significantly, between regions, but some generalisation is possible. After 400, there was drastic collapse of the Roman economy in the north-western provinces, and the situation did not begin to recover until the seventh century. Across northern Gaul and Britain, villas were abandoned almost universally, towns fell into drastic decline and widespread dereliction and abandonment; especially in Britain, fineware, mosaic and tile industries ended, the degree of craft specialisation was dramatically reduced, and the economy ceased to be monetary.[41] The local aristocracy seems to have retained its position with difficulty; archaeological data show the use of public competitive rituals such as burial rites to maintain social standing.[42] Support was maintained through costly display and gift giving. Settlement archaeology reveals that there was, unsurprisingly, as yet no differentiation of the aristocracy through the size of its buildings, let alone through the construction of separate élite dwellings. This was a poor economy. There was almost no long-distance trade. Agricultural techniques did not generate huge surpluses; economic surplus was accumulated with difficulty and quickly dissipated in necessary social strategies. Consequently, settlements were small. An army of 5,000 men could represent 100 times the population of a rural settlement, or more, and many times the permanent population of any 'town'. In this non-monetary economy, exchange was of necessity extremely local. Much of it was barter; more of it took place through socially embedded gift exchange (as discussed above). With no currency, exchanges had to take place between known and trusted people. To judge from the presence of balances in lavish burials, it seems that local aristocrats controlled weights and measures, but the word of such a 'big man' would not carry much authority in areas where he was not known. With this in mind, how could a large army be maintained? It would have difficulty foraging in a settlement pattern of dispersed small-scale settlements; an army of a few thousand men and their horses will have caused havoc, immediately consuming the accumulated food-stocks of every settlement it passed. The troops will have found it difficult to carry with them large quantities of food, even if they had the reserves at home to furnish these supplies, and in the non-monetary economy of the period, buying supplies from the locals cannot have been straightforward. If the centre of a *civitas* with its bishop, counts, clergy and supporting staff, their links to surrounding estates, and the ability to attract large numbers of people from the surrounding districts to periodic feast-days, could nevertheless only support a population of a few hundred, with how much more difficulty could a mobile body of a few thousand men be supplied? If the passage of an army caused local famine, it need not have been very large to have done so.

On the other side of the coin, however, is the importance of royal service in legitimating local authority. A major means of cementing local status was through employing links with the king and the patronage, in wealth and authority, which he could bestow. All this led to the situation described above, where the king held all the aces and thus was able to use his army as an effective coercive force; it also led, as we have seen, to the importance of direct links to the king, often maintained through military service, as this was a pathway to social betterment; a way of coming to royal attention and gaining all-important patronage. Offices in royal service were hotly competed for, a fact which strengthened the effectiveness of royal administration. The competition for, and frequent rotation of, such offices will probably have led to a certain amount of acquiescence in the demands of officials. After all, one day one might hold that same office and expect other people to comply with instructions. Local royal officers may have done what they could to facilitate the provision of supplies, in order to maintain royal favour.

Further south, although, as in northern Europe, the situation varied from region to region, the overall indications are that the situation was not quite as bad, although even here the economy had suffered considerable regression.[43] Generally, towns contracted but urban life remained. Cities around the Mediterranean coast were still keyed into the, albeit declining, Mediterranean exchange network. Villas appear to have continued for longer, in southern Gaul and Spain occasionally surviving into the seventh century, and finewares and other manufactures similarly fared rather better than in the north. In certain areas coinage was used. In Marseille, even a small denomination copper currency was known, though it does not appear to have been used far into Gaul itself. All of this implies a situation in which supplies could be gathered, both by soldiers before their departure and by royal officials. None the less, this was still a situation far removed from that of the late Roman Empire. Settlements, even towns, were still small, and the effect of a large army passing through could be devastating. In Spain and Italy the situation deteriorated drastically after the middle of the sixth century, which will have reduced the economic situation to something more like that in northern Europe. Although towns did not entirely disappear, there was serious contraction, especially as the Mediterranean trading network gradually declined through the seventh century. There was also widespread abandonment of villas, and the fine pottery forms disappear to be replaced with coarsewares. These changes must have had an effect on the ability to raise armies.

Contemporary sources can support the grimmer interpretations of the situation. Gregory of Tours describes the movement across the countryside of Princess Rigunth, her officials, baggage train and escort, as causing devastation like that of a plague of locusts.[44] Gregory talks of other occasions where armies created considerable damage to their own territory, as, given the general economic situation, is not surprising.[45] The passage of armies created much violent resentment even on the part of 'friendly' populations.[46] It has been argued that Gregory's accounts of the damage done by campaigning armies should not be taken seriously, because they stem from his contempt for worldly politicking, especially war.[47] Gregory did indeed wish to point out the futility of worldly activities, and was not fond of warfare.[48] Nevertheless, though it is likely that he played up their significance and told them in as much lurid, rhetorical detail as possible, whilst probably keeping quiet about campaigns or troop movements which were well conducted and did not cause much misery and disruption, this does not mean he invented such tales. It is well known that twenty years of warfare, although sporadic and uneven in coverage and frequently waged, to judge from Procopius' account, by small forces, nevertheless wrecked the classical Roman social and economic structures of the Italian peninsula. Theoderic the Great was concerned about the abuses carried out by his armies moving through Italy, and Visigothic legislators also discussed this situation.[49] However, Rigunth's entourage caused such damage essentially through wanton indiscipline. Gregory says that vast supplies had been stockpiled along the route in advance of their arrival; his complaint seems to have been that this was exacted as a tax, rather than being paid for by the king whose daughter was being married off. The story nevertheless suggests that such stockpiling could be carried out, and that this would ease the passage of armies. Such stockpiling is indeed implied by the requirements of Frankish taxation, and is legislated for in Visigothic Spain, although even here the concern is with officials who have not carried out this duty.[50]

To conclude, if well organised and planned in advance, the passage of an army might be managed without causing catastrophic damage. However, in the socio-economic conditions of the time, there would nevertheless be very strict limitations to the size of an army which could be supported even under these optimum conditions. Again, we can compare the supply of an army with that of a major settlement. Marseille, the boom-town of this period in Gaul, which, with its economic prosperity deriving from long-distance trade and its unusual small-denomination currency ought to have been able to create a market to provide food for a large number of inhabitants, probably had a population numbered in a few thousands. A town, of course, is static, whereas a campaigning army is mobile; to supply an army of several thousand men would be the equivalent of arranging one of the major periodic urban festivals every day in a different place. With all of these considerations in mind, except when the aim was local defence, the interests of a commander would have been in raising a smaller number of good, well-equipped troops and in getting them into hostile territory as quickly as possible, so that their depredations would damage the enemy. It may have been for this reason that the three recorded Marchfields of Childebert II were held close to his northern frontier.[51] Royal assemblies such as these may have brought together large numbers of warriors. If well planned, it may have been able to cope with the supply of such a force for a short time but, if a campaign were to follow, it would be as well to get the army rapidly out of the kingdom.

After about AD 600, the situation may have changed somewhat. As mentioned above, profound changes took place at this time, one effect of which was a slow revival of the economy in the north-west of Europe. The increase in aristocratic power discussed above[52] will have meant that through the period between 600 and 900 the surplus available to aristocrats steadily increased. By the end of our period, some Frankish magnate dynasties held far-flung estates, and were extremely rich. Even those at a lesser level had benefited from the increased prosperity of Charlemagne's reign to consolidate and manage their estates to maximise surplus. Hand in hand with these developments went an increase in the level of craft specialisation, organisation of manufacture and industry, and a reappearance of coinage and, to some extent, a monetary economy. The latter was, however, a fairly slow process. Not surprisingly, there was a resurgence of urban life. At first, in the seventh century, this was manifested by the creation of the *emporia*,[53] centres for aristocratic acquisition of overseas produce, for the concentration of surplus from their estates and for the manufacture of specialist items. Royal interest in, and sponsorship of, such centres stemmed from the fact that they took tolls there. Through time, they developed into more straightforward trading centres. As the period developed, internal market centres appeared in the hinterlands of the *emporia* at former Roman towns and lesser centres, and around monasteries. By the mid- to later ninth century these hinterland centres had eroded the pre-eminence of the *emporia*, to which Viking attacks sounded the death knell, and the stage was set for the urban explosion of the tenth century.[54]

We need to keep these developments in perspective, however. The population of the *emporia* at their height has been estimated at 1,000 people for Hedeby and 500 to 600 for Birka, though sites like Dorestad and Hamwic may well have been rather larger.[55] Some of the great monasteries may have approached and even exceeded this order of size, but the population of the former Roman towns in the Carolingian hinterland is similarly estimated at a few thousand souls at most.[56] There were now many more such places than before, and this and the other economic developments may have made the provisioning of an army easier. Thus what will earlier have seemed large armies, will have been made more practical. Yet it is unlikely that a single army in the field will have numbered tens of thousands. An army of 10,000 men – perhaps twice the size of a town like Paris – would have caused immense damage if put into the field for any length of time or over any sort of distance. Timothy Reuter, rejecting the notion of the 20,000 man army, has expressed the situation well: in a ninth-century context, the movement of an army four times the size of Paris would have had an effect on the settlement pattern and economy analogous to 'the down-wind ellipse of fall-out from a nuclear weapon'.[57] Another point, made by Reuter, concerns the damage that would be done to the economy if large numbers of farmers were taken away from their lands for months at a time on a regular basis. We might agree that several smaller armies could be set to campaign in different areas, and that one reason for Charlemagne's dramatic success was that he was able to put more, and better-equipped troops in the field than his enemies, but this should not lead us to overestimate the capability of the Frankish Empire to support concentrations of warriors.

Throughout the period, armies starved.[58] This does not necessarily mean that they were huge forces. As we have seen, in the economic context of the early

Middle Ages, a force of only 1,000 or so, or fewer, might soon find itself without access to sufficient sources of food and fodder to keep itself in the field. In 360, the Caesar Julian reduced an army of only 600 Franks to starvation.[59] Fodder for horses was equally important. Its absence could compel even one of Charlemagne's armies to retreat,[60] and as chapter 7 shows, Charlemagne seems to have taken greater care over logistics than most.

Three comparisons may be instructive. First of all, let us consider the armies of the contemporary Byzantine Empire, a far larger state than any western European kingdom in this period, with the exception of the Carolingian Empire at its height between, say, 796 and 840. The careful and detailed analyses of John Haldon have shown very clearly that the usual Byzantine campaigning army numbered only a few thousand men.[61] It may be countered that the terrain over which these forces campaigned, around the Taurus mountains and in the Balkans, was harsher than that of most of western Europe, although there are similarly large areas of the west in which it would be difficult to forage. But at the same time the Byzantine Empire was a taxing state able to maintain an independent coercive force in the form of a standing army, in a way that no early medieval western realm was.

The armies of the late Roman Empire may also stand as a comparison. The empire's total standing army has been estimated at around 400,000 men. This total was spread over a huge area and, after the economic crises (the seriousness of which admittedly varied from region to region) of the third century, had to be dispersed throughout the provinces for ease of supply and maintenance. Large concentrations of troops may have been comparatively rare. At Strasbourg in 357, Julian's army was 13,000 strong, according to Ammianus. Although Ammianus was not present, he may have had access to reliable official documents. The army defeated by the Goths at Adrianople in 378, in a catastrophe regarded as a second Cannae by contemporaries, has been estimated as about 20,000–30,000 men. The armies assembled during the fourth-century Roman civil wars may have been of this order of magnitude. Largest of all, probably, was Julian's expeditionary force assembled for the invasion of Persia, allegedly totalling 60,000 men. This, however, from contemporary accounts, was an extraordinary concentration of soldiers, and Ammianus tells stories of the incredible scale of the logistical preparations for the venture. Yet the Roman state was enormous, and with an economy, even in the fourth century, more complex than that of any successor state (even the Byzantine after about 620), and with the ability to extract the grain produce of fertile provinces such as Egypt and North Africa as tax to feed its armed forces. It was also a more urban society. Yet even here, many successful campaigns were waged with small armies of a couple of thousand men. Thus in comparison with the late Roman state, it seems most unlikely that any post-Roman kingdom could raise a campaigning army of between 10,000 and 20,000 troops.[62]

Finally, we may consider late medieval English armies. In spite of contemporary chronicle estimates which occasionally place field armies in the region of 40,000 men, the largest army recorded in detailed administrative documents, which of course are far more plentiful than in the early Middle Ages, numbers 32,303, although even this army may not all have been assembled before Calais, as the muster roll claims, but spread through the English territories in France. Most field armies appear to have been much smaller than that. The muster rolls reveal large expeditionary armies of between 9,000 and 20,000 men.[63] Again, we must think of the broader context. Late medieval England was more populous, more urbanised, more developed in terms of agricultural techniques and production, had a more advanced economy and was a more complex state, than any kingdom of the period 450–900.

A few other points militate against large armies in this period. The first is the distances over which wars were fought. This is clearly illustrated in the eighth-century campaigns of Charles Martel, his sons and grandsons. Armies campaigned over vast distances, sometimes from one side of the *regnum francorum* to the other, with frequent occasions when more than one campaign was launched per year. In 786–87 alone, Charlemagne travelled 3,500 km or more.[64] Apart from the time taken to assemble such forces (which, obviously, would increase with the size of the army), we need to consider the speed with which these forces moved. Speed of movement is related to the size of the column of troops on the march, a column increased correspondingly by attendant supply wagons and pack animals as the size of the army grows. A force of 5,000 horsemen riding two abreast, would, at 2.5 metres per horse,[65] have taken up over 6 km (nearly 4 miles) of road. Adding spare horses, pack animals and wagons to the above (but no foot-soldiers, attendants and other camp followers other than those needed to drive the supply wagons and animals), would probably about double the length of the column. We should, in addition, consider the time taken for the column to leave camp at the start of a day's march and arrive at a new campsite at the end of the day and the fact that 12 km probably means over an hour's difference (more if one included wagons and foot-soldiers) between the head of the column and the end of the rear guard. This implies two to three hours out of the day just to leave and enter camp. We should, furthermore, remember that Rigunth's party of about 4,000 (admittedly with a probably larger wagon train) managed only 5 miles in a day. Even with these generous parameters (minimal supply train and numbers of camp-followers) an army of 20,000–40,000 men, such as Bachrach envisages, could, like some Napoleonic armies, have covered barely 10 miles a day.[66] All this argues that forces much larger than a few thousand would be incompatible with the speed and distances covered in eighth-century warfare.

Another point arguing against large armies is the cost of equipment. As we shall see in chapter 8, though this has possibly been overestimated in the past, it still represented an outlay beyond the means of many. More importantly, campaigning was expensive. In 811, people complained to Charlemagne's *missi* that being sent on campaign every year was enough to ruin one and drive one into a relationship of dependence upon a magnate.[67] Perhaps more than anything else, this evidence is decisive in rejecting the idea of the large early medieval army.

In conclusion, it is pointless to be too dogmatic about this issue; the evidence does not allow us to be categorical, and many variables would affect the size of armies. It is extremely unlikely that all armies of the period were of a particular order of size. Yet we can say that, on balance, the field armies of post-Roman western Europe were comparatively small. Time and place would be one important variable. In the centuries immediately following the end of the Western Empire, large campaigning armies probably only numbered a few thousand men. Perhaps 5,000 to 6,000 would represent the upper end of the spectrum, especially if we had to add on numbers of non-combatant attendants. In the smaller and more economically undeveloped states of post-Roman Britain, Germany and Scandinavia, it is unlikely that they often if ever exceeded a couple of thousand men. In early medieval Ireland this sort of size, or less, will have been typical throughout the period. Later on in the period, economic and social developments would have made larger armies possible. Forces of 5,000 men would have been more practical, and large field armies may on occasion have reached the region of 10,000 men. For all of the reasons set out above, however, armies any larger than that would have been extremely impractical, if not impossible. These estimates would appear to be in line with contemporary reports of Viking armies' size.

However, it should be made clear that these are estimates for single, large mobile armies, raised for significant campaigns. A larger kingdom or empire, like Charlemagne's, might raise more than one such army at once, to campaign in different areas. Context would also be a key variable. Armies for small-scale endemic raiding warfare might well be very much smaller, and an awful lot, perhaps the majority, of early medieval warfare was of this type. As we have seen, an army of a hundred or so could cause serious disruption and damage, and would be much more mobile. On many if not most occasions, an army would comprise a small number of experienced, mounted and well-equipped warriors. At the other end of the scale, however, in unusually serious outbreaks of warfare, larger numbers might be levied. For a defensive campaign of short duration against a very serious threat, the call-up might be much more widespread, leading to an army rather larger than the usual mobile field force. In such circumstances it might be that armies could reach 10,000 or more, although such an army would need to disperse again fairly quickly.

It should be remembered, however, that there were very good reasons why, in most cases, all available warriors would not be called out. Apart from committing all of one's manpower to the lottery of battle, it might be counter-productive to call out every man theoretically liable to military service. Although, as will become clear,[68] in early medieval set-piece battles numbers did count, they were numbers of good seasoned troops. Untrained, inexperienced and badly equipped farmer-soldiers might do more harm than good. A clear example is provided by Nithard, telling strongly against the argument often made by those who believe in eternal principles of warfare, that armies would always be as big as possible.[69] In the 830s, a large force was raised by Emperor Louis the Pious' supporters to drive out Lothar's adherents from the Breton March. Lothar's men, says the experienced soldier Nithard, were less numerous than Louis' 'but at least they all moved as one man. Wido's [Louis' commander's] large army made him and his men secure but quarrelsome and disorganised. No wonder they fled when it came to battle.'[70] A similar point emerges from the *Earlier Annals of Metz*'s account of the battle of Vinchy, 124 years earlier.[71] They describe the Neustrian Frankish army as 'a huge army but one indeed mixed with the common people'. Charles Martel's Austrasian army, however, was 'a lesser host but [made up of] men very well tested for battle'. In 882, a crowd of locals from around the monastery of Prüm assembled to attack the Viking army. According to the abbot, Regino, the Vikings were not in the least bit frightened by this mob, 'denuded of any military discipline', but rushed upon them with a shout and slaughtered them like beasts.[72] The knowledge that the rear ranks were unreliable would distract even battle-hardened warriors. Panic spreads, and the flight of large numbers of understandably frightened peasants would probably spell doom for the whole army. As we shall see, the flight of one part of an early medieval battle-line usually brought about the defeat of the whole. If the expedient was used, as in other periods, earlier and more recent, of pinning the least experienced troops between a front rank of the best warriors and a rear rank of the next best, this would reduce the numbers of hardened warriors committed to fighting 'at the sharp end'.[73] Though Napoleon may have thought that God was 'on the side of the big battalions', in our period, as the *Chronicle of Alfonso III* put it, 'the Lord does not count spears but offers the palm of victory to whomsoever he will'.[74] The quote surely shows that early medieval commanders did consider the relative size of their armies but also, clearly, that things other than the supposedly eternal 'Doctrine of Overwhelming Force' could prey on their minds.

7

CAMPAIGNING

The history of medieval warfare has been described recently as a progression from 'random raids by warbands' to 'organised interstate war'.[1] This sort of grand narrative seems mistaken. There was nothing random, or even particularly disorganised, about early medieval campaigning. The impression again comes from the difficulties involved in studying the subject. Although many early medieval works describe the routes which armies took and mention misfortunes that befell armies on the way, very few give detailed accounts of campaigns. Nithard's eyewitness account of the Fontenoy campaign in his *Histories* is one exception. Julian of Toledo's *History of King Wamba* is another. Written shortly after the conclusion of the campaign, it describes Wamba's campaign against the usurper Paul in 673. Though the text is coloured by various ideological agendas, its account of that campaign seems plausible.[2] Another interesting exception, although very brief, is the *Annals of Fontenelle*'s account of a Viking raid on Normandy in 841.[3] Often we have only the tersest accounts of campaigns: 'This year King X led an army to Y.'

The nature of campaigns

The nature of a campaign would largely depend upon its aims. Booty was important in early medieval warfare. It was surely the lack of opportunity to acquire it that made the raising of armies so much more difficult for local defensive wars than for aggressive campaigns, as discussed in chapter 4. However, as we also saw, booty was far from the be all and end all of early medieval campaigning, and might be more important in some times, places and political circumstances than others. Warfare presented opportunities for social and political advancement. It enabled the reaffirming of ties of friendship and of dependence that bound early medieval society. Not surprisingly, therefore, as shown in chapter 4, gifts of military equipment were important in oiling the cogs of such politics.[4] With that in mind it will probably come as less of a shock to find that early medieval armies were frequently called out only for no serious military activity to ensue (see the Appendix).[5] Political matters might be discussed, laws might be passed,[6] and charters issued,[7] but sometimes the army subsequently simply returned home or made a rather half-hearted-looking journey towards a hostile frontier. The latter might provoke the threatened kingdom into offering some tribute or asking for peace but the primary motor for such 'campaigning' was internal rather than external politics. If the Marchfield was a regular component of Frankish and eighth-century Lombard political life, as we have suggested it was, then these gatherings were, as with Theoderic the Ostrogoth's regular assemblies of his Goths (the army), an occasion for the king to distribute and redistribute his patronage, rewarding those who had done well, punishing those who had not. Furthermore, repeated summoning of the army might enable a king to gauge the extent of his support. Put bluntly, if people did not show up, the king would see that he was in trouble. The mass 'stay-away' from Louis the Pious' Breton campaign of 830 showed the writing on the wall. As chapter 2 showed, many early medieval social and political identities were constructed around the ability to participate in the activities of the army. This, too, necessitated the mustering of the army on a fairly regular basis. There was thus a certain amount of what we might call 'fictive campaigning' in the early medieval west.

Nevertheless, if military activity did follow from the assembly of the army, most post-Roman warfare was at least to some degree concerned with the acquisition of loot – whether livestock, prisoners (to be used as hostages or slaves) or other valuables. Small-scale raiding warfare was often, as with the 'fictive campaigns' just discussed, not aimed at changing the political or military status quo. To the modern mind this perhaps seems odd, but such would seem to have been the case. If an army took booty, this would be shared amongst its leaders and then redistributed amongst their followers.[8] The sharing of loot seems frequently to have been carried out according to an agreed formula. In the early sixth century, a now lost hagiographic source known to Gregory of Tours related how the Frankish king, Clovis, at the behest of a bishop (possibly St Remigius of Reims), asked his warriors if he could take a silver vase above his normal share of the booty, in order to return it to the church.[9] Although the story is didactic, concerned with the retribution meted out to the one warrior who objected to Clovis' request, its implication is that such formal and schematic redistribution was normal (as, presumably, was acquiescence when the king asked for a little extra!). James Campbell has compiled suggestive evidence that the formula may have been based around a division into thirds.[10] The Laws of Hywel Dda, which purport to be of tenth-century date, although in their extant form they are much later, record a very elaborate formula for the distribution of loot between the king and his senior palatine officials after the annual cattle raid. Whether this can be projected in detail back into our period is doubtful, but it is certainly suggestive.

On the fringes of kingdoms, there was doubtless more cross-border raiding than was ever recorded in the major narrative histories. A series of pacts between the Carolingian rulers of Italy and the Doges of Venice makes clear that such formal 'peace treaties' had to ensure that there would be no more such raiding, kidnapping and horse- and cattle-rustling.[11] If the laws of Ine of Wessex and of Wihtred of Kent were issued together as part of a peace-making process, then the concern with the raids of armies in Ine's code[12] can be understood in a similar way. Small-scale raiding often escaped the attention of contemporary writers but sometimes it shows through. In between accounts of the major campaigns led by Pippin I, the Continuator of Fredegar makes it clear that other raids and counter-raids were going on. In 763 Count Chilping of the Auvergne set off to plunder the area around Lyons; Count Ammanugus of Poitiers was killed during a raid on the Touraine in the same year.[13] All this, said the Continuator, was going on whilst the Franks and Gascons kept on with their tit-for-tat warfare.[14] On coming of age at fifteen, the Anglo-Saxon saint, Guthlac, assembled a warband and spent the next nine years raiding his enemies.[15] None of the warfare in which he was engaged seems to have made it into the major historical records of the period, though it seems unlikely that Felix, Guthlac's biographer, made up the idea. As will be further suggested below, in small-scale raiding the practice of war may have differed from more serious warfare.

Successful raids demonstrated the war-leader's military competence, which was a principal requisite of good lordship and good kingship. In the socially embedded economy of the early Middle Ages, the booty taken and redistributed oiled the cogs of the politics of the day.[16] Furthermore, the campaign offered the opportunity for young warriors to demonstrate their own prowess or skill, come to the attention of the leaders and earn them promotion and other rewards. It was these opportunities which made the Frankish aristocracy so desirous of warfare in the sixth century that, according to Gregory of Tours, they staged a violent protest and even tore up the royal tent when Chlothar I wished to make peace with the Saxons, and on another occasion pressurised the equally formidable king Theuderic I into launching an unusually savage punitive raid on the Auvergne when the king refused to join his half-brothers' attack on the Burgundians.[17] In the case of the sixth-century north Gallic, or Frankish, aristocracy, warfare was particularly important as they were heavily dependent upon royal patronage for the maintenance of their social pre-eminence (see chapter 3). Once again we must remember that the rewards of warfare were not always material.

Let us take one particularly interesting example. When the Visigothic king, Wamba, heard that his general Paul, whom he had dispatched to quell an uprising in Septimania, had himself rebelled and been proclaimed 'king in the east', he was on campaign against the Basques. Wamba's position on the throne may have been fairly insecure. He had been elected, rather than inheriting the throne. After having himself anointed,[18] it seems that he had launched this Basque campaign to demonstrate his military capacity to those who doubted his ability, whilst consciously not troubling himself with the disturbances in Visigothic Gaul. Even after the news of Paul's usurpation reached him, Wamba led his troops on a week's ravaging of Basque territory.[19] This not only removed the possibility of Basque support for the rebels, it also gave his army (the political assembly) the chance to see that the king was a war leader who meant business, it gave them a period to hone their martial skills, and it enabled them to demonstrate their prowess to him, in the expectation of political and other rewards. It furthermore presented his troops with the opportunity for some loot (though not much in that territory, one imagines).

In Merovingian Gaul, warfare between the different kingdoms was often concerned with the capture of cities. This was not, as is occasionally assumed (against the weight of decades of historical and archaeological research), because these were populous and prosperous socio-economic centres but because Merovingian Gaul was administratively organised by *civitates* – city-districts, originally the pre-Roman tribal units. The towns were the administrative centres of these areas. Because these wars were usually fairly stylised conflicts between members of the Merovingian royal house, the process seems usually to have been relatively simple. An invading army would head for the *civitas* capital and call upon the inhabitants of the region to change their allegiance. Sometimes there would be some harrying of the surrounding rural areas to help the locals make up their minds. If the count who ruled the district, and his garrison (made up mostly of his *pueri*), decided to hold out, and especially if they could persuade the notables of the region and thus the military forces of which they formed the core to remain loyal then a siege or even a battle might ensue. Apparently, early Merovingian siege techniques were comparatively crude and, certainly, towns were rarely taken by direct military action (see chapter 10), so eventually the aggressors would return home. However, the locals seem usually to have preferred to swear an oath of loyalty to the attacking king rather than risk a siege. The resident count and his followers would then quietly leave the city, and the invading forces would install a replacement with his following. The taxes and other revenues from the city-district would then flow to the coffers of a different ruler, until the same process happened again in reverse. The Appendix gives a sample of such warfare from the 580s. The transfer of garrisons during the war in Aquitaine in the eighth century seems normally to have followed the same course, as sieges are very rarely mentioned although the garrisoning of strong-points is.

In more serious warfare, armies seem generally to have harried enemy territory until either they were challenged in battle or the enemy submitted and paid tribute or granted possession of the disputed territory. Ninth-century Frankish campaigns on the Slavic frontier, for instance, seem invariably to have followed this pattern[20] but this is typical throughout the early medieval period. The eighth-century reincorporation of Aquitaine into the Frankish kingdom has sometimes been portrayed as war 'of position', a steady campaign of siege-warfare.[21] This impression may result from too ready an acceptance of the Continuator of Fredegar's portrayal of the war as a simple one between conquering Franks on one hand and rebellious Gascons on the other. Instead, it seems to have been much more fluid, with counts wielding considerable local power and negotiating between the political poles represented by Waiofar, *princeps* of the Aquitanians, and Pippin I, king of the Franks. Closer reading of Fredegar's Continuator shows that although there was some concern with installing garrisons in towns and other places to overawe the locality these wars were, in addition to the raid and counter-raid already referred to, rather a matter of repeated harrying of territory.[22] Usually fortifications were by-passed and the lands around ravaged. Only two campaigns involved significant siege warfare, with the storming of Bourbon and Clermont in 761 and of Bourges and Thouars in 762.[23] This apparently persuaded the Aquitanians to abandon any hope of defending strong points, and they demolished the walls of their cities.[24] Five battles are mentioned,[25] which may have been very small-scale affairs but they brought about the deaths of key political players and so were important. Charlemagne's conquest of Saxony followed a similar pattern. Pippin I defeated the Lombards by, after defeating their army and penning it and King Aistulf in Pavia, ravaging the territory until Aistulf came to terms.[26] Wamba subjugated the Basques by harrying the valleys and destroying the settlements until their leaders came in and submitted.[27] The Mercian ruler Wulfhere harried as far as Ashdown and the Isle of Wight in 661, apparently establishing a southern English hegemony, as he was able to grant Wight to King Æthelwald of Surrey.[28] Examples could be multiplied endlessly. Nevertheless, there were apparently changes. In the seventh century, thirty-three wars are noted between the Anglo-Saxon kingdoms, twenty-two of which produced battles, and seven of which are recorded as harryings (see figure 2). In some cases certainly, and in others probably, the battles were preceded by harrying of territory. In the eighth century, though thirty-one outbreaks of war are recorded in the patchy sources, there were only eleven battles (again, possibly preceded by harrying), but eleven recorded harryings. Perhaps in the eighth century, a period of fairly well established Mercian supremacy, harrying by superior forces was usually sufficient to reduce the enemy to submission.[29]

In an interesting passage of his *Histories*, Gregory of Tours places a speech in the mouth of Aridius, a Burgundian envoy to Clovis.[30] Aridius tells Clovis that it is pointless destroying lands when his enemy, King Gundobad of the Burgundians, is holed up in an impregnable fortress (Avignon): 'You are destroying the fields, spoiling the meadows, cutting up the vineyards, ruining the olive-groves and ravaging the whole countryside, which is a very fruitful one. In this you are doing no harm whatsoever to Gundobad. Why don't you send an ultimatum to him to say that he must pay whatever annual tribute you care to exact?' Clovis does as he is advised, the Burgundians pay up and the Franks go home. It has been suggested that this speech represents the voice of the 'scientific' Roman tradition of military practice, and one which post-Roman rulers took to heart.[31] This is most unlikely. If, as seems probable, it is Gregory of Tours who is preaching here, he is not doing so as some sort of advocate of military science but as a bishop who was opposed to warfare within the Frankish realms and told his kings as much.[32] In any case, as the foregoing discussion shows, and as we shall see again, early medieval military leaders did

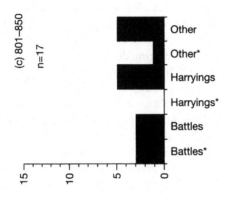

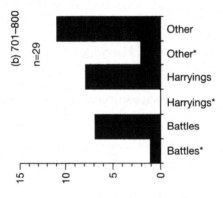

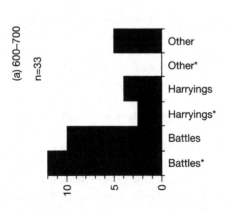

* = Involving the death of a Prominent Person

Figure 2 English warfare 600–850: changing patterns or changing traditions?

not take the slightest bit of notice. The destruction of territory (and Gregory's passage at least gives us a very good idea of what it involved) remained central to early medieval warfare (and beyond), for very good reasons. Furthermore, if there is any truth at all in the story, it is surely most likely that Gundobad paid the tribute because of the damage being done to his territory and perhaps more importantly to his political standing.

Harryings were not mere plundering raids. They struck directly at the enemy ruler's claim to be a good lord. Kings were supposed to defend their subjects and their property. The defending king could hold out in a fortification and wait for the enemy to go away, but such an abrogation of the ruler's role as war-leader could not be accepted indefinitely. Alternatively, if the defender did not feel strong enough to meet the aggressors in battle, he might submit and pay the attackers' tribute. This might reduce the damage and dissatisfaction to some degree. The attackers, however, might not be interested in this solution but instead want to remove the king from his throne and/or annex his kingdom. If enemy raids were not to turn into annual tribute-takings and if a king were not to become a mere subject ruler, sooner or later the issue would have to be put to the test of battle. Therefore, since the attacking army would have known this, harrying, rather than being a safer, strategically effective alternative to battle,[33] was a means of bringing one about. Harrying was a deliberate challenge to battle, aimed at producing confrontation. It might have been carried on only when one was fairly sure that one could defeat the enemy army. When the aim of a campaign was conquest, this was particularly the case. Campaigns aimed at outright conquest may simply have struck straight for the centre of the invaded territory and been aimed at killing or capturing its ruler. Something similar may have been the case in the smaller-scale Irish campaigning. Armies ravaged settlements and drove off the cattle, thus seriously undermining the rival king's political economy and claim to effective lordship. This would, similarly, either cause political unrest in the attacked kingdom or bring about the enemy king's submission and tribute payment, or battle.[34]

Thus warfare differed in scale and objectives. Long periods of endemic small-scale warfare would not ease all the tensions within a polity, and could create others. Where one kingdom had acquired a position of dominance over another this situation could only be reversed by a major war. These wars might deliberately eschew all the usual norms of warfare. For example, in 574–75, after repeated small-scale warfare between Chilperic and Sigibert, sons of Chlothar I, the Merovingian kingdoms were riven by a particularly serious conflict.[35] Its narrator, Gregory of Tours,[36] repeatedly describes the unusually severe ravaging of territory. A council of bishops was called to try to adjudicate in the affair, but the kings took no notice. Saint Germanus, bishop of Paris, intervened to try to dissuade the Austrasian king, Sigibert, from the war, but failed. Sigibert called in the 'peoples from beyond the Rhine', over whom he held hegemony. These peoples were apparently not normally involved in Merovingian internecine warfare, and Gregory tells of the seriousness of their harrying of Neustrian territory and the difficulty with which it was brought under control. Even the peace made at the end of 574, with Chilperic returning the territory his troops had taken, did not end the war. The next year it broke out again. Eventually a pitched battle took place in which one of Chilperic's sons was killed. Major set-piece battles were not very common in Merovingian civil warfare,[37] and this was the first time an adult member of the Merovingian family had been killed in warfare against his relatives. A fortnight or so later, Sigibert of Austrasia was assassinated at the moment of his victory over Chilperic, the first time an adult reigning Merovingian had actually been killed on the orders of one of his brothers.

Another serious outbreak of warfare came in 612–13, between the brothers Theuderic II of Burgundy and Theudebert II of Austrasia.[38] This again followed a spell of smaller-scale, normative warfare when tensions had been building up. In 605, Theudebert and Theuderic with their armies confronted each other near the royal villa of Quierzy, but something of a palace revolution took place within the Burgundian army, resulting in the murder of Theuderic's mayor of the palace, Protadius, and forcing Theuderic to make terms and return home without a fight.[39] In 610, the brothers squared up to each other in Seltz in Alsace. Theuderic was again forced to back down when he saw the size of the Austrasian host, and he ceded a number of territories to his elder brother.[40] In 612 Theuderic had his revenge. He attacked Theudebert in a major war, producing (as in the 570s) two serious pitched battles and again involving the Austrasians' use of troops from beyond the Rhine. As in 575, the war resulted in the death of a reigning king, Theudebert, and this time the slaughter of his family. The drama did not end there, however. Theuderic II died shortly afterwards, on his way to attack his cousin and erstwhile ally, Chlothar II of Neustria, and in the aftermath a faction of the Austrasian/Burgundian aristocracy called in Chlothar, who massacred Theuderic's children and their great-grandmother, Queen Brunichildis.

Within a polity, these outbreaks need not always happen. As mentioned above, in Merovingian Gaul there were mechanisms which could be employed to dissipate tensions. Councils of bishops were one such; a council failed to end the war in 574. When Chlothar II and his son Dagobert were about to fight each other in 625, a meeting was convened at Clichy, to which both parties sent twelve lords, including bishops.[41] It seems likely that the seventh-century Austrasian law-code Ripuarian Law emerged from this meeting. In 587 tensions between Childebert II of Austrasia and Guntramn of Burgundy[42] were lessened by the signing of the Treaty of Andelot,[43] which attempted to resolve the grievances between the two sides. A year later, when Guntramn and Childebert were still edging towards war, an embassy of bishops to Guntramn and a public reading of the treaty finally defused the situation. After the savage war of 613 Chlothar II, now ruling all Gaul, assembled a council at Paris in 614 and issued edicts for the church and the people of his realm. This again attempted to resolve the tensions which had brought the war about.

In Anglo-Saxon England between c.600 and c.850 there seem to have been major wars between major neighbouring kingdoms only once or twice per generation. In this period the Mercians fought the West Saxons every 17.85 years on average; the West Saxons fought the Welsh every 19.23 years; the Welsh fought the Mercians every 22.72 years; and the Mercians and Northumbrians fought every 25 years.[44] Most of the information upon which these figures are based is rather later than the events concerned. Warfare is recorded in some sources but did not merit mention in the major narrative or annalistic sources and there are other indications of repeated endemic warfare, for example the nine years' raiding by the young Guthlac discussed above and the 'many great battles against the Welsh' which the *Anglo-Saxon Chronicle* says were fought by Cynewulf of Wessex, none of which merited an individual entry. With these points in mind it does not seem unreasonable to view most of the outbreaks of warfare recorded in the narrative histories as major eruptions of warfare, against a back-drop of more limited endemic fighting.

The scale of warfare need not be reflected in the scale of open fighting, however. By 782, Charlemagne had been fighting the Saxons for ten years. In that year, he campaigned in Saxony once again, received the submission of most of the Saxon leaders and attempted to put an end to the Saxon war by issuing the harsh 'First Saxon Capitulary'. Nevertheless, shortly afterwards a Frankish army was badly beaten in the Süntel mountains, so Charlemagne assembled his army and attacked the Saxons a second time. The Saxons again came to submit but, doubtless to their horrified surprise, the king of the Franks had 4,500 of them killed on the spot. This act of savagery had the effect only of stirring up Saxon resistance to the Franks and three more years of campaigning, involving several full-scale pitched battles, were necessary before the Saxons were subdued (only to rebel again in 793–99).[45]

It seems, therefore, that there were various scales of warfare in early medieval Europe, although the differences between them were not clearly articulated and they shaded into each other in practice. If we accept the existence of different levels of warfare this might help us resolve certain problems which emerge in the study of the practice of warfare and the weaponry used, to which we shall return. The different types of war might have differed in the ways in which they were waged as well as simply in the scale of the violence employed or its results. There may have been accepted norms governing the usual practice of warfare. For example, churches, or at least certain areas within them, might normally have been spared attack. The Vikings certainly did not introduce church-burning to the early medieval west, but it was hardly usual practice amongst Christians nevertheless. Certain classes of people, for example those linked by ties of godparenthood, may have been spared if captured.[46] These norms were never written down or clearly articulated. Other norms may simply have emerged in the course of repeated campaigning. With a limited number of campaigning routes available to an attacker, the 'moves' in warfare may have been fairly well known, and the usual responses equally clearly understood. In chapter 1, this was referred to as a sort of grammar of warfare. Endemic warfare, such as that within the Frankish kingdoms and possibly elsewhere, could take on its own rhythms, as argued above for early Merovingian warfare.

Where armies deviated from the usual practices this would, one presumes, have made a clear statement about the nature of the war, intimating more serious intent. In 655, Penda of Mercia refused the tribute offered by Oswy of Northumbria, in a move which must have signalled his intention to fight a decisive war of subjugation even if (according to Bede) he had not declared that he wanted to wipe out 'the entire nation from the highest to the humblest'.[47] However, well-understood normative warfare would take place either within political systems such as the Frankish kingdom or perhaps the kingdoms of Anglo-Saxon England or across the land borders of long-standing neighbours. Outbreaks of more serious warfare would quickly be understood as such from the way in which they were waged. Problems might emerge when realms or cultures which had not previously come into contact encountered each other militarily. There the lack of shared or mutually recognised norms of behaviour could produce dramatic results. It can be argued that the reason for the widespread and genuine terror which the Vikings produced was a result not of deliberate 'terror tactics' but of the facts that, firstly, their sea-borne raids from unknown and distant homes could not be countered and retaliated to in the usual ways, and, secondly, the Vikings, although engaged in activity analogous to that carried out by western Christian rulers, did not follow the same norms of conduct. Their attacks seemed to be 'breaking the rules' and thus always seemed like the most serious types of war.[48]

Rituals of warfare

There were some foci for more clearly ritualised aspects of warfare. Ensuring divine backing for armies was a matter of crucial importance. Armies were accompanied by bishops in order to further ensure divine favour, where those bishops did not take part in the actual fighting. The procedures for the crowning of kings implored God to bestow victory and peace upon the king. When Charles the Bald was crowned at Metz in 869, for example, Archbishop Hincmar of Reims included in his benefaction 'may He always make you victorious and triumphant over visible and invisible enemies'.[49] Christian liturgies came to feature prayers for the victory of the army. Such prayers especially hoped for triumph over pagans and 'barbarians'. This is, in our period, especially clear in Visigothic Spain and in Frankish Gaul from the eighth century.[50] The Visigothic service for the departure of the king and his army included having the army's holy cross standard (with reliquary) and other banners blessed by the bishops, and Frankish armies seem, by the ninth century, also to have had standards similarly containing relics and thus imbued with numinous power.[51] The Visigothic service was still used in the kingdom of the Asturias, especially for warfare against the Moslems. Charlemagne ordered his bishops to say masses for the army[52] and, sixty years later, the emperor, Lothar, during his son Louis' campaign in the south against the Arabs, also set out lengthy procedures to ensure God's favour.[53] The latter was particularly important as the Saracens had just, after easily defeating a somewhat shambolic attempt to drive them away, sacked St-Peter.[54] What would the Lord think of those who had not defended the tomb of the Prince of the Apostles?

It was important to demonstrate to one's troops that the campaign was justified. This seems to have been particularly important in the warfare between rival Frankish kings in the ninth century.[55] In chapter 1 we noted the efforts by Louis the Younger to portray his campaign against Charles the Bald as his submission to a judgement of God. Before Fontenoy, the clear statements made by the two sides were also intended to display their belief in the justice and legitimacy of their cause to their followers, as well as to sway the opinion of waverers on the other side.[56] Such efforts were also necessary in other types of warfare against foreign neighbours. There may be a trace of this in Gregory of Tours' account of Theuderic I's war against the Thuringians in the early sixth century.[57] Although the exact details of Gregory's account, especially the speech he puts in Theuderic's mouth, are without doubt his own invention, there is something plausible about Theuderic's attempt to whip up his followers by referring to the Thuringians' recent faithless and brutal behaviour towards the Franks. In this case, and doubtless many others, warfare took on the nature of feud, with current military activity being justified by reference to previous wrongs done by the enemy. Theuderic's Franks were given the impression that their cause was just; they were avenging past wrongs. The same impression of warfare fought as vendetta justified by previous wrongs is given by the *Beowulf* poet in his account of the war between the Geats and the Swedes.[58]

When he decided to terminate the independent existence of the duchy of Bavaria in 787, Charlemagne prepared his ground very well. There were already several prominent landowners with pro-Carolingian leanings in Bavaria but in some ways the extent of the links between Bavaria and the Frankish *regnum* made the need to convince people of the justice of Charlemagne's actions all the more pressing. Thus Charlemagne obtained from the pope a declaration that the Bavarian duke, Tassilo, and all his adherents would be anathematised if they did not do as Charlemagne said. Furthermore, Charlemagne's troops would be absolved from any guilt in waging this war against such *infideles* (breakers of faith), and all blame would accrue to Tassilo if war did ensue. Charlemagne followed this up by publicly summoning Tassilo to obey the papal injunctions, and waiting for the duke to fail to comply before crossing into Bavaria with three armies.[59]

The Avars had been the major power in the Danube basin for over 200 years when Charlemagne launched his attack on them in the 790s. To ensure the success of his attack, launched late in the year, when the Frankish forces arrived at the frontier they decided to hold three days of prayer, celebrating mass and beseeching God to grant success to the army of the Franks. Interestingly, they portrayed the attack as seeking vengeance against the Avars.[60] This is not very surprising. The Visigothic service for a departing army used the phrase *ad ultionem* – 'to vengeance!' – almost as a chorus.[61] Once again, warfare was conducted as though it were feud.

The conduct of campaigns

How campaigns were carried out is, in detail, obscure. Some late classical texts such as Vegetius' *De Rei Militari* ('On Matters Military') were known and frequently copied in the period. As we have seen, however, the relationship between written source and everyday practice was a complex and in many ways surprising one in the early Middle Ages and it is doubtful that even Roman commanders used works like Vegetius in practice.[62] That a ninth-century version of Vegetius pauses to update some of its provisions for training[63] might seem to indicate that these texts were related to actual practice, but the copy was made in a monastery, as indeed were most of the extant manuscripts, and we cannot be sure that the popularity of Vegetius was not mainly a matter of antiquarianism and the desire to acquire classical learning. As has been noted, early medieval people were quite prepared to accord great authority to classical works, even while recognising that they had nothing to do with the world in which they lived.[64] There is no evidence at all that Vegetius' detailed tactical and organisational recommendations were ever put into practice, and it seems unlikely that his advice on campaigning was followed closely either. In many cases it is abundantly clear that it was not. Nevertheless we cannot rule out the possibility that some learned Carolingian commanders may have tried to apply the more general ideas to be found in works like these. However, to say that early medieval generals did not follow classical theoretical treatises is not to say that early medieval campaigns were conducted in haphazard fashion, with armies simply bumbling about the countryside hitting anyone who got in the way (though, as before and after, there were doubtless instances where this was the case).

In the early Middle Ages, as in other periods, summer appears to have been the campaigning season. The date of the Marchfield (1 March) derived from the fact that this was when campaigning began to be feasible. Fodder had to be available for the horses and pack animals, and food supplies assembled for the men, after the hard months of winter. The Continuation of Fredegar famously states that the Marchfield was moved to 1 May.[65] This is often taken as indicating a new reliance upon horses by the Franks. If so, the difference does not seem to have been tactical. It may rather be that armies were now somewhat larger, and possibly with larger mounted contingents. Campaigns in the eighth century were regularly fought over much longer distances than had been normal (though not unknown) earlier, which possibly also required more horses. In May, furthermore, the weather would be more suitable. Winter's rain and snow, apart from bringing illness and attrition, would often make roads unusable and rivers impassable, as would the immediate thaw after winter. The Frankish *Revised Annals*, therefore, repeatedly make clear that the political year (and thus the possibility of campaigning) began, usually after the celebration of Easter, in late spring or early summer for these sorts of reasons: 'As soon as the weather was seen to offer favourable opportunity, he set out for Saxony again, with a great army' (780); 'at the beginning of the summer. When fodder was at last plentiful enough to enable an army to march, he decided to enter Saxony' (782); 'in mild and smiling spring, when his preparations for a Saxon expedition were completed' (783); 'As soon as suitable weather arrived, the king . . . crossed the Rhine with an army' (784). In 798, the Saxons rebelled 'when Spring was already approaching but it had not yet proved possible, because of the lack of fodder, to bring the army out of winter quarters (*de hibernis*)'.

As the last reference shows, waiting for late Spring was all very well when an offensive was being planned, but sometimes the enemy might not be prepared to wait until conditions were at their most suitable. Winter campaigns were not unknown. Louis the German drove out Charles the Bald in November 858 and Charles, deploying his cunning to the full, regained his kingdom by attacking Louis 'when he least expected it', in January 859.[66] Campaigning at this time of year was, however, hardly desirable. The punishment for disloyalty meted out to the archchaplain, Hilduin, abbot of St-Denis, by Louis the Pious was that Hilduin spend the winter 'in a campaign tent near Paderborn'.[67] The undesirability of campaigning in winter – difficulty of communications would also make mustering the army more difficult – was what made attacks in mid-winter likely to succeed, at least in the short term. The Vikings campaigning in England made good use of this fact. These campaigns were usually short-lived drives at a political centre, forcing the enemy leader to retreat or to pay tribute. It was a high-risk/high-yield strategy, though. Defeat at this time of year would be catastrophic. The campaign of 871 between the West Saxons and the Vikings was fought in winter and was a hard one as a consequence. Battles arose, apparently, as and when the English had assembled enough troops to confront the Danes. The inclement season probably meant that it was taking longer to muster armies. Troops were coming in slowly and in dribs and drabs. At the same time, however, the English commanders' hands were forced by the difficulty of supplying a larger force for any period at that time of year, so it was difficult for them to wait until they had assembled a bigger army.

Thus the fact that political institutions such as the first gathering of the army required a muster on 1 March or 1 May did not mean that that was the only time of year when campaigns were begun. Many campaigns began rather later in the year. Charlemagne referred to summer as the hosting season, and regularly campaigned in June and, especially, July. He took his army into Saxony in late July 782 but, as discussed above, after he had returned to Herestal the war flared up again and must have gone on at least into September. A charter of 825, issued on 19 August, refers to Ecgberht of Wessex marching against the Britons.[68] He may possibly have defeated their army already, at Galford in west

Devon, but he still had to return to Wiltshire and face an invasion by Beornwulf of Mercia (whom he also defeated, at Wroughton).[69] This campaign seems equally to have gone on until the end of August at least. Indeed, Charlemagne's Avar campaign of 791 only began on 1 September. Campaigns could be fought, therefore, at most times of year but preferably, and for obvious reasons, in summer.

One key strategy was to attack the enemy, if possible, from several directions, forcing them to split their forces.[70] In 630, the Franks launched a three-pronged attack on the Wendish Slavs.[70] Charlemagne was skilful in bringing several different armies to bear on his enemies, for logistic and strategic reasons. For example, three armies attacked Bavaria in 787; three attacked the Avars in 791 and 796;[71] and four forces attacked the Saxons in 774. Charlemagne's son, Charles, also employed this strategy on the Slavic frontier in 805 and 806, and it continued to be used by Louis the Pious in the 820s against Liudewit, the rebellious south Slavic *dux*.[72] King Wamba moved his army across the Pyrenees in three columns, with a further one in reserve, presumably in order to keep his enemies guessing as well as to cross the mountains more rapidly. Armies would be strung out in longer and narrower columns than usual when crossing mountainous defiles, and thus more ripe for ambush. This was proved graphically by the two catastrophic Frankish defeats in the pass of Roncesvalles in 778 and (in a rather more significant battle) 824.[73] Wamba also appears to have used a naval force in conjunction with his columns.[74] In 773–4, Charlemagne similarly outflanked Desiderius' Lombard army by crossing the Alps in two columns, and crossed the Pyrenees in two columns in 778.

The use of allies, as mentioned in chapter 5, was an important aspect of the attack from several directions. The Northumbrians and the Scots attacked the Strathclyde Britons from different directions in 756. In an attempt to throw off Ecgbert of Wessex's overlordship, the Cornish appear to have allied with the Mercians in 825 and invaded Wessex separately.[75] The Lombard king, Liutprand, led an army against the Arabs in support of his ally Charles Martel, mayor of Francia, in 737, but he seems to have arrived in southern France too late to see action.[76] The allied Neustrians and Frisians attacked the Austrasians from separate directions in 715.[77]

An interesting strategy was adopted in Louis the Pious' early campaigns in Spain. In order to gain an element of surprise, a small Frankish force moved only by night and hid in the woods by day.[78] The cunning ruse was given away only by the fact that the observant Moorish commander noticed horse dung in the river downstream of the Franks' position. Whether this strategy was used on other occasions is unknown, but certainly possible. Presumably it was only really an option for a small force, and thus yet another objection to the argument for large early medieval armies.

Scouting seems to have been fairly minimal, to judge from the number of occasions when armies rode into ambushes or were attacked by surprise. Nevertheless, it is unlikely that no attempt at all was ever made to scout ahead of the army. There are some references to scouting. In an account written at the very start of our period, describing a campaign in Britain in c.429, Constantius of Lyons refers to scouts.[79] Similarly, in the campaign against the usurper Gundovald in 585, a force of horsemen was sent ahead of the main Burgundian army.[80] Wamba also despatched a force ahead of his main army when campaigning against Paul in 673.[81] Regino mentions Viking scouts (*speculatores*) provoking an undisciplined attack by a Frankish army in 891.[82] Just as the Vikings appeared, the utterly confused Franks, who (as discussed below) had been put at a severe disadvantage by harrying raids, were deciding to send out a select advance party of their own to find the Viking army. It is possible that the *explorationes* required of inhabitants of the Spanish March meant scouting duty.[83] *Exploratio* seems to have been a specifically Spanish obligation[84] but this is perhaps unsurprising. An army from the north wishing to cross the Pyrenees into hostile territory would be in great need of guides. When an army was located, though, commanders seem to have gone themselves and scouted out the terrain. According to the *Earlier Annals of Metz*, before the battle of Tertry Pippin of Herestal climbed up a nearby hill and selected the point to which his army would move in order to give battle with the morning sun behind them.[85]

Elsewhere the limits of geographical knowledge probably restricted campaigning armies to using a few, well-known principal routes.[86] Anglo-Saxon charters make repeated mention of *herepaths* (army paths). These routes seem to follow the tops of ridges, sometimes connecting old hillforts and later *burhs*, and do not seem to link contemporary rural settlements.[87] It seems most likely that they were so called because they were the usual roads used by armies on campaign. *Here* is the word usually used by writers in Old English to describe an offensive force (as in Ine's Laws, 13.1). Place-names like Hereford (ford of the army) might also designate the point where attacking armies usually crossed a river. Throughout early medieval Europe rulers tried to ensure that bridges were maintained, enabling their armies to move freely within their kingdoms (though, that said, the number of references to collapsed bridges suggests that these duties might not always have been carried out with the utmost rigour).[88]

Defence against an enemy attack largely turned upon fortifications, in which political leaders and their troops could shelter if battle was thought unwise, or from which they could sally if the opportunity presented itself (especially against supply trains or troops loaded down with plunder). As campaign routes were fairly few and well known, they could be blocked or controlled by fortifications. Another possibility was to make use of natural lines of defence such as mountains and rivers. Rivers played a significant part in the Frankish wars of the ninth century. A defender might destroy the bridges and remove all available boats to the other bank.[89] A system of watches could also be employed to provide immediate warning if and where an enemy tried to cross.[90] At a point of political crisis in 582, Chilperic of Neustria sealed the borders of his kingdom by positioning guards at the key river crossings and later on Guntramn of Burgundy closed his border with Austrasia.[91] Other sixth-century campaigns saw rivers play an important part. When Clovis marched against the Visigoths in 507 his campaign was held up at the river Vienne, swollen by recent floods, and he only got across because a ford was 'miraculously' revealed by a doe crossing the river.[92] Similarly, when Sigibert of Austrasia campaigned against his brother Chilperic in 574, he was held along the line of the Seine, and only able to cross by brow-beating his other brother, Guntramn of Burgundy, into allowing his army to march through his territory.

The early Middle Ages saw the construction of a number of long defensive barriers, the most famous being Offa's Dyke on the English–Welsh border and the Danevirke on the frontier between Saxony and Denmark. Others are also known, however. Many were constructed in the immediately post-Roman period in Britain.[93] These are unlikely to have been continuously manned frontiers in the way that Hadrian's Wall and Roman frontier lines had been, though we should probably imagine a certain monitoring and guard at key crossing points. The works would make cattle rustling very much more difficult, and might also channel raiding forces through a particular route, which could be watched, or even defended by an army (perhaps especially on the raiders' way home). The most difficult foes to defend against, however, were those who did not come via the well-worn land routes, but who descended upon one's territory from the sea: the Vikings.[94]

Logistics

There is very little evidence to tell us how an army was supplied in any detail. Some of the relevant issues were discussed in chapter 6. Gregory of Tours, as mentioned, bemoans the damage done by the movement of Princess Rigunth, her household and escort through the land. However, as discussed, what he seems really to have objected to was the use of public taxes rather than the private resources of the king to fund this procession. He says that the royal officials had organised and stockpiled the supplies along the way.[95] This is an interesting insight and suggests that this was, ideally at least, how Merovingian armies would have been fed and supplied. A similar situation would appear to have existed in Spain at the same date. The 'commissariat law' discussed in chapter 3 suggests that food and other provisions were to be collected by royal officers in towns and other fortifications.[96] These systems in some way probably descend from the late Roman situation.

Charlemagne seems to have taken an unusual interest in the supplying of his army, especially after 800. Earlier, his Capitulary 'Concerning Estates' (*De Villis*) also set out in some detail how the resources of the royal estates were to be harnessed to support his armies. Notably, the estates were to provide carts carry-ing 12 measures (*modii*) of wine and 12 measures of flour. The carts were to be capable of being floated across rivers and were to come with a shield, lance and a bow and arrows for the attendants to defend themselves. Those utensils that might be required by the army were also to be kept in a locked store room at the centre of each royal estate.[97] The carts were also mentioned in the Capitulary of Aachen of 802–3, which specified that they were to carry flour, wine, bacon and 'victuals in abundance', along with whetstones, stone-cutting tools, axes, augurs and 'slinging machines' (and there were to be men who could use these). Stones for the slinging machines were to be carried on pack animals.[98] The same capitulary instructed counts to reserve two thirds of the grass in their counties for forage, and to make sure that there were sound bridges and boats (if most bridges were pontoon bridges, this provision may have related to different aspects of the same obligation). The letter to Fulrad, lay abbot of St-Quentin, also specifies carts more or less as in the Aachen capitulary, but says all the monastic *caballarii* were to have provisions for three months. They were to keep discipline on the march and take only grass, water and firewood from the locals.[99] In 811, judging from Charlemagne's response, people were apparently alleging that their three months' supplies were used up and going home early. Charlemagne thus enacted that, for people living between the Loire and the Rhine, the three months began when the Loire or Rhine was crossed; Saxons campaigning on the Slavic front were to count their three months from the point at which they crossed the Elbe; and for Aquitanians fighting in Spain, three months began when the Pyrenees were crossed. The emperor also declared that all troops should bring clothing to last for six months.[100] The concern with logistics continued into the reign of Louis the Pious, who also enacted that carts were an essential part of military equipment.[101] A formula from his court specified the amounts of food to be provided for contingents sent to the army.[102] That this has survived in such a document, a model to be copied whenever needed, is probably clearer evidence than the legislation that the Carolingian rulers took these matters seriously.

Another means by which Carolingian rulers seem to have provided for the provisioning of their armies was by granting lands along major campaign routes to the more important monasteries of the realm, entrusting these houses with the supply of victuals to troops passing through.[103] The estates of the great religious houses could, by the ninth century, not only contribute sizeable military contingents, but also produce valuable quantities of supplies or monetary equivalents.[104]

The estimates about the speed of armies made in chapter 6 presupposed no significant baggage train or element of camp followers. In fact these featured prominently in early medieval warfare. The 'Astronomer' says that a Frankish *scara* campaigning in Spain moved more slowly because of an absence of pack-saddles.[105] Horses were vulnerable on campaign and wealthy warriors would take more than one, probably several in the case of the uppermost echelons. It seems, furthermore, likely that each warrior would have brought his own supplies on his own pack animals. Large contingents sent by monasteries and possibly those of very wealthy nobles may have carried their supplies on centrally organised wagons and pack animals but it seems more likely that an early medieval army was accompanied by far more beasts of burden than it technically required. Normalist analyses of the number of pack animals required to carry an army's food and fodder for horses probably considerably underestimate the numbers used. Such analyses, in calculating the weights of food required by an army and thus the animals and wagons necessary to carry it, also depend largely upon assumptions that food took the form of grain. This is entirely reasonable in some cases, such as classical armies and those of the Byzantines, but as Karl Leyser pointed out, early medieval warriors, especially aristocrats, needed meat too, as specified in Carolingian capitularies and other documents, and they often drove their food with them on the hoof.[106] In 810 one Carolingian army suffered badly when murrain struck the livestock it was bringing with it, 'almost no animals were left to feed such a large army'.[107]

These baggage wagons and pack animals and the herds of cattle needed attendants. Imma the thegn claimed to be a poor married ceorl who had followed the Northumbrian army to fetch and carry.[108] Aristocratic warriors would certainly not take the field on their own and perform all their own chores. Fairly frequent references to slaves and the half-free in the army make it clear that soldiers took attendants on campaign with them. Charlemagne's legislation assumes a sizeable number of carts, baggage animals and armed attendants following major armies, as does the *formula* emanating from the court of Louis the Pious.[109] Major armies, as will be discussed below, carried their wealth with them. Kings took elaborate tents with them, which would need transport, and tents for the rest of the army are mentioned frequently.[110] Interestingly, when campaigning in Aquitaine in 585, the usurper Gundovald moved his supplies with the aid of camels. Some of these beasts were captured by the pursuing Burgundians.[111] Charles the Bald's army in 876 was accompanied by merchants including shield-sellers.[112] This is unlikely to have been unusual, although the number of such people is likely to have risen with the increased monetisation of the economy in the latter part of our period. Carolingian armies often relied heavily upon their supply trains, especially, one assumes, when fighting on home territory. In 891, a Frankish army was harassed by the Vikings who kept attacking its supply trains, using the woods and marshes around Aachen as bases from which to attack, and capturing the wagons in which food was being brought to the army.[113] This utterly disoriented the Frankish commanders, who had no idea where the Vikings were or what their planned movements were. Eventually, in a shambolic attempt to bring about a battle (discussed above), the army was drawn into a rash attack and badly defeated, Bishop Sunzo (or Sunderolt) of Mainz being among the slain. Early medieval armies, therefore, required significant supply trains and, as mentioned in chapter 6, this can only have had a serious effect in limiting their size.

Problems of discipline

The bringing together of an army posed a number of problems. A large concentration of armed men whose social identities were, as shown in chapter 2, often based upon ideas of violence and martial valour could easily produce a surfeit of aggressive energy. Assembling armed men from across the realm, or at least a region, at a single point could raise tensions and rivalries which might otherwise have lain dormant. A vassal of the abbot of Fulda asked Einhard to intercede for him. He wanted to be excused military service (in the abbot's contingent) as he was involved in a quarrel with several other men who would be at the muster, not least the count in charge, and he feared he would be attacked.[114] Charles the Bald enacted at Pîtres that lesser men who owned horses should attend the muster and that they should do so without fear of attack.[115] Early medieval laws habitually penalised crimes, such as thefts and assaults, which took place in the army more seriously than would normally be the case.[116] And as the army was an armed gathering of the political community there was always a danger that political dissent might be fostered within its ranks. 'Sedition' within the army was thus another serious crime.[117]

Spiritual discipline was also a concern, and so, as mentioned, bishops frequently accompanied armies. Sometimes, especially towards the end of the period, they fought, and died, in the battle line but even when not serving as warriors bishops were important to ensure that the correct religious observation was made, without which military success was thought unlikely. In a similar effort to defend the souls of their troops, the Carolingians also enacted that transfers of land, gifts and donations to churches made whilst with the army should be accepted as fully legally valid.[118] Concern for divine backing may have been as important as precautions against carelessness and inefficiency when Charlemagne outlawed drunkenness in his armies in 811.[119]

What later generations would call march discipline was not a forte of early medieval armies. Clovis, when on campaign against the Visigoths in Aquitaine, took special steps to ensure that his troops behaved themselves.[120] Gregory of Tours, as has been noted, discusses occasions when Merovingian Frankish troops pillaged their own territory.[121] In 574 Sigibert stoned to death a number of his trans-Rhenan auxiliaries for plundering and in 583 Chilperic had to behead the count of Rouen for pillaging.[122] Cassiodorus' letters also describe situations where Theoderic's troops were looting the friendly population when on the march, and this was a concern in Visigothic law too.[123] Wamba was horrified by looting and rape carried out by his troops on the march, feeling, according to Julian of Toledo, that this could only harm his cause by incurring divine disfavour.[124] Things do not seem to have improved very much by the ninth century. In 868, for example, Hincmar of Reims drily noted that a *scara* under Charles the Bald's son Carloman, which had been sent to help the Bretons against the Northmen on the Loire, 'laid waste certain territory but did nothing useful against the Northmen whom they had been sent to resist'.[125]

Presumably the territory ravaged was friendly Neustrian land. Charlemagne had pronounced in 810–11 that troops who took more from the locals than they were allowed would have to repay threefold, as well as paying a fine or, if a slave (presumably in attendance on a warrior), receiving a thrashing.[126]

Attrition

Disease and starvation were serious foes for early medieval armies. In the sixth century, the Lombards rapidly learnt the tactic of shutting themselves up in their cities and waiting for malaria and other diseases to whittle down invading Frankish forces. Only Charlemagne's unusual tenacity and exceptional organisational skills brought about the failure of this strategy and the collapse of the Lombard kingdom in 773–74. Early medieval people built up a resistance to the water in their own locality but they were very susceptible to water-borne diseases when outside their homeland. Thus, unsurprisingly, Charlemagne required that wine be transported in the supply carts that were to accompany his armies.[127] Further north, Anglo-Saxon lists of food renders talk about ale.[128] The Vikings, however, soon developed a taste for wine so that, as mentioned in chapter 2, one force sent 200 men to Paris to acquire it.[129]

Nevertheless, disease frequently ravaged early medieval armies, especially in Italy. A few examples should suffice. In 539, the Frankish invasion of Italy was ended when the army was all but wiped out by dysentery; the same fate befell another Frankish invasion in 590. In 820, dysentery killed 'a considerable number' of a Frankish army campaigning in Upper Pannonia (what is now the Austrian/Hungarian border area). In 877 'a terrible malady' (possibly whooping cough) followed Carloman of East Francia's army back to Germany so that 'many coughed up their lives'. Six years later, Berengar of Friuli cut short a campaign against his rival, Guy of Spoleto, because of 'illness and weakness' among his army, and in 882 a Frankish army besieging a Viking force was decimated by disease.[130] Not only the rank and file suffered. Pippin I died of a fever which he appears to have contracted in Gascony, and his father, Charles Martel, seems to have died of a fever caught in Provence. Later Carolingians were also decimated by disease. Lothar II died of an illness in Italy which also carried off 'many of his magnates' and 'heaps' of other men. Lothar's uncle, Charles the Bald, was also finished off by a fever contracted in Italy (though it was rumoured to be poison administered by his doctor that actually killed him).[131]

An early medieval army's efficiency was not wholly reliant upon its human component, either. Disease among horses could have a serious effect on the course of a campaign, as three examples will suffice to illustrate. In 791, a Frankish force composed of Saxon and Frisian contingents, campaigning in Bohemia, allegedly lost nine out of every ten of its horses to disease. Nearly a century later, King Arnulf's army lost 'more horses than any mortal can remember' on a march into Friuli and in 896 it suffered so badly from the outbreak of disease among the horses that 'almost the whole army had to transport its baggage in unaccustomed fashion with oxen saddled like horses'.[132] When an enemy had stockpiled food in fortified centres an invading army might, furthermore, end up starving, as happened to one late sixth-century Frankish army.[133] Again, food for the horses was also important: absence of fodder for the horses could delay or terminate campaigns.[134]

Apart from disease, campaigning armies were doubtless whittled away by desertion. Early medieval law repeatedly proscribed leaving the army without permission, and envisaged the heaviest of punishments, often the death penalty.[135] Desertion from an army on campaign was called *herisliz* in Francia and was punishable by death. These laws should not be understood, however, as having had any success in stamping out the problem. Their frequency rather indicates the opposite. Accusations of desertion were also used in politics. Charles the Bald, when moving against the treacherous Bishop Wenilo of Sens, accused him of deserting the army, pretending to be ill but in fact going over to Louis the German.[136] A similar accusation was levelled at Duke Tassilo of Bavaria.[137]

Viking campaigning

Viking armies appear to have been particularly strategically adept, and deserve separate treatment.[138] Here, we are dealing with large agglomerations of warriors, kept in the field for years on end, such as appear from the 840s onwards. The *modus operandi* of such forces appears to have been a kind of land-based political piracy. In England, the strategy of the first Great Army (*micel here*) between 865 and 880 is particularly interesting. The army seems usually to have descended upon its foes after the harvest had been gathered in, at the onset of winter. *Churchscot* (dues paid to the church) and other renders would have been paid (*churchscot* was due on Martinmas, 11 November) and food stockpiled at the major administrative centres.[139] We are helped here by the fact that at this point the *Anglo-Saxon Chronicle* begins its year on 24 September.[140] The movements of the Great Army are usually listed as the first event of the year, immediately followed by the army taking winter quarters. The attack on East Anglia in late 869 appears to have taken place late in the year. The feast day of St Edmund, whom the Danes killed, is 20 November, and the *Chronicle* says that Edmund was killed in battle in winter. Late sources date the Viking attack on York to 1 November 866. The crisis of Alfred's reign came similarly when the Danes attacked Chippenham after Twelfth Night (5 January) 878. The army aimed unerringly for secular or ecclesiastical political centres where, as mentioned, there would be concentrations of wealth and stockpiled food renders. Thus they descended upon the political and economic centres of York in 866 and 868 and London in 870, the royal estate centres of Reading in 870–1 and Chippenham in 878, and the nunnery of Wareham in 875. These places, if not already defended, could easily be fortified, and the contemporary sources frequently mention the Danes' use of fortifications. Reading lies at the junction of two rivers, and Asser tells us that the Danes quickly constructed a rampart between the two.[141] Wareham lies at a narrow point between two rivers and the church there provided a strongpoint and a defensible perimeter wall, and York and London had the advantage of Roman and, possibly, Anglo-Saxon fortifications, as well as being partly defended by rivers.

The timing of the Danish attacks therefore made, on the one hand, these English lay and ecclesiastical centres particularly profitable targets. On the other hand, it made military response to the Viking attack more difficult. The components of the English army would usually have dispersed to their estates by this time of the year. Not surprisingly, therefore, the normal result was that the Anglo-Saxon rulers, accompanied, presumably, only by their immediate military households but faced with a large concentration of hostile Danish warriors, 'made peace', as the *Chronicle* has it, and paid the Danes tribute. Trying to resist in these circumstances was, as Edmund of East Anglia found to his cost, a far more dangerous alternative. Besieging the Danes in their fortifications in mid-winter would be unlikely to produce a more successful outcome. For some rulers the surprise and the consequent loss of face was too great. Burghred of Mercia was driven from his kingdom as a result of a Viking attack in Winter 873, though here we cannot rule out the possibility that the Danes were being used as mercenaries, as a tool in internal Mercian politics. Burghred's shadowy successor, Ceolwulf II, may have belonged to a rival dynasty.[142] Military counter-attacks usually came with the spring, and could be equally unsuccessful. The Northumbrian counter-offensive against the Great Army in York, launched on 21 March 867, led only to the death of two English kings and an 'immense slaughter' of their troops. The Mercians and West Saxons attacked the Viking army holed up in Nottingham in spring 868, with fewer celebrity casualties but no more success. The West Saxon response to the Danes' seizure of Reading in late 870[143] was piecemeal and resulted in a series of indecisive battles, mostly English defeats. Æthelræd and Alfred seem to have committed themselves to an engagement every time they had enough troops to hand, and as soon as such warriors had arrived, rather than waiting to acquire a decisive superiority in numbers. As has been mentioned, this probably stemmed from the difficulty of mustering and supplying troops in winter. In most cases, the Vikings seem to have stayed put in their stronghold, perhaps under the watchful eye of the local Anglo-Saxon army and fed by local renders (tribute) until the next autumn, and then moved on.

In Francia and elsewhere it does not seem that the Vikings operated precisely the same strategy. That may be because the Frankish realms were larger and more powerful than the English, and less likely to be browbeaten by an attack on a single political centre. On the whole, Viking attacks on Francia appear to have been based around pillaging and plundering regions until bought off, and in that sense they were not very different from much other early medieval warfare. The 'Northmen' do seem to have campaigned into the winter,[144] though, and there were other similarities in their strategy, most notably the use of fortified bases, sometimes on islands, from which to launch their attacks. Not for nothing has Eric Christiansen listed the spade as a key weapon of Viking warfare.[145] As in England, too, churches and royal *villae* were used as bases. Churches, as substantial stone buildings, made very useful strongpoints, as at Brissarthe in 866, where Robert the Strong was killed.[146] Churches and monasteries had eminently defensible walls defining their precincts. In Ireland, it seems that the initial Viking base (*longhport*) at Dublin was in the monastery at Kilmainham, upstream from the later town.[147]

The Viking attacks seem also to have been timed around Christian festivals: All Saints (if Simeon of Durham is to be believed) in 866; Christmas (probably) in 870; Christmas or Twelfth Night in 877–8; possibly Martinmas (11 November) in 869 (judging from the date of Edmund's death). This was not a practice limited to their activities in England. It has been suggested that the Viking attack on Armagh in 869 was timed to fall on the feast of St Patrick.[148] The Danish attack on Tours in 853 may also have been planned to arrive on the feast of Martin but it arrived three days early and the locals had heard of their approach and moved St Martin's body.

Bringing about a battle

A battle, as will become clear, was a very risky undertaking. In the ninth century, Sedulius Scottus put it very clearly:

> In the arms and rumblings of war there is great instability. What is more uncertain and unstable than military campaigns, where there is no sure outcome to the wearisome combat and no victory assured, where often illustrious men are overthrown by lesser ones, and where equal misfortunes sometimes befall both sides, who both expect victory but in the end enjoy nothing but calamitous miseries?[149]

As we have seen, quantitatively, most early medieval campaigning was probably small scale and aimed at the acquisition of booty, though the majority of such warfare escapes notice. However, as has also been shown, larger warfare, even when conducted through the raiding and harrying of territory, was usually carried out in order to bring the enemy to battle or force him to submit. Some wars had the outright military destruction of the enemy as a goal. Such wars were aimed at territorial conquest, at throwing off overlordship or at other significant changes in the political status quo. Years of harrying or raids, which had not been beaten off, would produce tensions which could only be resolved by large-scale military action or outright submission. Here a decisive battle might also be sought. As we shall see, it seems that warfare was conducted rather more through set-piece battles than, as would later be the case, through sieges, making early medieval warfare quite distinctive.

Though early medieval commanders doubtless sent troops out ahead of the main force to look for the enemy, it does not seem that early medieval scouting was a highly developed science.[150] So how were battles brought about? Possibly, locating the enemy was made easier by the fact that, as has been mentioned, campaigning routes were limited in number. Analysis of the location of battles might also help. In England between c.600 and c.850 the locations of twenty-eight battles are mentioned, two of which are unidentifiable (figure 3). Of these, no fewer than twenty-two are located either at river crossings or significant man-made features of the landscape, mostly Roman or prehistoric monuments, but also Roman towns.[151] Four of the remainder possibly lay by river-crossings, landmarks or both. Thus most, if not all, Anglo-Saxon battles lay by important features of the landscape. River crossings were obvious places for battles. One army attempted to restrict or prevent the passage of the other, which had to fight if it was to proceed with its campaign. The other Anglo-Saxon locations are in some ways more interesting. One army seems to have pitched its camp at a well-known landmark and waited for the enemy to attack it, possibly as a sort of challenge. As a comparison from after our period, in 1006 the Danish army camped at the barrow of Cwichelmslow (Cuckhamsley, Berkshire) for two weeks, challenging the English to make good their claim that no enemy who reached that spot would see the sea again. After all, it was located near the site of Alfred and Æthelræd's victory over the Great Army at Ashdown. No English troops showed up and the Danes proceeded on a looting spree right past the English capital at Winchester.[152] It is worth noting that this barrow was also the site of legal gatherings.[153] There was often an overlap between the places chosen for battles and those selected for other political meetings. We should perhaps see the battles fought by hillforts, throughout the British Isles, as having been brought about by the same means, rather than being sieges.[154] Possibly armies used such old fortifications as camps.

On the Continent, too, battles seem generally to have been located at river crossings or prominent landscape features. The Lombard battle of Coronate (c.688) was fought by the Adda, for example, and the battle in 843 between Asturian factions was fought at the bridge over the Narcea.[155] Many battles were fought outside or near the camp of one or other army, and others were frequently located by royal villas.[156] The Lombards stationed their armies in the Alpine passes in their defence against the Franks because these were very obvious invasion routes. All in all, it seems that battle was usually produced either by hindering the passage of the enemy or by camping at a very-well-known spot and awaiting the enemy attack. Ambushes were sited in passes, along river valleys or on other well-known routes. Chance encounters seem very rare. One possible example is the battle between Guntramn and Chilperic in 583, which began late in the day.[157]

One distinctive feature of ninth-century warfare within the Frankish polity was lengthy confrontation without battle being joined. The purpose of this seems to have been to test the strength of the support for the other side. As

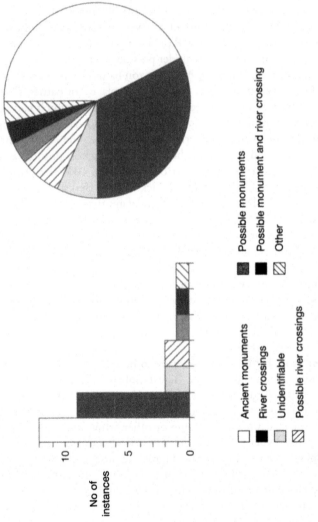

Figure 3 Locational analysis of Anglo-Saxon battles, 600–850

negotiations went on, formally and, one suspects, informally (as in many civil wars, it was not uncommon for families to be represented on both sides[158]), troops might desert one side for the other. Perhaps the best-known instance of this took place in 833 when the forces of Emperor Louis the Pious and those of his rebellious sons faced each other at Rotfeld in Alsace. During a confrontation of several days, the bulk of Louis' army went over to the rebels, bringing about the emperor's temporary deposition and humiliation. The encounter was, sourly, subsequently named that of the Field of Lies.[159] A similar occurrence took place later in the century when Charles the Bald was attacked by his brother Louis the German in late 858. Again the armies confronted each other, at Brienne, apparently for three days. Gradually Charles' troops deserted him to join Louis, forcing Charles briefly from his kingdom. Possibly the lengthy negotiations before Fontenoy were aimed partly at seeing if the supporters of one or other side would abandon their leaders. This may not have been limited to the ninth century. The early seventh-century confrontations between Theuderic II and Theudebert II discussed above may have been very similar.

As noted, normalist military historians have tended to assume that battle was rare, as it was in the twelfth century, for example. Partly this issue turns on a definition of battle related to its size. Thus battles are distinguished from skirmishes or other lesser encounters. However, as has already been mentioned, the scale of warfare can be measured by its political consequences as well as by the scale of fighting or the amount of investment of manpower and other military resources. The same is true of battle. The death in battle of a king, or one of his sons or relatives, or of major noblemen, had serious political repercussions. Yet in the early Middle Ages, commanders were prepared to commit themselves and their armies to the lottery of battle with unusual frequency. Battles are common in this period. As mentioned, twenty-two battles are recorded between seventh-century English kingdoms, twelve of which resulted in the death of one or more king or senior member of the royal family.[160] Sometimes battle was sought even in unfavourable circumstances. In 882, for example, Bishop Wala of Metz was killed at Remich when he and a small army (also including the archbishop of Trier and the count of Metz) 'rashly' attacked a Viking force campaigning in the Moselle valley.[161] In war it was often difficult to shake off the demands of a society wherein, as discussed in chapter 2, so many social identities were based around ideas of military ability and martial valour. The Frankish defeat in the Süntel mountains in 782 was brought about by the rash desire of some younger leaders to acquire glory ahead of the arrival of the more experienced Count Theoderic. 'They feared that the honour of victory might be Theoderic's alone if they should fight at his side. Therefore they decided to engage the Saxons without him.'[162] A similarly ill-advised and disastrous engagement occurred during an East Frankish campaign against the Sorbs in 849. Again the cause was jealousy, in this case of Thachulf, the experienced duke of the Sorbian March, who, it was feared 'wanted to be set above the others and to take over the supreme command'.[163] In the early eighth century, as a result of one commander accusing another of cowardice, a Friulan Lombard army was destroyed in an insane charge up a steep hill against the fortified camp of a Slavic army. The troops followed their squabbling leaders because 'they considered it base not to'.[164] The casualties were such that Paul the Deacon says that 'all the nobility of the Friulans perished'. A later duke of Friuli had to see to the bringing up of those orphaned in the battle.[165]

As we have noted, the harrying of territory was aimed to produce either submission or confrontation. Not all such battles were produced by the defenders having to drive off plundering attackers, either. There were good reasons for the attackers to seek out the defending army. Confrontation was all the more likely because, as just noted, martial ability and victory over enemies were central to so many early medieval social identities. To underpin kingship and other forms of lordship, and the military basis of nobility or (in other times and places) ethnic identity, relatively frequent battle was actually necessary. Admittedly, many of these engagements were small but, as stated, if they risked bringing about the death of leading social and political figures – and they did – this made them serious matters. Challenges to battle were made, as when in 577 Guntramn of Burgundy and Childebert II of Austrasia challenged Chilperic of Neustria either to return disputed territory or choose a spot for battle.[166] Battle could be seen as a judicial ordeal, a judgement of God in which the right-eousness or otherwise of one's cause would be decided.[167] As has been discussed above, judging from the location of battles, it is likely that most engagements were brought about by occupying a prominent location or barring the enemy route and inviting the opposition to give battle.

This does not mean that all early medieval commanders automatically gave battle whenever it was offered. The martial bases of their social and political identities were not so strong that they were always driven to fight regardless of the circumstances. A purely substantivist view does not explain early medieval military behaviour either. Generals manoeuvred to gain advantage over their enemies, they tried to take them by surprise, and on many occasions they simply refused to be drawn. The Slavic *dux* Liudewit remained in his fortifications and refused to negotiate or come out and fight the armies of Louis the Pious, in spite of the ravaging of his territories.[168] On one occasion, the Lombard army, having seen its champion killed by the Franks, simply wheeled away and declined battle.[169] In 584 Chilperic I prepared for war by ordering his counts to bring all valuables into the cities and make sure their walls were ready for attack.[170] Viking armies in England seem actively to have developed strategies aimed at producing success and profit at minimal risk, that is to say, without battle. In 577, Chilperic simply ignored Guntramn and Childebert's challenge and devoted his time to giving circuses to the people of Paris and Soissons. This was a clever stratagem. Although Childebert and Guntramn had aimed to strike at the martial underpinning of his kingship, and challenged Chilperic to prove his value as a war-leader, Chilperic made the challenge redound to *their* shame.

He did not even deign to reply. Furthermore, he ostentatiously demonstrated a superiority by claiming to be a more civilised heir of the Roman Empire, presenting spectacles to the people of the key political centres of Paris and Soissons.[171] In many cases where a formal challenge to battle was made, it is noteworthy that no battle ensued. This does not negate the importance of the challenge; the possibility that it would be accepted must have been real. Interestingly, we have the text of the challenge sent by the usurper Paul to Wamba in 672–3.[172] In that case the site specified as a site for battle did see confrontation between the two sides, but Paul's troops quickly fled. We have also seen that, when their strategy did not produce the desired results, Viking armies were more than willing, and able, to give battle. Sometimes they accepted being besieged but at others they came out and fought.[173] The same was true for other early medieval leaders. At times to sit tight and wait for the enemy to go away may have been a safe option; at others it may have been prudent to pay tribute; but eventually, if a ruler was to remain in control of his territory, the issue had to be put to the test of battle. Liudewit persistently refused to fight, and was eventually forced to flee and assassinated.[174] Mercian overlordship over Kent in the reign of Offa, attested via the charter evidence, must have been built up through regular raids and tribute takings. However, because of the generally hostile nature of the narrative sources to Mercian power, none of this is mentioned. The only such harrying referred to is that of Sussex in 771, recorded by Simeon of Durham.[175] The first set-piece military encounter is the battle of Otford in 774, when the Kentish ruler threw off Mercian domination.

Another, possibly more important, reason for the comparative frequency of battle in the early Middle Ages was the profit that could accrue to the winners. Kings took their treasuries on campaign with them and the booty taken from a defeated host could therefore be sumptuous. The supply trains captured from the usurper Gundovald in 585 included much gold and silver. The career of the luckless but fascinating Charles the Bald once again provides illumination. On one occasion, he temporarily lost three crowns and some fine jewellery whilst marching against the Vikings.[176] The Bretons captured much of his royal finery after Jengland,[177] and Charles again had his baggage, and that of the traders following his army, taken by the victorious East Franks after Andernach in 876.[178] Captured enemies might be ransomed or, more usually, sold as slaves. High-quality loot played a part in social advancement. The *Hispanus* John received lands from Charlemagne after sending his son Louis the pick of the spoils from a victory over the Moors: a horse and a mail shirt of the best quality and a sword decorated with silver.[179] Furthermore, the defeat of an enemy field army would leave the victors free for much more serious ravaging of the enemy territory. The Viking success at Remich was followed by particularly widespread plundering. If warfare was to be profitable, the best way of ensuring this was to defeat the enemy army in battle.

This point is underlined by brief reconsideration of the economy. As noted in the previous chapter, most of the early medieval period was an era of economic contraction, when towns were very small. Except perhaps on market days, they were not the great concentrations of wealth and loot that they would be later. Royal palaces might be the location for wealth but, as has just been mentioned, kings tended to take their wealth with them when they moved about their kingdom. The fortification of palaces was fairly basic. The same was true at other aristocratic levels too. Status was ostentatiously displayed in costume and jewellery, and military equipment was often lavishly ornamented.[180] Horses too would be captured, as in 762 when a Gascon army beaten by the Franks lost all its horses (presumably it had dismounted to fight, though the reference could be to spare horses or rustled animals).[181] Horses, as has been seen, were essential to the maintenance of a military identity, they were expensive items and campaigning could be expensive in horseflesh, so the capture of horses was important. Thus in this period a defeated army was likely to produce far more captured wealth than the seizure of a settlement. The plundering of churches might be the key exception to this, as the Vikings knew.

For all these reasons, it seems that, overall, battles were more frequent in the early Middle Ages than in many other periods. We will examine the nature of battle, when it *was* offered in chapter 9, but now we must look at the appearance and equipment of the warriors who participated in those encounters.

8

WEAPONRY AND EQUIPMENT

Before considering the nature of battle, it will be of use to consider the weaponry and armour of the early medieval western warrior.[1] Here we have pictorial and archaeological as well as documentary evidence to help us. The technology of warfare remained fairly constant throughout the early medieval period but this should not lull us into believing that the nature of battle remained similarly constant, as we shall see.

The most plentiful sources of information about early medieval military hardware are the grave-goods of the fifth to earlier eighth centuries in most of northern Europe and parts of Italy and Spain, and the continuation of the grave-goods tradition in some cemeteries of the Viking Age. Whilst these sites provide numerous examples of actual weapons and thus give an idea of the types of weapon available there are important problems involved in the use of such evidence. As Heinrich Härke has shown,[2] it is not possible to extrapolate actual weapon combinations from the assemblages found in Anglo-Saxon graves, and his conclusions apply to the mainland continental evidence too. The deposition of grave-goods was a ritual act, wherein weaponry could symbolise age, ethnicity or rank; at various times and places a token weapon might be used to illustrate such concepts. In the seventh century in Gaul and England, weapon deposits became more standardised, and sometimes a single spear or scramasax might be used to make the same statement as had been made by fuller weapon sets in the preceding century. Regional variations in ritual were significant too. In northern Gaul, shields were much rarer than in Anglo-Saxon England or Alamannic southern Germany, and are found mainly in lavish graves.[3] This does not mean that only Frankish chieftains carried shields. Swords are more common in sixth-century Frankish graves than in Anglo-Saxon ones but it is difficult to deduce from this that swords were in shorter supply on the English side of the Channel. Similarly, deposits of armour are far more common, and lavish, in the Alamannic region in the sixth and seventh centuries than anywhere else in Europe at that time, and probably later. This fact cannot be used to conclude that the Alamannic warrior was typically more heavily armoured than his contemporaries in Francia or England; the explanation has to be sought in the much higher degree of competition in the funerary rite in Alamannia, on the political fringe of the Frankish world. It is equally difficult to make confident statements about the appearance of warriors from the written sources, which are again highly stylised and tend to use classical models. Nevertheless, a reasonable general survey is possible.

Weaponry

The most treasured item of early medieval military equipment was the sword.[4] Swords are of a fairly standard form throughout our period, so that dates can be assigned only through the artistic style of designs occasionally found on their pommels, guards and scabbard fittings, and from the shape of the pommel and guard. The latter was usually straight, although in ninth-century England a fashion developed for a downward-curving guard.[5] Early medieval swords are long, straight, two-edged weapons, such as are referred to in Roman sources as *spathae*, designed mainly for cutting, but which could also be used to thrust or jab. The design of such weapons means that they need a certain amount of room to be used to full effect. Unlike the early Roman short stabbing sword, the *gladius*, they are not weapons which are particularly suited to close formations, and may have been developed primarily for mounted use. The blades were made using a technique known as pattern welding, which balanced flexibility with strength.[6] Towards the end of our period, as better-quality steel became available, the technique became less common. Swords represent the apex of early medieval military technology, were probably expensive and as a result highly prized.[7]

Probably the most common weapon of the period, however, was the spear. At least until the Viking Age, most if not all warriors, whether on foot or on horseback, would have carried at least one spear. Spears are the most common weapons found in graves, and they were symbolically important too: 'He placed Childebert on his throne and made over to him his entire realm. "Let one single shield protect us both", he said, "and a single spear defend us."'[8] Anglo-Saxons referred to the male half of a family as 'the spear side'; their poetry often talks of battles as clashes of spears. The stereotypical warrior figure, throughout the period, carries a spear: 'Cuthbert dismounted, gave his horse and spear to a servant (he had not yet put off secular dress) . . .'[9]

Spears vary enormously in shape and size.[10] Some smaller examples are most likely to have been throwing spears or javelins,[11] whereas others with long, broad leaf-shaped blades may have been used two-handed to slash the enemy, as well as to thrust with, rather like the 'halberd' described in later Icelandic Sagas. Some found in lowland England are 'corrugated', allowing the blade to be lightened without weakening it; these were probably designed for throwing, are of fifth- and sixth-century date, and, it has been suggested, may have been of insular, British manufacture.[12]

Another specialised type of throwing spear is known as the *ango*, and was used apparently by élite warriors in the earlier Merovingian period. It was, according to the *Fragmentary Chronicle of Saragossa*, an *ango* that killed King Amalaric of the Visigoths.[13] This weapon was based upon the classical Roman *pilum*. It had a long, slender iron shank and a barbed head, and was thrown at close range, just before the two sides came into contact. Designed to punch through a shield and transfix its bearer, it would also weigh down any shield into which it was embedded, and would bend if it hit the ground, preventing it from being thrown back. Though described as the typical Frankish weapon by Agathias,[14] *angones* are rare and found mainly in lavish burials.[15] The *ango*, like the English 'corrugated' blades, had fallen out of use by the seventh century.

In the seventh century and later, spearheads developed 'wings' projecting from their sockets (they are depicted in rather exaggerated form in manuscript illustrations).[16] These were sometimes interpreted as designed to prevent the blade from penetrating too far, or as being designed for boar-hunting, to help absorb the boar's rush. Neither explanation is convincing. The blades of such spears are often so long that an enemy's body would have been completely transfixed by the time the wings contacted it; at the same time, the wings are rarely broader than the widest point of the blade, and are sometimes rather narrower, and are unlikely to have been able to stop a charging boar! It seems more likely that these wings were either for decoration (some are inlaid), or for catching enemy blades.

One of the weapons widely thought to have been common in this period is the axe, frequently supposed to have been double-headed. In fact the axe was far less common than the spear, and was popular only in restricted times and places. The sixth-century Franks seem to have made much use of the axe. Two general types appear in the archaeology of Merovingian cemeteries: a battle-axe apparently wielded with one hand, and the more famous throwing axe, or *francisca*, which Isidore of Seville supposed had given the Franks their name.[17] The latter has a top edge of characteristically 'upswung reversed S' shape, and the top point has often been broken off by impact. Tests have shown that it required skill and training to use, but had quite fearsome penetrating power.[18] However, this axe seems to have developed in northern Gaul during the fifth century, quite probably from prototypes common in the late Roman army; it was not an ancestral weapon brought by the Franks when they settled in this region. These axes are also found to a lesser extent in southern England and in the Alamannic region of southern Germany. Both the *francisca* and the battle-axe drop from the archaeological record in the seventh century and the fact that axes had lost their popularity may be confirmed by the absence of the axe from the list of weapons given in the probably early seventh-century Frankish *Ripuarian Law*.[19] The demise of the throwing axe may indicate that battle involved more tightly arrayed formations, and that fighting styles were less open and individual, with the attendant decrease in the room needed to throw axes. The battle-axes may have been replaced by the scramasax.

The axe was, however, reintroduced into early medieval warfare by the Vikings in the late eighth and ninth centuries. The association of Viking raiders with their dreaded axes is illustrated graphically on the Lindisfarne tombstone, which shows a line of Viking warriors brandishing swords and one-handed axes.[20] In the period covered by this book, these axes appear to have been used single-handed; the long, two-handed axe which is commonly associated with later Viking and eleventh-century English *huscarls* does not seem to have been introduced until the tenth century. Note that, Hollywood to the contrary, no double-headed axe has ever been found from early medieval Europe! It has, however, been suggested[21] that the association of the Vikings with axes may have been overstated. Spears are, again, the most common weapons found, and axes are not often found in grave deposits with other weapons.

More common than the axe was the single-edged seax or scramasax, a long knife, found in various forms throughout our period, and probably the typical early medieval side-arm, especially for those who could not afford swords.[22] Early scramasaxes are generally short and narrow. They become broader in the seventh century and then increase in length too, so that they are effectively one-edged swords by about 700. The Vikings similarly developed one-edged swords akin to this type.[23]

Early medieval warriors also fought at a distance with bows. These survive rarely, as they were made of wood, but Alamannic bows were found at Ober-flacht, and Viking bows have been found at Hedeby.[24] Small arrowheads are found quite commonly on the Continent, often used as 'token' weapons in the graves of young Alamannic males, but it is difficult to know when a large 'arrow-head' might instead come from a light javelin or dart. The remains of bows and arrows are, however, sometimes found in the lavishly equipped weapon graves. Gregory of Tours describes his old foe, Count Leudast, as carrying a quiver[25] but his description is somewhat stylised. Procopius' account of the Byzantine campaigns in Italy makes clear that the Ostrogothic warriors were commonly equipped with bows, and that their archery could be significant.[26] Visigothic law also implies that archery was important; as we saw in chapter 3, slaves brought to the army were to be equipped with bows; legal evidence from the Lombard kingdom of Italy likewise suggests that warriors who did not own a horse should bring a bow; and Carolingian Frankish capitularies imply that archery featured in their tactical planning.[27] Sometimes the capitulary evidence, which requires Frankish nobles to appear at military musters with the usual heavy cavalry equipment and a bow and quiver of arrows, has been assumed to mean that the cavalryman brought along a bow-armed dismounted retainer. However, this assumption stems from modern ideas about rigid functional distinctions between 'cavalry' and 'infantry', 'light infantry' and main line-of-battle troops. The trained early medieval warrior was expected to be a master of numerous skills, including mounted and dismounted, distant and close-quarters fighting.

Evidence of archery is rarer in early Anglo-Saxon cemeteries.[28] Härke mapped thirty-seven finds of arrows or the remains of bows in early Anglo-Saxon England, but few of these were from modern, 'scientifically' excavated sites, and those which were were from child burials.[29] This differs interestingly from the continental situation. None the less the symbolic nature of the grave-goods display ought to imply that archery had at least some significance on the post-Roman British battlefield. It is possible that Anglo-Saxon archery played a minor role and was practised by young men or adolescents (*geoguþ*) who had not yet acquired full warrior status.

Shields

For defence against the weapons just described, warriors relied upon a shield,[30] in this period almost invariably round, or perhaps oval; the classic high medieval knight's 'kite shield' did not come into use in the west until after the close of our period, possibly adapted from the Byzantine 'teardrop shields' depicted in manuscripts from the mid-tenth century. As far as can be ascertained, most shields seem to have been constructed as flat boards. Shields appear to have been less commonly convex than the manuscript and other pictorial evidence would imply; the apparent convex shape may be a convention for depicting flat shields from the side. Lightly convex circular shields are, nevertheless, known from sites such as Niederstotzingen in southern Germany,[31] and evidence suggests that convex shields became more common through our period. According to some of the carved stones, Pictish shields could be rectangular, sometimes with projecting, rounded corners.[32]

A circular hole was left in the centre of the shield, and a grip placed across this. The fist holding the grip was then protected by a metal dome, or boss, which covered the hole. The shield-boss is the principal datable element of early medieval shields. Most shields were held by this single 'fist grip', with the board perpendicular to the axis of the fore-arm, and thus differed from earlier and later shields where the board was held by passing the fore-arm through two small loops and gripping the second, laying the shield flat along the fore-arm. The single grip behind the boss precludes a small loop for the fore-arm, as this would make the shield very uncomfortable to carry, bending the fist back at the wrist. It does, however, allow the shield to be moved about freely, and the iron boss could be used to punch the enemy. A larger, looser fore-arm loop may nevertheless have been used, to prevent the shield from being dropped completely, and perhaps to permit it to be slung or suspended over the shoulder or from the saddle bow.

Many sixth-century shield-bosses from Germany, northern Gaul and Britain terminate in a circular disc, rather like a golf tee. This was probably designed to catch the blades of enemy weapons.[33] When coupled with the fact that earlier post-Roman shields in northern Europe appear to have been smaller than later examples[34] this seems likely to suggest that sixth-century fighting styles may have been rather looser. Some other evidence supports this idea. Seventh-century bosses become longer, and lose the terminal disc. Viking shield-bosses are simple domes. Shields, contrary to many popular reconstructions and illustrations, do not seem to have had broad metal rims, though their edges may have been bound in leather.

It seems likely that the shield was painted with designs identifying its owner. The Welsh epic, the *Gododdin*, mentions lime-washed white shields on several occasions.[35] When combined with decoration of those metallic fittings visible on the shield's surface, including decorated, inlaid metal ornaments fixed to it, such as found at Sutton Hoo in England, and at various sites on the Continent,[36] the shield was probably an important indicator of status. Shields may well have been hacked away in combat, and thus have been reasonably expendable items; the final line of the *Hildebrandslied* mentions how the participants in the tragic fight between father and son fought until their shields were 'ground away by weapons' and the motif occurs in much later Norse literature too. Anglo-Saxon poetry frequently mentions the shattering or splintering of shields, usually in the context, however, of the defeat of an army, and especially (and plausibly!) as a circumstance in which a warrior might be killed. In the elegy composed for him, Duke Eric of Friuli was killed 'his shield having been shattered'.[37] That this is more than a simple literary device is suggested by the *Annals of St-Bertin's* invaluable reference to shield-sellers in the baggage train of Charles the Bald's army.[38] None of this disproves the notion that shields were elaborately painted and decorated, however. The Roman army's shields – no more indestructible than those of the early Middle Ages – were very intricately painted with designs specific to particular units. We must, furthermore, remember the psychological value of weaponry. The impact of facing a row of brightly painted and distinctive shields – especially if designs were known to belong to renowned warriors or war-leaders – must have been very daunting.

Armour

The question of defensive armour for the head and body is a vexed one. Contemporary written sources imply that helmets and armour were quite plentiful. Written sources refer fairly frequently to helmets and armour, although often in rather stylised fashion. Agathias states that armour was rare in Frankish armies in Italy.[39] He was, however, a prisoner of the traditions of Greek ethnography, which demanded that northern 'barbarians' like the Franks be described as half-naked, fur-clad savages. Gregory of Tours describes his arch enemy, Count Leudast, as wearing body armour and a helmet, carrying sword, shield, lance and quiver. His language is highly classical, however, and makes little sense if taken too literally. Nevertheless, he uses one of these phrases about armour to describe a Lombard champion in the Frankish invasion of Italy in 590,[40] and in several other instances mentions body armour; in at least one case it is clear that he means mail.[41] In the list of items given in *Ripuarian Law* referred to above, mention is made of the *byrnie* (mail shirt) and 'leggings', which would seem to represent some sort of protection for the legs – perhaps the splint greaves[42] which are known from other parts of the early medieval world. Late Lombard legislation required that the strike force of the armies of the kingdom of Italy be armoured, and Carolingian Frankish legislation makes a similar point. In Spain, as we have seen, even some slaves brought to the army were required to be equipped with armour.[43] In Britain, the poetry of Aneirin, purporting to belong to the years around AD 600, though of rather uncertain date (and possibly later than the close of our period), mentions armour on a number of occasions and, from the use of 'blue' or 'blue-grey' as a synonym for armour, it would seem that this was of metallic construction.[44]

Thuringian Law mentions that the eldest son was to inherit a father's mailshirt.[45] This would imply that there might be one suit of armour per household. Nevertheless, it should not be assumed that such armour was universal. As was noted in chapter 4, Carolingian kings required that certain ecclesiastical institutions furnish them with mailcoats. Whilst this must, on the one hand, have meant that Carolingian royal armies were fairly well equipped with armour, it also implies that a large number of those who answered the kingly call to arms would turn up without armour, and that there was a concern to ensure that the royal troops were better protected than their enemies (also suggesting that body armour was not universal).[46]

Body armour was often of mail construction, but lamellar armour, constructed from many small iron plates laced together at the top and bottom, has been found at a number of Merovingian period sites in France and Germany.[47] This type of armour was probably easier to make than mail and may well have been much more common than is often supposed. It was used by the late Roman army in the west and appears to be depicted on the seal ring of the late fifth-century Frankish king, Childeric I.[48]

Manuscript illuminations support the idea that ownership of helmets and body armour was common, though far from universal. As one might expect, helmets are more often shown than body armour, but the latter is nevertheless frequent. In this, these illustrations differ from their classical models so we can perhaps take this evidence seriously. It has often been thought that Carolingian manuscripts depict the use of scale armour, but it seems far more likely that the apparent 'scales' are in fact the artist's way of portraying interlinked mail rings. Stone carvings frequently show helmets,[49] and not uncommonly show body armour as well.[50] To this list we might add other forms of illustration. The Franks Casket clearly shows helmets and mail armour.[51] An incised Merovingian phalera from Ittenheim (Alsace) depicts a spearman in helmet and, apparently, a muscled leather cuirass with pteruges[52] whilst the plaque from Stabio in Switzerland shows an armoured warrior on horseback, wielding his lance two-handed, and the Agilulf plaque from Val di Nievole shows the king wearing a helmet and lamellar armour, and is itself apparently from a lamellar helmet like the Niederstotzingen helmet (see below).[53] Another depiction of lamellar comes from the Isola Rizza dish, which depicts a lance-armed armoured horseman riding down two (possibly Lombard) foot soldiers.[54] The list could be greatly extended but the essential point is that early medieval artists, working in various artistic traditions and in diverse media, all imagined the warrior as wearing a helmet and, very often, armour.

Armour survives rarely from this period, however, superficially contradicting the written and pictorial evidence, but the archaeological data, as mentioned, cannot be taken simplistically as a representative sample. Arguments that armour was simply too expensive to bury are unconvincing. They are in glaring contradiction with the fact that, for the late fifth to seventh centuries, we have about three dozen helmets from western Europe. All but two or three are 'top of the range' expensive decorated helmets. If helmets were too expensive to bury, why do almost all of the known buried examples come from the costliest end of the scale? Once again we run up against the fact that grave deposits are the result of ritual, and armour may only exceptionally have had a symbolic role in such rituals. As mentioned, helmets and body armour are found most commonly on the fringes of the Merovingian world, where graves were often more lavishly, and competitively, furnished, underlining the point that we need to understand the political and social context of grave-goods, and not just read them off as mirrors of a static reality.

Expensive helmets of the late fifth to seventh centuries were commonly of a type called *Spangenhelme* ('clasp-helmets', though the German term is always used), where the bowl of the helmet was made of several parts, held together by reinforcing clasps which covered the joins. Many examples had mail aventails protecting the neck.[55] The helmets are generally believed to have been made in Ostrogothic Italy, but are found throughout Europe, probable fragments of one even being found as far north as Dumfriesshire.[56] It has been claimed that it was still being worn in the Carolingian period[57] but, although helmets which are technically *Spangenhelme* are known, the precise form known in the sixth century seems to have died out in the early seventh century. Although the gradual decline of the furnished burial rite makes the survival of helmets less common, the surviving examples from the period after c.625 are of rather different types, as are those depicted in art. One ninth-century *Spangenhelm* has been found at Groningen in the Netherlands.[58] This is made up of four plates clasped together, with a further band running around the base of the helmet 'bowl'. The latter has a very slight brim, and the rivets used are tall and pointed, giving the helmet a distinctive 'spiny' appearance. The original also had cheek plates.

In northern Europe a different helmet tradition emerged, developing out of two-piece late Roman 'ridge helmets', where the bowl of the helmet is made of two pieces, held together by a clasp which takes the form of a ridge. This type is exemplified by the helmets of the Vendel-Valsgärde culture in Sweden, and Sutton Hoo in England.[59] These often sport elaborate facemasks as well as protection for the neck. In England a helmet found at Benty Grange was apparently made largely of bone plates within an iron frame, and carried a boar crest.[60] A very similar type of helmet has recently been discovered in Northamptonshire and dubbed (from the firm on whose land it was found and who are paying for the restoration) the 'Pioneer Helmet', and an object found in a woman's grave at Guilden Morden seems to be the boar crest of a third.[61] An illumination in a St Petersburg manuscript of the poems of Paulinus of Nola also shows this type of helmet and, given the symbolic importance of the boar in 'Celtic' as well as 'Anglo-Saxon' areas of Britain, this could be an insular British type, common to 'Britons' and 'Saxons'.[62] However, helmets with boar crests and cheek guards are also shown on the plaques from Torslunda (Sweden), though they are somewhat larger.[63]

A currently unique helmet was found at Niederstotzingen (Baden-Württemburg) and dates to c.600.[64] This was made up of many overlapping long iron bands, laid vertically and laced together, had a nasal guard, cheek-plates and mail aventail, and seems to have been inspired by Avar 'steppes' fashions. After the seventh century, with the widespread abandonment of grave-good deposits, our evidence for helmets dries up. In the eighth century the best known northern helmet is now that found at Coppergate in York, with its long nasal and mail aventail.[65] The probably slightly earlier 'Pioneer Helmet' is of comparable design, but with a boar crest, and similar helmets may be depicted on the Franks Casket and Aberlemno Stone. A famous Viking-age helmet is known from Gjurmundbu in Norway, which had spectacle-like rings protecting the eyes.[66] Carolingian manuscripts appear to show a two-piece helmet held together by a single clasp running across the dome of the helmet, and with another reinforcing band running around the bottom of the cap.[67] Helmets seem to have been gradually developing into the simple and effective 'Norman' types depicted on the Bayeux Tapestry: conical skullcaps with reinforcing bands or clasps. The Bayeux Tapestry helmets' famous nasal bars may, however, not have appeared until after the end of our period – or rather reappeared, since the 'Pioneer' and Coppergate helmets and those depicted on a number of carvings, not least the Franks Casket and the Hornhausen Stone, also have nasals. Throughout the period many more warriors must have worn helmets of simpler construction like those found at Bretzenheim near Mainz or Trivières in Belgium, or even simple iron skull-caps. Others still may have worn leather helmets or cloth caps with iron reinforcing bands.[68]

Where metallic armour was not available, warriors probably made use of boiled leather or padded protection; such armour appears to be depicted in contemporary manuscripts. As we shall see in chapter 9, early medieval battle was a horrific business, fought out, especially from the seventh century, mostly at very close quarters. It would seem foolish to enter such an affray without some form of protection, at least for the head. Ancient Greek warfare between phalanxes of hoplites was probably, in some ways at least, quite similar to combat between early medieval spearmen drawn up in 'shieldwalls' and as the classical period progressed Greek warriors increasingly abandoned heavy body armour, first in favour of linen armour and then, often, of no body armour at all. They did not, however, discard the helmet. A helmet and a large shield were held to be sufficient protection in close combat between densely drawn-up bodies of troops, whilst also allowing speed of movement to close with lighter armed missile troops. However, heavier body-armour reappeared in the Hellenistic and Roman periods. In the end, attitudes to body-armour are neither timeless, nor technologically determined, nor governed by supposedly eternal, 'logical' exigencies of particular types of warfare; they are culturally specific. In most times and places covered by our period it would seem that warriors wanted to acquire as much armoured protection as possible, but this need not have been universal. Irish warriors, for example, seem to have scorned heavy armour in this period. Another factor to consider, in connection with this, is the type of warfare. Highly mobile raiding warfare or skirmishing probably required less (or lighter) armour than a major campaign which was likely to result in a set-piece encounter.[69] It may in part have been the predominance of this type of warfare in Ireland that led to the Irish attitude to armour.

There could be change through time, too. The possible tactical changes in warfare around 600, towards less open and fluid warfare,[70] may have led to changes in attitudes to armour but whether they did, and whether towards more or (with perhaps less likelihood) less protection, is unknown. Nicholas Brooks, in two interesting articles, suggested that the late tenth-century English army was lacking in defensive armour until a general reform of the early eleventh century.[71] Individually, the evidence cited in support of the argument is not decisive, but cumulatively it is extremely suggestive and the claim is difficult to refute, also finding some support in late Anglo-Saxon manuscript illuminations. However, we should not assume that this state of affairs reached far back into Anglo-Saxon history. As has been argued repeatedly above and as will be further expounded below, Anglo-Saxon armies did not differ greatly from their contemporaries in mainland Europe in the fifth to ninth centuries and, as has been shown, these armies were on the whole well armoured. Furthermore, Anglo-Saxon armies generally acquitted themselves well in ninth-century warfare against Viking armies that posed considerable problems for contemporary, well-armoured Frankish forces. They did so, moreover, as will be discussed in chapter 9, in what was often dismounted close combat, wherein armour was especially valuable.

Body armour, however, was hot and uncomfortable. Regino of Prüm says as much when he describes the death of Robert the Strong at Brissarthe.[72] Thinking that the Vikings he was attacking had been safely penned into a church, Robert, 'boiling in the great heat' (*nimio calore exaestuans*), took off his helmet and mail shirt in order to 'cool down for a little while' (*paulisper refrigeraretur*). At this point the Vikings launched a counter-attack and Robert, running up to help without helmet or armour, was killed. In the generation following the conquest of the north of England (more or less complete by the mid 950s at the latest), Anglo-Saxon forces were rarely engaged in warfare other than tribute-taking and excursions against the generally light-armed and mobile Welsh and Scots. With that in mind, it seems plausible that, in the type of expedition to which English armies had become accustomed in the latter half of the tenth century, uncomfortable armour may have become unpopular or even unfashionable and been discarded. This does not imply that the same was true in the wars of Alfred, Edward the Elder or Athelstan.

On the whole, though, when we look at the decorative metalwork, often of breathtaking complexity, sponsored by post-Roman aristocrats and their followers, and remember the technical complexity of the pattern-welded sword, the argument sometimes presented that metal helmets and armour were too complex or expensive for the early medieval west is very unconvincing.

Horses and horse furniture

The final element of the early medieval warrior's equipment was his horse. The question of the extent to which post-Roman armies relied on cavalry on the battlefield will be further considered in chapter 9. For now, though, it will suffice to say that almost everywhere from Scandinavia and Scotland down to the Mediterranean coasts, most early medieval warriors at least campaigned on horseback. Whether or not, or in what circumstances, they dismounted to fight, the bulk of post-Roman armies travelled by horse.[73]

Little is known of the appearance of the post-Roman war-horse, however. It does not seem that the fully-fledged later medieval war-horse had yet been bred. It is difficult to say very much about saddles, as few examples are known. From what is known they appear to have been quite simple, though the front panel could be quite high. The front pommel was sometimes adorned with decorative plaques. Indeed the harnesses of early medieval horses were often vehicles for the display of wealth, with decorated gold, silver and bronze plaques.[74] The bridle was similarly decorated, and sometimes the occasion for real inventiveness. Examples are known of the use of boar tusks and other horns to adorn bridles, to attempt to give the horse a fearsome, monstrous appearance.[75] Early in the period, boar tusks also seem occasionally to have been mounted on the horse's harness so as to project from the horse's chest.[76] A good rider controls his horse with his knees rather than the reins, though, enabling freer use of his arms in combat. Simple spurs were used, often only one, if we can judge from grave assemblages (though the deposit of a single spur may have been symbolic and representative). Stirrups appear to have been introduced into Europe from the late sixth century by the Avars, although they did not catch on everywhere for a long time. Carolingian manuscripts still appear to depict some warriors riding without stirrups.[77] The importance of the stirrup in warfare has in some ways been overstated. Lynn White Jr[78] proposed that the introduction of the stirrup was a key technological innovation allowing the appearance of the true medieval knight employing the crashing shock charge with couched[79] lance. This thesis has been rejected.[80] Experiments have shown that the stirrup does not materially affect the ability to perform such a charge. The key change was the development of the saddle, with very pronounced front and, especially, back panels which gripped the rider in place, and this did not take place until after the end of our period. By concentrating on the frontal charge with couched lance, however, the debate has possibly missed the point of the stirrup's advantages. The stirrup does help keep a rider in the saddle and permits a warrior to strike with much more force to his sides or the rear during a mêlée. It also makes downward sword-strokes more powerful, enabling the mounted warrior to stand in his stirrups. Stirrups can also make long rides less tiring by enabling 'light riding', where the rider stands in the stirrups for certain beats of the horse's gait. Finally, the stirrup allows easier mounting and dismounting.[81]

Horses were not armoured in this period. Horse armour had been used on occasion in the later Roman Empire and in the Sassanid Persian Empire, and continued to be used by some élite units of the Byzantine army and their eastern enemies. There is no evidence of true horse-armour in the early medieval west, however. It was suggested that the Bretons used horse armour,[82] but this suggestion stemmed from a misreading of Ermold the Black's poem on Louis the Pious.[83] A small piece of armour for a horse's forehead has been found in a grave in the Netherlands, but this is bronze, and may have been as much for show as defence.[84]

Counting the cost

It is difficult to know how much the panoply of an early medieval warrior cost. A text often cited is *Ripuarian Law*, which sets out a price for the items of a warrior's equipment. Here, the cost of a warrior's equipment comes to 40 *solidi*.[85] As has often been done, one can compare this with the cost of a cow in the same list. If one does, this comes to twenty oxen or forty cows – a small herd. Later, in Carolingian times, twelve wheaten loaves cost a penny and a horse seems to have cost about 10 shillings.[86] At *Ripuarian Law's* prices, this would make a sword worth 1,008 wheaten loaves and, by ninth-century standards, a top-quality horse the equivalent of 2,280 loaves! It is difficult to know what to make of such comparisons. As noted, swords are not uncommon in the sixth-century cemeteries of northern Gaul.[87] This evidence implies that sword ownership was fairly widespread and probably that such people could afford to dispose of swords in public ritual (which does not imply that those items not disposed of in ritual were too expensive to be buried). As we have seen, the early medieval economy was not a modern commodity economy, working according to laws of supply and demand and prices based upon labour and material costs. Nor was it monetised in the modern sense. This multilayered economy was very often socially embedded; artefacts were imbued with value according to their social usage, often to their history as objects (the renown of previous owners, for example), the prestige of the donor, when they were received as gifts, and so on. Thus it is clear that we cannot similarly convert the value of a sword into that of a number of cows by reference to a standard scale represented by a single currency, in the same way that today one might (were one so inclined) represent the value of a house as a multiple of the value of a chocolate bar by reference to pounds sterling or US dollars, in which salaries are paid. The possession of a sword, especially if it had once been given by a king or renowned magnate, marked one out as the member of a particular, prestigious social group and as a person who might be involved in high-status activities or prestigious political assemblies such as warfare and the army, in a way that ownership of a herd of cattle – or a barn full of wheaten loaves – did not. It would be mistaken to think that a full set of equipment – helmet, armour, sword, shield, spears and harnessed war-horse – did not represent a huge outlay, beyond the means of most of the population, but one should beware of simplistic statements which equate the cost of such gear with the income from a small village.

Nevertheless, some values emerge from study of the charters and other texts. In ninth-century Breton charters, horses seem to be worth about 9–10 *solidi* (presumably a unit of account actually paid in silver *denarii* – pennies), and a horse and a mail coat were held to cost 20 *solidi*.[88] Similar values are found in slightly earlier Bavarian charters. A document of 829 mentions a horse worth 10 *solidi* whereas one of 828 refers to a horse, clothes and a flitch of bacon valued at 12 *solidi*.[89] Charlemagne imposed an annual tribute of a horse worth a pound (20 *solidi*) on the bishop of Konstanz and the abbot of St-Gallen.[90] This must have represented the very best kind of warhorse and been part of Charlemagne's concern that his troops be the best equipped. Though there are exceptions, the usual price of a horse seems to have remained fairly stable, around 10 *solidi*, throughout the period.[91] Nevertheless, these are significant sums usually seen in the context of the sale of parcels of land.[92] At the same time, it is worth remembering that many warriors would have been far less well equipped than this. None the less, those who could afford it doubtless spent as much as they could, not just on the weaponry and armour itself but also on its embellishment, and on fine, brightly coloured clothing. They did this for very good reasons.

Practicality: the moral and the physical

The Ostrogothic King Totila's change from very highly decorated parade armour, which certainly left an impression on his enemies, to simpler battlefield equipment before the battle of Busta Gallorum (552) is an interesting possible exception,[93] but on the whole early medieval military equipment cannot be divided into 'practical' and 'parade' items. The battlefield effectiveness of weaponry is as much about its moral effect on the enemy as about its physical efficiency. Even in modern periods, it is known that fearsome instruments of firepower – multibarrelled rocket-launchers, Stuka dive-bombers, napalm – have had a greater impact in terms of their effect on enemy morale than through their sheer killing-power. Similarly, the impression of rows of gleaming bayonets in the Napoleonic and other wars was considerable, frequently inducing troops to flee before actual contact, but the numbers of troops killed by bayonet wounds was, where figures are available, minimal when compared to other causes of death. In fact, in Napoleon's Egyptian campaign of 1798, such was the quality of French bayonets that the soldiers were able to bend them into hooks to fish in the Nile for dead Mamelukes to strip of their valuables. None of that reduced the psychological impact of several hundred such bayonets bearing down upon an enemy. For all those reasons, highly ornate sword-hilts, decorated helmets (especially with face-masks, eye-rings, nasal bars and mail aventails), painted and adorned shields, inlaid spearheads, and gleaming bridles with boar tusks – and with the overall effect doubtless rounded off with feather and horsehair plumes, which increase the apparent size of the warrior – were all intensely, grimly, practical items. The Sutton Hoo helmet may have been uncomfortable to wear, but it would be very fearsome to behold, especially when its wearer was surrounded by other well-armoured and equipped warriors. Victims of modern crime attest that when an assailant disguises or conceals his or her face, even with a simple stocking mask, it makes him or her particularly frightening. This fact was surely not lost on the early medieval warrior. The extra protection afforded by the Gjurmundbu helmet's eye-rings was minimal, but they create an imposing effect. Items like these proclaimed the approach of a renowned, experienced and fearsome warrior, or at least aimed at giving the enemy the impression that the approaching soldier was experienced and formidable.

9

BATTLE

The problems of the sources

Of all the problems facing the student of early medieval warfare, the most intractable is that of finding out what actually happened on the battlefield; here our perennial problem of the inadequacy of the sources becomes particularly acute. All we can say with any certainty is that the early medieval battle was a dense concentration of the most intense and extreme human emotions: men killed and maimed, died and experienced horrendous pain, felt terror and rage, showed bravery, heroism, cruelty and cowardice.

The sources' accounts are usually stereotypical; descriptions of battles were very often the occasion for archaic language, literary borrowings and other devices designed to show off the writer's skill. Asser[1] describes King Alfred attacking the Viking Great Army at Edington *cum densa testudine* ('in a dense testudo'), but it is unlikely that any precise formation is meant, or that any significance is to be deduced from the fact that the Vikings are not described as forming a *testudo*, as they are earlier in the work (see below). The word is chosen simply to illustrate classical learning, though it may have been selected because it was a reasonable approximation to a ninth-century shield-wall. It is certainly not possible to deduce that the English had actually formed a Roman *testudo* (a formation where legionaries' shields were locked to the front, sides and above their heads, to make a shelter almost impervious to missile fire), and possibly not even that the English were fighting on foot.

At the beginning of the era, we still have narrative political and military histories written in the classical tradition. However, in the accounts of East Roman or Byzantine writers like Procopius and Agathias, describing wars in Italy against Goths, Franks and Lombards, the use of archaic words and phrases is especially pronounced. These writers wrote in a tradition which held it as axiomatic that one must write in language as close as possible to the great practitioners of classical narrative history: Herodotus, Thucydides and Polybius. Words unknown to these models, thus all Latin or Christian terms, were to be avoided if at all possible, or introduced with tortuous circumlocutions.[2] Words and even whole phrases from their ancient models were to be used freely and without acknowledgement; their educated audience would immediately pick up on both reference and resonance. In Latin as well as Greek sources, 'new' peoples were given old names, and often given the characteristics associated with the earlier people. Thus Huns and Goths are called 'Scythians' in fourth-century sources; the sixth-century Avars, on the other hand, are called 'Huns'; eventually the Magyars were called Avars![3] Not all such borrowing was slavish and unimaginative 'lexicon-bashing'. Old words were used where they were appropriate, and could also be turned around and given new, sometimes ironic meanings.[4] Nevertheless, this shows the difficulty in trying to be too precise in the interpretation of these sources.

Towards the end of the era covered by this volume, fuller annalistic accounts also provide more detailed discussions. However, even these are often stereo-typical. Consider the following, unusually detailed, examples:

> After breaking off these negotiations, Louis and Charles rose at dawn, occupied the peak of a mountain near Lothar's camp with about one third of their army and waited for Lothar's arrival and the striking of the second hour, as their men had sworn. When both had come, they fought a violent battle at the brook of the Burgundians. Louis and Lothar were engaged in heavy fighting in a place called *Brittas*; there Lothar was overcome and fled. The troops which Charles confronted at the place called *Fagit* immediately took flight. But the part of our army which attacked Adalhard and others at *Solennat*, and to which I gave vigorous assistance with God's help, fought bitterly. There the fight was a draw, but in the end all of Lothar's party fled.[5]

> [F]our days later, with all their might and in a determined frame of mind, they advanced to battle against the aforesaid army at a place called Ashdown (which in Latin is *mons fraxini* [hill of the Ash]). But the Pagans, splitting up into two *turmae* [lit. units], organised *testudines* of equal size (for they then had two kings and a large number of *comites* [counts – earls]), assigning the core of the army to the two kings and the rest to all the *comites*. When the Christians saw this they too split their army into two *turmae* in exactly the same way, and established *testudines* no less keenly. But as I have heard from truthful authorities who saw it, Alfred and his men reached the battlefield sooner and in better order: for his brother, King Æthelræd, was still in his tent at prayer, hearing Mass and declaring firmly that he would not leave that place alive before the priest had finished Mass, and that he would not forsake divine service for that of men; and he did what he said. The faith of the king counted for much with the Lord, as will be shown more clearly in what follows.

> Now the Christians had decided that King Æthelræd and his forces should engage the two Pagan kings in battle, while his brother Alfred and his *cohortes* should submit to the fortunes of war against all the

Pagan *comites*. Matters were thus firmly arranged on both sides; but since the king was lingering still longer in prayer and the Pagans were ready and had reached the battlefield more quickly, Alfred (then *secundarius* ['heir apparent']) could not oppose the enemy battle lines any longer without either retreating from the battlefield or attacking the enemy forces before his brother's arrival on the scene. He finally deployed the Christian forces against the hostile armies, as he had previously intended (even though the king had not yet come), and acting courageously, like a wild boar, supported by divine counsel and strengthened by divine help, when he had closed up the *testudo* in proper order, he moved his army without delay against the enemy.

But it should be made clear at this point, to those unaware of the fact, that the battlefield was not equally advantageous to both contending parties. The Pagans had taken the higher position first, and the Christians were deploying their battle-line from a lower position. A rather small and solitary thorn-tree (which I have seen myself with my own eyes) grew there, around which the opposing battle lines clashed violently, with loud shouting from all, one side acting wrongfully and the other set to fight for life, loved ones and country. When both sides had been fighting to and fro, resolutely and exceedingly ferociously, for quite a long time, the Pagans (by divine judgement) were unable to withstand the Christians' onslaught any longer; and when a great part of their forces had fallen, they took to ignominious flight. One of the two Pagan kings and five *comites* were cut down in that place, and many thousands on the Pagan side were slain there too, or rather over the whole broad expanse of Ashdown, scattered everywhere, far and wide: so King Bagsecg was killed, and Sidroc the Old *Comes*, Sidroc the Younger *Comes*, Osbearn *Comes*, Fræna *Comes*, and Harold *Comes*; and the entire Pagan army was put to flight, right on until nightfall and into the following day, until such time as they reached the stronghold from which they had come. The Christians followed them till nightfall, cutting them down on all sides.[6]

Both examples are from the ninth century, albeit separated by thirty years, and both are near contemporary with the events related. Indeed the first is one of the period's very few eyewitness accounts of a battle by an active participant: it is Nithard's account of the battle of Fontenoy (841), with whose writing this book opened. Asser, the author of the second passage, about the battle of Ashdown (871), makes clear use of first-hand reports, and has visited the scene of the battle. Asser's is possibly the longest Latin description of a battle written in this period. The accounts are similar in many respects. Those who arrive at the field first take control of the high ground; the armies form up in several divisions which square up against each other; these then come into contact and apparently fight long and hard; the collapse of part of the line seems to spell doom for the whole, and pursuit can be close and bloody. However, the sources say very little about how the fighting was done, whether on foot or on horseback, whether with swords, spears, axes, bows or javelins, or whether mainly hand-to-hand or using missiles from a distance, and they describe no manoeuvres. Their similarity is especially interesting given that Fontenoy was fought by Carolingian Frankish forces, which we assume to have been largely mounted, whereas Ashdown was fought out between English and Viking armies usually believed to have been dismounted infantry, with no horsemen. Similar stereotyping is to be found in other genres of writing, such as Old English 'heroic' poetry.[7] Most accounts of battles in chronicles or other narrative sources offer far less detail than is to be gleaned from these two accounts. In fact, Lars Lönnroth's fine comment on early skaldic verse may stand for the textual study of almost all early medieval accounts of battle:

> [I]n most cases, we only learn, after having straightened out the inverted syntax and deciphered the intricate metaphors, that some great ruler, attended by brave warriors, defeated his enemies at such-and-such a place, thus making the life of local corpse-eating wolves and ravens a little happier.[8]

The standardised and laconic nature of battle descriptions makes it difficult to make precise statements about tactics, and received wisdom, such as just referred to, about whether armies did or did not use cavalry, is often based upon no more than *a priori* assumption.

Cavalry and infantry

We may in fact begin with a discussion of this issue, which is of double historiographical significance. In the first place, as has been mentioned, it has been of concern to those interested in the development of 'feudalism', with it being argued that the greater need for mounted and heavily armed troops led to significant social change.[9] The second instance is rather more parochial, though it has some connection to the first: there has been much argument over whether the Anglo-Saxons fought on foot or on horseback, and this in turn was part of the old debate about the Normans' introduction of 'feudalism' into England in 1066.[10] The broader debate has subsequently moved on, become much more refined and complex and left the issue of mounted warfare behind. Nevertheless the question of Old English mounted warfare has continued to provoke discussion.[11]

The viewpoints in these debates, like those in discussion of army size, are too rigidly held and stem from a series of presuppositions. The first is the anachronistic importation into the period of ideas about cavalry and infantry which derive ultimately from early modern and modern warfare. From the seventeenth century, if not earlier, regular armies were divided into formal regiments of cavalry and infantry with clearly defined tactical usages, weaponry, formations and drill. Infantry, obviously, could not fight on horseback, and cavalry rapidly saw it as beneath their dignity to fight on foot. A third category, troops who were mounted for mobility but who dismounted to fight, was introduced in the form of dragoons. Though, as is clear from the history of the British army, dragoons eventually became fully-fledged cavalry, the notion of the 'mounted infantryman' resurfaced during the American Civil War and the Boer War and those twentieth-century cavalry who retained their horses (rather than being converted into tank regiments) soon adopted this role. Early medieval warriors, however, did not see themselves as divided into such clear-cut categories. The anachronistic formal concept of the 'mounted infantryman' in particular has bedevilled the study of early medieval, especially Anglo-Saxon, warfare. There were troops who owned horses and those who did not, and there were military tasks which were better suited to dismounted warriors than to those on horseback. Similarly, some situations called for combat on horse; in other circumstances a commander might think it better to dismount. A warrior would expect to be able to perform most if not all of these tasks and fight in all circumstances. In what follows I have used the words 'cavalry' and 'infantry', but these should be understood simply as meaning 'warriors fighting mounted' and 'warriors fighting on foot' respectively.

The idea that Anglo-Saxon warriors travelled on horseback but fought on foot is based upon several preconceived notions, and arises especially from the long isolation of Anglo-Saxon history from studies of the contemporary continent. To evaluate the theory of the 'Anglo-Saxon mounted infantryman', we have to leave our chronological period and move on, temporarily, into the tenth and even eleventh centuries. R. Allen Brown declared that there was 'more than sufficient' evidence to demonstrate this notion[12] but in fact the support for his position is flimsy indeed. The idea derives very largely from the indisputable fact that the Anglo-Saxons fought on foot at Hastings in 1066. At Hastings, however, King Harold's position was at the top of a steep ridge. Facing, as he knew from having campaigned with them, the Normans' excellent shock cavalry, he chose a position to negate their knights, and dismounted his army. As the unusually long, hard-fought and bloody course of the battle shows, his decision was a wise one, which very nearly proved successful. That apart, there are only three battles, all of the tenth or eleventh century, whose descriptions support the idea that Anglo-Saxon troops fought dismounted. The first is the battle of Hereford in 1055.[13] Here the English army fled, according to the *Anglo-Saxon Chronicle*, 'because it was on horseback'. However, this statement may mean simply that the English *were able to flee* because they were on horseback. After all, at Maldon in 991 Earl Byrhtnoth had dismounted and sent away his troops' horses precisely because he wished to prevent flight. Much has been made of John of Worcester's twelfth-century gloss that the English fled at Hereford because they were fighting on horseback 'contrary to their custom'.

Yet John was writing sixty years after the event, when 'English' troops did indeed fight on foot, the army's mounted component being provided by the 'Norman' aristocracy. Furthermore, however, John says that 'Earl Ralph and his Frenchmen [Normans] began the flight.' Are we therefore to assume that the Normans were unused to mounted combat? Herefordshire is not prime cavalry terrain; a mounted force seems to have been caught at a disadvantage by the Welsh and put to flight. The instance is hardly decisive.

Fifty years before Hastings, the English suffered another catastrophic defeat at Ashingdon at the hands of Cnut's Danish army. The author of the *Encomium Emmae Reginae* states that this was a hard-fought infantry battle. The phrase used, *prelium pedestre*, probably comes from Suetonius' *Lives of the Twelve Caesars*.[14] The Encomiast seems to have been aware of this work; certainly he was familiar with work which did make use of Suetonius. Nevertheless, he has significantly omitted the phrase *ac equestre* (and on horseback) from his model, and this probably implies that the battle was fought on foot. There is another side to the problem, however. *Pedestre* means not simply on foot, but also, by extension, on land. In the previous chapter the Danish army has disembarked from its ships, so the Encomiast may have adapted Suetonius' phrase to mean that this was a hard-fought land battle. Certainly that was how he used the word in chapter 1.4 of his work.

The context is, once again, important, as it is in the third instance, the battle of Maldon (991), where an English army was (again) defeated by an invading force, this time of Norwegians and Danes. The source is the elegiac poem on the battle, composed some time after the event.[15] Earl Byrhtnoth, commanding the Essex *fyrd*, dismounted and sent the horses to the rear. The implication is that up until that point the earl and his warriors stayed with their horses, and presumably that mounted combat was an option. The Vikings, as was also the case at Ashingdon, had just disembarked from their ships and may not yet have acquired many horses. They would be fighting on foot. As Hastings demonstrated, a dismounted army of well-equipped and experienced infantry was difficult to defeat with cavalry. Thus the horses were sent away. There may have been other reasons for Byrhtnoth's decision. Long before, at the battle of Strasbourg (357), the Alamannic nobles had been faced with grumbling foot soldiers saying that if things went wrong it would be all right for the mounted nobility, who would be able to escape.[16] Thus the king of the Alamans and his cavalry dismounted to fight with the rest of the army. Similarly, at the siege of Rome (537) the poor performance of the Roman infantry was explained by the fact that their officers 'alone ride on horseback in the battle-line and are not willing to consider the fortunes of war as shared by all, but as a general rule each one of them by himself takes to flight before the struggle begins'.[17] As a result most of the infantry had acquired horses and 'were now mounted'.[18] Perhaps the distinction between mounted and dismounted troops had already begun to blur. Again the Roman solution was for the infantry to be led into combat by trusted leaders on foot.

As well as demonstrating the fact that the commanders were going to lead by example, dismounting an army also showed, by abrogating the ability to flee, that the army intended to fight to the death. In the Gothic Götterdämmerung, the battle of *Mons Lactarius* (Milky Mountain), the final, climactic engagement of the Gothic wars, King Teïas ordered his troops to fight on foot.[19] This displayed the Goths' decision to fight to the last breath and the hard-fought nature of the battle, which went on tooth and nail for a day even after Teïas was killed, showed that this was no empty gesture. Byrhtnoth may well have had a similar display in mind, demonstrating to his own troops that he would share the risks of battle, and making clear to the Vikings his intention to stand, fight and, if need be, die where he was. Byrhtnoth had decided upon committing his army to a decisive battle. Indeed, if he were to prevent further harrying by the more mobile Viking army, Byrhtnoth *had to* commit to a decisive battle. Thus he allowed the Viking army to cross from the island where it had encamped, across the causeway which the English had up to that point easily held against them, and on to the mainland. Although often criticised, and indeed a perilous strategy (as the outcome showed), Byrhtnoth was taking a calculated risk. If the Vikings lost they would have the sea to their backs, and no escape possible. Byrhtnoth also wished to show his determination; there would be no flight.

Thus none of the instances discussed above really demonstrates that the English always fought on foot; the laconic nature of almost all battle accounts means that the absence of many statements about cavalry (though, as we shall see, there are some) is hardly significant. In some of the cases just discussed the sources may be read in a different way and every battle had special circumstances which favoured dismounted combat. Given the scarcity of evidence, one might mischievously suggest that the Anglo-Saxons' defeat in every battle where they are specified to have fought on foot argues that they were better fighting mounted! There are two further possible instances. At the battles of Ashdown (871) and Edington (879), Asser describes Alfred's army, and at Ashdown the Vikings too, as forming a *testudo*.[20] Technically this is an infantry formation; it would certainly be an apt description of a densely packed early medieval shield-wall. However, as we have seen, classical Latin heavily influences Asser's language, so it is difficult to place much technical weight on the term. After all, he also describes the English and Vikings as being divided into *turmae*, which in technical classical usage meant cavalry units. If Asser wanted his term to convey the image of closely drawn up troops, as his use of the phrase *cum densa testudine* at Edington implies, this may suggest infantry but, as will become clear, it was thought that cavalry too should properly form up closely and advance slowly. It is impossible to reach a definite conclusion from this data. Two further pieces of evidence support the traditional view, however. The more suggestive of the two is the *Canterbury Hexateuch*, which juxtaposes two illustrations, one of an army riding and one showing them dismounted in the ensuing battle.[21] Secondly, the poem *Elene*, whilst making clear reference to horses in the army, and apparently warhorses at that, at the beginning of the campaign, does not refer to them during the battle (though it does not say that the army had dismounted or sent away its horses either).[22]

The four tenth- and eleventh-century examples discussed above have been enough to make historians generalise from their testimony and project the supposed fact of English dismounted combat back throughout the Anglo-Saxon period. Not only that, it has forced them to explain away all the evidence which describes Anglo-Saxon warriors on horseback, owning horses, and even fighting mounted, by reference to the anachronistic concept of the 'mounted infantryman'. Yet there is considerably more evidence for the idea that Anglo-Saxon warriors could fight mounted than there is for the idea that they always dismounted to fight. We may begin in the seventh century. There are Anglo-Saxon graves with horse-harness, and some accompanied by the interment of whole horses.[23] This is less common than on the Continent, but the Anglo-Saxon weapon burial ritual was, overall, less lavish than in the continental areas where horses and horse gear are found, so it is difficult to conclude very much from this. On the other hand, this does seem to indicate that the horse was considered an integral part of a warrior's equipment. This impression is only strengthened when we turn to the written evidence. As noted, Saint Cuthbert's 'secular dress' included horse and spear, the symbols of the aristocracy.[24] Other stories also illustrate that the Anglo-Saxon nobility and royalty were every bit as 'horsy' as their contemporary continental counterparts.[25] One of the very few stories to shed any light upon early Anglo-Saxon war demonstrates that this extended to warfare. When Ecgfrith of Northumbria defeated the Picts in 672, he did so with 'an army of horsemen'.[26] The same point is suggested by some of the early Welsh poetry, which refers to their apparently English enemies as on horseback.[27] The distances covered by early Anglo-Saxon armies suggest the use of horses, and so on. If we move later within the Anglo-Saxon period, there is clearer evidence yet. In 894, for example, Alfred's English army rode after, overtook and defeated a Danish force. The poem, *Maxims I*, states that 'an earl belongs on a charger's back; a mounted troop should ride in regular array, and the foot soldiers stand firm', which implies that both mounted and dismounted warriors took their place in an Old English army.[28] This impression is underlined by the poem on the great English victory at Brunanburh, which states that 'all through the day long the West Saxons in mounted troops pressed on in pursuit of the hostile peoples'.[29] By the eleventh century we even have legal requirement, as on the Continent, that a warrior's equipment include a horse.[30]

If we look at pictorial sources the argument is strengthened further. It has been suggested that the Pictish symbol stone at Aberlemno depicts the defeat of Ecgfrith's Northumbrian army at nearby Nechtansmere.[31] Though this cannot be proven, it seems likely and the stone certainly depicts the defeated side fighting on horseback. In the eighth century, the carved stone found at Repton portrays an armoured warrior on horseback.[32] Later Anglo-Saxon manuscript illuminations depict mounted warfare as well, often in ways which cannot be ascribed to classical models.[33]

Only the handing down from generation to generation of the received idea, indeed the construct, that Anglo-Saxon warriors never fought on horseback, has led to this substantial body of evidence being perversely explained away as evidence of 'mounted infantry', whereas the same sorts of data on the Continent are read simply as evidence of mounted combat. The weight of the evidence is overwhelming. This should not be taken as an argument that Anglo-Saxon warriors always fought on horseback; for one thing, there are plenty of manuscript illuminations showing Anglo-Saxons fighting on foot.[34] It may be that, especially since all of our explicit evidence for warriors dismounting to fight is late within the period, the Viking attacks led to a change in the practice of warfare. As we shall see, Viking fighting methods did bring about tactical changes on the part of their enemies. Dismounted shield-wall warfare possibly became more common in the later Anglo-Saxon period than earlier (when, as noted, the one explicit statement on the matter describes Anglo-Saxons fighting on horseback). It may be the case that throughout the era the Anglo-Saxons fought mounted less commonly than continental warriors, though this is impossible to ascertain. It may also be that the English were slower in developing true shock cavalry than their Frankish and Norman contemporaries, though that lies outside the scope of this book. What is clear is that the Anglo-Saxon warrior, like his continental counterpart, could and did fight on horseback when the occasion demanded. He could also dismount and fight on foot if that was what was required.

On the Continent, as mentioned, it has been supposed that the eighth century saw an upsurge in the use of mounted troops. This seems unlikely. As we have far more plentiful, and better, evidence on the Continent than in Anglo-Saxon England, the use of warriors fighting mounted is attested throughout the period. Procopius makes clear that the strike force of the Gothic, Vandal and Lombard armies often fought mounted.[35] He claims, as does his Continuator, Agathias, that the Franks had fewer mounted warriors, but he nevertheless makes clear that they did use such troops. Gregory of Tours, writing slightly later, states that Frankish armies as far back as he knew deployed cavalry, often as the spearhead of their attacks.[36] Seventh-century sources also describe mounted warfare.[37] Pictish, Irish and continental stone carvings show mounted warriors; manuscripts from continental Europe depict horseborne warfare. Horse furnishings accompany lavish weapon burials of the fifth to seventh centuries in northern Gaul, Germany and Scandinavia. Occasionally (especially in Germany) whole horses are found buried near these graves.[38] The most extreme instance is the veritable herd of stallions slaughtered and interred in pits around the grave of the Frankish King Childeric I.[39] Carolingian and Lombard legislation required warriors of any wealth to be horsed.[40] The Danish army of King Godfred is described as cavalry;[41] once they began to campaign Viking armies rapidly tried to acquire horses; and so on. Examples of the association of the early medieval warrior and his horse could be multiplied endlessly. It is clear that warriors from across Europe were usually horsed, and it is difficult to see the evidence for any dramatic upsurge, or change, in the use of cavalry between 450 and 900. As in England, the warrior could fight on horse or on foot according to the situation. A late sixth-century Byzantine treatise in fact describes western warriors as all too willing to dismount and fight on foot if the occasion demanded.[42] Lupus of Ferrières, writing to Bishop Pardulus of Lyon 250 years later, in 849, professed his (as an abbot, perhaps unsurprising) inability as a soldier, never having learnt to strike or parry, or 'execute the other duties of the infantry and cavalry'.[43] This suggests that a true warrior still learnt both.

The argument put forward here enables us to make better sense of some military legislation of the period. The Lombard law of King Aistulf discussed in chapter 4[44] is a case in point. If we follow the traditional assumptions about rigid distinctions between cavalry and infantry we would envisage a Lombard army as including only bowmen in its dismounted contingents; all the troops armed with spears and shields were mounted. Indeed this has frequently been the assumption made. However, Aistulf's law surely implies instead that warriors wealthy enough to own the full panoply of weaponry should also bring a horse; those who could not afford a horse should simply bring a bow and arrow. The law has no necessary implications about tactical usage. Earlier, Ostrogothic armies had included apparently large numbers of dismounted bowmen. On occasions, these were rapidly outdistanced by their mounted forces, but on others, says Procopius, they entered battle protected by what he calls their 'hoplites', which must mean close-fighting foot soldiers.[45] These troops (archers as well as close-fighters) were probably the same men as might, in other circumstances, charge into combat on horseback. A similar tactical flexibility for the Lombard warriors should probably be envisaged. In the precise context of Aistulf's Laws we might assume that dismounted bow-armed soldiers were only summoned in case of military emergency, such as appears to have prompted Aistulf's legislation. Aistulf's brother, Ratchis, had earlier, after all, envisaged that the sort of freemen who might attend a judge in a posse or in a contingent to the royal army would all be mounted and armed with lance and shield.[46] Some Carolingian Frankish legislation was also concerned to ensure that the poorest warriors be armed with a bow, although, well-equipped warriors were expected to bring bows too.[47]

A celebrated passage held to show the dominance of cavalry in later Frankish warfare is that in the *Annals of Fulda* for 891. King Arnulf and his East Frankish army was faced by a Viking force which had constructed a palisaded camp with its back to the River Dyle at Louvain, and with marshes on another side. Compelled to attack these fortifications on a comparatively narrow front, where, as the annalist says, there was no room for cavalry, Arnulf ordered his troops to dismount.[48] Cavalry would in any case have been at a severe disadvantage attacking a defended ditch and palisade; this is a good example of how the Vikings' tactical practices brought about changes in their enemies' tactics. However, Arnulf was not happy at having to make this decision for, say the *Annals of Fulda*, the Franks 'are not used to attacking *pedetemptim*'. The interpretation of this last word has been a matter of great debate. Traditionally it was understood simply to mean 'on foot', and thus used to show how the Frankish armies had become so entirely cavalry based that the Franks had forgotten how to fight dismounted. In 1970 Bernard Bachrach pointed out that *pedetemptim* technically means something more precise than just 'on foot': 'step by step'.[49] He suggested that it was the slow 'step by step' advance, necessitated by the terrain, which alarmed Arnulf's troops. This interpretation does not seem entirely satisfactory. The whole tenor of the *Annals'* account makes it clear that the key aspect of the battle was Arnulf's decision to fight on foot, something supported by Regino of Prüm's contemporary report. Furthermore, a dismounted Frankish army of armoured warriors, drawn up in close formation and advancing through a bog, could hardly fight other than *pedetemptim*. One might assume that when a Frankish warrior dismounted he usually did so to skirmish, particularly with the bow, rather than to engage in close fighting. This is not unlikely, but it would hardly refute the traditional theory that when it came to pitched battle the Franks were happier on horseback. Moreover, Regino of Prüm's account of Charles the Bald's hapless 851 campaign against the Bretons[50] makes it clear that the Franks' preferred means of fighting even while mounted was a steady, formed advance to hand-to-hand combat, and that they had great difficulty dealing with fast-moving Bretons; even the Saxon light troops placed in the front line were driven in at the first volley of Breton javelins.

Nevertheless, Bachrach was right that there is something more to the account than simply a decision to fight on foot. Three years later, in Italy, Arnulf's troops attacked the walls of Bergamo on foot, and Bachrach also correctly drew attention to the sieges which feature in Carolingian warfare; sieges, especially assaults, are the business of dismounted troops. It can hardly be postulated that the Franks were unaccustomed to attacking a field fortification on foot. We need to look again at the whole context but the whole context is not to be found in the *Annals of Fulda*. It is provided by Regino of Prüm in his *Chronicon*. Earlier that year a Frankish army had been drawn into a rash battle against the Vikings on the river Geule. The attack was easily beaten off by the dismounted Vikings, whose cavalry then arrived unexpectedly in the Frankish rear, causing rout and massacre. Regino says that the Danes in their fortifications on the Dyle taunted Arnulf's men about this defeat.[51] Here, as the Fulda annalist said, Arnulf's troops were going to have to attack in a confined space with, once they reached the Danish rampart, a marsh at their backs. The army's baggage train would further impede movement to the rear.[52] If the battle went badly escape would be very difficult: more difficult still if the warriors were on foot, as they would be if they were to avoid the fate of their rash predecessors on the Geule. That the difficulty of escape if things went wrong lay at the root of the Franks' wariness about fighting dismounted is driven home by their request, granted by Arnulf, to post screens of horsemen to ensure that no flanking movements by the Vikings could hem them in further. Clearly the Franks were aware, generally, of the Vikings' 'elastic' use of field fortifications as bases from which to launch surprise counter-attacks and, specifically, of the way the disaster on the Geule had been brought about by a Viking mounted force falling on the Frankish rear.[53] To send away the horses was indeed the sign of a decision to fight to the death. The Vikings had chosen their position carefully and invited Arnulf to lead his army into a potential death-trap. Fortunately Arnulf prepared his attack well and his army stormed through the marsh, over the Vikings' defences and into their camp; it was the Danes who found themselves penned in by marsh and river and butchered, though many escaped in their boats. This instance demonstrates clearly that an early medieval commander had a number of options open to him at the beginning of battle, including mounted or dismounted combat, which he would choose according to the situation. Sometimes, as here, the decision was difficult. One of the factors governing a decision as to whether or not to fight mounted was the nature of the encounter. The case of the battle of the Dyle is also instructive as a cautionary tale for the study of Anglo-Saxon combat. If we had fewer and less full sources, and only a cursory reference to Arnulf's decision to fight on foot (as in Regino's account), we might mistakenly assume that dismounting to fight was the rule and that the Franks did not use cavalry.

Types of encounter

As Sedulius Scottus knew,[54] battle is indeed a lottery; the early medieval battle was possibly more of a lottery than most. No matter how one tried to stack the odds, it was a game of chance, played for stakes that were high and terrible. It is small wonder, when the efforts of man to predetermine the result of battle, no matter how 'scientific', so often came to nothing, that contemporaries believed that its outcome lay entirely with the will of God. Wise commanders accompanied even their most carefully laid tactical plans with attempts to ensure divine favour. Arnulf, according to the *Annals of Fulda*, spoke to his warriors at the Dyle exhorting them to avenge insults to God's church and to attack in His name. As well as strategic and devout attempts to reduce the element of chance involved in battle, there were tactical means of increasing the odds in one's favour. A common one was to attack at dawn, hoping to catch the enemy, at worst, off balance, and at best possibly even asleep or only half awake. Strong oblique early morning sunlight might shine into the enemy's eyes, further increasing the odds in favour of success. This seems to have been the case when the Northumbrian King Oswald attacked Cadwallon of Gwynedd at Haefenfelth in 634. With the sun in their eyes, the Welsh troops and their king were slaughtered by the numerically inferior Bernicians.[55] As was mentioned in chapter 7, according to the *Earlier Annals of Metz*, the Austrasian Frankish leader, Pippin of Herestal, took similar considerations into account before the battle of Tertry in 687. He looked over the potential battlefield from a hilltop the evening before, and ordered his army to move to a position so that the Neustrian Franks would have the sun in their eyes during the battle.[56]

However, dawn attacks involved risk, and could go badly wrong. Charles the Bald tried to launch one upon his nephew Louis the Younger at Andernach (876), moving his army forward under the pretence of seeking peace – much to the disgust of the *Annals of Fulda*.[57] However, a lack of familiarity with the terrain led to his troops getting lost in the dark on the narrow tracks, and by dawn the next day they were exhausted and soaked by rain. Charles' problems were compounded by the fact that Louis had been belatedly warned of his attack and had his army drawn up in battle order – or that part of it which was at hand, since much of it was scattered at the time, foraging for horse fodder. A catastrophic defeat for Charles' army followed, yet he had come very close to pulling off what would doubtless have been hailed as one of the tactical masterstrokes of medieval military history.[58] He had caught his nephew off-guard, with much of his army dispersed. By moving his own army forward at night under cover of peace feelers he very nearly brought about battle with a strong numerical advantage and a treble element of surprise (the dawn attack, and the facts that Louis had thought him to be some way away, and was not expecting an attack in any case) in his favour. As it turned out, because of bad luck, or possibly a failure to plan the movement properly, Charles' army was slaughtered and he was fortunate to escape with his life. Such is the gamble of battle.

Another tactic occasionally used to increase the chances of success was the feigned retreat. The idea here was to draw the enemy into an undisciplined attack, wherein his troops would be dispersed in pursuit, rather than drawn up in a formed line of battle, and thus incapable of mutual support or organised resistance. In addition to this there would be the element of surprise, as the 'retreating' army unexpectedly turned to face its pursuers; more often a second, larger, formed force would emerge from ambush to attack the disorganised enemy. Byzantine military writers claimed that the Franks were particularly susceptible to such stratagems,[59] and indeed the Visigoths destroyed a Frankish army invading Septimania in 589. A small force of Goths attacked the Franks whilst the latter were having a meal; clearly Frankish scouting left something to be desired! The Franks leapt to arms, mounted up and chased the Goths, only to be attacked by the main force of the Visigothic army, under Duke Claudius. The Franks, caught by surprise and in poor array, were massacred. Spanish sources claimed that most of an army of 60,000 was killed, although Gregory of Tours puts the Frankish losses in the region of 7,000. Both figures are probably inflated but the Frankish defeat was complete. In the seventh century the Franks again fell victim to this tactic. Rather than chance his army in battle – and the Franks tended to beat the Lombards in open battle – the Lombard King Grimoald devised a cunning stratagem. He abandoned his camp in feigned flight, leaving it 'filled with divers good things and especially an abundance of excellent wine'. The Franks fell to looting the camp and soon got blind drunk. During the night, Grimoald's troops returned and slaughtered them.[60] Things had not improved much by the ninth century when a Frankish army came across the Viking scouts on the river Geule and chased after them in confused order and without consulting their leaders.[61] As mentioned above, the attack was easily beaten off by the Viking foot soldiers, whose cavalry (*equites*), hearing the clamour of battle, then arrived on the scene, taking the Franks by surprise and routing them.[62]

Ambush, rather than formal battle, was a further means of employing surprise. As we have just seen, sometimes this was used in conjunction with feigned flight. On occasions the ambush was used by forces that were unable to face the enemy in open battle, either because their opponents were more numerous or because they were better armed and equipped. Knowledge of the terrain would make up for this disadvantage. When King Arnulf raided Moravian territory in 893, his army was severely harassed by ambushes on its way back.[63] Probably the most famous such ambush was that launched in the Pyrennees in 778 by the Basques against the rear-guard of Charlemagne's army. The lightly equipped Basques inflicted heavy casualties on the Franks, including a number of leading commanders, not least a certain Hruotland.[64] This event gave rise to the great *chanson de geste*, *The Song of Roland*.

On other occasions a defending army might employ an ambush simply to increase its chances of winning a decisive victory, using knowledge of the country to gain an important element of surprise. This tactic was used to great effect by Mummolus, probably the most skilful general in Merovingian employ in the sixth century, commanding a Burgundian army against invading Lombards in 572.[65] Mummolus felled trees and created various obstacles to impede Lombard movement through, and indeed trap them within, the woods of south-eastern France. Caught strung out along forest tracks, the Lombards were heavily defeated by the Burgundian warriors who launched ambushes from several directions. Less successful were the ambushes launched by the Spoletan Lombards, apparently with southern Italian Byzantine allies, against the army of the Lombard King Liutprand in 740. The Spoletans and the Romans seem to have repeatedly attacked Liutprand's rear-guard, composed of men from Friuli, under the command of the brothers Ratchis and Aistulf (both of whom later became kings of the Lombards) in a wood and also as it crossed a river. The latter was an excellent place to ambush an army, as the river would enable the attackers to isolate and (with luck) annihilate a portion of the enemy force. However, luck was not with the Spoletans, the Friulan rear-guard beat off their attacks, and Ratchis and Aistulf brought their troops out of the dangerous situation, 'except for a few who were wounded'.[66] Liutprand had chosen wisely in selecting as his rear-guard the Friulan contingent, which, as frontier troops, was probably fairly battle-hardened. From study of the terrain it seems likely that the great Pictish triumph at Nechtansmere may also have involved an element of ambush but ultimately we shall never know exactly what happened at that battle.[67]

An army on its way back home from a campaign, laden with loot and prisoners, was especially vulnerable to ambush and attack. Its speed was slower and we may suspect that, thinking the war was as good as over, its guard may have dropped slightly. The Roncesvalles ambush of Charlemagne's rear-guard took place during the return from a Spanish campaign in 778. Later, in 862, Robert the Strong attacked and defeated a Breton army laden with booty. In the later fifth century a similar fate befell a Suevic army raiding neighbouring territory in Spain. The local population ambushed it and forced it to free the prisoners it had taken.[68]

Commanders could make use of ambushes and raids to weaken the enemy before battle, or to drive them off without having to commit the army to a risky set-piece encounter. Campaigning against his rebellious son Pippin in 832, Emperor Louis the Pious was eventually driven back over the Loire into winter quarters by a combination of bad weather and repeated raids by the Aquitanians.[69] Fifty years later, his grandson Charles the Fat led a large army against the Vikings. He dispatched a smaller force of Franks and Bavarians, under markgraf Henry and the future king, Arnulf, ahead of the main army, to try to catch the Vikings by surprise and wear them down with raids and ambushes. Unfortunately the plan was betrayed and the detached force returned to the main body having 'killed a few men'.[70] The same campaign witnessed another trick designed to do as much damage to the enemy as possible at as little risk as possible. The besieged Danes raised a shield as a sign of truce, and a number of Franks went into their fortification to trade and generally have a look around; the Danes then lowered the shield, closed the gates and killed or captured the Franks who had entered their fort.[71] The Lombard duke, Romuald of Benevento, leading the defence of Benevento in 663 against a besieging Byzantine force, too numerous to face in battle, led a number of sallies into the Byzantine camp, killing many of the besiegers, and prolonging the defence until his father, King Grimoald, was able to bring up a relieving army.[72] On another occasion the Lombard royal army, under King Perctarit, was put to flight by a night-time sortie by the rebel Duke Alahis besieged in Trento.[73]

Small-scale encounters of this sort must have been the norm in early medieval warfare. In the dramatic 841 campaign between the sons of Louis the Pious, Charles the Bald managed, with some skill and inventiveness, to get his army across the Seine and put detachments from Emperor Lothar's army to flight 'and did so a second and third time too'.[74] In the famous 'Year of Battles', 871, the Anglo-Saxon Chronicler reported nine battles and countless skirmishes between the Vikings and the West Saxons; a similar situation is recorded in 894. As discussed in chapter 7, in 891 the Viking army in the Rhineland was able utterly to disorientate King Arnulf's first attempt to defeat them by constant raiding against his army's supply trains.[75] In the many small-scale raiding campaigns this sort of small encounter may have been common, but never deserving of much comment from contemporary writers. Clashes between scouting, foraging and plundering parties must also have been fairly frequent in all types of warfare. It seems likely that the practice of these forms of smaller encounter was different from that of the major battles. Perhaps it was in less formal fights like these that Frankish warriors used their bows. Perhaps also, these encounters were more fluid and more usually suited to open mounted combat even in cultures, or at times, when dismounted fighting was the norm. The scale of war may have governed its tactical conduct. There is little or no evidence to substantiate these possibilities but they remain the best way of reconciling problematic apparent contradictions within the evidence.

Before the battle

For an early medieval commander, the stages immediately preceding the opening of a battle were tactically as important as what he did once battle had commenced, and his conduct during them was equally vital. It could be argued that at this point he had a greater ability to affect the outcome of battle than he did once the armies closed. Before the warriors engaged each other their leaders attempted to gain a moral advantage over their opponents. Largely this was carried out within the field of ritual: rituals to reassure one's own troops of the righteousness of their cause and the unrighteousness of their enemies' cause; rituals to shame the enemy. Religious ritual could be staged to claim divine sanction, and call divine aid; more secular ritual could be employed to shame or overawe one's opponents and thereby encourage one's own side. One of the most interesting and celebrated examples of this comes from the climactic battle of *Busta Gallorum*, fought near Capua in 552 between an East Roman (Byzantine) army under Narses and the Italian Ostrogothic army of King Totila. Totila was outnumbered by Narses' army, but expected a further contingent of reinforcements. Donning elaborate armour, Totila rode out into the space between the two armies and began a display of elaborate riding and military exercises. Let Procopius, the battle's narrator, take up the story:

> And he himself, sitting upon a very large horse, began to perform the dance under arms skilfully between the armies. For he wheeled his horse round in a circle and then turned him again to the other side and so made him run round and round. And as he rode he hurled his javelin into the air and caught it again as it quivered above him, then passed it rapidly from hand to hand, shifting it with consummate skill, and he gloried at his practice in such matters, falling back on his shoulders, spreading his legs and leaning from side to side, like one who has been instructed with precision in the art of dancing from childhood.[76]

Dismissed by Edward Thompson[77] as a blunt show of barbarism summing up the easy choice between civilisation and savagery facing the Italian civilians, there was far more to Totila's 'dance of death' than that. In addition to playing for time, the Ostrogothic king's display of military prowess will have inspired his followers and impressed, even overawed, Narses' troopers. Judging from the force of Procopius' account, probably derived from eyewitness reports, it must have succeeded. Nevertheless, Totila still lost the ensuing battle and was killed in the rout.

A similar occurrence seems to have occurred during the ill-fated Frankish invasion of Italy in 590; again the event appears to have been sufficiently noteworthy to have merited particular report. The Frankish army encountered the Lombards drawn up on the far side of a river. A heavily armed Lombard rode forward and challenged the Franks to single combat. He was slain but when the Frankish army crossed the river they found the Lombards had gone. Whether the death of their champion had dispirited the Lombard army, or whether his self-sacrifice was a ploy to cover the withdrawal of the army we shall never know. Gregory's account of the affair makes it sound as though the Lombard was killed by a number of Franks. It is intriguing to wonder if there may have been a conflict of different codes of conduct, with the Lombard expecting the Franks to fight him one at a time. If he did, he was to be fatally disappointed. During the battle of Coronate (c.688) between King Cunincpert of the Lombards and rebel Duke Alahis of Trento,[78] challenges to single combat are mentioned twice. In both cases Alahis refused single combat, and in the first instance Paul the Deacon says he lost the support of one of his followers as a result. It is difficult to know what to make of Paul's account, however, as it seems suffused with folkloric and miraculous elements.

Pre-battle challenges might be of a more general nature. In the campaign leading up to the battle of Fontenoy (841), a number of challenges were made by the commanders of both sides. At one point the two armies found themselves near Auxerre, separated by a marsh and a forest.[79] Louis the German and Charles the Bald arranged a truce for one night with their brother, Emperor Lothar, commanding the other side. The next day, Louis' and Charles' envoys expressed their dismay at Lothar's rejection of peace, and asked for a straight fight; if he would allow their troops to cross the swamp without harassment, they were happy to submit the dispute to trial by battle, and put the outcome in God's hands. If Lothar was unwilling to do this, their emissaries swore that Charles and Louis were happy to allow Lothar's army to cross over.

Similarly, before battle, a commander might wisely take precautions to ensure divine favour. As well as being very important in contemporary mentalities, this would improve his troops' morale. Before the battle of Andernach, Louis the Younger undertook elaborate preparations to show that God was on his side. He had men undertake ordeals, all of which worked out satisfactorily.[80] Andernach is valuable in showing that neither the normalist nor the substantivist approach to early medieval warfare is entirely satisfactory. Louis was stacking the odds in his favour by serious attempts to ensure divine support, just as his uncle, Charles the Bald, was using low cunning, deceitful peace feelers and a dawn attack, to make sure *he* won. In this case, it was appeals to the Almighty rather than to eternal strategic principles, which were successful! To the early medieval mind this was hardly surprising; King Æthelræd delayed the start of the battle of Ashdown until he had finished hearing mass, leaving his brother Alfred's division unsupported for some time.[81]

Generals also appear to have ridden up and down the lines before battle, speaking reassuringly to their troops, reminding of the basics of weapon-handling which, like the sensible injunction to 'wait until you see the whites of their eyes', might be forgotten in the heat of battlefield emotion, and telling them, as Arnulf did at the Dyle, of the justice of their cause.[82]

Formations and tactics

Little is known about western European early medieval tactics. Foot and Wilson's comment on Viking warfare is valid for most tactics in this period: they consisted 'largely of bashing hell out of the opposing side'.[83] As far as can be told, set-piece battle was decided by the brutal expedient of an advance to contact followed by a more or less lengthy period of hand-to-hand combat. Nevertheless, whilst simple when compared with the complex manoeuvres of other historical periods, such warfare was far from being mindless or without its own form of skill. Leadership was vitally important. We have just seen the role of the commander before battle, and we have noted that a decision to remain mounted when the bulk of one's command was fighting on foot could undermine the troops' morale. The importance of being led by a known commander is illustrated by a couple of examples. In the seventh century, under attack by the Mercians under Penda, the East Angles dragged their king, Sigbert, from the monastery to which he had retired, and force him to lead them once again. Sigbert refused to carry a weapon and was killed.[84] In the late ninth century, a sick Breton commander had himself carried on a litter in front of his battle-line (*acies*) rather than leave his troops leaderless.[85]

It is not known, in any detail, in what sort of formation an early medieval army might be drawn up. As far as can be ascertained, in set-piece battle warriors were assembled in dense masses, such as Old English literature described as 'shield-walls'. Warfare on the continent too would seem to have been similar, if there is more than mere rhetoric to the phrase that the warriors were packed so tight that the dead could not fall to the ground.[86] The Franks at Poitiers (732–3) 'remained immobile like a wall, holding together like a glacier in the cold regions'.[87] The terminology for battlefield formations is vague and, as we have seen, riddled with classicisms: phalanxes, *testudines*, *turmae*, *acies*. It cannot be used to distinguish between different types of formation, as known in earlier and later periods, such as columns, lines, squares and wedges. The same point can be made of poetic, especially vernacular, sources' references to shield-walls, shield-*burhs*, battle-enclosures, war-hedges and so on. The general sense of all, however, is of closely packed bodies of warriors.

It has occasionally been argued that there was some use made of a wedge-shaped formation, which would be aimed at breaking through the enemy line. There is no good contemporary evidence for this. Largely the assumption derives from classical authors' description of Germanic barbarians deploying in a *cuneus* or wedge. However, the word is much more flexible than that. It could mean no more than 'wedged together'; it could also be used simply to mean a body of troops. *Cuneus* was a term used for 'regiment' in the Roman army, and Gregory of Tours used it in this sense, for a 'body of men', sometimes with slightly disparaging undertones.[88] Agathias seems to describe a 'wedge' at the battle of Casilinium in 554.[89] He says that the centre of the Frankish line was like a boar's head, a common way of talking about a wedge formation. The wings of the army seem to have been angled back from this centre, as arrows fired by archers on one side of the Byzantine army hit Frankish warriors on the other flank in the back. It is possible, however, that the 'boar's head' refers simply to a densely formed body of men at the centre of the Frankish line, around the Frankish general, Buccelin. The angled wings may have stemmed from the fact that Buccelin charged rapidly straight for a weak point in the Byzantine line, a hole left by a Herul contingent being late to arrive. As this body set off at full speed, and possibly unexpectedly, the troops on either side will have started forward when they realised that an attack had been launched, leading to a progressive time-lag in beginning the advance, as one moved outwards from the centre to the flanks. The V-formation of the Frankish army may then have been somewhat accidental.

How these close-order formations were organised is impossible to establish. It is not normal even to know whether mounted troops were formed up separately from foot-soldiers, in front of them or to one side. It seems like a reasonable guess to suppose that the best armoured and equipped troops would have formed the front ranks. These would usually be the best trained and the most experienced warriors, too, and probably mounted. At Rimini in the 550s, Agathias describes the Frankish horsemen as forming the flanks of a densely drawn-up formation.[90] Within the division or shield-wall, it again seems likely that local contingents, aristocratic retinues and other groupings would stand together. It was important to stand alongside people whom you knew and trusted. Here we must distinguish between organisational units, which might, like Penda's 'thirty legions' at Winwæd,[91] be numerous, and battlefield, tactical units, which seem to have been few. We do not even have evidence about how deep such a formation was likely to be; we have to retreat into *comparanda*. Snorri Sturluson describes a shield-wall in 1161 as 'long and no more than five men deep'.[92] A battle-line would have to be sufficiently deep to prevent the enemy being able to cut straight through it as a result of a small local advantage. If this happened, the opposing warriors would be able to start striking at the flanks and rear of the troops on either side of this breach, and disaster would ensue.

Armies may have been deployed in more than one body, or division, though the evidence is, as ever, vague. From Nithard's account, at Fontenoy the two sides both seem to have drawn up in three divisions. At two battles in 871, Ashdown and Merton, the English and their Danish foes each formed up in two divisions. Reference to the death of the ætheling Theodbald 'and all his army' at the battle of Degsastan in 603, between Northumbrians and Scots, possibly implies a separate unit.[93] After the close of our period this remained common practice. The Ottonian armies frequently deployed in a series of battlefield divisions.[94] These units may commonly have been formed of troops from different regions or even nationalities.

Dense formations like these seem to have been used by mounted and dismounted troops equally. Given the shortage of detailed information, the Frankish examples referred to above may have been mounted troops. Certainly, in the eighth century, cavalry were expected to be drawn up in close array and to advance cautiously. The *Revised Annals'* account of the serious Frankish defeat in the Süntel mountains say that this was brought about by rash warriors, unwilling to share potential glory with the experienced and prudent Count Theoderic:

> Each individual . . . charged with as much speed as he could muster, just as fast as his horse could carry him . . . they acted as though their task was to pursue a fleeing enemy and seize booty rather than to take on an enemy standing marshalled to face them.[95]

A description of a cavalry battle in the epic poem *Waltharius* supports this view.[96] Here the two sides form up closely, advance to close range and throw spears at each other before closing to fight it out with swords. This seems fairly indistinguishable from the ways in which infantry battles were fought.

Once deployed and closed up, the armies would have been within but a short distance of each other. Their divisions would square up to face one another. Doubtless an eerie silence fell, as the two sides eyed each other. Concentrations of well-equipped warriors, horses and banners would mark the centre of each body of troops. Then one or both sides would begin to grind slowly forward. Now the noise would begin: shouts, battle cries and taunts, trumpet and horn blasts, all designed to frighten and overawe the other side.[97] Periodically, the divisions would halt to straighten the line. Older, more experienced warriors would restrain those who, like the Franks in the Süntel mountains, wanted to respond to the psychological strain and the fear by rushing forward towards the enemy. This response, to drive away the threat at all costs, the 'flight to the front' as nineteenth-century French military theorists would call it, would only break the line and spell doom, as in the Süntel. 'Since the approach had gone badly, badly went the battle', said the anonymous author of the *Revised Annals*, who appears to have known what he was talking about. Snorri's thirteenth-century account of an infantry shield-wall at Stiklestad (fought in 1030 between a Norwegian royal army and a rebel force of 'bonders', landowners) may stand as useful comparanda:

Now when the battle order of the farmers was established, the landed-men spoke to them exhorting the troops to watch their position, where each one was stationed, beneath which standard was his place, how far from his banner or how near to it. They asked the men to be alert and quick to take their places when the trumpets sounded and they heard the signal, and then keep step; because they still had to advance their army a very long distance and there was a chance that their lines might break during the march.[98]

Thus, in set-piece battle, the advance to combat was slow and steady, whether on foot or horse, again leading to the impossibility of distinguishing between mounted and dismounted warfare in our terse sources. The full cavalry charge appears to have been developed after the close of our period in the tenth and, especially, the eleventh century. Too rapid advances split up units and sometimes left rash leaders dangerously exposed. This nearly spelt doom for the seventh-century leader, Berthar, during a battle between two Frankish aristocratic factions.[99] His son saved him, but Duke Desiderius was less fortunate during pursuit of a possibly feigned flight by Visigothic troops. Separated from his men, he was trapped by a sally of another group of Goths from Carcassonne, and killed.[100] Sixty years earlier, the same fate befell the Frankish king, Chlodomer, during battle with the Burgundians, and in the 670s some of Wamba's Visigothic troops were likewise caught by a sally by Paul's rebel warriors from the amphitheatre in Nîmes when they pursued too far.[101] The cohesion of formed bodies of troops, on foot or on horseback, seems thus to have been paramount. A ragged line would allow the enemy to break into, or even right through, the formation and strike at the unprotected or unshielded sides or backs of warriors engaged to their front. It would also prevent the troops from mutually supporting each other, each man protecting the man to his left with his shield, and rob them of the moral effect of knowing that there was a warrior close to either side.

The role of archery and other missile fire on the battlefield is equally unclear. It may well have been used to break up the enemy's formation prior to contact. Certainly, the use of missiles in the sixth century seems to have had this aim. The heavy spears like *angones* were sophisticated items which, if they did not kill their target, would weigh down his shield, allowing the advancing warrior to strike down the comparatively defenceless enemy with sword or thrusting spear. Franciscas, too, were designed to split shields and render the enemy warrior more vulnerable. As noted in chapter 8 and discussed further above, the infantry component of Italian Ostrogothic and, later, Lombard armies included numerous archers, at least when the full host was called out, and Frankish, Visigothic and Lombard legislation required the provision of warriors with bows. Archers seem to have been important in Asturian armies as well. Especially in the early part of the period, missile fire played an important role in major battles. Gregory's probably fairly stylised account of Vouillé refers to troops throwing spears from a distance.[102] There was a considerable degree of fluidity though. At Busta Gallorum, Totila ordered his warriors not to use spears or bows but to rely on their swords.[103] This suggests that Gothic warriors could serve as close-fighting troops (on foot or horseback) or as archers, depending on the occasion. As will be argued below, battlefield tactics may well have been different before about 600, but it seems that warriors retained their ability to fulfil more than one battlefield role. Later sources also describe the use of missile weapons from within the shield-walls. Archers may sometimes have been positioned in vantage points to shoot at enemy leaders. Count Ranulf, Robert the Strong's co-commander at Brissarthe, was picked off by a Viking bowman 'sniping' from the window of the church.[104] There are no references to light horse-archers in early medieval western European battles. The St-Gall 'Golden Psalter', however, shows one Frankish cavalryman firing a bow from the saddle.[105] Possibly, Frankish cavalry stationed in the rear ranks used their bows to shoot overhead into the ranks of the enemy, like their dismounted colleagues.

Once close fighting was joined, a full-scale, early medieval set-piece battle was a terrible affair. Getting the two sides to close and begin this maelstrom may not have been easy. Whether troops drank before battle to deaden the nerves, as the ancient Greeks did, and later generations were to, in the form of a 'rum ration', is unknown but hardly implausible.[106] The psychology of this stage of battle is now, like so many other aspects of early medieval battle, outside our purview. In many other periods, hand-to-hand fighting has been comparatively rare. In spite of the weight given to sword and bayonet practice, actual fatalities and wounds from 'cold steel' were comparatively rare in the Napoleonic and American Civil Wars, except in pursuit. Usually the defenders broke before contact, if their volleys failed to stop the attack, or the attackers would be stopped, forced to take cover or driven off by the defenders' firepower. Precipitous flight by one side was known in this period, but the majority of early medieval battles were decided by fighting at close quarters. This seems to give us some proof that battlefield psychology is not timeless. It is unlikely, however, that armies very often crashed straight into each other unless one side or other seemed to be flinching. Perhaps the two sides would halt facing each other, a few yards apart, and trade insults and missiles until one side achieved sufficient psychological superiority over its opponents to charge home. Perhaps it was at this point that leadership and the aspects which gave rise to 'heroic' verse came into their own. Leaders would taunt the enemy and try to inspire their warriors to close. Possibly charges by brave leaders produced a general engagement, as their warriors followed to protect them, or were inspired by their example. Given that early medieval combat was so different from that in later, better documented periods with different cultures and mentalities, it seems dangerous to resort to comparisons with more recent fighting, but this reconstruction does seems to tally with modern works on the psychology of units in action.[107]

Once the two sides closed, then it would be difficult for a leader to exert much control over a battle at all. Fighting would be too close. Whether battles like this were decided by a rugby-scrum-like shoving match,[108] or whether there was more room for individual weapon play, is, yet again, unknown. The latter would be suggested by the use of horses. The emphasis on 'heroic' combats in poetry might also suggest the latter alternative, though it is difficult to press this possibility too far. Either way, warriors would be trying to jab or cut over their shields, at their enemies' heads, necks and shoulders, with little room to do much else. Mounted warriors might try to disable their opponents' mounts. On foot, in this type of fighting, casualties may have been comparatively few, but they would be horrendous. When a warrior fell, the other side would try to exploit the gap, whilst his comrades tried to close it.[109] Again, there is scope for active leadership, if not exactly generalship, here. Leaders would try to inspire their men by fighting hard and attempting to force their way into the enemy line. This appears to be the implication of Procopius' accounts of officers distinguishing themselves in battle.[110] They would attempt to cut their way through to, and kill, leading warriors on the other side, for the death of a commander could dispirit the whole army, especially if the common but gruesome expedient was resorted to of hacking off the head and mounting it on a spear. The personalised elements of battle in the 'heroic' poetry, and the 'heroic' culture, which has attracted so much attention from literary scholars of the period, might also have a relevance to actual battle, if, again, we adopt the possibly risky strategy of analogy with later military psychology. Analyses have shown that it takes only a comparatively small number of soldiers actually, conspicuously doing any fighting to keep a unit involved in battle.[111] Thus the actions of 'heroic' warriors and leaders could maintain the morale of their side, when most warriors may have settled into a rather passive involvement in the fighting. This might also explain how these personal elements were transmitted to the poets, and why the audience of such verse was able to accept these accounts of fighting even if, overall, they bore little relationship to what a battle was like.[112]

An alternative form of leadership might have been to command from the rear, keeping a reserve and moving up and down the line exhorting and encouraging the troops, and intervening with this reserve at points of danger or crisis. This would allow greater control of the battle to be retained. Though this does not seem unlikely, there is little evidence for it. In battle outside Rome in 537, the Roman and Gothic commanders stationed themselves behind their lines, urging on the troops.[113] A later instance is perhaps also instructive. In his attack on Bergamo in 894, King Arnulf remained mounted with his battle-standard on top of a hill, prepared 'to give assistance to those attacking the wall'.[114] This might have been an approach to open battle as well.

The reference to standards is important. These appear to have been important in early medieval battle. The approach of the royal banner to their sector of the line would doubtless inspire troops fighting there. The *Annals of Fulda* record triumphantly that Charles the Bald's standard bearers were killed at Andernach, and that this brought about the defeat of Charles' army.[115] Certainly the sight of a banner falling appears to have depressed the morale of an army, just as the capture of such a standard boosted that of the other side. Some banners were invested with numinous power and had relics associated with them.[116] This was not only true of Christian armies. The *Anglo-Saxon Chronicle* records the capture of the 'banner called Raven' from a defeated Viking army in Devon.[117] The 'Raven Banner' features in later Scandinavian sagas as a quasi-magical object.[118] King Arnulf sent sixteen captured Viking royal banners to Bavaria as proof of his victory on the Dyle.[119] As an illustration of a similar phenomenon in more recent times, we need think only of the iconic status of the eagles which Napoleon gave to his regiments and, conversely, the delight and pride which their enemies took in their capture. As the banner would, for these reasons, be the focus of the hardest fighting, banner bearers would be the best and most experienced warriors, and probably given some responsibility for command: Lothar I, in his capitulary for the 847 campaign against the Saracens in Italy, names commanders and *signifers* (standard bearers) for each of the army's *scarae*.[120] In a strange story about the battle of Burford (752), the twelfth-century chronicler Henry of Huntingdon describes a single combat between standard bearers as opening the engagement. This might well be a twelfth-century fiction based around the practices of Henry's own day, and is more probably an example of Henry's classicising elaboration of bald early texts, but it would also fit with what is known about the early middle ages.[121] Thus the *Annals of Fulda's* delight in the killing of Charles the Bald's standard bearers.

Not surprisingly, some battles were over very quickly. Stories circulating about the battle of Vouillé (507) in the late sixth century held that the Goths soon fled.[122] Sometimes one side would flee before contact. In 841, the Emperor Lothar's forces in Germany, led by Adalbert, 'fled in fright before they had come to lance-point, and by this cause innumerable men were killed in this flight'.[123] Three years later, in the battle in which Nithard was slain, an army marching to support Charles the Bald's forces in south-western France was set upon by the troops of Pippin II of Aquitaine. The inexperienced component of the army ran away immediately, leaving its leaders to be rapidly killed or captured.[124] Three years previously at Fontenoy, fortunes had been reversed. The implication of Nithard's account would seem to be that the key factor was the immediate rout of the troops facing Charles' division. Engilbert's poem about the battle suggests the same, when it states that Lothar had been let down by his dukes, who had not fought so hard. If it is possible to reconcile the accounts, it would appear that Lothar's division was successful at first, driving Louis back towards the stream, but that the early flight of the other division led to his defeat.[125] Other accounts speak of enemies who fled at the first charge.[126] Doubtless those battles recorded where the victorious army lost few or no men, were of this character, as indeed the *Annals of St-Bertin* confirm for the 844 encounter mentioned above. On occasion, apparently, the sight of a well-trained, experienced and successful army led by a feared commander might alone be too much. According to the *Revised Annals*, in one of the last campaigns of the Saxon wars, the Saxons drew up an army on the plain of the Sindfeld and awaited battle, but when Charlemagne's forces arrived they simply threw down their arms and surrendered: 'hope of the victory which, mistakenly, they had shortly before been promising themselves deserted them'.[127]

Otherwise the fighting would go on until one side could take no more and fled. Local successes might lead to one side breaking into and through the enemy, shattering its cohesion and allowing the slaughter to begin. Experienced warriors might learn to give ground in order to maintain the line. Hardened warriors would have known the penalties of allowing the enemy to break into the shield-wall. Stepping back and closing up the gaps, whilst maintaining a continuous front, was preferable to flight and being cut down from behind. The difficulty of moving backwards in close formation might be offset against the fact that the advancing side would have the bodies of the dead and wounded to negotiate. In spite of the ground lost, one might still wear down the enemy psychologically. Even if the rest of the line fled, a formed body of troops prepared to sell itself dearly might fight its way off the battlefield. The victorious enemy would probably be happier chasing fugitives than risking further death and injury in trying to cut down a formed remnant.

It is easy to see how, if one segment of the line fled, disaster would often overtake the whole. With its opponents in flight, if a commander could rally and bring under control even a portion of the winning division, he could turn it against the flank and rear of the other parts of the enemy line. This might not be easy, as the opportunity for easy kills and plunder might surpass concern for the greater tactical situation, and tight discipline does not appear to have been a strong suit for early medieval western European troops. But because warriors knew that in these circumstances there was a possibility of this happening, the flight of one part of the line might infect neighbouring divisions and lead to widespread flight even without the active intervention of victorious troops from that sector.

The moment of apparent victory was also, however, a dangerous moment, as troops broke formation to pursue and cut down their enemies, and loot their bodies and baggage. This cost the East Roman army victory in battle outside Rome, for example.[128] The intervention of fresh troops or a reserve might bring disaster upon an army even as it thought the battle won. It was for this reason, too, that the tactic of feigned flight was sometimes employed.[129] It might be another reason for commanding with a reserve behind the main line. However, such forms of leadership were risky. Apart from abdicating the possibility of exercising the important aspect of leadership by example, a sizeable reserve might mean that not enough troops were placed in the battle-lines. A small reserve of good troops might mean that valuable warriors were kept out of the fighting where it mattered, and such a reserve, even of seasoned warriors, could be overwhelmed and infected by the flight of troops in front of them.

If neither side broke, it seems unlikely that this sort of 'hard pounding' could go on for long. The weight of full early medieval warrior panoply, especially when combined with the mental exertion of battle, would rapidly become very heavy, and the effort to make a real attack correspondingly great. After a while, warriors will have fought to defend themselves rather than to kill the enemy, and then conserved their strength, falling back into the early medieval warrior's *en garde* position, with shield high and sword or spear levelled, waiting either to defend an attack and kill with the riposte or for a sign of weakness on the part of his enemy, perhaps for the enemy line to break somewhere else, thus creating distraction and an opening on his sector. With the ground covered in corpses or the writhing bodies of the wounded and dying, an attack would become increasingly difficult and risky: tripping over a corpse would be fatal. On foot, the feet would be planted firmly; on horseback, the shield held to protect the horse's head (as described in the *Strategikon*).[130] This was where the example of experienced warriors and leaders continuing hard fighting was important, as noted above. After a while, however, both sides might gradually fall into this stance, and fighting would cease along the line. At this point the two sides might back away from each other, to lick wounds, send, or drag, the badly wounded to the rear, and attempt to rest and build up energy for a second attack.

There might be a certain tacit agreement between the two sides at this point, as suggested by an interesting episode during Charlemagne's Saxon Wars, which, again, we only hear of from the fuller and more 'open' *Revised Annals*.[131] In 775, a division of Charlemagne's army, posted on the Weser at Lübbecke, was attacked by Saxons who mingled with returning foragers – an interesting feature in itself – and thus forced a way into the camp, causing considerable damage. However, a proportion of the Frankish army roused itself and put up a spirited defence. Eventually, with the battle having been fought to a standstill and neither side having gained a decisive advantage, the two sides, 'being in such dire straits', made an agreement and the Saxons were allowed to withdraw. It is interesting to speculate further on this incident. Where neither army had been able to break the other and inflict a decisive defeat, there may often have come a point where the two sides made such an agreement, allowing one side to leave the field unmolested. The Saxons, tactically, would appear to have been in an unenviable position, inside the Frankish camp. On the other hand, the Saxons had clearly not been beaten, and the Franks were disorganised and tired. To try to break down a still coherent body of troops would have been difficult and would certainly have cost more casualties, in dead and wounded, and might perhaps even lead to a defeat. Battles are occasionally recorded as long and hard fought but with neither side being victorious. The third component of Fontenoy, where Adalhard's troops faced those including Nithard, also fought itself out without a decision. One wonders whether Adalhard's division made a similar agreement to leave the field.

Where no such agreement was made to end the battle, the two sides would draw back and slowly work up the courage for a second attack. One imagines, however, that after each such phase of mêlée, it became progressively harder to force the troops (and more especially the horses) to recross that open space between them and the enemy. At this point, a less experienced army might become vulnerable. Troops might disperse to loot the dead, or sneak away with the wounded. A sudden counter-attack by an enemy which had thus far slowly been driven back might furthermore snap the morale of an army and lead to flight, or simply take them by surprise as they halted to rest and recover. The death of Robert the Strong and the precipitate flight of his army at Brissarthe took place at just such a moment.[132] At the battle of Saucourt (881), the Danes retreated into a royal villa and then launched a surprise counter-attack on the Franks as the latter looted and took care of their wounds. About 100 Franks were killed in this late counter-charge and many others took to flight. Here, though, the presence of mind of Louis III meant the Franks were able to rally and complete their victory. Interestingly, Louis rallied the Franks by dismounting to fight. Nevertheless the temporary reverse meant that the *Annals of St-Bertin* wrote up the battle as a defeat.[133] We must again note the fluidity characteristic of early medieval fighting.[134] The Danes used exactly the same tactic at Reading around New Year 871, with greater success.[135] Indeed Viking tactics usually were successful. The *Anglo-Saxon Chronicle* describes battles against the Danes in which the English were victorious 'far into the day' but 'the Danes had possession of the field of battle'.[136] If this is not propaganda we might wonder whether we are not faced with a similar situation. The English, in spite of success, were unable to break down the enemy and were eventually forced to withdraw. It is possible that the undoubted psychological strain of a long battle in which a stubborn enemy refused to break in spite of one's best efforts might eventually become too much and result in the sudden flight of the hitherto 'winning' army, especially if prompted by this sort of counter-attack by the more experienced enemy.

Some battles, however, appear to have been fought over a long period of time. Old English sources, notably the *Anglo-Saxon Chronicle*, frequently record day-long battles. In the eighth century, a battle between the Lombards and the Bavarians was only halted by nightfall.[137] Sometimes battles went on even longer. Gregory of Tours reports a battle between the Franks and the Bretons lasting for three days.[138] Nearly three centuries later, the battle of Jengland between Charles the Bald and the Bretons also went on for several days.[139] Paul the Deacon discusses a four-day confrontation between the Lombards and the Avars.[140] The great battle of *Mons Lactarius* (552), lasted for two days.[141] Some of these lengthy battles were fought against opponents, like the Avars and the Bretons, who appear to have used skirmishing hit and run tactics. A 'battle', in these circumstances, might rather be a long series of skirmishes and minor attacks fought over several days. Either the other side would eventually be worn down, as was the case with the Lombards in their struggle with the Avars, or in the Frankish–Breton encounters, or eventually the raiding side would be dispirited by repeated failure and leave the field. Alternatively it might be caught against a natural obstacle where it had no room to manoeuvre, and cut down. Charles the Bald attempted to defeat the Bretons by opening the battle of

Jengland with a night attack, which seems to have gained some local success, though he still ended up abandoning the battlefield.[142] *Mons Lactarius* was fought in the sixth century, when tactics may have been more fluid. Otherwise, long battles might take place because of the nature of close-order combat discussed above, when periods of fighting were indecisive. Perhaps, even after several clashes, neither side was able to make a decisive impact on the other. Simeon of Durham records an eighth-century battle in Northumbria lasting for three days.[143] It is possible that this too was made up of a long period of skirmishing rather than set-piece battle; after all, as we have seen, the Anglo-Saxons too fought mounted, and it is often argued that the Northumbrians may have had more in common with their British, Pictish and Scottish neighbours, who often seem to have employed skirmishing hit and run tactics. If not, then it may be that the armies repeatedly squared up against each other and advanced to combat but without result. Perhaps on some occasions, especially since this was a civil war, they could not be brought to close. Possibly, after an indecisive bout of hand-to-hand combat, the two sides withdrew and simply faced each other for the rest of the day, before trying again the next day. Only on the third day was a decisive encounter forced.[144] The idea that battle was made up of short bouts of close fighting between longer spells of rest and recuperation, and perhaps skirmishing and exchanges of missiles, seems the best way of reconciling the sources' accounts of very long battles with the practicalities of hand-to-hand fighting.[145] The battle of Coronate, which if we can believe Paul the Deacon's account fell into two phases of fighting, may have conformed to this model.

Tactical variations

Mention of battles against foes who did not fight in the usual set-piece 'slogging match' style leads to discussion of variations from this tactical norm. As noted, Breton troops appear to have used mobile skirmishing and harrying tactics, employing light cavalry. Similar tactics were apparently used by the Basques, at least in their homelands;[146] in the wars against Pippin I the *Vascones* seem to have fought in similar ways to other warriors, probably dismounting to fight on at least one occasion.[147] This might lend support to the idea that *Vasco* (Gascon – Basque) was becoming a political identity in Aquitaine at the time. Skirmishing fighting methods may, as mentioned, have been used by most western European warriors in small-scale warfare and raiding. What seems to be at stake is the Bretons' and Basques' refusal to follow suit and deploy for conventional formal battle once the Franks had set out their stall for that kind of engagement. This would seem to be proved by contemporary Frankish response to the first defeat at Roncesvalles. A clear account of the Basques' refusal to fight fair is given by the author of the *Revised Annals*. 'Although the Franks were manifestly superior to the Basques in both weapons and courage, yet they were rendered their inferiors by the steepness of the terrain and the character of the battle, which was not fought fairly', he whines. Einhard, in a very similar passage (unsurprisingly, he was once thought to have written the *Revised Annals*), points out that the terrain and light arms of the Basques gave them an advantage whilst the heavy equipment and unevenness of the ground hampered the Franks.[148] Similar skirmishing tactics seem to have been used by the Avars, who appear, unlike western armies, to have used mounted archers. It is an intriguing possibility that when Gregory of Tours refers to the 'Huns' (meaning Avars) magically making figures dance before the eyes of an Austrasian Frankish army this stems from skirmishing, harrying and feigned flight tactics by the Avar light cavalry.[149] It has been proposed from analysis of archaeological data that horsemen in Vendel period Sweden (from the end of the sixth century) used tactics wherein heavy cavalry charged home after gaps in the enemy line had been opened up by the use of archery.[150] It is suggested that the horsemen used their bows mounted, protected by screens of foot soldiers. This is very plausible but perhaps relies too heavily upon preconceived ideas of rigid distinctions between mounted and dismounted soldiers, and on a possibly too direct comparison with Sassanid Persian heavy cavalry (*clibanarii*).

Feigned flight has repeatedly been mentioned above. This was a useful tactic for breaking an enemy army's cohesive formation, making them think the battle won and drawing them into unformed pursuit. As we have seen, it seems to have been used by Visigothic armies in the later sixth century, in conjunction with ambush or second forces placed in fortifications. Agathias describes the Franks in Italy succumbing to this tactic in battle against an allegedly smaller Byzantine force at Rimini in 554.[151] Such a tactic was difficult, however. If the enemy caught up with the withdrawing troops, feigned flight might easily become real. Real panic might overtake troops in feigned flight, with their backs exposed to the enemy. A second, reserve force was needed to strike the unformed pursuers; the 'fleeing' troops would need time to halt their 'flight', reform and face the enemy. If not, the attackers would catch them at a disadvantage. Without care, it was possible that the reserve troops might think the feigned flight was genuine and take to their heels too. Fear can be infective. Frankish troops, as noted in chapter 5, were trained in the use of feigned flight, but they rarely seem to have used it in formal battle. One possible instance appears in the *Earlier Annals of Metz*'s account of Charles Martel's battle at Amblève.[152] Perhaps the Franks used this tactic mostly in small-scale fighting.

As we have seen, closely packed bodies of troops were the norm, advancing slowly and deliberately towards the enemy. Manoeuvre and changes of formation are not recorded. Turning a body of men like this to one flank or to face another threat would be very difficult. Even in other periods where there were drill-books and complex procedures for formation change, such changes, where actually employed on the battlefield, were often difficult and risky. Flank attacks would be decisive against such formations, but they were rarely employed in the early Middle Ages. This could only really be accomplished by surprise.

A division of early medieval troops could only with immense difficulty, or utter loss of formation, be 'wheeled' out of line to attack the flank of enemies facing the front of another part of the line. More to the point, as we have seen, armies squared up to face each other. It would be unlikely that an army would deploy so that its enemies overlapped a flank to this degree. Thinning but lengthening the shield-wall, as at Stiklestad, was preferable.[153] It was even less likely that a division would be drawn up in the open, to one side of the main line of battle, but facing the flank of any enemy line of attack, without the enemy guessing the tactic and taking preventative measures, or, worse, just attacking that division itself, flank on. Thus flank attacks seem only, as mentioned, to have occurred when one segment of the line had beaten the troops to its front. Otherwise, such flanking forces might be deployed out of sight of the enemy. Fighting the Andalusian Moslems in 815, the Christian Spanish deployed flanking forces in ambush at the side of a valley, but without success.[154] In a battle in Northumbria just after the close of our period, a Scandinavian army deployed in four divisions, but kept one out of sight. This division surged out of its ambush and turned the tables on its enemies, who had been winning up to that point.[155] Such tactics required skill; deploy too soon and the enemy would spot the trick, or might flee before the flank attack could do much damage; deploy too late and the battle might already be lost. Nevertheless, if successful, the results could be dramatic. Once again we see the skill of battle-hardened Viking armies.

Field fortifications

A number of battles in seventh- to mid-ninth-century England took place at or near fortified sites, usually dating from earlier periods: Iron Age hillforts or Roman walled sites. This could result from the use of those fortifications in battle, or indeed from attempts to carry the fortification by assault. It is also possible, however, that the occupation of the defensive site was, as discussed in chapter 7, a strategy designed to bring about battle. The army would position itself at the site of this well-known monument as a challenge.

The Vikings made excellent use of fortifications in battle. They also employed difficult terrain to hamper their opponents and to negate their greater use of cavalry.[156] The Vikings used their defended camps in much the same way. This use of fortifications seems to have been, as military historians term it, 'elastic'. In other words, the Scandinavians did not sit passively behind their ramparts but used them as a base from which they could launch counter-attacks. Occasionally they allowed their attackers to penetrate the defences, whereupon they could be entrapped and killed. In 867 the Northumbrians were heavily defeated in this way. The Danes, apparently making use of the Roman walls of York, allowed the English to fight their way into the enclosure, but once inside the Danes were able to trap and slaughter them, the Northumbrians losing both of their kings in the disaster. The *Anglo-Saxon*

Chronicle gloomily records 'an immense slaughter . . . of the Northumbrians there, some inside, some outside'. Another classic example comes from the battle of Brissarthe (866), when the Vikings and their Breton allies withdrew into a church – presumably again used as the focus for a fortification – only to launch a surprise counter-attack which routed the Frankish army. Very similar tactics were used at the Battle of Reading (871), and Saucourt (881). As noted, this attack cost Robert the Strong his life. Perhaps, like many less-well-recorded western European victims of the tactic, he assumed that the battle had ended, at least for the time being, once the Vikings had been pinned in their encampment. As mentioned, it was probably Frankish wariness of the Viking use of fortifications that prompted King Arnulf to post screens of cavalry on his flanks before assaulting the Scandinavian camp on the Dyle. The Danes may not have been alone in this kind of fighting – earlier, the Goths appear to have been capable of similar withdrawals, sometimes into fortifications, and counter-attacks, and we shall see in chapter 10 that sorties and sallies were a common feature of sieges – but they certainly made the most repeatedly successful use of it.

The Danes were not the only armies to use field defences, however. In the early sixth century the Thuringians, according to Gregory of Tours, dug pits in front of their battle-line, into which the advancing Frankish cavalry fell. The Franks were able to reform, however, renew the attack with more circum-spection, and win the day.[157] The problem with such field fortifications is that they can commit an army to too static a defence, and prevent them from following up advantages. A Slavic force attacking the Duchy of Benevento in the late seventh century enjoyed greater success; they too surrounded their camp with pits, and in this case this resulted in the death of the attacking Lombard Duke Aio.[158] Similarly, the Vikings killed the East Frankish markgraf Henry when he fell into a pit outside their camp.[159] We have noted the Burgundian general, Mummolus' use of barricades in forests. Early in the sixth century, Frankish King Chlothar I, outnumbered by the joint armies of his brother, Childebert I, and nephew, Theudebert I, took up a position in a wood, and similarly made barricades and fortifications in the terrain. No battle ensued, as Childebert and Theudebert's forces were dispersed by a bad storm. Spanish Christians also used field fortifications, palisades and ditches, in conjunction with their mountainous terrain, to negate the Moslems' probable superiority in numbers, especially cavalry. On one occasion a ford was further defended by the construction of a palisade.[160]

Tactical change

Most of what has been said above is derived from ninth-century sources. Whilst much of this may have applied to the whole period we should not assume this. Evidence suggests that tactics did not remain static through the period. First of all, it appears that the nature of battle differed before c.600. Study of the weaponry of the period shows that there was much more emphasis on missile weapons in the immediately post-Roman centuries. As we saw in chapter 8, it is in this period that we find the throwing axes (*franciscae*) and specialised throwing spears like *angones* and the 'corrugated' British types. Also it is to this period that belong the shield-bosses with disc terminals, which, as discussed in chapter 8, suggest open 'fencing' styles of combat. These shields seem to have been smaller than later ones, and were designed to be 'mobile', used to catch and deflect blades. In this period, too, we find the best evidence for battlefield archery, especially in the Italian Gothic armies. Indeed, in the accounts of the Byzantine writers Procopius and Agathias of battles during the Italian wars, battles do seem to have been more open and fluid. This reliance on missile fire may very well be an inheritance from the Roman army, out of which, after all, most 'barbarian' armies evolved (see chapter 3). The late Roman army, too, had made heavy use of missile weapons, especially spears and heavy javelins and darts thrown just before contact. The *ango* is derived from the Roman *pilum*, and the *francisca*, too, is probably a late Roman weapon. Battle in the fifth and sixth centuries seems therefore to have been rather different from that after about 600. Formations may, though still fairly dense, have been rather looser than later, to enable rapid charges, the throwing of this array of weapons, and the use of the small shield.

After 600, as we have seen, weaponry changes. Shields become bigger and heavier, and bosses eventually lose their terminal discs. At the same time, spearheads become longer and heavier, as do sidearms like the scramasax. The heavy scramasax, designed for chopping, may have become more popular as a weapon too. A shorter, chopping weapon would be more use in close dismounted combat than a long slashing sword, whilst the often elongated point of the scramasax also gave it an advantage over the battle-axe. Thus it seems to be only from this period that the classic close-fighting infantry phalanx, or shield-wall, became the battlefield norm. Why this change in tactics took place is difficult to fathom. As we have seen, there were also important social, economic and political changes at about this time, and thus changes in the ways in which armies were raised. Nevertheless there seems to be no straightforward link between the two. One might expect that, as armies became raised down 'vertical' chains of lordship and dependence rather than 'horizontally', across broader bands of landowners, warfare became a more specialised occupation. Yet the throwing axes of the later fifth and sixth centuries, especially, and other throwing weapons to a lesser degree, need training and skill to use effectively. Possibly, though we can never know, shock tactics slowly emerged, to smash through more open formations using missile weapons, especially, perhaps, if the training needed to use these weapons was in increasingly short supply. Another possibility is that the warrior retinues of the seventh century were indeed, as has been suggested, trained in the full range of military skills, on foot and on horseback, with missile weapons, and in hand-to-hand fighting, but in battle opted for the decisive battle at close quarters. As we have seen, mounted and dismounted combat appears to have been fought by densely packed bodies. Nor should we assume that such fighting was without skill, as we have seen. This kind of battle required real nerves. Less-well-trained warriors might indeed flee from the approach of an enemy shield-wall, on foot or on horseback. On the other hand, perhaps armies grew in size after the seventh century. We have noted that the social and economic background made larger armies more feasible from this period. Larger armies might have been more easily used in this kind of tactical fashion. Certainly this is the sort of fighting in which numbers could tell, although not, as we have seen, in any crude fashion. Experienced warriors would be deployed at the front of these dense formations but would have to fight in the same way. Ultimately, however, we can do no more than suggest possible links between social change and the apparent change in battlefield usages. Nevertheless, these changes make it impossible to back-project details from the better-documented seventh to tenth centuries into the fifth and sixth or, conversely, to push forward details from Procopius' and Agathias' detailed accounts of sixth-century battles in Italy into the seventh to tenth centuries. It is also important to note that the changes in weaponry take place in Anglo-Saxon England at the same time as they occur in mainland Europe,[161] something else which makes it unlikely that English armies differed radically from their contemporaries in tactical practice.

It has sometimes been suggested that the Arab conquests, in the west, led to changes in battlefield tactics and in the nature of armies. Traditionally, it has been held that the Arabs' light-armed and fast-moving cavalry produced a need for 'rapid-response' western cavalry which was heavily enough armoured to break through the Arab lines. This in turn, it was argued, led to the growth of 'feudalism'. We have discussed various related aspects of this broader thesis before, and generally found them wanting. This argument seems no more satisfactory. We know little about the armies of the Arab conquest in Spain. A large portion, however, appears to have been made up of Berber infantry and much of our stereotypical image of the light cavalry of Moslem armies may actually derive from much later accounts of crusader battles in Syria. In the period that concerns us, Spanish Islamic cavalry does not appear to have been any lighter than its Spanish and Frankish contemporaries. Furthermore, the Basques had been deploying light skirmishing cavalry in the region for centuries, leading to their use as mercenaries and their growing political importance. As far as can be told, battles between Christian and Moslem armies in Spain seem to have been decided, as elsewhere, by hand-to-hand fighting, although infantry archers appear to have been important (as they had been under the Visigoths). It does not seem that there was any significant change in the weaponry in use. Overall, the first phase of Islamic expansion is unlikely to have brought about any significant tactical change.

Much more significant, as will have become clear, were the Vikings. We have seen that the Viking armies had acquired significant tactical skill and, from long periods of serving together, their warriors acquired experience, knowledge and skill, and were very difficult to beat. Viking troops appear to have been hardened enough to give ground in the face of a determined attack, without breaking. They also made clever use of terrain and field fortifications, including existing buildings, most notably churches. On the battlefield they acquired a certain tactical fluidity, and an ability to launch unexpected counter-attacks. They seem to have affected the tactics of their enemies too. Because of the Vikings' use of terrain, Frankish, and possibly Anglo-Saxon, armies had to be prepared to dismount and fight on foot. It may well be that the use of the densely formed infantry shield-wall became more prominent still after the Viking attacks. Although the Vikings rapidly sought out horses once they had landed, and sometimes fought mounted, they usually seem to have fought on foot in close order, and, as we have seen, such formations were difficult to beat with cavalry at this date.

After the battle: casualties, rout, pursuit and plunder

When an army did not break at the first charge or, later in the battle, as a result of a sudden counter-attack or its nerve breaking after several phases of close fighting, such as we have discussed, then battles were won, simply enough, by killing more men than the enemy. In shield-wall fighting a fully exploited local success could lead to the advancing side cutting its way into the less-well-protected and experienced rear ranks, possibly causing panic and more casualties. If it cut right through the division, warriors could be fed through this breach to slash and hack at the sides and rear of the enemy warriors. Such a breach might be closed, possibly by falling back and closing ranks, or by the rear ranks being able to stop the surge, whilst those further forward could strike at the flanks of the enemy warriors in the salient. Casualties could therefore be quite heavy during hand-to-hand fighting, though probably caused mostly in sudden dramatic bursts. Such fighting was probably therefore decided ultimately by who could kill the most of their enemies and exploit the advantage created by such killing. As Asser puts it in his account of Ashdown, 'when a great part of their forces had fallen, they took to ignominious flight'. The more stubborn, experienced or well-drilled the enemy, the higher the casualties would be before a decisive situation was reached.

As we have seen, experienced warriors will have known that it was often better, and perversely often safer, to keep fighting, and to 'sell yourself dearly', than to try to make a run for it. Nevertheless, the results would often be the same, surrounded by a victorious enemy with its 'blood-lust' raised. This might be especially true if the enemy were able to close in on flanks and rear before the ranks could be closed and a tight, outward-facing 'knot' formed, which might deter the enemy from pressing the issue too hard. This practical battlefield knowledge might have given rise to the 'heroic' notion that it was better to avenge or die with one's lord than to survive him, though close study has shown that evidence for this notion is sparse and usually late within the early medieval period.[162] It may also be that once the core of a beaten army saw that it stood no chance of escape, it made a consciously 'heroic' show of its determination to 'go down fighting', praying, saying farewell to old friends, burying old differences and so on. Let us not forget, however, that there is precious little 'heroic' about death brutally administered by spear, axe and sword. We must disabuse ourselves of notions derived from epic poetry, sanitising modern works or Hollywood. The final demise of an early medieval army was accompanied by hideous screams, pleas for mercy, crushed skulls, hacked limbs, ripped bodies and faces, gallons of blood, and spilt brains and intestines.

Though the casualties caused in hand-to-hand fighting were often those which decided the battle, the most numerous casualties were those caused once one side was beaten and broke in flight. Now the slaughter really began. Fleeing troops would discard their shields and be unable to defend themselves. Sometimes, as at Andernach, they became caught up in the baggage train and were cut down even more easily. It would not have been easy to take prisoners. After a burst of hand-to-hand fighting, terrible as it was, emotions could have been whipped to the highest possible pitch, and these would have been released when the enemy broke. Warriors would have hacked down their enemy and gone on doing so. This was not the result of innate blood-lust. Partly it stemmed from the pent-up release of emotion; partly it stemmed from the desire to make sure that a threat, once removed, is removed for good. Warriors who lost comrades in hard fighting wanted to see them avenged. Surrender immediately after close fighting was a risky business even when 'close fighting' was usually actually done with guns and grenades at some distance rather than actually face-to-face.[163] In the early Middle Ages as we have seen, bands of warriors, like later soldiers, often lived in close proximity to each other for long periods, drinking and feasting and engaging in other rituals designed to promote solidarity. Warbands and contingents of levied warriors would also have included many men related to each other by blood, marriage and other 'fictive' kinship ties. This would have promoted feelings of vengeance, and throughout early medieval western Europe vengeance, and vengeance killing, were held to be entirely legal concepts, which must have exaggerated the mood. As Imma's captor said at the Trent, he ought to have Imma killed in vengeance for those of his kin who had fallen in battle.[164] Luckily for Imma, this exchange took place on the day after the battle, when emotions had cooled. In this situation, killing out of hand was rather less likely.

Palaeopathological evidence shows what can happen to an army which has been beaten. In close fighting, when a warrior falls, a new threat to his killer will present itself, as the ranks close. However, when a warrior goes down in flight, without the distraction of the appearance of new threats, his pursuers will keep cutting and hacking to make sure he stays down. The undated Anglo-Saxon cemetery of Eccles in Kent is very instructive.[165] The events which produced the 'Eccles massacre' are unknown but the skeletons are nevertheless interesting. Three were killed by single blows to the front of the skull; the remainder were cut to the head from behind, but suffered multiple wounds. One skeleton, the sadly otherwise anonymous Eccles II, raised his hands to defend himself and had his arms dreadfully cut as a result. His assailants then delivered at least eight separate cuts to his body once he had fallen. The stratigraphy of this site does not allow definite conclusions about how many violent incidents were represented by the burials; nevertheless, for our purposes, the site is a very interesting illustration. We can understand the first group (skeletons I, V and VI) as being indicative of the sorts of horrific fatal head wounds produced in close combat. The deaths of warriors in this way produced tactical advantage and possibly victory. Then in pursuit we see the multiple hacking and stabbing to the other victims (skeletons II, III and IV) as they broke and fled. Those who fell during the hand-to-hand fighting may have been the lucky ones. Imma was knocked unconscious during the battle of the Trent (yet another blow to the head), but survived. One imagines that this took place in close fighting rather than in pursuit.

Absolute numbers of casualties are just as impossible to establish as the size of armies.[166] A beaten army might suffer extremely heavily as a percentage of the original. As we have seen, their casualties would largely be fatal, too. If there had been anything like a hard fight, the winning side too would have suffered badly, though a higher percentage of its losses would be wounded and disabled. Nithard describes the situation following the battle of Fontenoy when the winners, eschewing close pursuit, comforted 'those felled by blows and only half-alive'.[167] 'Many were killed on both sides', say the *Annals of St-Bertin*.[168] The frequency with which this phrase is encountered in contemporary sources makes clear that close fighting was a bloody affair for the winning side as well as for the losers.

Casualties could be particularly high amongst leaders. These would usually be leading from the front, and thus be in the thick of the fighting. If an army broke, however, they would be at the rear and thus the most exposed. The kudos derived from killing a known leader would also make them the focus of fighting. Thus, not surprisingly, death in action was a common fate for early medieval western European aristocracy and royalty. Twelve of the twenty-two battles recorded in seventh-century Anglo-Saxon England resulted in the death of at least one royal figure. Ten ninth-century West Saxon ealdormen (of the shires between Kent and Devon) were killed in warfare. In 827 King Ludeca of Mercia and five ealdormen were killed in battle in East Anglia.[169] As we have seen, the losing Viking side at Ashdown lost six named leaders: one king and five earls. The Irish annals are filled with records of the deaths of kings in action. In the battle of Almain, fought on 11 December 722, no fewer than ten notables were slain.[170] In the one-sided battle which killed Nithard, the *Annals of St-Bertin* mention four other leading aristocrats and 'a great many others' amongst the dead.[171] On the other hand, leaders would probably be well armoured, and surrounded by the best-equipped and most experienced warriors. This may have offset the fact that they were in the thick of the fighting, and meant that they could fight their way off the battlefield if necessary. At Fontenoy, for all that the sources claim it was a great field of slaughter, no leader of any note was killed.[172] Overall, then, whilst a battle in which a large number of named leaders were killed probably saw the demise of many lesser men, we should not assume that battles in which no leaders are mentioned as killed were any less bloody for the 'rank and file'.

Pursuit could be long and close, especially if the winners were mounted, or able to have their horses brought up rapidly. Here again we see why the decision to dismount was a signal of serious battle. A beaten army might not only suffer huge losses but be utterly dispersed by this hue and cry. Sometimes, as at Fontenoy, close or extensive pursuit was abandoned, but this was a somewhat unusual battle during a civil war. Where pursuit of a beaten foe was not pressed, it was more likely because of the onset of night, or because the winners themselves were too exhausted. The presence of readily available loot in the enemy's baggage train might also rapidly divert the victorious warriors from chasing beaten and frightened enemies. The baggage accompanying an early medieval army could be sumptuous, as we saw in chapter 7, and might now be augmented by loot taken earlier in the campaign.[173]

Battle, for all its risks and undoubted horror, need not be decisive. We have noted that some battles simply produced no clear winner at the end of the day. Ironically, both of the battles whose descriptions were quoted at the start of this chapter were quite indecisive, in spite of the accounts of their ferocity and descriptions of the losing side fleeing the field. Fontenoy had no long-term strategic effect. By the end of the year, the defeated Lothar was still on the offensive. After Ashdown, the Danes were reinforced by a *micel sumer lida* ('a great summer hosting') and defeated the English twice. When king Æthelræd died, perhaps of wounds, apparently leading to something of a succession crisis,[174] the English had to buy off the Danes. The disappointing overall outcome of the campaign may be why Asser discusses the only significant English success in such detail, and probably means that he overstated the extent of the Danish defeat. This does not appear to have been unusual; the Vikings were difficult armies to beat, and such was their effect on contemporary mentalities that quite inconclusive victories like Ashdown (871), Saucourt (881) and the Dyle (891) were written up as triumphs or celebrated in verse.[175]

The fate of captives taken in the pursuit or later – as has been seen, there will have been few taken in battle itself – is unclear. King Sigibert of Austrasia managed to negotiate his release from captivity among the Avars. The Vikings ransomed captives, though not often those taken in battle. The 2,000 prisoners taken by the Visigoths after their triumph over a Frankish army in 589 were eventually released and found their way home.[176] Sometimes captured warriors might be released on a promise not to fight against their captors again. Chilperic's son Theudebert swore an oath to that effect when captured by Sigibert in 562, and his later death in battle against Sigibert's troops was seen as a sort of divine retribution for breaking the oath.[177] Nearly 300 years later, some of those taken in battle in the Angoumois were also released after being bound by oath.[178] During the Gothic wars in Italy, captured troops repeatedly enlisted in the winning side, though that was a fairly unusual war within the early medieval west. Otherwise the fate of those captured in war could be grim. Many were doubtless sold as slaves. Others were executed, though this is not commonly reported. The Vikings massacred the prisoners they took in the battle of the Geule in 891.[179] As has been mentioned, Imma's captor after the battle of the Trent declared that he should have him killed in vengeance for relatives lost in battle. In this light, it is an intriguing possibility that the executed people whose bodies were interred in the ditch around Sutton Hoo mound 5[180] were killed in vengeance for the death of the subject of the main grave. The precise circumstances here will always be unknown, but Raedwald of East Anglia, still the most plausible occupant of Sutton Hoo mound 1, lost a son during a victorious battle against the Northumbrians at a date not incompatible with that of mound 5. Some wars were waged with more savagery than others. Those between Christians and Moslems in Spain were such. Fruela I of the Asturias himself beheaded a captured Moorish commander on the battlefield of Pontubio (757).[181] Moslem soldiers were butchered when towns were taken by the Christians.[182]

The other main activity consequent upon battle was the looting of the defeated army's dead and baggage train. It was suggested in chapter 7 that defeating an army in battle was the most potentially profitable military action in the early Middle Ages, more likely to produce important quantities of plunder than the capture of settlements, even at the end of the period. This, it was suggested, was one reason for the relative importance of set-piece battle in the early Middle Ages. In order to examine that proposition further it is necessary to consider the other half of the equation and make a brief survey of fortifications and siege warfare.

10

FORTIFICATION AND
SIEGE WARFARE

Although, as we have seen, large-scale military activity was fairly common, the fortification of settlements was relatively rare. Two methodological points need making at the outset. The first is that we must distinguish *defended* sites from *defensible* ones; as we shall see, although the former may be comparatively few, the latter are perhaps much more numerous than is immediately apparent. The second point, related to, and in some ways the converse of, the first, is that we should not automatically assume that the primary purpose of every walled, palisaded or bank-and-ditched line or enclosure was defensive. Some such apparent 'fortifications' might have been intended as markers, delineating different social or economic zones, within which different actions were possible. It has, for instance, been argued that the purpose of walls around Merovingian *villae* was social control, marking a point beyond which slaves would be considered runaways.[1] Perhaps more plausibly, and certainly more commonly, these walls, fences or ditches could simply define the extent of a private *curtis* (courtyard), household or property, an area within which early medieval law generally penalised offences more seriously. Similarly, ditches, banks or walls around larger settlements may exist primarily to define the extent of such a settlement, where the settlement lay under special royal protection,[2] or where certain activities where only permitted within such an enclosure.[3] Although town walls may take on a very military appearance, as with the ritual use of weaponry, the primary purpose of such building may have been the display of social status or wealth or the power of the ruler. Having made these important points, though, we must still recognise that even a wall designed primarily for legal or social rather than defensive purposes may well have been defensible.

Our survey of early medieval fortification begins with a consideration of the lowest level of rural settlement. Characteristically, this period's farmsteads, hamlets and villages do not seem to be defended. Anglo-Saxon, Merovingian and Carolingian rural settlements are collections of timber buildings, halls and ancillary structures, without any sign of defensive walls, banks, ditches or palisades. However, some of the hall-like structures may well have been defensible. With limited points of access, usually pairs of opposed narrow doors mid-way along the long walls of the structures, a handful of determined warriors with shields and spears could easily have prevented an enemy from gaining entrance. Damp thatch is difficult to ignite and without large axes the load-bearing walls of these buildings may not have been easy to breach. With time, a determined enemy could have broken in, but in many cases the attacker will have found it both less trouble and less costly to pen in the inhabitants with some warriors whilst the remainder rounded up the cattle, other livestock, food and whatever loot could be found in the undefended structures; this, after all, rather than slaughter of farmers, will usually have been the objective of the attack. If slaves were sought, if the enemy's armed forces had been defeated and scattered or were otherwise no threat to the attackers, or if it was a particularly severe outbreak of warfare, then the inhabitants' situation might become much grimmer.

These points may be pursued with regard to rural sites of slightly higher social status. The Roman villa was rarely fortified, but some late Roman Gallic examples may have been. In northern Gaul, to judge from their ground plans, a number of higher-status rural settlements may have been fortified, but these had largely been abandoned in the decades around 400. Further south, near Bordeaux, the mid-fifth-century author, Sidonius Apollinaris, described the villa, appropriately called *Burgus* ('Fort'), belonging to his friend Pontius Leontius, with its walls and towers.[4] Some of these sites may have been used in our period, although, as Ross Samson[5] has pointed out, the narrative of Gregory does not often refer to such defended habitations. Gallo-Roman aristocrats under attack appear to have made their homes defensible, but they did not apparently have the benefit of defensive fortifications. Further south, in Spain, impressive villa sites were certainly occupied into the sixth and some-times the seventh centuries, and a number of these do seem to have been designed to be defensible. Similarly, in Italy, some high-status sites seem to have been fortified in the late Roman period, and to have been occupied into the post-Roman era.[6]

New types of high-status settlement do not, on the whole, appear to have been fortified. Again, they may have been defensible, but early medieval 'palaces' do not appear to have been fortified. The Anglo-Saxon palace at Yeavering lay next to an enclosure which was eminently defensible, but, rather like other types of contemporary settlement, it was not situated within those ramparts. Surrounding ditches and fences were not substantial, even at major Carolingian palace sites such as Aachen, and appear to have served other purposes. The defence of such sites resided in the personnel of the occupant's bodyguards and their ability to hold doors and gateways of the buildings themselves. The *Anglo-Saxon Chronicle*'s famous entry for 757, relating events of thirty years later, shows how a high-status hall could be held for a while, although not against serious odds and a determined enemy. Here the situation was, or may have been, different, as the aim of such attacks was to take the buildings and kill the occupants.[7]

The towns and more important villages of the Roman Empire had been fortified by the later Roman period. This happened at different times in different areas, and with different results. British towns were fortified earlier than most and consequently have quite extensive walls. On the Continent, most towns were only fortified after the 'third-century crisis'. This normally resulted in very short walled circuits. At Paris, for example, only the Île de la Cité and the left bank's forum were walled.[8] This has usually led to conclusions about hastily built defences thrown up as an emergency response to barbarian invasions. In fact these walls are very difficult to date, and may have been built over quite long periods of time. Although the foundations were usually built from *spolia* from tombs and public buildings, surviving examples above ground seem to show careful construction. The short length of these walls may also reflect the urban contraction of the period; certainly, occupation outside the reduced enceintes is not always easy to find, although doubtless it existed. However, it is more likely to result mainly from the reluctance of urban councils to pay for public building. These walls seem to have been high, built of stone, and with projecting towers, though the evidence is far less clear than is often supposed. The fate of these town walls in the post-Roman period is not always certain. They do not always appear to have been properly maintained, as a number of instances of collapsing walls, and the need for rebuilding, indicates.[9] Bishops very often took over responsibility for their upkeep in the immediately post-Roman centuries, though kings, obviously, were concerned to maintain the defences of the administrative nodes of their kingdoms. In the Carolingian period, however, the walls of a number of cities were allowed to decline. The inhabitants of ninth-century Mainz demolished a section of their town walls to gain access to the river and to trade.[10] The archbishop of Rheims gained permission to knock down a portion of the walls of his city so that he could extend his cathedral.[11] Even in eighth-century Aquitaine, the site of repeated campaigning, the Aquitanians apparently slighted their city walls because of their failure to hold them against Frankish attack and, as discussed in chapter 7, this was a war fought out mostly by raids and harryings.

This once again reveals a profound difference in attitudes towards walled areas in the post-Roman period. Although walled areas were valued as administrative centres and, presumably, as refuges, it is clear that occupation had a tendency to drift away from the often derelict walled zones, and especially to areas with Christian associations. This is partially indicative of a change in mentalities which led to greater faith being placed in spiritual protection. Thus occupation at Tours concentrated around the unwalled, extra-mural Christian complex around the church of St Martin.[12] A similar shift, leading to a bifocal town, took place at Limoges with its shrine of St Martial.[13] The acquisition of numinous protection was not the only factor in these shifts, however. Merovingian occupation at Trier was largely to be found between the old inhabited area and the walls (an early circuit which was always too long and enclosed uninhabited areas), although some major late Roman buildings appear to have been turned into small strongholds (such as the 'Barbarathermen' public baths, and the amphitheatre).[14] At nearby Metz, too, occupation appears to have drifted to the south, and perhaps the amphitheatre there was also used as a defensive redoubt. The same feature can be observed on the sites of the former Roman *castra* and *castella* (walled villages), which also seem to indicate a shift of settlement away from the formerly defended zone.[15] In a period of economic contraction, like the fifth and sixth centuries, large stone buildings were difficult to maintain and therefore will rapidly have become derelict and dangerous. The occupants of the sites of the *civitas* capitals were also now largely involved in subsistence activities, which meant that occupation became less dense and areas were turned over to use as gardens and vineyards. The need for such land also presumably contributed to the shift to extra-mural areas.

In the fifth to ninth centuries, then, people do not appear to have wanted to live within walled zones. This is further underlined by the development of the *emporia*, trading centres, which were invariably unfortified in this period. The English sites at Hamwic (Southampton) and Ipswich lacked walls; Hamwic having only a small boundary ditch.[16] The middle Saxon sites at York and London were located outside the former walled areas, upstream in the case of *Lundenwic*, and downstream at *Eoforwic*.[17] Continental emporia, at Dorestadt, Quentovic, Domburg, and Hedeby for example, were likewise undefended.[18] When the trading centres, usually referred to as *portus* in the sources, emerge near Roman towns and *castra* on the Continent, these too lie away from the walled areas. Most emporia had a defensible refuge nearby – the old Roman walled sites at York and London, Roman forts near Hamwic and Dorestadt, a hillfort at Hedeby, and so on – but the towns themselves remained unwalled. This is a common feature of towns in this period: we can often trace a defended redoubt, perhaps containing a royal and ecclesiastical presence, but this seems to be separated from the main social and economic zone. Sometimes cult centres form another separate area, thus leading to polyfocal settlements.

Given the ubiquity of warfare in this period this apparent lack of concern with fortification is surprising. The deliberate dereliction of walls in early ninth-century Francia was clearly born of over a century's internal peace and stability; the Vikings (followed by the Magyars and the Arabs in the south) were to change that. Otherwise, in Anglo-Saxon England, warfare does not appear to have turned much on sieges. The capture of cities was, as we have seen, the aim of much sixth-century Merovingian warfare, but there are no instances in Merovingian Gaul where a walled town was captured by straightforward assault. Either there was collaboration (or treachery) within the town, or the walls were in such dilapidated state that defence was impossible (which is perhaps how we should read accounts of collapsing walls, such as at Angoulême in 507, written up with clear echoes of Joshua at Jericho).[19] Most such warfare was fairly stylised in any case, as discussed in chapter 7. The inhabitants of towns (who were never very numerous in any case, especially in the earlier part of our period) seem to have been content, on the whole, to take themselves and whatever movables they could into the shelter of a small refuge or, if they could, perhaps flee the area altogether. This was probably the safer option. The slaughter of such people was not the aim of most warfare but the inhabitants of a town which was captured after a siege, however rarely this happened, could find themselves in serious trouble. In the Gothic wars in Italy, a terrible fate befell the inhabitants of Milan when it surrendered to the Goths, and the citizens of Naples suffered a severe sack by Belisarius' Roman troops when it was stormed.[20] The people of Vienne were slaughtered when their town was stormed (with the aid of treachery) during a Burgundian civil war in 501.[21] As with troops in battle, emotions ran high among troops engaged in the dangerous, costly and usually fruitless business of an assault, and these could not easily be switched off. This would lead to similar sprees of hot-blooded killing as followed the defeat of an army in the field. In 585, although their town was surrendered rather than being taken by assault, the inhabitants of Lugdunum Convenarum (St-Bertrand-de-Comminges) were still butchered by the army of Guntramn of Burgundy.[22] This probably resulted from the fact that the siege of St-Bertrand had been a fairly long one, which had involved numerous failed attacks on the walls; there were slates to be cleaned. It had also been held by the army of a pretender, whose supporters were hunted ruthlessly. Such occurrences do not appear to have been common in the sixth to eighth centuries, however. On the whole, it seems to have been a comparatively safe option to 'hole up' in a walled refuge until the enemy went away, or negotiations for a peaceful solution were concluded.

Only with the advent of the Vikings does this pattern of dispersed and largely defenceless urban or proto-urban sites begin to change. In its last, mid-ninth-century phase, *Lundenwic* was given a much more substantial and clearly defensive ditch. The Viking attacks, and the new type of warfare which they introduced, led to a new concern with fortification. The earliest response was the construction of circular fortresses along the coast of the Netherlands by Louis the Pious.[23] These were not especially successful, however, and were soon replaced by attempts to defend the area by giving it, as benefice, to Scandinavian leaders, an expedient which was not very much more successful.[24] In the 860s Charles the Bald experimented with fortified bridges, which would deny passage of the Scandinavian fleets into the heartland of West Francia.[25] There were fewer of these than has sometimes been supposed; some instances seem rather to have been occasions when the Frankish army stationed itself at a bridge to prevent the Vikings from passing. Nevertheless there were at least two more permanent fortifications, the best known being at Pont-de-l'Arche. Here a bridge at the lowest bridgeable point of the Seine connected one large forti-fication and one smaller bridgehead. The nature of the bridge itself is a matter of contention. It is usually supposed that the bridge was of the type one usually imagines, constructed as a series of arches across the river. It is then assumed that these arches would somehow be blocked when the Vikings attacked to stop their ships from sailing through. Another possibility, however, which may be more plausible, is that the bridges were pontoon bridges. These would be low enough to present a barrier in themselves. Many (possibly most) bridges in post-Roman Gaul, even those across major rivers, were of this type.[26] One imagines that central sections were removable, to allow river traffic to pass, and replaced when people wished to cross the river.

In England, the famous response to the Viking incursions, and the most successful, was the network of *burhs* (fortified towns, whence the modern word 'borough').[27] This network was created by King Alfred in the 880s, after the damaging, free-moving raids of the Viking army in the later 860s and 870s. The nature of the burghal forts was diverse. Some reused Roman fortifications (Winchester), others were reused prehistoric forts (e.g., Lydford), and others still seem to have been of new construction (e.g., Wareham and Wallingford). Some sites were moved back inside the old Roman walls, as happened at London, where *Lundenwic* became *Lundenburh*. It does not seem that there was any constant feature of the layout of these sites or of the construction of their defences. Alfred appears simply to have fortified a network of high-status sites within his kingdom, be they major churches ('minsters') or royal administrative centres (either former Roman towns or royal *vils*). These types of site had been major targets for Viking attacks in the past.[28] The sites seem to have been selected so that all the inhabitants of Wessex were within a day's walk of one, and so as to minimise the ability of an attacking army to move freely about the kingdom. Therefore, many *burhs* are at river crossings, denying passage up or down the river by boat, or across the river by the bridge or ford. Alfred also drew up a system to provide for permanent garrisons in these fortifications.[29] The full development of the burghal 'system', and the development of these sites into planned towns, may belong to the reigns of Alfred's successors, notably his son Edward the Elder, and grandson, Athelstan, but the success of the defences can be judged easily by the fact that the Great Army of the 890s was able to make no significant inroad into Wessex and rapidly moved elsewhere. The expansion of the burghal system and its use in the West Saxon wars of conquest in the midlands and the north lie outside the scope of this book. At about the same time, towns appear to have begun to be more extensively fortified. The Anglo-Scandinavian site at York was moved so that it lay within one defensible circuit defined by the northern and eastern walls of the Roman fortress and the rivers Ouse and Fosse.[30] The centres of Danish rule in the 'Danelaw' were also fortified. This tendency increased in the tenth century, as enclosing walls were thrown around the trading centres of Birka and Hedeby.[31] This development also lies beyond the present volume's coverage.

Cities and other larger settlements were not the only fortifications in this period. Hillforts were also used from time to time, most frequently in the west and north of Britain.[32] At the end of the Roman period in what is now Wales and western England, a number of Iron Age hillforts were reoccupied and their defences refurbished.[33] South Cadbury in Dorset is possibly the best known of these sites, largely because of the fact that its excavator cannily played upon a sixteenth-century antiquarian's report that legend had it that the site was

King Arthur's Camelot![34] These sites usually only have a single bank and ditch enclosure, even if the original Iron Age phase had several; they are thus termed univallate. The ramparts were, depending on the region, either timber fences or stone walls. The defences at South Cadbury have been reconstructed as being formed by a stone-revetted rampart topped with a timber palisade. On occasion, however, where the fort lies on a promontory, the main approach to the enclosure is barred by a series of ramparts.[35] In what is now Scotland, a number of forts were composed of a series of enclosures, though again usually with only a single bank and ditch. Walls appear to have been of dry stone construction. These were high-status sites, which have yielded evidence of specialist craft-working, and involvement in long-distance trade. Judging from the laconic sources, they also played an important role in the warfare of the period in these regions;[36] sieges and 'burnings' of strongholds are repeatedly mentioned, although it is sometimes difficult to know whether the engagements which took place there were sieges or open battles. In 685, for example, the Northumbrian army and its king, Ecgfrith, were destroyed at the battle of Nechtansmere (Nechtan's Lake), or Llyn Garan (the Lake of Cranes). Although the sources place the battle clearly by the lake (now dried up) the site lies at the foot of a hill crowned by a small hillfort, Dunnichen (Nechtan's Dun, or fort). Either the Northumbrians were ambushed whilst marching on the fort,[37] or they were attacked whilst besieging the place, or the Pictish army simply chose its ground by the hillfort. Either way, the fort played an important strategic role in the campaign. If the Northumbrians had won the battle, it is likely that Dun Nechtan would have been burnt in the aftermath.

Very similar hillforts were used in the middle and upper Rhine valley, in the land of the Alamans, in the fifth century.[38] These, too, were high-status centres, with evidence of craft specialisation. Like the British examples, they are usually univallate and quite small, though some larger examples are known. Most were abandoned at the beginning of the sixth century, when important changes took place in Alamannic society, but some were reoccupied in the eighth century. At about the same time there is some evidence that Frankish aristocrats were also constructing their own hilltop fortifications. For example, Count Wulfoald, an enemy of the Arnulfing dynasty, seems to have constructed a hillfort (*castrum*) at St-Mihiel in the Argonne.[39] This was doubtless a response to the troubled, and violent politics of the period.[40] In the next century, as Frankish internal politics became more stable and as the inhabitants of some Frankish towns even demolished their town walls, the need for such fortifications declined. The situation was different on the frontier. Charlemagne made much use of forts as bases for his campaigns of conquest in Germany and there were more sieges during the wars against the Saxons than was usual within the period 450–900. Indeed the eastern frontier of the Frankish realm relied heavily on fortified strongpoints. Hamburg and Frankfurt owe their origins in part at least to such fortifications. The use of fortifications on the frontier went back as far as the eighth century, when Franks and Saxons strengthened their side of the frontiers with hillforts. In the ninth century river lines were used, though not exclusively, and some use was made of other natural features such as forests to bar the frontier to enemy forces.[41]

Recent archaeological evidence has suggested that the Anglo-Saxons may also have made some use of prehistoric hillforts, at least as refuges. Many such sites are linked by the major routes known as *herepaths* ('army paths').[42] Though functionally different, these sites may be the precursors of the later *burhs*.

Another area where small hilltop fortifications were common is Italy.[43] The fortification of such sites goes back to the Ostrogothic period, when at least one high-status site was located on the top of a hill. This seems to have been a process accelerated by the Gothic wars and underlined thereafter in the political fragmentation of the Italian peninsula. The troubled times of our period led to the relocation of many villages to fortified hilltop sites, a process known as *incastellamento*.[44]

In western Britain and Ireland forts on islands, sometimes man-made, were used, called crannogs.[45] Most of the defence was left to the natural obstacle of the lake's waters, but timber ramparts and gatehouses were constructed. Irish forts were usually small and fairly simple. They are known as raths or cashels depending on the region and whether stone or timber was used for the defences. They sheltered small groups of people, and were usually univallate. Although such fortifications provided adequate defence against small raids, such as was the norm in Irish warfare, they could not hold out against a major attack by an army.[46]

Fortifications could have other tactical and strategic uses. The possible tactical use of field fortifications and the possibility that the occupation of such sites may have been a ploy to control or bring about battle have already been discussed. These defences could also of course have provided a base, and protection against surprise attack for an encamped army. The past masters of the strategic use of fortifications were, as has been noted, the Vikings. Viking armies repeatedly either used existing fortifications as bases or rapidly made key points defensible, as can be seen repeatedly in the Great Army's attacks on England. As we have seen, the Danes usually homed in upon a high-status settlement – be it a royal *vil* or *tun* or a monastery or prestigious church. The use of monasteries and other major churches was not just because they were centres of moveable wealth; monastic communities were enclosed with walls to delineate the monastic enclosure from the secular world. In 867–8, the Danes' employment of fortification at Nottingham meant that the combined armies of Wessex and Mercia had had to disband and buy peace because they were unable to mount a successful attack.[47] In 870 the army fortified the English royal *vil* at Reading, by enclosing the spit of land between Thames and Kennet with a bank and ditch.[48] In 875 they moved quickly from one fortified site to another, making use of the natural defensibility of the minster church at Wareham, between two rivers. Archaeologically a similar process has been revealed clearly by excavations at Repton, which have shown how the Great Army built a small defended enclosure, which appears to have used the church as a gatehouse or strong point.[49] Later, in the 890s, the Danes again occupied a half-finished English fort when they landed in Alfred's kingdom, and used this as a base.[50]

The use of fortifications in campaigns was another area within which the Vikings had an impact. Although, as mentioned, fortifications played an important role in warfare on the Frankish eastern frontier since the eighth century, as the last century of our period wore on, their use became increasingly common. As has already been pointed out, these changes do not seem to have been fully carried through until the tenth century. In that century, tactical and strategic developments may well have combined with the fragmentation of the Carolingian empire to produce increased reliance upon local aristocratic fortifications and their garrisons.

Siege warfare appears to have varied in intensity and importance from place to place and from time to time within the period under review. This variation probably also reflects differences in the nature of warfare. In Italy during the Gothic wars sieges were frequent and often vicious affairs; this war was a long, protracted and extremely destructive one, which shattered the classical social structures of Italy for ever. We have already noted the fate of the inhabitants of Naples and Milan. The massacre of the latter stemmed from a rather shameful deal done by the East Roman garrison, the Goths allowing them to leave, but treating the inhabitants of the city as traitors for having welcomed the 'Greeks'. Cities in this war were important bases for the control of regions which were retaken by the armies of the Emperor Justinian. Recognising this, the Gothic king, Totila, demolished the walls of cities recaptured from the Byzantines, to prevent their use in this way.[51] Similarly, the Visigothic campaigns against the Byzantine enclave of *Spania* were concerned with the capture of cities, sometimes followed by serious sackings. The Byzantine military does not appear to have had the capability to wage open warfare against the Goths.[52] The campaign by the Visigothic king, Leuvigild, against his rebellious son Hermenigild was also concerned with the steady reduction of those cities which had declared for the rebel.[53] On the other hand, as we have seen, siege warfare in Merovingian Gaul was fairly stylised.

On the whole, early medieval siege-craft was basic. There were only a few simple techniques. One could harry the surrounding area and hope that the defenders chose to surrender rather than lose more of their property; one could surround the place and starve it into surrender; or one could try to carry the defences by storm, usually conducted with a minimum of finesse. Siege warfare seems nevertheless to have been rather fluid in form. One should not regard it as a case where one side was strictly penned in within its defences, whilst the other sat outside and periodically attacked the walls. The defenders made sallies, and sometimes ventured out to engage in major battles.

Trying to starve out a besieged site was a risky business. Disease was a frequent visitor to the encampments of besiegers as well as the besieged. As has been mentioned before, the Lombards habitually shut themselves up in their cities when confronted by Frankish invasion (as in 590), because they knew that dysentery and malaria would be more likely to decimate the Frankish armies before they had managed to capture any of the Lombard cities. Periodic sallies and raids could also undermine the besiegers' will to continue the operation. One example where the besiegers tried to ensure that the besieged were truly hemmed in came in 873, when Charles the Bald constructed an earthwork ring around Angers, which was held by a Viking army. A Breton army was held in reserve, and, according to one report, diverted the river Mayenne to increase the besieged army's hardship.[54] This siege was successful and produced the Vikings' surrender, but this level of complexity does not seem to have been frequent.

Probably the most detailed description of a siege is Procopius' account of the Gothic siege of Rome in 537.[55] Procopius was an eye-witness of the events, but it should be remembered that, whatever notes he took at the time, the final polished version was written up to a decade or more after the event, and Procopius has clearly enmeshed his account in the rhetoric of classical military history, as well as embroidering other aspects for their rhetorical and even ironic potential. The Goths constructed a number of camps mostly on the east side of Rome, facing the gates of the city. There was no attempt to construct any serious lines of circumvallation, and access into and out of the city was not entirely prevented. Indeed, Belisarius' Eastern Roman army appears to have done more to confine the Goths to their camps by aggressive sorties and raids. A number of large-scale encounters were fought outside the walls, too, in which sometimes the Goths, sometimes the Romans, came off best. The Goths made several serious assaults on the walls, on one occasion using large siege towers. This event is made into an occasion of ridicule by Procopius, who describes Belisarius standing on the walls of Rome laughing at the Goths' stupidity. The Goths were hauling their siege towers towards the walls with oxen, which the Roman garrison promptly shot down, leaving the towers helpless. At this distance it is impossible to weed out the elements of truth from an account which so clearly plays upon the stereotypical inability of barbarians to wage siege warfare in Graeco-Roman ethnography.[56] The Goths tried to use siege towers later in the campaign, at Rimini, where this time they did not use oxen, but hauled the tower themselves from within.[57] Once again, the Byzantines got the better of them, however, by digging a ditch between the tower and the walls, during the night. Once again the Gothic attempt at siege-craft was left looking ludicrous. At Rome, most attacks were carried out with much less complication, but no more success. After camping against the city for a year, the Gothic king, Wittigis, broke up the siege.

Assaults against defences seem generally to have been of a basic nature. Siege artillery was not unknown in the post-Roman west, and may have been more common than is often supposed, but it was not very commonly deployed to any significant success. The tragicomic references to the Goths and their towers constitute the only evidence of that type of complex machinery. The bolt-shooters positioned on the walls of Rome by Belisarius appear to have seriously damaged the morale of the Gothic forces,[58] but most Gothic attacks were repelled by far more basic means. In one instance, the East Roman defenders defeated a Gothic attack by the desperate expedient of heaving the statues from the parapet of the tomb of Hadrian (the later Castel Sant' Angelo) onto the heads of their assailants.[59]

There are other references to siege engines. There is a reference to the Vikings using stone-throwers at the siege of Paris in 886 in the poem *De Bello Parisiaco* (On the Parisian War) by Abbo. Paul the Deacon describes the Lombard king, Aripert, besieging Bergamo with battering rams and 'weapons of war'.[60] More precise, however, is Paul's reference to a stone-thrower somewhat earlier.[61] The *Royal Frankish Annals* mention the use by the Saxons of catapults during an attack on a Frankish fort, although they say that these were not very effective.[62] Another reference to a stone-thrower comes in Venantius Fortunatus' account of Bishop Nicetius of Trier's fortress on the Moselle.[63] Siege engines are mentioned in Charles Martel's and Pippin I's wars in southern France whenever a formal siege seems to have taken place. In these wars, when the Franks did not simply take a place by assault, they appear to have employed fairly sophisticated siegecraft. Charles Martel threw up lines of circumvallation around Avignon and Narbonne during his 737 campaign against the Moors. He used battering rams at Avignon and what appear to have been stone-throwers at Narbonne.[64] Charles' son Pippin employed similar techniques at Bourges in 762, surrounding the town with a fortified line, equipped with siege engines.[65] The reference to the Franks camping around Thouars in the same campaign might hint at a similar procedure. Otherwise the Franks simply seem to have taken Aquitanian strongholds by storm. These techniques seem much more advanced than those mentioned in accounts of sixth-century Frankish warfare.

Gregory of Tours gives an unusually detailed account of the attack by a Frankish Burgundian army on St-Bertrand-de-Comminges, held by the forces of the usurper Gundovald.[66] Again the picture is fairly crude. The attackers attempted to make battering rams. These had shelters constructed from wagons, and roofs cobbled together from planks, old saddles and bits of wickerwork. These makeshift contraptions were, unsurprisingly, not very effective, being crushed by rocks dropped from the ramparts of the city. The defenders' tactics consisted largely of dropping things from the walls; we are told of boxes of stones, rocks and, interestingly, barrels filled with pitch and fat, which were set alight. The siege was ended by treachery, itself produced by the collapse of morale on the part of the defenders. Gregory says that the town could easily have held out for a long time if the garrison had had the will. A similar occurrence took place earlier in the sixth century.[67] The occupants of the fortress of Chastel-Marlhac, says Gregory, could also have held out indefinitely, had they not launched an ill-advised sortie against the besieging army of Theuderic of Austrasia. A number of them were captured, giving the attackers a useful bargaining chip, and the defenders eventually ransomed themselves. During the same campaign, the Austrasians stormed the fortress of Vollore, putting large numbers of defenders to the sword and enslaving the rest (this was a notably savage campaign which ravaged the Auvergne, and about which Gregory, as a local, knew many stories). How this came about is difficult to know; Gregory is cryptic. He says that the place had never been captured before, and that Theuderic's troops were on the verge of giving up and going home. This led the defenders into a false sense of security, and the fortress fell. Does this imply that they stood down their guards, and fell victim to an unexpected attack?

When we have detailed accounts of attacks upon fortifications they seem to be of uncomplicated attempts to rush the gates. Wamba's troops took Narbonne and Nîmes by burning the gates.[68] Charles Martel's troops used rope ladders and battering rams in their attack on the walls of Avignon (737).[69] The Viking attacks on Paris seem, from Abbo's account, generally to have been fairly simple attempts to storm the walls, sometimes by setting fire to the defences. The seventh-century Spanish Visigothic assaults described in Julian of Toledo's *History of King Wamba* were similarly unsophisticated assaults covered by showers of missiles and resisted in like manner.[70] In 896, Rome fell to King Arnulf in just such an attack. The *Annals of Fulda* describes the attack in some detail. The defenders were driven off the walls by the throwing of stones (this seems to have been by hand – the attack appears to have been somewhat spontaneous) and 'a mass of men hurled themselves at the gates'. Iron bars and clubs were used, as well as the troops trying simply to hew their way through the wood. Other men used ladders to scale the walls, and the city fell. Another assault by Arnulf's troops, on Bergamo, is described in 894.[71] The troops held their shields over their heads and tried to dig their way through the ancient walls. The inhabitants, like the defenders of St-Bertrand-de-Comminges three centuries earlier, emptied containers of rocks onto them, threw spears and even pushed the battlements down on the attackers, all without success. The town fell and its commander was hanged from the tower where he made his last stand. As mentioned earlier,[72] Arnulf appears to have controlled his attacking army much as though it were engaged in an open battle. On the other hand, the combined Mercian and West Saxon armies attacked the Viking fort at Nottingham in 869, but were unable to breach the walls.[73]

In 852 an attacking force gave up at the point of victory in a case which illustrates some of the imperatives of early medieval campaigning. The future Emperor Louis II was attacking Bari, held by an invading Arab army. Having made a breach in the walls, he called off the attack, fearing that the army might get out of control and thus deprive him of his full share of loot. How he had effected the breach is not specified, though we might suspect the use of engines of some sort. It would not be easy simply to call off an army in the middle of an assault which had broken the defences. In the meantime, the Arabs repaired the breach with balks of timber and 'had nothing to fear'. Consequently Louis gave up the siege and marched away.

On the whole, early medieval western siege warfare was fairly crude, though not as basic as is sometimes supposed. The importance of fortifications varied through time and place, as did the importance of sieges. When trying to drive a raiding enemy force, like those of the Vikings or the Saracens, from a fortified base, sieges were essential. In other cases the political centre of a region had to be stormed before its conquest or subjugation could be deemed complete. Certainly, fortification of key centres, political and economic, was becoming more important at the end of our period than it had been earlier. This helped to produce a change in the nature of warfare. Between 450 and 900 it was more usual, however, for sieges to be far less important in military thinking than harrying and the battles it was aimed at producing. Given the relative unimportance of sieges and the generally low socio-economic scale of even the major settlements at the end of the period, the paradox with which the chapter began – the frequency of warfare and large-scale violence but the infrequency of major fortifications – is more apparent than real.

EPILOGUE

Ending a war

War and peace were, as was noted in chapter 1, polarities. When the fighting was concluded peace did not automatically ensue. A beaten army might straggle home. Disputed territory or a defeated kingdom might be incorporated in the victor's realm. Otherwise hostages might be given or, more usually, oaths of fidelity sworn by the losers, and tribute could be paid;[1] until the next time. The endemic raiding might go on just as before. All formalities, however, required shared values. For oaths to be binding they had to be sworn on objects or deities venerated by both sides. The penalties for defaulting on promises made with divine sureties had to be accepted by all those who were swearing the oaths. One reason why some peoples, most notably the Vikings, were regarded as habitual liars and oath-breakers was, probably, simply that they did not see themselves bound by the objects or the divine powers upon which they had been forced to swear. Thus Christian kings worked hard to bring pagan enemies within the Church, to avoid these problems, and to create common ground, shared norms and accepted rules of behaviour.[2]

The victors would return home, and perhaps church services would be held in thanksgiving for their triumph. In Visigothic Spain, the defeated parties could be maimed and publicly humiliated in front of the army and the people.[3] Executions might take place. Only occasionally were formal treaties of peace drawn up. Before the Treaty of Verdun in 843, which temporarily ended the warfare between the sons of Louis the Pious in which Nithard had been involved, complex negotiations took place.[4] After some to-ing and fro-ing of emissaries, the three brothers met, with equal numbers of followers, on an island near Mâcon in June 842. Later in the year, hostages were exchanged before a second meeting at Koblenz in October, with the two sides' armies camped on opposite sides of the Rhine. There, just as the negotiations at Mâcon had taken place in a geographically neutral spot, an island in the river, the talks took place in a location whose neutrality was spiritually guaranteed: the church of St-Castor. A truce was agreed until 14 July 843. Eventually the three brothers met at Verdun in 843 and signed a treaty dividing their father's empire between them.

Peace and law, following from Roman equations of the two, meant a similarity between law-codes and peace treaties. It has been suggested that the Laws of Ine of Wessex and of Wihtred of Kent were promulgated at the same time as part of the peacemaking process when they ended their war in 694.[5] A more famous treaty was that made between Alfred of Wessex and the Viking leader Guthrum, after Alfred's victory in 879.[6] The series of treaties made between the Carolingian and post-Carolingian rulers of Italy and the Doges of Venice take a not dissimilar form.[7] In these cases all cross-border conflict was to be ended and any infractions were to be compensated for. The parties undertook to help each other maintain law and order within their realms, by not receiving fugitives from justice. There are other references to warfare between kingdoms being ended by the payment of compensation.[8] Bishops were often used as go-betweens in these processes, just as, in some political systems, they could be used to try to defuse situations when they threatened to erupt into more serious outbreaks of warfare.[9] One such instance resulted in the Treaty of Andelot between the Merovingian kingdoms of Austrasia and Burgundy, which set out to resolve long-standing issues, which were threatening to blow up into full-scale war. Even that did not entirely end the tension. Gregory of Tours himself had to go on an embassy to Guntramn of Burgundy and have the treaty read out again in public before the crisis passed.[10] Formal states of peace were unusual, though. Wars usually ended with the victory of one side and the *de facto* conquest or submission of the other, or it simply justified the next attack. Warfare was too important to too much of early medieval politics, economics and social structure to be ruled out for very long.

By way of conclusions

The present volume has presented a series of conclusions, which, it is hoped, might form the basis of future discussions of early medieval warfare. Warfare varied in scale, and its practice varied accordingly. However, one thing which has become apparent was the distinctiveness of warfare in the period between 450 and 900. Warfare was carried out through harrying enemy territory. The ravaging of land was carried out as a challenge to the opposing army, enticing it to come out to battle. As a result of that, encounter in the field was much more important a component of early medieval warfare, and sieges less important, than would be the case from the tenth century onwards. Changes in economy and society appear to have made siege warfare, especially of small private fortifications, and the ransoming of captives, more important in the conduct of warfare than open battle by the twelfth century.

Another lesson to emerge is the similarity of developments across Europe, including Anglo-Saxon England. There was, however, variation too. Warfare in Ireland and in northern and western Britain retained a distinctive character and tactical practices were not everywhere the same. We have seen change through time as well. There seems to have been important change around AD 600, which has not hitherto received much attention. Further change appears to have come with the Vikings. One conclusion drawn from the present work is that Viking armies *were* distinctive, even if often acting within a recognisably similar framework. They were difficult enemies to beat for a number of reasons; they adopted distinctive strategies (at least in England) and they seem to have inspired tactical change, making good use of fortifications and bringing about an increase in the battlefield importance of dismounted combat. In all areas we have also seen the intricate interrelation of warfare with the rest of early medieval society, politics and economics and, in particular, how the raising of armies was one of the most important and dynamic points of contact between local societies and royal authority.

But one of the main lessons of this book has been that to search for an understanding of warfare in the early medieval west does not and cannot involve the simple quarrying of texts for facts about numbers of men, weapons, form-ations, strategies and tactics. Instead it involves a complex engagement with medieval mentalities as manifested through many and diverse forms of evidence. This means that rather than seeking dry statistics and information from sources, we must study them carefully for what they were trying to say, how and why. In turn, doing so implies that authority on the subject indeed comes from exegesis and understanding rather than simple 'factual knowledge'. Thus we return to where we began, with Nithard and his approach to writing the history of war and we see that, in the end, Nithard's shade has had the last laugh.

APPENDIX: MILITARY ACTIVITY IN THE FRANKISH REALMS, 581–90

Dramatis Personae

Austrasia (north-east Gaul + Auvergne and various parts of Aquitaine and Provence): King Childebert II.

Neustria (north-west Gaul + various parts of Aquitaine): Chilperic I (to 584, then minority of Chlothar II).

Burgundy (central Gaul + various parts of Aquitaine and Provence): King Guntramn.

Visigothic Spain (included Septimania, around Narbonne): King Liuvigild (to 586), then King Reccared.

Lombard Italy: King Authari.

Bretons – Waroch.

581 (*LH* 6.1–13)

(a) Rebellion of the Burgundian duke, Mummolus, who flees to Avignon in Austrasian territory and fortifies himself there.

(b) Civil strife in Austrasia between factions competing for control of the court. Factional armies confront each other but Queen Brunechildis defuses the situation.

(c) Childebert II breaks off his alliance with Guntramn and makes a treaty with Neustria.

   Civil strife in Marseille, and accusations against Bishop Theodore. Childebert demands that Guntramn demand his share of the revenues from the city.

(d) Duke Desiderius attacks the Burgundians, defeats Duke Ragnovald and occupies Périgueux. He takes Agen and all other Burgundian cities in the region.

(e) Duke Berulf (Neustria) takes an army to Berry and devastates areas of Yzeures and Barrou.

(f) Duke Bladast (Neustria) invades Gascony with his army, and loses most of it.

231

582 (*LH* 6.14–24)

(a)   Asclepius, a former duke, kills Chilperic's border guards on the River Orge. Chilperic prepares an invasion of Burgundy but is dissuaded. Guntramn asks for peace.

583 (*LH* 6.25–32)

(a)   Attack on Duke Mummolus at Avignon, by an Austrasian army raised from Clermont and Le Velay, in association with a Burgundian force. A siege ensues until the Austrasians are sent home by orders of Childebert. The Burgundians return home too.

(b)   Chilperic leads an army to Paris.

(c)   Duke Berulf (Neustria) attacks Bourges with the men of Tours, Poitiers, Angers and Nantes. The Neustrian dukes, Desiderius and Bladast, also attack. Chilperic attacks Melun. Battle is joined between the men of Bourges and Desiderius' army. The territory of Bourges is devastated. The Burgundian army defeats Chilperic's army. Peace is made between Guntramn and Chilperic.

(d)   Mutiny breaks out in Childebert's army.

584 (*LH* 6.33–7.23)

Peace is made between Guntramn and Childebert.

(a)   Chilperic raises armies and orders his cities to be put in readiness.

(b)   Childebert invades Italy and the Lombards submit.

(c)   Childebert raises an army to invade Spain but campaign ensues. (Chilperic is assassinated)

(d)   The men of Orleans and Blois attack Châteaudun. A counter-attack is launched by the men of Châteaudun and the men of Chartres. Peace is restored by the counts of the area, and compensation paid.

(e)   Childebert and Guntramn both lead armies to Paris.

(f)   Campaign of the usurper Gundovald in Aquitaine.

(g)   Guntramn campaigns in the Loire valley. Ravagings ensue. The men of Tours and Bourges attack Poitiers.

585 (*LH* 7.24–8.30)

(a)   Men of Orleans and Bourges attack Poitiers and Tours.

(b1) Army moves from Poitiers against Gundovald.

(c)   Guntramn and Childebert raise armies and meet for a conference. Peace between Guntramn and Childebert.

(b2) Campaigns against Gundovald culminate in siege of St.-Bertrand-de-Comminges. Death of Gundovald.

(d)   Childebert sends an army to Italy.

(e)   Rebellion against Duke Wintrio in Champagne.

f)   Guntramn sends an army into Septimania. Defeated by the Goths.

586 (*LH* 8.31–42)

(a) Goths invade Aquitaine.

(b) Unauthorized attack on Rennes by Guntramn's followers.

587 (*LH* 8.43–9.19)

(a) A Frankish attack is launched on Carcassonne. A battle ensues and the Franks are defeated after early success. The Goths and the Austrasians (but not the Burgundians) make peace.

(b) A raid on Aquitaine is launched by the Gascons.

(c) The Goths attack Arles.

(d) The Revolt of the Dukes takes place in Austrasia.

(e) The Bretons attack Nantes. The Treaty of Andelot between Guntramn and Childebert is signed.

588 (*LH* 9.20–25)

(a) The Bretons raid Nantes.

(b) Childebert orders an invasion of Italy. This is defeated by the Lombards.

589 (*LH* 9.26–44)

(a) Childebert raises army to attack Lombards but halts when the Lombards offer to make peace.

(b) Guntramn sends an army to attack Septimania. This is defeated.

(c) The 'Nuns' Revolt' breaks out in Poitiers.

590 (*LH* 10.1–23)

(a) Childebert orders an invasion of Italy. Ravaging of territory (friendly and hostile) ensues. There is one confrontation between Frankish and Lombard forces, ended when a Lombard champion is killed. The Lombards then retreat to their cities and the Franks are decimated by disease. The Lombards ask for a truce.

(b) The Bretons attack Nantes. The Neustrians counter-attack the Bretons. Part of their army is defeated in battle. The Bretons make peace. The retreating Franks are nevertheless harried.

(c) The 'Nuns' Revolt' in Poitiers is quelled by a force called out by the local count, Macco.

NOTES

1 WARFARE AND VIOLENCE IN THE EARLY MIDDLE AGES

1 Nithard, *Histories* 2.10. For Nithard himself, see, above all, J.L. Nelson, 'Public *Histories* and private history in the work of Nithard', in J.L. Nelson, *Politics and Ritual in Early Medieval Europe* (London, 1986), pp. 195–237. For the battle in which Nithard was killed, see *AB s.a.* 844 and *The Annals of St-Bertin. Ninth-Century Histories, Volume 1*, trans. J.L. Nelson (Manchester, 1991), p. 58, n. 9. Nelson refutes the early view that Nithard was killed in battle against the Vikings in 845.

2 His account is quoted in full below, p. 178.

3 *HE*, Preface.

4 On this, see J.L. Nelson, 'The quest for peace in a time of war: the Carolingian Brüderkrieg, 840–43', in J. Fried (ed.), *Träger und Instrumentarien des Friedens im hohen und späten Mittelalter* (Vorträge und Forschungen 43; Sigmaringen, 1996), pp. 87–114; Nelson, 'The ritualisation of Frankish warfare in the ninth century', in G. Halsall (ed.), *Violence and Society in the Early Medieval West* (Woodbridge, 1998), pp. 90–107.

5 See also T. Reuter, 'Carolingian and Ottonian warfare', in M. Keen (ed.), *Medieval Warfare. A History* (Oxford, 1999), pp. 13–35, at pp. 18–19.

6 E. John, 'English feudalism and the structure of Anglo-Saxon Society', in his *Orbis Britanniae and Other Studies* (Leicester, 1966), pp. 128–53, at p. 132.

7 *ARF s.a.* 792. See also *AF s.a.* 847 for another report of this rare state of affairs. Again, the statement was not entirely true, as there was a Viking raid on what is now Holland.

8 *Rev. Ann. s.a.* 790.

9 *Lorsch Annals, s.a.* 793; Astronomer, *Life of Louis*, ch. 6; Lorsch charter 257. The expedition is also mentioned in Manaresi 32 (August, 821).

10 Below, pp. 231–3.

11 G. Williams, 'Military institutions and royal power', in M.P. Brown and C.A. Farr (ed.), *Mercia: An Anglo-Saxon Kingdom in Europe* (London, 2001), pp. 295–309, thinks that warfare was recorded because it was unusual and noteworthy. This seems unlikely. Some of the Mercian wars listed above escaped all attention in contemporary or near-contemporary annals, chronicles or histories, occurring only in later recensions of chronicles, or as chance references in sources such as saints' lives.

12 ICERV no. 287; On the text, see J. Fontaine, 'Une épitaphe rythmique d'un contemporain d'Isidore de Séville: l'éloge funèbre du Visigot Oppila', in M. Van Uytfanghe and R. Demeulenaere (eds.), *Aevvm inter Vtrvmque. Mélanges offerts à*

Gabrial Sanders, professeur émérite a l'Université de Gand, (*Instrumenta Patristica* 23; The Hague, 1991), pp. 163–86. Obscure Basque campaigns are also referred to in Venantius Fortunatus, *Poems* 10.19; Braulio of Saragossa, *Letters* 3 (to Isidore; *c*.610–20); Taio of Saragossa, *Letter to Bishop Quiricus of Barcelona* (654). I am grateful to Dr Mark Handley for many of these references.

13 C. Sánchez-Albornoz, 'El ejército y la guerra en el reino Asturleones 718–1037', *SdS*15, pp. 293–428, at p. 337, n. 181.

14 H.M. Chadwick, *The Heroic Age* (Cambridge, 1912).

15 V. Hanson, *The Western Way of War. Infantry Battle in Classical Greece* (2nd edition; Berkeley, 2000).

16 See, e.g., Hanson, *The Western Way of War* on Greek battle; A.K. Goldsworthy, *The Roman Army at War 100BC–AD200* (Oxford, 1996) on Roman battlefield actualities.

17 Notker, *Deeds of Charlemagne* 2.12.

18 See M. Innes, '"He never even allowed his white teeth to be bared in laughter": The politics of humour in the Carolingian renaissance', in G. Halsall (ed.), *Humour, History and Politics in Late Antiquity and the Early Middle Ages* (Cambridge, 2002), pp. 131–56.

19 Augustine's *The City of God* represents the clearest, though far from the earliest, example of this thought.

20 For Prudentius' work, see *Prudentius*, ed. and trans. H.J. Thompson (2 vols.; London 1949–53); for Carolingian illustrations, see, e.g., J. Hubert, J. Porcher and W.F. Volbach, *Carolingian Art* (trans. J. Emmons, S. Gilbert and R. Allen; London, 1970), pp. 177, 189, 287.

21 See, for example, the Old English poems *Elene* and *Judith*, which in many ways bring us closer than many other sources to a glimpse of what Anglo-Saxon battles were actually like.

22 See M. Innes, 'Teutons or Trojans? The Carolingians and the Germanic past', in Y. Hen and M. Innes (ed.), *The Uses of the Past in the Early Middle Ages* (Cambridge, 2000), pp. 227–49, for an interesting argument against the idea that these poems represent age-old oral traditions, as opposed to new forms of literature written in response to the precise demands of the ninth century. However, see C. Edwards, 'German vernacular literature: a survey', in R. McKitterick (ed.), *Carolingian Culture: Emulation and Innovation* (Cambridge, 1994), pp. 141–70, at p. 152, for important caveats. Nithard himself, when he recorded the oaths sworn by the armies of Charles the Bald and Louis the German at Strasbourg, gives us the earliest precisely dated texts in Old High German and Old French. In an important article, M. Lapidge, 'The archetype of Beowulf', *ASE* 29 (2000), pp. 5–41, discusses palaeographical methods whereby old originals may be detected behind the manuscripts of poems which might otherwise be considered late compositions.

23 Engilbert, *Poem on the Battle of Fontenoy*.

24 By far the best work on western early medieval warfare has been done by historians who would not consider themselves primarily (or at all) military historians. Amongst the current generation of British academic medieval historians one might cite the work of, for example, Timothy Reuter and Nicholas Brooks. Reuter's tutor, Karl Leyser, was another exception. The oeuvre of Janet Nelson is of greater value to the subject of early medieval warfare in theory and practice than almost anything written by a specialist military historian. Similarly, in six beautifully concise and well-informed pages (pp. 182–8) of E. Christiansen's *The Norsemen in the Viking Age* (Oxford, 2002), one may find more good sense on the subject of Viking battle than in the entire corpus of early medieval military history in the strict sense.

25 As an indicative sample of such writing over the past twenty or so years, see
I. Heath, *Armies of the Dark Ages 600–1066* (2nd edition; Worthing, 1980);
S. Macdowall, *Germanic Warrior 236–568 AD* (Osprey 'Warrior' Series 18;
London, 1996); R. Underwood, *Anglo-Saxon Weapons and Warfare* (Stroud, 1999);
J.K. Siddorn, *Viking Weapons and Warfare* (Stroud, 2000).

26 See E.C. May, G.P. Stadler and J.F. Votaw, *Ancient and Medieval Warfare. The
History of the Strategies, Tactics and Leadership of Classical Warfare (West Point Military
History Series)* (Wayne, NJ, 1984). For a not particularly successful attempt by a
War Studies academic (though one specialising in a completely different era) to
apply an extreme normalist view to the early medieval period, see P. Griffith, *The
Viking Art of War* (London, 1995). For a judicious discussion of the latter, see
G. Williams' review in *EME* 6.1 (1996), p. 106.

27 See F. Lot, 'Études sur la bataille de Poitiers de 732', *Revue Belge de Philologie et
d'Histoire* 26 (1948), pp. 33–59 for a hard-hitting, and in places exasperated,
critique of such approaches.

28 B.S. Bachrach, *The Anatomy of a Little War: A Military and Diplomatic History of the
Gundovald Affair* (Boulder, 1994), p. xx.

29 See below, ch. 9.

30 See below, ch. 7, ch. 9.

31 Nithard, *Histories* 2.8.

32 *AB s.a.* 876.

33 The classic, here, is J. Keegan, *The Face of Battle* (London, 1976). See P. Sabin,
'The face of Roman battle', *JRS* 90 (2000), pp. 1–17, at p. 4 for a clear statement
of the view of timeless military psychology

34 B.H. Rosenwein (eds), *Anger's Past. The Social Uses of an Emotion in the Middle Ages*
(Ithaca, 1998). See also C. Cubitt, B.H. Rosenwein, S. Airlie, M. Garrison and
C. Larrington, 'The history of emotions: a debate', *EME* 10.2 (2001), pp. 225–56,
with G. Halsall, review of Rosenwein (ed.), *Anger's Past* at pp. 301–3.

35 Recent attempts to apply the Keegan model to ancient warfare include
Goldsworthy, *The Roman Army at War*. For similar attempts, see Hanson, *The
Western Way of War* and Sabin, 'The face of Roman battle'.

36 Nelson, 'Public *Histories* and private history in the work of Nithard'.

37 My approach is heavily indebted to the work of Pierre Bourdieu and Anthony
Giddens. See, e.g., P. Bourdieu, *Outline of a Theory of Practice* (trans. R. Nice;
Cambridge, 1977); A. Giddens, *The Constitution of Society: Outline of the Theory of
Structuration* (London, 1984).

38 C. von Clausewitz, *On War* (ed. and trans. M. Howard and P. Paret; Princeton
1984), 1.24, p. 87, for his famous dictum that war is 'the continuation of policy
by other means'; for Karl Leyser's canny statement that the reverse was often true
in the early Middle Ages – 'policy was a continuation of war by other means' –
see K. Leyser, 'Early Medieval Warfare', in his *Communications and Power in
Medieval Europe: The Carolingian and Ottonian Centuries*, ed. T. Reuter (London,
1994), pp. 29–50, at p. 50.

39 For the reasoning behind this methodology, see G. Halsall, *Settlement and Social
Organisation. The Merovingian Region of Metz* (Cambridge, 1995), pp. 1–4; Halsall,
'Social identities and social relationships in Merovingian Gaul', in I.N. Wood
(ed.), *Franks and Alamanni in the Merovingian Period: An Ethnographic Perspective*
(Woodbridge, 1998), pp. 141–65.

40 For this methodology see Halsall *Settlement and Social Organisation*, pp. 3–4; Halsall,
'Archaeology and historiography', in M. Bentley (ed.), *The Routledge Companion
to Historiography* (London, 1997), pp. 807–29.

41 The *New Cambridge Medieval History*, for example, contains only a very brief
and superficial discussion: H.-W. Goetz, 'Social and military institutions', *NCMH*,

pp. 451–80, at pp. 479–80 – thus only something like one fifteenth of the chapter ostensibly devoted to the subject. P. Linehan and J.L. Nelson (eds.), *The Medieval World* (London, 2000) has no treatment of the subject at all, in spite of containing sections on 'Power and power structures' and 'Elites, organisations and groups'.

42 For the sanitisation of early medieval warfare, see the oeuvre of Bernard S. Bachrach, esp. B.S. Bachrach, *Early Carolingian Warfare: Prelude to Empire* (Philadelphia, 2000). Bachrach believes that armies were numbered in many tens of thousands (see below, ch. 6) but that these hordes had little damaging effect upon the landscape or civilians. It is interesting to speculate upon the role which modern United States right-wing political culture and vocabulary, with its dangerous euphemisms like 'collateral damage', 'friendly fire' and 'surgical strikes', has had in producing this approach to past warfare. One hopes that, if anything good might come of the assault on New York and Washington on 11 September 2001, it might include a serious rethinking of these attitudes. So far such does not, alas, appear to have been the case.

43 See, e.g., S.S. Evans, *Lords of Battle: Image and Reality of the Comitatus in Dark-Age Britain* (Woodbridge, 1997).

44 The tradition of trying to identify the great battles of history is best exemplified in J.F.C. Fuller, *The Decisive Battles of the Western World and their Influence upon History* (2 vols. abridged and revised edition, ed. J. Terraine; London 1954–56). Fuller saw the battle of Poitiers (732/3) as the decisive engagement in our period, turning back the 'tide' of Islam.

45 F. Braudel, *The Mediterranean and the Mediterranean World in the Age of Philip II* (2 vols; London, 1975), p. 21, 1241–2.

46 K.F. Drew (trans.) *The Laws of the Salian Franks* (Philadelphia, 1991), p. 94; A.C. Murray (trans.), *From Roman to Merovingian Gaul: A Reader* (Peterborough, Ont., 2000), p. 552.

47 Cp. *LH* 8.6.

48 N. Gradowicz Pancer, *Sans Peur et sans Vergogne: De l'honneur et des femmes aux premiers temps Mérovingiens* (Paris, 2001) discusses this law at pp. 112–15 but accepts the translation of *cinitum* as pederast.

49 See H. Kennedy, *The Armies of the Caliphs Military and Society in the Early Islamic State* (London, 2001) for excellent discussion of early Islamic warfare and military organisation. See also A. Cameron (ed.), *The Byzantine and Early Islamic Near East 3: States, Resources and Armies* (Princeton, 1995).

50 J. Haldon, *Warfare, State, and Society in the Byzantine World, 565–1204* (London, 1999). Haldon is one of very few writers on the early Middle Ages to incorporate detailed military historical writing into a sophisticated wider political, social and economic framework.

51 H. Elton *Warfare in Roman Europe, 350–425* (Oxford, 1996); P. Southern and K. Dixon, *The Late Roman Army* (London, 1996); R.S.O. Tomlin, 'The army of the late empire', in J.S. Wacher (ed.), *The Roman World* (London, 1987), pp. 107–23; B.D. Shaw, 'War and violence', in G. Bowersock, P.R.L. Brown and O. Grabar (ed.), *Late Antiquity. A Guide to the Postclassical World* (Cambridge, MA, and London, 1999), pp. 130–69; M. Whitby, 'The army, *c.*402–602', in A. Cameron, B. Ward-Perkins and M. Whitby (eds.), *The Cambridge Ancient History vol. 14: Late Antiquity: Empire and Successors, A.D. 425–600* (Cambridge, 2000), pp. 288–314.

52 B. Kreutz, *Before the Normans. Southern Italy in the Ninth and Tenth Centuries* (Philadelphia, 1996), p. 67.

53 See J. France, *Western Warfare in the Age of the Crusades, 1000–1300* (London, 1999).

54 The works cited in this paragraph are: J.F. Verbruggen, *The Art of Warfare in*

Western Europe during the Middle Ages (2nd rev. edn, trans. S. Willard and R.W. Southern; Woodbridge 1997); P. Contamine, *War in the Middle Ages* (trans. M. Jones; Oxford, 1984); C.W.C. Oman, *A History of the Art of War in the Middle Ages, vol. 1:378–1278AD* (London, 1924; reprinted 1991); H. Delbrück, *History of the Art of War, Volume II: The Barbarian Invasions* (trans. W.J. Renfroe, of German 3rd edition of 1909; Lincoln, NE, 1980); J. Beeler *Warfare in Feudal Europe, 730–1200* (Ithaca, 1971). J. Keegan, *A History of Warfare* (London, 1993), pp. 282–90, deals with the early Middle Ages, but in very ill-informed and out-of-date fashion.

55 The technological determinist view was most famously presented by L.T. White, *Medieval Technology and Social Change* (Oxford, 1962), pp. 1–38.

56 Beeler, *Warfare in Feudal Europe, 730–1200*, pp. 9–13.

57 Most famously, or possibly infamously, expressed by E. Gibbon in his *History of the Decline and Fall of the Roman Empire*, ch. 52.

58 R. Abels, *Lordship and Military Obligation in Anglo-Saxon England* (London, 1988). See also S. Chadwick-Hawkes (ed.), *Weapons and Warfare in Anglo-Saxon England* (Oxford, OUCA Monograph 21, 1989); C.W. Hollister, *Anglo-Saxon Military Institutions on the Eve of the Norman Conquest* (Oxford, 1962); E. John, 'War and society in the tenth century: the Maldon campaign', *TRHS*, 5th series, 27 (1977), pp. 173–91; the works of N.P. Brooks collected in his *Communities and Warfare 700–1400* (London, 2000).

59 G. Williams is working on this volume.

60 The obvious exceptions, ironically, are the nuclear attacks on Japan and the strategic bombing offensives of the Second World War, all of which, like the New York attack, predominantly involved civilians.

61 T. Renna, 'The idea of peace in the West, *c*.500–1150', *Journal of Medieval History* 6 (1980), pp. 143–67.

62 See G. Halsall 'Violence and society in the early medieval west: an introductory survey', in Halsall (ed.), *Violence and Society in the Early Medieval West*, pp. 1–45, at pp. 16–29, and references. For treatments of various forms of early medieval violence, see Halsall (ed.), *Violence and Society in the Early Medieval West*.

63 Halsall 'Violence and society in the early medieval west: an introductory survey', pp. 14–16.

64 *Ibid.*, pp. 7–16 and references; below, pp. 50, 56.

65 See, e.g., P. Fouracre, 'Attitudes towards violence in seventh- and eighth-century Francia', and M. Bennett, 'Violence in eleventh-century Normandy: feud, warfare and politics', in Halsall (ed.), *Violence and Society in the Early Medieval West*, pp. 60–75 and 126–40 respectively.

66 See, e.g., the treaty between Lothar I and Doge Peter of Venice of 840, chs. 1 and 6: Boretius 233.

67 See below, pp. 140–1.

68 Isidore, *Etymologies* 18.1.5.

69 See further below, pp. 57–9.

70 *Sacramentary of Gellone*, pp. 429–30; Nelson, 'The quest for peace in a time of war', p. 87 for discussion.

71 Nelson, 'The ritualisation of Frankish warfare in the ninth century', pp. 93–5. K. Leyser 'The battle at the Lech, 955', in his *Medieval Germany and its Neighbours* (London, 1982), pp. 43–67, at p. 43, for tenth-century Ottonian usage, and Sánchez-Albornoz, 'El ejército y la guerra en el reino Asturleones 718–1037', pp. 396 ff. for comparable usage in Christian Spain. For the earlier part of the period and the inheritance of Roman ideas about levels of warfare, see W. Pohl, 'Konfliktverlauf und Konfliktbewältigung: Römer und Barbaren im früheren Mittelalter', *FmS* 26 (1992), pp. 165–207.

72 J.E. Cross, 'The ethic of war in Old English', in P. Clemoes and K. Hughes (eds.), *England Before the Conquest. Studies in Primary Sources Presented to Dorothy Whitelock* (Cambridge, 1971), pp. 269–82.

73 G. Fasoli, 'Pace e guerra nell'alto medioevo', *SdS*15, pp. 15–47, is still useful, though readier than most writers would be today to identify Germanic 'barbarian' traditions. See also J.M. Wallace Hadrill, 'War and peace in the early Middle Ages', in his *Early Medieval History* (Oxford, 1975), pp. 19–38. J. Flori, *L'Idéologie du Glaive: Préhistoire de la Chevalerie* (Geneva, 1983), pp. 2–40; more recently, Flori, *La Guerre Sainte* (Paris, 2001).

74 See, especially, Ambrose, *On the Christian Faith* 2.16; Ambrose, *On the Duties of the Clergy* 1.27, 29, 35, 40. See also F. Prinz, *Klerus und Krieg im früheren Mittelalter: Untersuchungen zur Rolle der Kirche beim Aufbau der Königsherrschaft* (Monographien zur Geschichte des Mittelalters; Stuttgart, 1971), pp. 1–35. S. Muhlberger, 'War, warlords, and Christian historians from the fifth to the seventh century', in A. Callander Murray (ed.), *After Rome's Fall: Narrators and Sources of Early Medieval History: Essays presented to Walter Goffart* (Toronto, 1998), pp. 83–98.

75 Augustine may ultimately have sanctioned the use of state force against heretics, employing the Gospel of St Luke (14.22–23) with its (potentially) chilling instruction to 'compel them to come in' (*On the Correction of the Donatists* (= *Ep.* 185) 6.24–26; *Ep.* 93; see P.R.L. Brown, 'Religious coercion in the Later Roman Empire: the case of North Africa', *History* 48 (1963), pp. 283–305; Brown, 'St. Augustine's attitude to Religious coercion', *JRS* 54 (1964), pp. 107–16; Brown, *Augustine of Hippo: A Biography* (London, 1967), pp. 233–43, but nearly 400 years later Alcuin counselled Charlemagne against using force alone to bring about the conversion of the Saxons (Alcuin, *Letters* 56, 57 (Allott)).

76 R. Markus, 'Saint Augustine's views on the "Just War"', *SCH* 20 (1983), pp. 1–14, at p. 13.

77 See Augustine, *Against Faustus the Manichaean* 22.74.

78 Isidore, *Etymologies* 18.1.2, copied by Hrabanus Maurus in his *On the Nature of Things* 20.1. According to Isidore there are four types of war, just, unjust, civil and more than civil.

79 For the penitentials see below. In one of Charlemagne's pronouncements, killing a brigand (*latro*) was no crime 'unless motivated by enmity or evil' (*per odium aut male*); Capitulary issued at Herestal, 779 (King 2; Boretius 20), *c.* 11.

80 The *locus classicus* of Gregory's thought on war is *LH* 5.preface. For local vengeance killing as *bellum civile* see *LH* 7.47.

81 *Penitential of Theodore* 4.6; 'Pseudo-Bede I' 2.6; 'Old Irish Penitential' 5.4; Regino: Handbooks, p. 317; Halitgar, *Roman Penitential* 79.

82 Nithard, *Histories* 3.1; see Nelson, 'The ritualisation of Frankish warfare in the ninth century', p. 101.

83 *ARF s.a.* 787.

84 S. Airlie, 'Narratives of triumph and submission: Charlemagne's mastering of Bavaria', *TRHS* 6th series 9 (1999), pp. 93–119.

85 B.D. Shaw, 'Bandits in the Roman Empire', *P&P* 105 (1984), pp. 4–52; B. D. Shaw, 'The bandit', in A. Giardina (ed.), *The Romans* (Chicago, 1993), pp. 300–41.

86 Ermold the Black, *In Honour of Emperor Louis* [the Pious], Book 4, lines 277–82.

87 See, e.g., P. Veyne, 'Humanitas: Romans and non-Romans', in Giardina (ed.), *The Romans*, pp. 342–69; P. Geary, 'Barbarians and ethnicity' in Bowersock, Brown and Grabar (eds.), *Late Antiquity. A Guide to the Postclassical World*, pp. 107–29; G. Halsall, *Barbarian Migrations and the Roman West* (Cambridge, forthcoming), ch. 2.

88 On Bretons, see, e.g., J.M.H. Smith, *Province and Empire: Brittany and the*

Carolingians (Cambridge, 1992), pp. 17–19. On the Basques, see, e.g., R. Collins, 'The Basques in Aquitaine and Navarre: problems of frontier government', in J. Gillingham and J.C. Holt (eds.), *War and Society in the Middle Ages: Essays in Honour of J.O. Prestwich* (Cambridge, 1984), Collins, 'The *Vaccei*, the *Vaceti*, and the rise of *Vasconia*', *Studia Historica* 6 (1988), pp. 211–23; Collins, *The Basques* (Oxford, 1986). See also *HW* 9–10 for the severe ravaging of Basque territory by the Visigothic king Wamba, which brought about their submission; below, p. 136.

89 *LH* 9.7.

90 See, e.g., *AF s.a.* 849, on the Bohemians. Warfare against the Slavs was equally regarded as the suppression of rebellion; e.g., *AF s.a.* 844, 848, 850.

91 Astronomer, *Life of Louis*, ch. 18.

92 On which see P. Kershaw, '*Rex Pacificus*: Studies in Royal Peacemaking and the image of the peace-making king in the early medieval west' Ph.D. Thesis, University of London (1999). Kershaw's forthcoming book arising from this thesis will be definitive.

93 *HE* 2.16. See also, for an analogy, *HL* 3.16, on the Lombard king, Authari. For discussion of similar concepts and exemplars, see T. Reuter, 'Die Unsicherheit auf den Strassen im europäischen Früh- und Hochmittelalter: Täter, Opfer und ihre mittelalterlichen und Modernen Betrachter', in Fried (ed.), *Träger und Instrumentarien des Friedens im Hohen und Späten Mittelalter*, pp. 169–201.

94 As in an inscription erected for Theoderic, Ostrogothic king of Italy: M. McCormick, *Eternal Victory: Triumphal Rulership in Late Antiquity, Byzantium and the Early Medieval West* (paperback edition; Cambridge, 1990), p. 278.

2 WARFARE AND SOCIETY

1 My thinking on this issue has been stimulated by J. Haldon, *The State and the Tributary Mode of Production* (London, 1993), a valuable study from a Marxist perspective of the mechanisms of the earlier medieval state, which uses this survey to contribute to broader historical and sociological issues. Another key work which has inspired these thoughts is C.J. Wickham, 'The other transition: from the ancient world to feudalism', *P&P* 103 (1984), pp. 3–36.

2 Haldon, *The State and the Tributary Mode*, pp. 32–3, in turn drawing upon other recent studies of states and state formation.

3 J. Glete, *War and the State in Early Modern Europe: Spain, the Dutch Republic and Sweden as Fiscal-Military States, 1500–1650* (London, 2002), p. 121.

4 G. Halsall, *Settlement and Social Organisation: The Merovingian Region of Metz* (Cambridge, 1995), p. 24.

5 Legal recognition (that is to say that the existence of an élite group within the free population is recognised in certain legal provisions) should not be confused with legal definition. When laws set out to define élite status this normally indicates that in fact the group has become open to entry from other groups. It is usually an attempt to end such social mobility.

6 See, e.g., R. Le Jan, *Famille et Pouvoir dans le Monde Franc (VIIe–Xe siècle): Essai d'anthropologie sociale* (Paris, 1995); S. Airlie, 'The aristocracy', *NCMH*, pp. 431–50; T. Reuter, 'The medieval nobility in twentieth-century historiography', in M. Bentley (ed.), *The Routledge Companion to Historiography* (London, 1997), pp. 177–202; A.J. Duggan (ed.), *Nobles and Nobility in Medieval Europe: Concepts, Origins, Transformations* (Woodbridge, 2000). For collections of classic studies, see F.L. Cheyette (ed.), *Lordship and Community in the Middle Ages. Selected Readings* (New York, 1968); T. Reuter (ed. and trans.), *The Medieval Nobility* (Amsterdam, 1979).

7 Airlie, 'The aristocracy'; P. Fouracre, 'The origins of the nobility in Francia', in Duggan (ed.) *Nobles and Nobility in Medieval Europe*, pp. 17–24.

8 See, e.g., T. Reuter and C. Wickham, 'Introduction', in W. Davies and P. Fouracre, (eds), *Property and Power in the Early Middle Ages* (Cambridge, 1995).

9 These points are not given due consideration in my previous meanderings around the subject: Halsall, *Settlement and Social Organisation*, pp. 22–5; Halsall, 'Social identities and social relationships in Merovingian Gaul', in I.N. Wood (ed.), *Franks and Alamanni in the Merovingian Period: An Ethnographic Perspective* (Woodbridge, 1998), pp. 141–65.

10 *LH* 6.46. The passage is an elaborately constructed diatribe and the charges levelled against Chilperic by Gregory of Tours may not have been meant very seriously. G. Halsall, 'Nero and Herod? The death of Chilperic and Gregory's writing of history', in K. Mitchell and I.N. Wood (ed.), *The World of Gregory of Tours* (Leiden, 2002), pp. 337–50. Nevertheless the point is surely that these were held to be concerns that a 'bad' king might have, simultaneously showing the resentment of such an attitude by the élite.

11 In the case of Theoderic the Ostrogoth, this is demonstrated very clearly by P. Heather, 'Theoderic, king of the Goths', *EME* 4.2 (1995), pp. 145–73. Similar policies seem to have been employed by sixth-century Merovingian rulers to similar effect: Halsall, 'Social identities and social relationships in Merovingian Gaul'. For ninth-century attempts, see J. Martindale, 'Charles the Bald and the Government of the kingdom of Aquitaine', in M.T Gibson and J.L. Nelson (ed.), *Charles the Bald. Court and Kingdom* (2nd edition; Aldershot, 1990), pp. 115–38.

12 See, e.g., P. Fouracre, 'Carolingian justice: the rhetoric of improvement and contexts of abuse', *La Giustizia nell'Alto Medioevo Secoli V–VIII, Settimane di Studio* 42 (1995), pp. 771–803.

13 E.g. P. Fouracre, 'Cultural conformity and social conservatism in early medieval Europe', *History Workshop Journal* 33 (1994), pp. 152–61; Fouracre, 'Space, culture and kingdoms in early medieval Europe', in P. Linehan & J.L. Nelson (ed.), *The Medieval World* (London, 2001), pp. 366–80.

14 See the now classic volume, W. Davies and P. Fouracre (eds.), *The Settlement of Disputes in Early Medieval Europe* (Cambridge, 1986).

15 Wickham, 'The other transition: from the ancient world to feudalism', p. 15.

16 For a convenient brief summary see J. Glete, *Warfare at Sea, 1500–1650: Maritime Conflicts and the Transformation of Europe* (London, 2000), pp. 9–13.

17 Another key component in the analysis of the early modern situation: Glete, *War and the State in Early Modern Europe*.

18 M. McCormick, *Eternal Victory: Triumphal Rulership in Late Antiquity, Byzantium and the Early Medieval West* (paperback edn; Cambridge, 1990).

19 For examples of such exemplars, see Y. Hen, 'The uses of the Bible and the perception of kingship in Merovingian Gaul', *EME* 7.3 (1998), pp. 277–89, and the literature cited there.

20 For example, *pietas* was regarded as an essential feature of legitimate political leadership in the early Roman period. There was little difficulty in translating this into Christian 'piety' in the later empire, and this *pietas* was easily assimilated with the God-fearing kings of the Old Testament.

21 See, for a radical and important treatment of this topic, T.S. Burns, *Barbarians within the Gates of Rome. A Study of Roman Military Policy and the Barbarians, ca.375–425* (Bloomington, IN, 1994).

22 See, e.g., Heather, 'Theoderic, king of the Goths'.

23 P.S. Barnwell, *Emperor, Prefects and Kings. The Roman West, 395–565* (London, 1992), p. 82.

24 G. Halsall, 'Childeric's grave, Clovis' succession and the origins of the

Merovingian kingdom', in D. Shanzer and R. Mathisen (eds.), *Society and Culture in Late Roman Gaul. Revisiting the Sources* (Aldershot, 2001), pp. 116–33.

25 H.W. Böhme, 'Das Ende der Römerherrschaft in Britannien und die angelsächsische Besiedlung Englands im 5. Jahrhundert', *RGZM* 33.2, pp. 469–73; S. Suzuki, *The Quoit Brooch Style and Anglo-Saxon Settlement: A Casting and Recasting of Cultural Identity Symbols* (Woodbridge, 2000). I hope to follow up the implications of the data presented in these studies in a future article.

26 See, e.g., Angilbert, *On the Conversion of the Saxons*; anonymous *On King Pippin's Avar Victory*; Ermold the Black, *In Honour of Emperor Louis*; Ermold the Black, *In Praise of King Pippin*; *Ludwigslied* on Louis III.

27 O. Bouzy, 'Les armes symboles d'un pouvoir politique: l'épée du sacre, la Sainte Lance, l'Oriflamme, aux VIIIe–XIIe siècles', *Francia* 22.1 (1995), pp. 45–57.

28 Sedulius Scottus, *On Christian Rulers*, 2 (prudence in war), 3 (the dangers of committing the fortunes of the kingdom to warfare; see below, p. 156). See J. Flori, *L'Idéologie du Glaive: Préhistoire de la Chevalerie* (Geneva, 1983), pp. 65–84.

29 G. Mac Niocaill, *Ireland Before the Vikings* (Dublin, 1972), p. 47; D. Ó Corráin, *Ireland Before the Normans* (Dublin, 1972), p. 37.

30 G. Scheibelreiter, *Die barbarische Gesellschaft, Mentalitätsgeschichte der europäischen Achsenzeit 5.–8. Jahrhundert* (Darmstadt, 1999), pp. 285–376, for in-depth analysis of the role of warfare in Merovingian politics.

31 E.g. Venantius Fortunatus, *Poems* 6.1a, 9.1.

32 *PLS* Capitulary 6.1 (Decree dated at Andernach 1 March 594) 6.2 (Decree dated at Maestricht, 1 March 595) and 6.3 (Decree dated at Cologne, 1 March, 596).

33 *AMP s.a.* 690 [recte 687], 717.

34 P. Fouracre, *The Age of Charles Martel* (London, 2000), p. 119.

35 The classic works on this subject are T. Reuter, 'Plunder and tribute in the Carolingian empire', *TRHS*, 5th series, 35 (1985), pp. 75–94; Reuter, 'The end of Carolingian military expansion', in P. Godman and R. Collins (ed.), *Charlemagne's Heir. New Perspectives on the Reign of Louis the Pious* (Oxford, 1990), pp. 391–405.

36 Fredegar, *Chronicle*, 4.87.

37 Sawyer 96 (755–757); Birch 181.

38 S. MacLean, 'Charles the Fat and the Viking Great Army: the military explanation for the end of the Carolingian empire (876–88)', *War Studies Journal* 3.2 (1998), pp. 74–95.

39 Manaresi 66 (March, 864); C.J. Wickham, *Early Medieval Italy. Local Society and Central Power, 400–1000* (London, 1981), p. 136.

40 Thus weapon burial is most lavish, including armour and whole horses, on the northern and eastern fringes of the Merovingian kingdom. The lavish Scandinavian burials of the Vendel/Valsgärde type are also found on the fringes of the permanently settled area, and the location of the famous cemetery of Sutton Hoo, on the fringes of East Anglia and Essex, might also be suggestive.

41 Below, chs 3–4.

42 *Life of Arnulf*, 4. The *Life* itself is of disputed date, though certainly written well before the 780s, when Paul the Deacon made use of it. Its subject lived in the late sixth and earlier seventh centuries.

43 Felix, *Life of Guthlac*, 16.

44 *Life of Benedict of Aniane* 1.

45 See below, pp. 164, 184.

46 Freising charter 634.

47 J. Hubert, J. Porcher and W.F. Volbach, *Carolingian Art* (trans. J. Emmons, S. Gilbert and R. Allen; London, 1970), pp. 22–3.

48 Paulinus, *On Duke Eric*, verse 6.

49 *Maxims I.*

50 G. Duby, 'Les origines de la chevalerie', *SdS*15, pp. 739–61. *Pugnatores* and *pugnare* appear in such formulae by the eleventh century.

51 *AB s.a.* 859. This is J.L. Nelson's interpretation of the somewhat ambiguous text.

52 Detailed and sophisticated analysis by Heinrich Härke has made this interpretation very plausible. See, e.g., H. Härke, 'Early Saxon weapon burials: frequencies, distributions and weapon combinations', in S. Chadwick-Hawkes (ed.), *Weapons and Warfare in Anglo-Saxon England* (Oxford, OUCA Monograph 21, 1989), pp. 49–61; Härke, '"Weapon graves"? The background of the Anglo-Saxon weapon burial rite', *P&P* 126 (1990), pp. 22–43; Härke, *Anglesächsische Waffengräber des 5. Bis 7. Jahrhunderts* (Zeitschrift für Archäologie des Mittelalters, Beiheft 6; Cologne, 1992); Härke, 'Changing symbols in a changing society: the Anglo-Saxon weapon rite', in M. Carver (ed.), *The Age of Sutton Hoo: The Seventh Century in North-western Europe* (Woodbridge, 1992), pp. 149–65. I would differ slightly from Härke's interpretation in not seeing this identity as necessarily reflecting actual immigration from northern Germany. Clearly some, perhaps many, of these individuals were, or were descended from, immigrants, but ethnic identity, especially in the post-Roman period, is more a matter of belief than of genetics.

53 See G. Halsall, 'Violence and society in the early medieval west: an introductory survey', in G. Halsall (ed.), *Violence and Society in the Early Medieval West* (Woodbridge, 1998), pp. 1–45, and G. Halsall, 'Reflections on early medieval violence: the example of the "Blood Feud"', *Memoria y Civilización* 2 (1999), pp. 7–29, for the idea that 'feuds' were resolved by the *threat* of violence more often than its actual perpetration, and indeed that the institution of *faida* (formally declared hostility or enmity) was designed to bring about arbitration and settlement. R. Fletcher, *Bloodfeud: Murder and Revenge in Anglo-Saxon England* (Harmondsworth, 2002), has not taken full account of more recent studies of the phenomenon, and his analysis consequently remains somewhat problematic.

54 G. Halsall 'Archaeology and the late Roman frontier in northern Gaul: the so-called Föderatengräber reconsidered', in W. Pohl and H. Reimitz (eds.), *Grenze und Differenz im früheren Mittelalter* (Österreichische Akadamie der Wissenschaften: Vienna, 2000), pp. 167–80.

55 E.g., Council of Mâcon I (581–3), ch. 5; Council of Losne (673–5), ch. 2; Austrasian Council of 742, ch. 2; Council of Reisbach (798), ch. B.1, C.7; Council of Reisbach (799–800), ch. 3. Council of Toledo IV (633), ch. 45.

56 F. Prinz, *Klerus und Krieg im früheren Mittelalter: Untersuchungen zur Rolle der Kirche beim Aufbau der Königsherrschaft* (Monographien zur Geschichte des Mittelalters; Stuttgart, 1971), p. 14.

57 *PLS* 30; Rothari's Edict; see above, p. 11.

58 *The Fortunes of Men*, ll.48ff.

59 See, e.g., *LH* 10.5 for the defence of her house by Magnetrude, the former wife of the bishop of Le Mans. Cassiodorus, *Variae* 5.32, concerns a murderous attack by one woman upon another. R. Balzaretti '"These are things that men do, not women": the social regulation of female violence in Langobard Italy', in Halsall (ed.), *Violence and Society in the Early Medieval West*, pp. 175–92.

60 E.g., *LHF* 53; Nithard, *Histories*, 3.4; *AF s.a.* 896.

61 *LHF* 36.

62 *LH* 7.42.

63 See, e.g., Felix, *Life of Guthlac* 16.

64 See below, pp. 50–1, 52.

65 K. Leyser, 'Medieval canon law and the beginnings of knighthood', in his *Communications and Power in Medieval Europe: The Carolingian and Ottonian Centuries* (ed. T. Reuter; London, 1994), pp. 51–71, esp. at pp. 55–8; J.L. Nelson,

'Ninth-century knighthood: the evidence of Nithard', in her, *The Frankish World, 750–900* (London, 1996), pp. 75–87.

66 Lorsch charters 252, 257, 259; M. Innes *State and Society in the Early Middle Ages; The Middle Rhine Valley 400–1000* (Cambridge, 2000), pp. 147–50. It is possible that the date of the 792/3 charter is wrong, but this assumption stems mostly from the fact that, whilst Ripwin says he was following the elder King Charles to *Longobardia*, the major annals do not mention Charlemagne campaigning in Lombardy that year. However, the *Lorsch Annals* (appropriately enough) and The Astronomer (*Life of Louis*, ch. 6) do record that Charlemagne sent an army under his sons Louis and Pippin against Benevento in winter 792/3. When he made his grant to Lorsch Ripwin may have been unaware of the exact details. For Ripwin's career, see further below, pp. 77–81.

67 J.J. O'Donnell, 'Liberius the patrician', *Traditio* 37 (1981), pp. 31–72.

68 *LHF* 41; Bachrach translates the phrase incorrectly, and with a certain amount of unintentional humour, as 'wrapped in a cloak of dog skins'. Whether the war itself ever took place, which can be doubted, is here irrelevant. G. Scheibelreiter, 'Vom Mythos zur Geschichte: Überlegungen zu den Formen der Bewahrung von Vergangenheit im Frühmittelalter', in A. Scharer and G. Scheibelreiter (eds.), *Historiographie im frühen Mittelalter* (Vienna, 1994), pp. 26–40.

69 *LH* 7.38.

70 See Halsall, 'Violence and society in the early medieval west', pp. 16–19 for discussion of relationships of violence.

71 J.L. Nelson, 'The Frankish Empire', in P. Sawyer (ed.), *The Oxford Illustrated History of the Vikings* (Oxford, 1997), pp. 19–47, at p. 37.

72 Edict of Pîtres (Boretius 273), ch. 25.

73 A.A.M. Duncan, *Scotland: The Making of the Kingdom* (Edinburgh, 1975), p. 44; A.P. Smyth, *Warlords and Holy Men: Scotland AD 80–1000* (London, 1984), pp. 116–18.

74 M.O. Anderson, 'Dalriada and the creation of the kingdom of the Scots', in D. Whitelock, R. McKitterick and D.M. Dumville (eds.), *Ireland in Early Medieval Europe* (Cambridge, 1982), pp. 106–32 at pp. 109–10; Smyth, *Warlords and Holy Men*, p. 180.

75 *Fragmentary Chronicle of Saragossa, s.a.* 531.

76 See, e.g., R. Collins, *Early Medieval Spain: Unity in Diversity, 400–1000* (2nd edn; London, 1995), pp. 41–53 for Leuvigild's reign.

3 RAISING AN ARMY (1): POST-ROMAN EUROPE

1 See J. Haldon, *Warfare, State, and Society in the Byzantine World, 565–1204* (London, 1999).

2 A. Ferrill, *The Fall of the Roman Empire: The Military Explanation* (London, 1986); J.H.W.G. Liebeschuetz, 'The end of the Roman army in the western Empire', in J. Rich and G. Shipley (ed.), *War and Society in the Roman World* (London, 1993), pp. 265–76.

3 For this process, see G. Halsall, *Barbarian Migrations and the Barbarian West* (Cambridge, forthcoming); T.S. Burns, *Barbarians within the Gates of Rome. A Study of Roman Military Policy and the Barbarians, ca.375–425* (Bloomington, IN, 1994); P. Amory, *People and Identity in Ostrogothic Italy, 489–554* (Cambridge, 1997).

4 *Theodosian Code* 7.8.5 (issued 398).

5 For a classic statement, see J.B. Bury, *History of the Later Roman Empire from the Death of Theodosius I to the Death of Justinian* (2 vols; New York, 1958 – reprint of 1923 edition), vol. 1, pp. 205–6.

6 W. Goffart, *Barbarians and Romans AD 418–585: The Techniques of Accommodation* (Princeton, 1980), pp. 40–102.

7 Most famously Sidonius, *Poems* 12; Paulinus of Pella, *Thanksgiving*, lines 287–8, only implies the billeting of troops; *Thanksgiving*, lines 571–81 mentions that someone else had acquired usufruct of Paulinus' lands in Bordeaux in his absence (Paulinus, it should be remembered, left under a political cloud, as a supporter of a failed usurper), but the Goth who eventually acquired the land paid Paulinus for it. Gildas, *On the Ruin of Britain*, 23 should probably be included in the list.

8 See *Theodosian Code* 7.4, esp. 7.4.22 (30 May, 398), 7.4.35 (14 Feb., 423).

9 See the judicious comments of P. Heather, 'Theoderic, king of the Goths', *EME* 4.2 (1995), pp. 145–73, p. 159, following S.J.B. Barnish, 'Taxation, land and barbarian settlement in the western empire', *Papers of the British School at Rome* 54 (1986), pp. 170–95.

10 In addition to Barnish's article cited in the previous note, see, e.g., J.H.W.G. Liebeschuetz, 'Cities, taxes and the accommodation of barbarians: the theories of Durliat and Goffart', in W. Pohl (ed.), *Kingdoms of the Empire. The Integration of Barbarians in Late Antiquity* (Leiden, 1997), pp. 135–51; I.N. Wood, 'Ethnicity and ethnogenesis of the Burgundians', in H. Wolfram & W. Pohl (ed.), *Typen der Ethnogenese unter besonderer Berücksichtigung der Bayern* (Vienna, 1990), pp. 53–69. Other contributions to the debate include H. Wolfram, 'Neglected evidence on the accommodation of Barbarians in Gaul', in Pohl (ed.), *Kingdoms of the Empire*, pp. 181–3.

11 For *possessio* and *dominium*, see above all E. Levy, *West Roman Vulgar Law: The Law of Property* (Philadelphia, 1951). Levy argues that the words themselves were losing their technical force in the late Roman period. A distinction between full ownership and other forms of possession seems, however, to have remained and the terms will thus be used in this sense here. I.N. Wood, 'The barbarian invasions and first settlements', in A. Cameron and P. Garnsey (ed.) *Cambridge Ancient History, Vol.13: The Late Empire, A.D. 337–425* (Cambridge, 1998), pp. 516–37.

12 Heather, 'Theoderic, king of the Goths', is excellent on this. See also P. Heather, *The Goths* (Oxford, 1996), pp. 235–48.

13 B.S. Bachrach, *Merovingian Military Organisation, 481–751* (Minneapolis, 1972), argues interestingly and at length for extensive continuity with Roman military structures. Bachrach's argument is based upon a very full knowledge of the sources but he uses them in a very literal and uncritical way, so that, in their fully developed form, his views are somewhat unreliable and have consequently found little support. As I have taken a very different, indeed entirely divergent, approach, there seems little to be gained from confronting Bachrach's arguments in detail.

14 Eugippius, *Life of Severinus* 20.1–2.

15 See E. James, *The Merovingian Archaeology of South-West Gaul* (2 vols.) BAR(S.) 25 (Oxford, 1977), pp. 200–2, for discussion of the Taifals in Aquitaine. Gregory of Tours mentions them at *LH* 4.18 and *Life of the Fathers* 15.1.

16 In the absence of any detailed evidence, it is just as likely that their settlement near the Loire, the effective frontier of Roman Gaul from about 418 at the latest, took place when the Visigoths (a political entity descended from a 'Gothic' army commanded by Alaric) controlled Aquitaine (418–507), as that it took place under Roman rule. Given their previous association, it seems quite feasible that a 'Taifal' unit may have existed within the Gothic army. Another possibility is that their settlement took place *at the same time* as the Goths were settled further south, in 418.

17 By way of parallel, we might note the persistence of the Hwicce and Magonsaete as political identities on the Anglo-Saxon Welsh frontier until late into the Anglo-Saxon period.

18 See Halsall, *Barbarian Migrations and the Roman West*, ch. 3; E. James, 'The militarization of Roman society, 400–700', *MASS*, pp. 19–24, for a very useful and succinct survey.

19 Sidonius Apollinaris, *Letters* 8.6 (serving in the Visigothic navy), 3.3 (defending against the Goths).

20 For the 'Senate of Cantabria', see Braulio of Saragossa, *Life of Aemilian*, 11, 15, 17, 22, 26; S. Castellanos, *Poder social, aristocracias y hombre santo en la Hispania Visigoda: La Vita Aemiliani de Braulio de Zaragoza* (Logroño, 1998). For the military power of the aristocracy of Cordoba, see Isidore, *History of the Goths*, 45–6; John of Biclaro, *Chronicle*, 20. Hydatius, *Chronicle* 81[91], reveals the locals of Gallicia inflicting defeats upon the Sueves.

21 Though K.R. Dark, *From Civitas to Kingdom: British Political Continuity, 300–800* (Leicester, 1994), assembles suggestive evidence for the possible continuation of the *civitas* unit in post-Roman Britain too.

22 For an early sixth-century mobilisation order, see Cassiodorus, *Variae*, 1.24.

23 E.A. Thompson, *The Goths in Spain* (Oxford, 1969), pp. 264–5.

24 A.H.M. Jones, *The Later Roman Empire, 284–602* (Oxford, 1964), p. 256; J. Moorhead, *Theoderic in Italy* (Oxford, 1992), p. 254.

25 *Wars* 8.35.24–28.

26 When Procopius is compelled to use a current Latin technical term for 'guards', he has to use a circumlocution to excuse his employment of a word not found in the models of Attic Greek historical writing: Herodotus, Thucydides and Polybius. Thus, 'Solomon commanded the excubatores, for thus the Romans call their guards': *Wars* 4.12.17.

27 For a survey of post-Roman administrative structures, see P.S. Barnwell, *Emperor, Prefects and Kings: The Roman West, 395–565* (London, 1992); Barnwell, *Kings, Courtiers and Imperium: The Barbarian West, 565–725* (London, 1997).

28 D. Pérez Sánchez, *El Ejército en la Sociedad Visigoda* (Salamanca, 1989), pp. 69–73, 113–21 with refs., although Pérez Sánchez believes in the existence of a Visigothic regular army in the sixth century (p. 117). My thanks to Chris Wickham for lending me his copy of this useful volume.

29 Cassiodorus, *Variae* 8.28; Goffart, *Barbarians and Romans AD 418–585*, pp. 93–102.

30 *Theodosian Code* 7.4.34.

31 *LH* 3.36, 7.15. See (for alternative readings) W. Goffart, 'Old and New in Merovingian Taxation', *P&P* 96 (1982), pp. 3–21; C.J. Wickham, 'The other transition: from the ancient world to feudalism', *P&P* 103 (1984), pp. 3–36, at p. 21; J. Durliat, *Les Finances Publiques de Dioclétien aux Carolingiens (284–890)* (Beihefte der Francia 21; Sigmaringen, 1990). For a possible analogue, see Cassiodorus, *Variae* 4.14.

32 G. Halsall, *Settlement and Social Organisation: The Merovingian Region of Metz* (Cambridge, 1995), p. 258.

33 The reference to Roman soldiers in a later sixth-century capitulary (*PLS* 117) may refer to troops from the south, or more likely it shows us a stage in the process. It is likely that Romans acquired the right to perform military service and then gradually adopted or passed to their heirs the Frankish identity which was associated with such service.

34 See, e.g., Halsall, *Settlement and Social Organisation*, p. 32, for further discussion of this.

35 See, e.g., Heather, *The Goths*, pp. 276–98, for this process.

36 *HL* 2.32. On the Lombard invasion, see W. Pohl, 'L'Armée romaine et les Lombards: stratégies militaires et politiques', in F. Vallet and M. Kazanski (eds.), *L'Armée Romaine et les Barbares du IIIe au VIIe Siècle* (Paris, 1993), pp. 291–5.

37 See above, n. 33.
38 James, 'The militarisation of Roman society, 400–700', p. 21, names Count Claudius, mentioned in Isidore of Seville, *History of the Goths*, ch. 54 and the *Lives of the Fathers of Mérida*, 5.10–11, as an example.
39 *LH* 7.42. Above, p. 35. Even with Gregory's episcopal gloss, I interpret the passage as showing that the defence of those charged with neglect of military duties was that, as tenants, they were not liable to military service, even if their landlord, St Martin, could not reasonably be expected to carry out such obligations in a conventional sense. Another possibility would be that the tax exemption granted to St Martin's church also covered other obligations such as military service.
40 J. Durliat, '*Episcopus, civis* et *populus* dans les *Historiarum Libri* de Grégoire', in N. Gauthier and H. Galinié (eds.), *Grégoire de Tours et l'Espace Gaulois* (Tours, 1997), pp. 185–93.
41 *LH* 6.31.
42 Gregory, *Life of the Fathers* 8.11.
43 Thompson, *The Goths in Spain*, pp. 264–5.
44 *LV* 5.3.1–4.
45 This is certainly the case in seventh-century Spain: P.D. King, *Law and Society in the Visigothic Kingdom* (Cambridge, 1972), pp. 55–9; see also the documents about *antrustiones* in Marculf's late seventh-century formulary. C.J. Wickham, *Early Medieval Italy: Central Power and Local Society, 400–1000* (London, 1981), pp. 132–6; Lombard charters about *gasindii*: Schiaparelli 163 (early 762); 293.
46 Fredegar, *Chronicle* 3.89; *Austrasian Letters* 25. The latter reference is from a letter to the Byzantine court, which gives some grounds for caution that the term was current in Merovingian Gaul; the *spatharius* in question was on an embassy to the imperial court and would need to be given a title which would be recognised at the Constantinopolitan court. Fredegar's reference goes some way to alleviating these doubts.
47 The author of the *Life of Eligius* describes himself as *puerolus* at the royal court: *Life of Eligius* 1.6.
48 P. Riché, *Education and Culture in the Barbarian West* (trans. J.J. Contreni; Columbia 1976), pp. 236–46, is an excellent discussion of the Merovingian court as an educational centre.
49 *Wars* 5.12.50–54. Again, Procopius uses a classical term: *doryphoroi*. Spanish legal evidence would suggest that they were actually called *bucellarii* or *saiones*.
50 See also, above, pp. 35–6.
51 *LH* 5.3, is a clear case of the abuses which a lord might inflict upon his *pueri*. Here Duke Rauching buries alive one of his *pueri* who had dared to marry without his permission. Cp. Gregory of Tours, *Life of the Fathers* 12.2.
52 Halsall, *Settlement and Social Organisation* pp. 255–6.
53 *PLS* 42.
54 *Life of Desiderius of Cahors* 1. This is problematic text and the author may have derived the term from Desiderius' own letters. Desiderius (*Letters* 1.5, to Dagobert I, 1.9 to Abbo of Metz) recalled being a member of the *contubernium* of young men at the royal court. See also *Passion of Leudegar* 7; *Life of Menelaus* 1.4.
55 *Life of Desiderius of Cahors* 6, 9.
56 H. Härke, *Angelsächsische Waffengräber des 5. bis 7. Jahrhunderts* (Zeitschrift für Archäologie des Mittelalters, Beiheft 6; Cologne, 1992), p. 67.
57 See, p. 26, n. 25, above.
58 Härke, *Angelsächsische Waffengräber des 5. bis 7. Jahrhunderts*, pp. 182–90; D.F. Clark, 'A methodological examination of aspects of chronological and social analysis of early Anglo-Saxon cemeteries with particular reference to Cemetery I, Mucking, Essex' (Ph.D. Dissertation, University of London, 2000).

59   L. Alcock, *Economy, Society and Warfare among the Britons and Saxons* (Cardiff, 1987), pp. 274, 310–11.

60   Gildas, *On the Ruin of Britain* 23.

61   I hope to deal with this in a future study.

62   See, e.g., Alcock, *Economy, Society and Warfare among the Britons and Saxons*; Alcock, 'The activities of potentates in Celtic Britain, AD 500–800', in S. Driscoll and M. Nieke (eds.), *Power and Politics in Early Medieval Britain and Ireland* (Edinburgh, 1988), pp. 22–46; Alcock, 'Message from the dark side of the moon: western and northern Britain in the age of Sutton Hoo', in M.O.H. Carver (ed.), *The Age of Sutton Hoo: The Seventh Century in North-western Europe* (Woodbridge, 1992), pp. 205–15; P.A. Rahtz, 'Celtic society in Somerset, A.D. 400–700', *Bulletin of the Board of Celtic Studies* 30 (1982–83), pp. 176–200; Rahtz, 'Pagan and Christian by the Severn Sea', in L. Abrams and J.P. Carly (eds.), *The Archaeology and History of Glastonbury Abbey: Essays in Honour of the Ninetieth Birthday of C.A. Ralegh Radford* (Woodbridge, 1991), pp. 3–37; C. Snyder, *An Age of Tyrants: Britain and the Britons, A.D. 400–600* (Stroud, 1998), esp. pp. 137–216 for discussion of sites.

63   Patrick, *Letter to Coroticus*.

64   R. Christlein, *Die Alamannen: Archäologie eines lebendigen Volkes* (3rd edn; Stuttgart, 1991), pp. 43–9; H. Steuer, 'Handwerk auf spätantiken Höhensiedlungen des 4./5. Jahrhunderts in Südwestdeutschland', in P.O. Nielsen, K. Randsborg and H. Thrane (eds.), *The Archaeology of Gudme and Lundeborg: Papers Presented at a Conference at Svendborg, October, 1991* (Copenhagen, 1994), pp. 128–44; Steuer, 'Germanische Heerlager des 4./5. Jahrhunderts in Südwestdeutschland', *MASS*, pp. 113–22.

65   See, e.g., L. Jørgensen, K.W. Alt and W. Vach, 'Families at Kirchheim am Ries: analysis of Merovingian aristocratic and warrior families', *MASS*, pp. 102–12; a similar picture can be drawn from the best-recorded section of the large cemetery of Schretzheim: U. Koch, *Das Reihengräberfeld bei Schretzheim* (Germanische Denkmäler der Völkerwanderungszeit, Serie A, Band 13; 2 vols.; Berlin, 1977).

66   B. Schmidt, 'Die Thüringer', in B. Krüger (ed.), *Die Germanen*, vol. II (Berlin, 1983), pp. 502–43; D. Claude, 'Universale und partikulare Züge in der Politik Theoderichs', *Francia* 6 (1978), pp. 19–58; see Cassiodorus, *Variae*, 3.3, 4.1; *LH*, 2.27, 3.3, 3.7, 4.10.

67   An excellent overview can be found in J. Hines, 'The military context of the *adventus saxonum*: some continental evidence', in S. Chadwick Hawkes (ed.), *Weapons and Warfare in Anglo-Saxon England* (Oxford University Committee for Archaeology monograph 21; Oxford 1989), pp. 25–48.

68   B. Myrhe, 'Boathouses and military organisation', *MASS*, pp. 169–83, which has very interesting implications.

69   See, e.g., *LH* 9.12.

70   Halsall, *Settlement and Social Organisation*, pp. 262–70.

71   R. Le Jan, *Famille et Pouvoir dans le Monde Franc (VIIe–Xe siècle): essai d'anthropologie sociale* (Paris, 1995) for the development of the Frankish nobility from the seventh century and discussion of the vocabulary of power.

72   R.A. Gerberding, *The Rise of the Carolingians and the Liber Historiae Francorum* (Oxford, 1986), esp. pp. 167–8.

73   W. Goffart, 'Old and new in Merovingian taxation', *P&P* 96 (1982), pp. 3–21.

74   Kölzer 99 (for Speyer cathedral).

75   Wissembourg charter 12 (731–739).

76   H. Ebling, *Prosopographie der Amtsträger des Merowingerreiches von Chlothar II (613) bis Karl Martell (741)* (Beihefte der Francia 2; Munich, 1974), p. 183.

77   Fredegar, *Chronicle* 4.87.

78 *Ibid.*, 4.74.
79 Halsall, *Settlement and Social Organisation*, p. 49; M. Innes, *State and Society in the Early Middle Ages: The Middle Rhine Valley 400–1000* (Cambridge, 2000), p. 156.
80 See, recently, P. Fouracre, *The Age of Charles Martel* (London, 2000); I.N. Wood, *The Merovingian Kingdoms 450–751* (London, 1994).
81 Kölzer 143 (Compiègne, 23 Dec. 694). Innes, *State and Society in the Early Middle Ages*, p. 145, says the document shows that 'a free man [Ibbo] was forced by the abbot of St-Denis to sell a piece of land to escape military service'. This is very clearly not the case. Thus the document does not necessarily (though of course it *might*) represent evidence of 'the close relationship between these criteria [identifying certain individuals as liable for military service] and local patronage systems'. See also T. Reuter, 'The end of Carolingian military expansion', in P. Godman and R. Collins (eds.), *Charlemagne's Heir: New Perspectives on the Reign of Louis the Pious* (Oxford, 1990), pp. 391–405, at p. 396, who points out that Ibbo cannot have been a simple free man.
82 *Lex Ribv.* 68.1–2.
83 Innes, *State and Society in the Early Middle Ages*, pp. 154–6. This is an important discussion, though too hard and fast in its conclusion.
84 See further below, p. 100.
85 Even B.S. Bachrach, the main proponent of mass armies drawn from broad sections of the free population, points out that the *haribannus* can only have been imposed from those specifically selected to attend but who refused, rather than from all those of the classes liable to military service who did not come to the muster. B.S. Bachrach, *Early Carolingian Warfare. Prelude to Empire* (Philadelphia, 2001), p. 58.
86 Fredegar, *Chronicle* 4.74. Fredegar notes, however, that the promise had little effect.
87 Fouracre, *The Age of Charles Martel*; Gerberding, *The Rise of the Carolingians*.
88 This may be seen particularly clearly in the *Passion of Leudegar*. For discussion, see Fouracre-Gerberding, pp. 166–79.
89 For the royal *contubernium*, see n. 54, above. *Life of Audoin* 1 describes education at the royal court.
90 A useful guide is M. Rouche, *L'Aquitaine des Wisigoths aux Arabes, 418–781: Naissance d'une Région* (Toulouse, 1979), pp. 350–61; B.S. Bachrach, 'Military organisation in Aquitaine under the early Carolingians', *Speculum* 49 (1974), pp. 1–33, should be used with care but cites the relevant primary sources.
91 R. Collins, 'The *Vaccei*, the *Vaceti*, and the rise of *Vasconia*', *Studia Historica* 6 (1988), pp. 211–23 (repr. in Collins, *Law, Culture and Regionalism in Early Medieval Spain* (Aldershot, 1992), no. XI).
92 See, e.g., C.W. Hollister, *Anglo-Saxon Military Institutions on the Eve of the Norman Conquest* (Oxford, 1962); E. John, 'English feudalism and the structure of Anglo-Saxon Society', in E. John, *Orbis Britanniae and Other Studies* (Leicester, 1966), pp. 128–53; H. Härke, 'Early Anglo-Saxon military organisation: an archaeological perspective', *MASS*, pp. 93–101. I have largely taken my lead from R. Abels, *Lordship and Military Obligation in Anglo-Saxon England* (London, 1988), although with minor differences of interpretation.
93 Eddius Stephanus, *Life of Wilfrid* 2; *Life of Guthlac* 16.
94 H. Härke, 'Changing symbols in a changing society: the Anglo-Saxon weapon rite', in M. Carver (ed.), *The Age of Sutton Hoo: The Seventh Century in North-western Europe* (Woodbridge, 1992), pp. 149–65.
95 Ine's Laws 50, 51. For discussion, see Abels, *Lordship and Military Obligation in Anglo-Saxon England*, pp. 12–19; T.M. Charles Edwards, 'The distinction between land and moveable wealth in Anglo-Saxon England', in P.H. Sawyer (ed.),

Medieval Settlement. Continuity and Change (London, 1976), pp. 180–7. For discussion of Ine's code, see C.P. Wormald, '"Inter cetera boni genti suae": law-making and peace-keeping in the earliest English kingdoms', in his *Legal Culture in the Early Medieval West: Law as Text, Image and Experience* (London, 1999), pp. 179–99.

96 As noted above, the *Life of Wilfrid* uses the term *puer*, common on the continent. Abels, *Lordship and Military Obligation in Anglo-Saxon England*, pp. 26–7, is mistaken to see *puer* as denoting inferior social origins, as will have become clear.

97 Charles Edwards 'The distinction between land and moveable wealth in Anglo-Saxon England'.

98 Eddius Stephanus, *Life of Wilfrid*, ch. 2 (fourteen); Felix, *Life of Guthlac*, ch. 16 (fifteen).

99 An intriguing possibility recently mooted is that the Old English term *Hlafeata* ('loaf-eater') for a dependant may be a translation of the continental term *bucellarius*: P.S. Barnwell, *Kings, Courtiers and Imperium: The Barbarian West, 565–725* (London, 1997) pp. 45–6. It may be simplest to assume that the term simply means someone who eats at his lord's table; as we have seen, although *bucellarius* does mean 'biscuit-eater' the phrase has a more technical meaning than the superficial similarity with the meaning of *hlafeata* might suggest.

100 *HE* 4.22.

101 This is also the conclusion of Abels, *Lordship and Military Obligation in Anglo-Saxon England*, p. 28, one of the few scholars to note Imma's mention of his marital status.

102 Ine's Laws, 19.

103 Ine's Laws, 6.3.

104 Abels, *Lordship and Military Obligation in Anglo-Saxon England*, pp. 112, 114.

105 Territories are assessed in *hides* by Bede, *HE* 2.9, 3.24 and 4.16, and also, famously, in the *Tribal Hidage*, as well as in the charters if the period.

106 Abels, *Lordship and Military Obligation in Anglo-Saxon England*, p. 23, makes this very clear.

107 T. Reuter, 'The recruitment of armies in the Early Middle Ages: what can we know?' *MASS*, pp. 32–7, at p. 36; Härke, 'Early Anglo-Saxon military organisation', p. 97.

108 G. Halsall, 'Violence and society in the early medieval west: an introductory survey', in G. Halsall (ed.), *Violence and Society in the Early Medieval West* (Woodbridge, 1998), pp. 1–45, at p. 8, relates the clause to a tripartite view of violent crime, with membership of a band occupying a grey area between low-level crime and affairs of state.

109 On the Visigothic army, see, above all, Pérez Sánchez, *El Ejército en la Sociedad Visigoda*. For brief discussion in English, see Thompson, *The Goths in Spain*, pp. 145–7, 262–7.

110 A reference to a *dux exercitus hispaniae* (*Life of St Fructuosus* 2) is probably to be understood as a general and rather vague description (Fear, p. 124, n. 8) rather than an exact title (*pace* King, *Law and Society in the Visigothic Kingdom*, p. 75).

111 Isidore, *Rule for Monks* 4.2; M. De Jong, *In Samuel's Image: Child Oblation in the Early Medieval West* (Leiden, 1996), pp. 41–2. My thanks to Mark Handley for drawing my attention to this reference.

112 *LH* 7.42; above, pp. 35, 48. For tax-lists, see, e.g., *LH* 9.30, 10.7; Goffart, 'Old and new in Merovingian taxation'; S. Sato, 'The Merovingian accounting documents of Tours', *EME* 9.2 (2000), pp. 143–61.

113 *Life of Fructuosus of Braga*, 3. The *Life* (ch. 14) also mentions the local *dux's* concern that recruitment into the monasteries would affect his ability to find troops for the army. The concerns may echo those of Bede somewhat later.

114 *LV* 9.2.6; King, *Law and Society in the Visigothic Kingdom*, p. 72.

115 Pérez Sánchez, *El Ejército en la Sociedad Visigoda*, p. 117, goes too far in describing the sixth-century Spanish army as a permanent regular army.

116 *LV* 9.2.8–9.

117 *LV* 9.2.9.

118 L.A. García Moreno, 'Legitimate and illegitimate violence in Visigothic law', in Halsall (ed.), *Violence and Society in the Early Medieval West*, pp. 46–59.

119 *LV* 5.3.1–4.

120 *PLS* 26.1 refers to *laeti* (half-free) men with their masters in the army, but on balance this seems to imply that such people attended their lords as servants (Halsall, *Settlement and Social Organisation*, p. 42). The *cause célèbre* of Imma and his claim to be a *ceorl* and thus a non-combatant is discussed above (p. 58).

121 In Visigothic Spain, all dependants of landowners, slaves, *coloni*, half-free and free, may have become submerged in a single 'slave' class, which might have thereby had a slightly different character to that elsewhere in late and post-Roman Europe. I am grateful to Chris Wickham for his thoughts on this issue.

122 See, e.g., P. Bonnassie, 'Society and mentalities in Visigothic Spain', in his *From Slavery to Feudalism in South-Western Europe* (Cambridge, 1991), pp. 60–103; García-Moreno, 'Legitimate and illegitimate violence in Visigothic law'; Sánchez, *El Ejército en la Sociedad Visigoda*, pp. 192–3. A modified view can be found in P. Díaz and M.R. Valverde, 'The theoretical strength and practical weakness of the Visigothic monarchy of Toledo', in F. Theuws and J.L. Nelson (eds.), *Rituals of Power. From Late Antiquity to the Early Middle Ages* (Leiden, 2000), pp. 60–93.

123 See, e.g., in English, R. Collins, *Early Medieval Spain: Unity in Diversity, 400–1000* (2nd edn; London, 1995), pp. 107–28 (for analysis of Visigothic kingship), 143, 158–9.

124 See *Chronicle of 754*, ch. 36.

125 *HW* 27; M. de Jong, 'Adding insult to injury: Julian of Toledo and his *Historia Wambae*', in P. Heather (ed.), *The Visigoths: From the Migration Period to the Seventh Century* (Woodbridge, 1999), pp. 373–89; M. McCormick, *Eternal Victory: Triumphal Rulership in Late Antiquity, Byzantium and the Early Medieval West* (paperback edn; Cambridge, 1990), p. 313. Whether *decalvatio* meant tonsuring, simple cutting of the long hair which symbolised freedom or, with less likelihood, scalping, has given rise to a long-running but not especially interesting debate.

126 *Chronicle of 754*, ch. 52, 54, R. Collins, 'The Basques in Aquitaine and Navarre: Problems of Frontier Government', in J. Gillingham and J.C. Holt (eds.), *War and Society in the Middle Ages: Essays in Honour of J.O. Prestwich* (Cambridge, 1984), pp. 3–17, at p. 12.

127 M. Handley has argued very cogently that the use of the 'Spanish Aera' (a chronology beginning in the year we think of as 38 BC) was, in the seventh century, promoted to enhance Spanish unity. Handley demonstrates the Visigothic kings' promotion of Spanish martyr cults. M. Handley, 'Tiempo y identidad. La datación por la Era en las inscripciones de la España tardoromana y visigoda', *Iberia. Revista de la Anigüedad* 2 (1999), pp. 191–201.

128 See, e.g., R. Stocking, *Bishops, Councils and Consensus in the Visigothic Kingdom, 589–633* (Ann Arbor, 2000) for the situation up to the early seventh century. For the acts of these councils see J. Vives (ed.), *Concilios Visigóticos e Hispano-Romanos* (Barcelona, 1963).

129 P. de Palol and G. Ripoll López, *Die Goten: Geschichte und Kunste in Westeuropa* (Augsburg, 1999); G. Ripoll López, 'The arrival of the Visigoths in Hispania: population problems and the process of acculturation', in W. Pohl and H. Reimitz (eds.), *Strategies of Distinction. The Construction of Ethnic Communities, 300–800*

(Leiden, 1998), pp. 153–87; Ripoll López, 'Symbolic life and signs of identity in Visigothic times', in P. Heather (ed.), *The Visigoths: From the Migration Period to the Seventh Century* (Woodbridge, 1999), pp. 403–31.

130 I hope to return to this in a separate study.

131 Pérez Sánchez, *El Ejército en la Sociedad Visigoda*, pp. 129–74, 192–3 for conclusion.

132 Although, perhaps ironically, the Visigoths' 'Ummayyad successors *were* ultimately to create precisely this sort of independent, tax-funded coercive force, raised from slaves of usually foreign extraction.

133 Fredegar, *Chronicle* 4.82.

134 Above, p. 3, n. 12.

135 Collins, 'The Basques in Aquitaine and Navarre', p. 12, with n. 48.

136 The fundamental study is O. Bertolini, 'Ordinamenti militari e strutture sociali dei Longobardi in Italia', *SdS*15, pp. 429–607. To this must now be added S. Gasparri, 'Strutture militari e legami di dipendenza in età longobarda e carolingia', *Rivista Storica Italiana* 98 (1986), pp. 664–726.

137 This is one problem with the very detailed and useful analysis by D. Harrison, *The Early State and the Towns: Forms of Integration in Lombard Italy, 568–774* (Lund, 1993), which essentially applies only to the eighth-century situation.

138 Rothari's Edict, 20, 23, 24. The reader should note that Fischer Drew's translation (*The Lombard Laws* (Philadelphia, 1973), pp. 56–7) completely obscures the situation by inserting the word 'soldier' into Rothari's Edict 22, where *exercitalis* does not appear, and omitting it from clauses 23 and 24 (translating *exercitalis* as 'his man'), where it does!

139 L. Jørgensen, 'Castel Trosino and Nocera Umbra; a chronological and social analysis of family burial practice in Lombard Italy (6th–7th centuries)', *Acta Archaeologica* 62 (1991), pp. 1–58.

140 *HL* 2.9.

141 A. Callander Murray, *Germanic Kinship Structure: Studies in Law and Society in Antiquity and the Early Middle Ages* (Toronto, 1983), pp. 89–97.

142 Rothari's Edict, 225.

143 Lombard law was thorough on the nature of gift and counter-gift; see Rothari's Edict, 172–5. One law discusses the return of gifts to dukes or freemen by other freemen (Rothari's Edict, 177). This occurs in the context of a freeman moving from one part of the kingdom to another with his *fara* (the only use of the term in Lombard law, and where it does seem to mean family). This law does not seem to imply that land-grants were made in return for service, and could be revoked if that service was terminated, in the way which would be the case slightly later (the clause looks, superficially at least, comparable to Ine 63–8). I think the law's concern is rather, firstly, with lands which would be abandoned and/or have an absentee owner, and secondly, with the rupture of 'horizontal' ties within local society which such a move would produce. Nevertheless, it is far from impossible that this is the first reference to land granted 'beneficially' (see ch. 4), in return for service.

144 The most famous case is that of Droctulf, recorded in his inscription as an exterminator of his own people. *HL* 3.19; N. Christie, *The Lombards* (Oxford, 1995), pp. 84–6.

145 Rothari's Edict 6.

146 Bavarian Law 2.4–6; Alamannic Law 26–27.

147 *LHF* 41 refers to a duke of the Saxons in the early seventh century, but the passage is very problematic. It is possible that repeated processes of subjugation by the Franks and incorporation into their hegemony, followed by successful attempts to break free of such overlordship, produced significant social change. For discussion of the tale, see G. Scheibelreiter, 'Vom Mythos zur Geschichte: Überlegungen zu den Formen der Bewahrung von Vergangenheit im Frühmittelalter', in A. Scharer

and G. Scheibelreiter (eds.), *Historiographie im frühen Mittelalter* (Vienna, 1994), pp. 26–40.

148 T. Capelle, *Die Sachsen des frühen Mittelalter* (Darmstadt, 1998); a brief but excellent discussion with full bibliography can be found in M. Becher, 'Die Sachsen im 7. und 8. Jahrhundert: Verfassung und Ethnogenese', in C. Stiegemann and M. Wemhoff (eds.), *Kunst und Kultur der Karolingerzeit: Karl der Grosse und Papst Leo III. in Paderborn 799* (3 vols., Mainz, 1999), pp. 187–94. W. Lammers (ed.), *Entstehung und Verfassung des Sachsenstammes* (Darmstadt 1967) remains fundamental. See also H.-J. Hässler (ed.), *Sachsen und Franken in Westfalen* (Studien zur Sachsenforschung 12; Hildesheim, 1999). A useful, brief discussion of early Saxon society in English can be found in E. Goldberg, 'Popular revolt, dynastic politics and aristocratic factionalism in the early middle ages: the Saxon *stellinga* reconsidered', *Speculum* 70 (1995), pp. 467–501 at pp. 470–5.

149 *HE* 5.10.

150 See below, p. 88, n. 91.

151 See p. 62.

152 A. Nørgård Jørgensen, 'Sea defence in Denmark AD 200–1300', *MASS*, pp. 200–209, at pp. 205–6.

153 V.I. Evison, 'The Dover ring-sword and other sword-rings and beads', *Archaeologia* 101 (1967), pp. 63–118 and plates VIII–XV.

154 L. Hedeager, *Iron Age Societies. From Tribe to State in Northern Europe, 500 BC to 700 AD* (London, 1992).

155 On this period in Sweden, see, above all, J.P. Lamm and H. Nordstrom (eds.), *Statens Historiska Museum, Studies 2: Vendel Period* (Stockholm, 1983). For a very brief introduction to the sites at Vendel and Valsgärde see G. Halsall, *Early Medieval Cemeteries: An Introduction to Burial Archaeology in the Post-Roman West* (Glasgow, 1995), pp. 35–6.

156 J. Engström, 'The Vendel chieftains – a study of military tactics', *MASS*, pp. 248–55.

157 See, e.g., *HE* 1.34 for Northumbrian aggression *c.*600; *ASC s.a.* 584, 597 for traditions of West Saxon expansion at the same time.

158 See, e.g., E. Campbell, 'The archaeological evidence for external contacts: imports, trade and economy in Celtic Britain, A.D. 400–800', in K.R. Dark (ed.), *External Contacts and the Economy of Late Roman and Post Roman Britain* (Woodbridge, 1996), pp. 83–96.

159 N. Hooper, 'The Aberlemno stone and cavalry in Anglo-Saxon England', *Northern History* 29 (1993), pp. 188–96; G.D.R. Cruickshank, 'The battle of Dunnichen and the Aberlemno battle-scene', in E.J. Cowan and B.A. McDonald (eds.), *Alba: Celtic Scotland in the Medieval Era* (East Linton, 2000), pp. 69–87.

160 Rather like the *Tribal Hidage* in England, this document exists only as a later version, with many difficulties of interpretation, but seems to relate to the seventh century.

161 M.R. Nieke and H.B. Duncan, 'Dalriada: the establishment and maintenance of an early historic kingdom in northern Britain', in S. Driscoll and M. Nieke (eds.), *Power and Politics in Early Medieval Britain and Ireland* (Edinburgh, 1988), pp. 6–21; for hillforts, see above, n. 62.

162 S. Foster, 'The state of Pictland in the age of Sutton Hoo', in M.O.H. Carver (ed.), *The Age of Sutton Hoo: The Seventh Century in North-western Europe* (Woodbridge, 1992), pp. 217–34.

163 Welsh evidence is sparse and intractable. For the most sophisticated attempts to extract information and detect development and change, see W. Davies, *Wales in the Early Middle Ages* (Leicester, 1982), with pp. 130–1 on military service; also W. Davies, *Patterns of Power in Early Wales* (Oxford, 1990), pp. 22–4, 60, 76–8, 86–87.

164 J.T. Koch (ed. and trans.), *The Gododdin: Text and Context from Dark-Age North Britain* (Cardiff, 1997); this argument has not commanded universal assent, however.

165 A wonderful evocation of annual cattle raiding and the formal rules for its redistribution may be found in the laws of the tenth-century king, Hywel Dda. Unfortunately, this text is much later than the period it purports to describe, being compiled in the thirteenth century, and its evidential value for our period is dubious.

166 *HE* 2.20.

167 For Irish politics, see F.J. Byrne, *Irish Kings and High Kings* (London, 1973); G. Mac Niocaill, *Ireland Before the Vikings* (Dublin, 1972); D. Ó Cróinín, *Early Medieval Ireland 400–1200* (London, 1995); for an archaeological approach see H. Mytum, *The Origins of Early Christian Ireland* (London, 1992).

4 RAISING AN ARMY (2): THE CAROLINGIAN WORLD

1 F.L. Ganshof, *Feudalism* (3rd edn; London, 1964).

2 L.T. White, *Medieval Technology and Social Change* (Oxford, 1962), pp. 1–38; J. Beeler, *Warfare in Feudal Europe, 730–1200* (Ithaca, 1971), pp. 9–13.

3 The best concise treatment of the problem is P. Fouracre, *The Age of Charles Martel* (London, 2000), pp. 137–54. For more detail see J. Jarnut, U. Nonn and M. Richter (eds.), *Karl Martell in seiner Zeit* (Beihefte der Francia 37; Sigmaringen, 1994).

4 See chapters 8 and 9, this volume.

5 B.S. Bachrach, 'Charles Martel, mounted shock combat, the stirrup and feudalism', *Studies in Medieval and Renaissance History* 7 (1970), pp. 49–75; Bachrach, 'Charlemagne's cavalry: myth and reality', *Military Affairs* 47 (1983), pp. 181–7. Both articles are reprinted in B.S. Bachrach, *Armies and Politics in the early Medieval West* (London, 1993).

6 For more thorough and scholarly treatment, see S. Reynolds, *Fiefs and Vassals: The Medieval Evidence Reinterpreted* (Oxford, 1994), pp. 17–74, for discussion of concepts, and pp. 84–114 for analysis of the Carolingian evidence.

7 See, e.g., Council of Orléans I (511), ch. 7.

8 Evidence for lay land tenure, always less plentiful than that for ecclesiastical, is especially so at this date in Francia. The habit of giving the previous deeds regarding an estate to a church along with the estate itself, had not become common. We must look for references to tenurial arrangements within grants to the church by secular aristocrats. For benefices held by laymen from other laymen, see, e.g., Wissembourg charters, nos. 9 and 10, dated 735/6 and 739.

9 Halsall, *Settlement and Social Organisation*, p. 273.

10 F. Theuws, 'Landed property and manorial organisation in Northern Austrasia: some considerations and a case study', in N. Roymans and F. Theuws (eds.), *Images of the Past: Studies on Ancient Societies in North-Western Europe* (Studies en Prae- en Protohistorie 7; Amsterdam, 1991), pp. 299–407.

11 See above, pp. 54–6.

12 Fouracre, *Age of Charles Martel*, pp. 155–66.

13 *Ibid.*, pp. 150–4.

14 Though this is what the ninth-century *Earlier Annals of Metz* claim.

15 *CFred* 24. *Pippinus dux, commoto exercito, cum auunculo suo Childebrando duce et multitudine primatum et agminum satellitum plurimorum* . . . : 'Duke Pippin, having called out the army, with his uncle Duke Childebrand and a multitude of leaders and crowds of their followers . . .'

16 Council of Estinnes (Boretius 11), ch. 2; Fouracre, *Age of Charles Martel*, pp. 139–40.

17 This is clear in the later eighth-century charters to the abbeys of, for example, Gorze, Fulda and Lorsch; M. Innes, *State and Society in the Early Middle Ages. The Middle Rhine Valley 400–1000* (Cambridge 2000), pp. 13–34 for analysis. The term *Lex Beneficium* appears in documents of the middle eighth century.

18 Classic studies of military service in Charlemagne's realm are: F.L. Ganshof, 'L'Armée sous les Carolingiens', *SdS*15, pp. 109–30, reprinted as 'Charlemagne's army', in his *Frankish Institutions under Charlemagne* (trans. B. Lyon; Providence RI, 1968), pp. 59–68; J.F. Verbruggen, 'L'Armée et la stratégie de Charlemagne', in H. Beumann (ed.), *Karl der Grosse: Lebenswerk und Nachleben, vol. 1, Persönlichkeit und Geschichte* (Düsseldorf, 1965), pp. 420–36.

19 See the excellent survey by S. Airlie, 'The aristocracy', *NCMH*, pp. 431–50, for the point that the dynasty was also the *creation* of a certain group of aristocratic families, rather than the *creator* of a new, powerful aristocracy,

20 On the Frankish aristocracy in this period, see R. Le Jan's exemplary study, *Famille et Pouvoir dans le Monde Franc (VIIe–Xe siècle): essai d'anthropologie sociale* (Paris, 1995).

21 See, in particular, M. Becher, *Eid und Herrschaft: Untersuchungen zum Herrscherethos Karls der Grossen* (Vorträge und Forschungen Sonderband 39; Sigmaringen, 1993).

22 See Pippin, Capitulary of Soissons, 2 Mar., 744 (Boretius 12), ch. 3.

23 Mühlbacher 91: *de tribus causis: de hoste publico, hoc est de banno nostro, quando publicitus promovetur, et wacta vel pontos componendum . . .*

24 Mühlbacher 20, of Pippin I for Worms cathedral. This is a confirmation of a Merovingian charter, and seems to reserve cases of especial need. Another is Mühlbacher 143, of Charlemagne for Speyer cathedral, and this too is a confirmation of a Merovingian grant – Kölzer 99.

25 J.L. Nelson, 'The Church's military service in the ninth century: a contemporary comparative view?', *Studies in Church History* 20 (1983), pp. 15–30, reprinted in her *Politics and Ritual in Early Medieval Europe* (London, 1986), pp. 117–32.

26 *ARF. s.a.* 806. J.F. Verbruggen, *The Art of Warfare in Western Europe during the Middle Ages* (2nd rev. edn, trans. S. Willard and Mrs R.W. Southern; Woodbridge, 1997), p. 314.

27 *CFred* 29; Fouracre, *Age of Charles Martel*, p. 169.

28 E.g. *Rev. Ann. s.a.* 785, 792.

29 Innes, *State and Society*, p. 151, says that the Carolingian army was not simply an 'agglomeration of personal followings' but this seems to hold only if one assumes precisely the sort of rigid or even institutional nature of such followings which Innes' work does so much to question. His book seems to me to show clearly that 'personal followings' were loose and fluid collections. I see nothing in the evidence to suggest that these were not the building blocks of Carolingian armed forces. See below.

30 On all this, see Fouracre, *Age of Charles Martel*, pp. 150–4.

31 Innes, *State and Society*, pp. 143–56. This section in essence attempts to flesh out the argument presented by Nelson, 'The Church's military service in the ninth century', esp. pp. 126–7. Nelson's case is thorough and convincing for the ninth-century situation she discusses but the slightly earlier data from the Lorsch cartulary cannot simply be forced into the framework of her argument. Though Innes' work is largely concerned with bigger issues, his discussion of military service still lies at the core of his argument.

32 Above, p. 55.

33 Above, pp. 54–5, where we also saw that the case of Ibbo, cited as an instance of the intervention of local patronage networks in the working of royal government and military service is nothing of the sort.

34 Lorsch charter 247, dated to between October 768 and October 769; Innes, *State and Society*, pp. 148–9. It is not entirely clear who the recipient of the horse was to be. Although the main text only mentions Ripwin, the witness list begins with the names of 'Ripwin and Giselhelm, who made this sale' (*Ripphuuini et Giselh[elmi] qui hanc uenditionem fecerunt*).

35 Innes, *State and Society*, p. 148.

36 Lorsch charter 257, 9 Oct., 792–8 Oct., 793.

37 Lorsch charters 260 and 597, dated 22 July 817, and 10 June 808, respectively. Ripwin's last appearance is dated 1 August 806 (Lorsch charter 259). Whilst not in Ripwin's company, someone called Giselhelm witnessed a further fourteen Lorsch charters, during the same general period (767–801), six of which are dated to the May–August campaign period mentioned above. It is not clear that this Giselhelm is Ripwin's brother (he never refers to a family connection – such as his father or mother's name – to show this). He attests in villas where Ripwin is never found, and never in the company of any of Ripwin's other known family members. As regards the summer months, this Giselhelm's pattern of attesting charters is not significantly different from Ripwin's in any case. However, see below, n. 47.

38 Campaigns of course took place outside this period. For example, Charlemagne's 775 and 780 expeditions only seem to have begun in late July or early August. Nevertheless, May–August seems to have been the usual time for warfare. Charlemagne, Capitulary of Aachen, late 802/early 803 (King 14; Boretius 77), ch. 9, referred to summer as the hosting season.

39 Ripwin (and Giselhelm and Stahal) attested Lorsch charter 249, dated 12 June 775, whereas Charlemagne's Saxon campaign that year seems to have begun after 3 August, when he was still at Düren (Mühlbacher 103), and ended by 25 October, by which time the king was back at that palace (Mühlbacher 104). Ripwin (and his brothers) also attended the inquisition recorded in Lorsch charter 228 (6 June 782), which probably gave him (and his brother) time to join the king for his Saxon expedition which began from Lippspringe in late July (Mühlbacher 143; *ARF s.a.* 782). Charlemagne was back at Herestal by 18 August (Mühlbacher 146), and Ripwin and Stahal witnessed Lorsch 230 on 1 September 782. Any or all of the brothers could have served on this campaign.

40 See below, ch. 7.

41 Pace Innes, *State and Society*, pp. 148, 149, n. 34.

42 Ripwin and Stahal, alongside Giselhelm, donate land to Lorsch in Lorsch charter 252 (3 May 767); Giselhelm and Stahal give land in Lorsch charter 234 (6 May 766); Stahal also appears in Lorsch charters 231 (766–68), 236 (30 December 766), 235 (27 May 766), and 240 (15 June 767).

43 Innes, *State and Society*, p. 148.

44 Stahal (who refers to Ripwin as *germanus meus* [my brother] in Lorsch charter 252) refers to their father as *Liutherus* [*sic*] *quondam* (very loosely, 'the late Liuther') in Lorsch charter 234 and as *Liutwinus quondam* in Lorsch charter 240. Innes, *State and Society*, p. 149, n. 34, says that Ripwin's father last appears in Lorsch charter 245. Although Ripwin's two brothers and his mother all attest this document (but in no instance for the last time) this charter contains no mention of Ripwin's father, who indeed never appears in his own right in the Lorsch charters.

45 Most significantly in Lorsch charter 228, where he appears in a list of local witnesses in an inquiry.

46 See also Halsall, *Settlement and Social Organisation*, pp. 70–1, for discussion of the use of patronymics and matronymics in early medieval charters from a neighbouring region.

47 The pattern is not altered at all by the inclusion of the 'other' Giselhelm, who

might not be the same as Ripwin and Stahal's brother (above, n. 37), possibly strengthening the argument that the two are indeed one and the same.

48 On which see, e.g., H. Mordek, 'Karolingische Kapitularien', in H. Mordek (ed.) *Überlieferung und Geltung normativer Texte des frühen und hohen Mittelalters*, Quellen und Forschungen zum Recht im Mittelalter 4 (Sigmaringen, 1986), pp. 25–50.

49 See note 5, and p. 94, for other instances.

50 See below, pp. 93–5.

51 See, for discussion of the historiography, F. Staab, 'A reconsideration of the ancestry of modern political liberty: the problem of the "King's Freemen" (Königsfreie)', *Viator* 11 (1980), pp. 51–69.

52 This situation was so well known in early ninth-century Italy that Lothar I issued a law which decreed that, where brothers had decided not to divide an estate so that only one of them would have to perform military service, at least one brother was always to go to the army, and one (but no more than that) was to stay behind to manage the estates. Capitulary of Corteolona, 825 (Boretius 165), ch. 6. It was presumably this sort of situation which prompted Bede's concerns in his Letter to Ecgbert; see below.

53 The same trend can be seen in the charters of Gorze Abbey in Lorraine, for which see Halsall, *Settlement and Social Organisation*, pp. 194–5, 276.

54 For brief but excellent discussion, see P. Delogu, 'Lombard and Carolingian Italy', *NCMH*, pp. 290–319 and, now, C. La Rocca (ed.), *Italy in the Early Middle Ages, 476–1000* (Oxford, 2002).

55 Here I follow the analysis of C.J. Wickham, 'Aristocratic power in eighth-century Lombard Italy', in A. Callander Murray (ed.), *After Rome's Fall: Narrators and Sources of Early Medieval History: Essays presented to Walter Goffart* (Toronto, 1998), pp. 153–70.

56 It is difficult to know for sure that this was a new development. However, the two seventh-century law-codes, Rothari's and Grimoald's, both of which were issued at public gatherings, are dated to 22 November and 'the month of July' respectively.

57 Alfrid the *exercitalis*, for example, appears in CDL4 14 (Rieti, February, 761).

58 O. Bertolini, 'Ordinamenti militari e strutture sociali dei Longobardi in Italia', *SdS*15, pp. 429–607, is an exhaustive discussion of the terms *exercitalis* and *armimannus*.

59 Liutprand's Laws 62.

60 Schiaparelli 50 (Siena, 1 December, 730; *exercitum Senensium civitatis*).

61 Ratchis' Laws 4.

62 Delogu, 'Lombard and Carolingian Italy', p. 291.

63 Liutprand's Laws 83.

64 Memorandum on military affairs, 811 (King 27; Boretius 73), ch. 4; Capitulary of Boulogne, October 811 (King 28; Boretius 74), ch. 9; Capitulary on mobilisation for the use of the *Missi*, 808 (King 24; Boretius 50), ch. 4.

65 Aistulf's Laws, 2–3.

66 *Ibid.*, 7.

67 S. Gasparri, 'Strutture militari e legami di dipendenza in età longobarda e carolingia', *Rivista Storica Italiana* 98 (1986), pp. 664–726.

68 Ratchis' Laws 10–11. Ratchis' Laws 10 also shows that some royal officials could use their patronage to interfere in the workings of the law.

69 C. Wickham, *Early Medieval Italy. Local Society and Central Power, 400–1000* (London, 1981), p. 46; Wills: Schiaparelli 114 (Lucca, July 754), 117 (August 755).

70 For summary, see R. Collins, 'Spain: The northern kingdoms and the Basques, 711–910', *NCMH*, pp. 272–89.

71 The area around Narbonne in southern France, which remained under Gothic control after the Franks had destroyed the Gothic kingdom of Toulouse in 507.

72 *CA3* 8–10.

73 Though very out of date in approach and assumptions, there is nevertheless much useful information in C. Sánchez-Albornoz, 'El ejército y la guerra en el reino Asturleones 718–1037', *SdS*15, pp. 293–428. See, more recently, J. Escalona Monge, 'Las prestaciones de servicios militares y la organización de la sociedad feudal castellana: los infanzones de Espeja', *Castillos de España* 94 (1987), pp. 55–60.

74 Attempts to argue for a Roman or Visigothic frontier in the region have not been entirely successful. See: A. Barbero and M. Vigil, 'Algunos aspectos de la feudalización del reino visigodo en relación con su organización financiera y militar', in their *Sobre los orígenes sociales de la Reconquista* (Barcelona, 1974), pp. 107–37; J.M. Blazquez, 'Der Limes im Spanien des vierten Jahrhunderts', in D.M. Pippidi (ed.), *Actes du IXe Congrès International d'Études sur les Frontières Romaines, Mamaïa 6–13 Sept., 1972* (Cologne, 1974), pp. 485–502; J.M. Blazquez, 'Der Limes Hispaniens im 4. und 5. Forschungsstand. Niederlassungen der Laeti oder Gentiles am Flusslauf des Duero', in W.S. Hanson and L.J.F. Keppie (eds.), *Roman Frontier Studies 1979. Papers presented to the 12th International Congress of Roman Frontier Studies* (BAR(S) 71; Oxford, 1980), pp. 345–96; A. Dominguez Monedero, 'Los ejércitos regulares tardorromanos en la Península Ibérica y el problema del pretendido "limes hispanus"', *Revista de Guimaraes* 93 (1983), pp. 101–32; L.A. García Moreno, 'Zamora del dominio imperial romano al visigodo. Cuestiones de Historia militar y geopolítica', *I. Congresso de Historia de Zamora* (1990), pp. 455–66.

75 *CA3* 13.

76 As in the previous chapter, I have largely taken my lead from R. Abels, *Lordship and Military Obligation in Anglo-Saxon England* (London, 1988), but with some differences in interpretation. See also the insightful survey by N.P. Brooks, 'The development of military obligations in eighth and ninth century England', in P. Clemoes and K. Hughes (eds.), *England before the Conquest* (Cambridge, 1971), pp. 69–84, reprinted in his *Communities and Warfare 700–1400* (London, 2000), pp. 32–47. I cite the reprint.

77 The splendid isolation of Anglo-Saxon history, the fifth- and sixth-century Anglo-Saxons kings' paganism and the convenient *deus* (or at least *servus dei*) *ex machina* of Augustine's mission in 597 have obscured the fact that, although the earliest Anglo-Saxon charters and other legal documents are Christian and date to after Augustine's mission, this does not mean that such things were absent before 597. In Merovingian northern Gaul, the earliest charters and similar documents also belong to the period after *c*.600, but we know from Gregory of Tours' writings that the sixth-century administration of region was literate and made use of many written instruments. See Halsall, *Settlement and Social Organisation*, pp. 46–8.

78 Brooks, 'The development of military obligations in eighth and ninth century England'.

79 Abels, *Lordship and Military Obligation in Anglo-Saxon England*, pp. 43–57.

80 N.P. Brooks, 'The development of military obligations in eighth and ninth century England', pp. 69–84; P.A. Rahtz, 'The archaeology of west Mercian towns', in A. Dornier (ed.), *Mercian Studies* (Leicester, 1977), pp. 107–29; J. Haslam, 'Market and fortress in England in the reign of Offa', *World Archaeology* 19.3 (1987), pp. 76–93.

81 See also Brooks, 'The development of military obligations in eighth and ninth century England'.

82 Here I am in agreement with T.M. Charles Edwards, 'The distinction between land and moveable wealth in Anglo-Saxon England', in P.H. Sawyer (ed.), *Medieval Settlement. Continuity and Change* (London, 1976), pp. 180–7, who sees grants of land, additional to inherited estates, as necessary to maintain the warrior status of the next generation. This would be especially necessary in the conditions of partible inheritance. Abels, *Lordship and Military Obligation in Anglo-Saxon England*, p. 29, rejects this idea, but on uncertain grounds. See also the discussion of Ripwin and Italian analogues, above, p. 80, and n. 52.

83 Brooks, 'The development of military obligations in eighth and ninth century England', p. 44; for the meaning of the term *comes*, see above, p. 58.

84 *Ibid.*, p. 38.

85 *ASC s.a.* 757.

86 Mondsee, charter 5. For context, see C.I. Hammer, 'Land sales in eighth- and ninth-century Bavaria: legal, social and economic aspects', *EME* 6.1 (1996), pp. 47–76. We do not know, *pace* Hammer, 'Land sales', p. 66, that the three were brothers, though this seems likely enough.

87 Mondsee charter 63.

88 C.R. Bowlus, *Franks, Moravians and Magyars: The Struggle for the Middle Danube, 788–907* (Philadelphia, 1995), pp. 33–45.

89 R. Christlein, *Die Alamannen: Archäologie eines lebendigen Volkes* (3rd edn; Stuttgart, 1991), pp. 9–49.

90 *Rev. Ann. s.a.* 775.

91 M. Hardt, 'Linien und Säume, Zonen und Räume an der Ostgrenze des Reiches im frühen und hohen Mittelalter', in W. Pohl and H. Reimitz (eds.), *Grenze und Differenz im früheren Mittelalter* (Österreichische Akademie der Wissenschaften: Vienna, 2000), pp. 39–56, and literature cited there.

92 N. Lund, 'Scandinavia, *c.*700–1066', *NCMH*, pp. 202–27, at p. 205.

93 E.g. N. Lund, 'If the Vikings knew a *Leding* – What was it like?', in B. Ambrosiani and H. Clarke (eds.), *Developments around the Baltic and the North Sea in the Viking Age* (Birka Studies 3; Stockholm, 1994), pp. 98–105; Lund, 'Allies of God or man? The Viking expansion in a European perspective', *Viator* 20 (1989), pp. 45–59.

94 *Memorandum on Military Affairs* 811 (King 26; Boretius 73), ch. 9. For the *missi*, see above, p. 75.

95 T. Reuter, 'Plunder and tribute in the Carolingian empire', *TRHS*, 5th series, 35 (1985), pp. 75–94; Reuter, 'The end of Carolingian military expansion', in Godman and Collins (eds.), *Charlemagne's Heir*, pp. 391–405.

96 Charles the Younger: *ARF s.a.* 805–6; Louis: Astronomer, *Life of Louis*, ch. 5–19. The Carolingians were, in military terms, a consistently very able dynasty.

97 E.g., Capitulary of Nijmegen, March 806 (King 20; Boretius 40), chs. 2–3; Capitulary of Boulogne, Oct. 811 (King 28; Boretius 74), ch. 8.

98 Reuter, 'Plunder and tribute in the Carolingian empire'; E. Goldberg, '"More devoted to the equipment of battle than the splendor of banquets": Frontier kingship, military ritual and early knighthood at the court of Louis the German', *Viator* 30 (1999), pp. 41–78.

99 Thegan, *Life of Louis*, 28, 55. Thegan says that even Hugh's own bodyguard ridiculed him on this account.

100 *AB s.a.* 830.

101 *Ibid.*

102 The term is not without problems but appears to have remained in use as a form of shorthand for the class of Carolingian 'super-aristocrats'.

103 See, e.g., R. Le Jan Hennebicque, 'Domnus, illuster, nobilis: Les mutations du pouvoir au Xe siècle', in M. Sot (ed.), *Haut Moyen-Age: Culture, Education et Société* (La Garenne-Colombes, 1990), pp. 439–48; J.L. Nelson, 'Nobility in the ninth

century', in A.J. Duggan (ed.), *Nobles and Nobility in Medieval Europe: Concepts, Origins, Transformations* (Woodbridge, 2000), pp. 43–51.

104 Probably the most striking example is that of the family of Bernard of Septimania. Several members, male and female, were killed by the Carolingians in the ninth century but in the early tenth century his descendant, William, could still style himself 'Duke of the Aquitanians'. J. Martindale, 'The French aristocracy in the early middle ages: a reappraisal', *P&P* 75 (1977), pp. 5–45, at pp. 17–19.

105 This has been shown above all in the *oeuvre* of J.L. Nelson (see bibliography). See also S. MacLean, 'The Carolingian response to the revolt of Boso, 870–887', *EME* 10.1 (2001), pp. 21–48, for the way in which this was shown when a magnate not of the direct Carolingian line made a bid for royal power.

106 Airlie, 'The aristocracy', p. 445.

107 J. Martindale, 'Charles the Bald and the government of the kingdom of Aquitaine', in M.T. Gibson and J.L. Nelson (eds.), *Charles the Bald. Court and Kingdom* (2nd edn; Aldershot, 1990), pp. 115–38.

108 MacLean, 'The Carolingian response to the revolt of Boso, 870–887', p. 46. The quote could apply equally well to most early medieval rulers.

109 Capitulary of Boulogne, October 811 (King 28; Boretius 74), ch. 2.

110 Capitulary on various matters, Nijmegen, March 806 (King 20; Boretius 49), ch. 3, referring to Frisia; Memorandum on mobilisation, Aachen before August 807 (King 23; Boretius 48), ch. 1.

111 Memorandum on mobilisation, Aachen before August 807 (King 23; Boretius 48), ch. 2.

112 Capitulary on mobilisation, for the use of the *Missi*, 808 (King 24; Boretius 50), ch. 1.

113 Double Capitulary of Thionville, 806 (King 17; Boretius 43–4), ch. 22/6.

114 Capitulary of Aachen, late 802/early 803 (King 14; Boretius 77), ch. 9.

115 In the ninth century, abbeys were often controlled, as far as their estates and affairs in the secular world were concerned, by 'lay abbots', secular noblemen (Nithard, for example, was lay abbot of St-Riquier), leaving spiritual authority to a prior. As Charlemagne's letter to Fulrad of St-Quentin shows, lay abbots were expected to lead monastic contingents. Then again, even ordinary abbots were expected to attend the army.

116 Probably better (if more clumsily) translated as 'warriors possessing a horse' than as 'horsemen'; though the word, obviously, is the root of the modern term 'cavalry', to use this word would create a misleading impression. See below, ch. 9.

117 Letter to Fulrad, mid-April 806 (King 22; Boretius 75).

118 See also, for most detail, Capitulary concerning Estates (*De Villis*), 800 (Boretius 32), ch. 64; and Capitulary of Aachen, late 802/early 803 (King 14; Boretius 77), ch. 10; also Memorandum of mobilisation, Aachen before August 807 (King 23; Boretius 48), ch. 3.

119 See also, e.g., Capitulary of Boulogne, October 811 (King 28; Boretius 74), ch. 8.

120 See, for a selection: 'Programmatic' Capitulary, March 802 (King 13: Boretius 33), ch. 7; Capitulary of Aachen, late 802/early 803 (King 15; Boretius 77), ch. 17; Double Capitulary of Thionville, 806 (King 17; Boretius 44), ch. 22/6, 31/15; Capitulary on mobilisation for the use of *Missi*, 808 (King 24; Boretius 50), ch. 2, 5; Aachen Capitulary, 810 (Boretius 64), ch. 12.

121 E.g., Italian Capitulary of 801 (Boretius 98), ch. 2, 3; Capitulary on mobilisation for the use of the *Missi*, 808 (King 24; Boretius 50), ch. 2; Aachen Capitulary, 810 (Boretius 64), ch. 12, 13.

122 Capitulary on mobilisation for the use of the *Missi*, 808 (King 24; Boretius 50), ch. 7.

123 Memorandum of agenda, 811 (King 26; Boretius 71); Memorandum on military affairs, 811 (King 27; Boretius 73).

124 Capitulary of Boulogne, October 811 (King 28; Boretius 74), ch. 9. Also Capitulary on mobilisation for the use of the *Missi*, 808 (King 24; Boretius 50), ch. 4.

125 See, e.g., G. Tabacco, 'Il regno Italico nei secoli IX–XI', *SdS*15, pp. 763–90, which, though now rather old, contains much of use and analyses the data in fairly subtle fashion.

126 Most notably the use of the term *arimannus/exercitalis*, which became particularly common under the Spoletan dynasty which reigned (sporadically) after Charles' deposition. See, e.g., Pavia Capitulary issued by the Emperor Guy, 1 May 891 (Boretius 224), ch. 4; Ravenna Capitulary issued by Lambert of Spoleto, 898 (Boretius 225). Tabacco, 'Il regno Italico'. Dr Marios Costambeys has pointed out to me that the term *arimannus* is very commonly used in Spoletan documents.

127 For the problems of defending southern Italy from the Moslems, see B. Kreutz, *Before the Normans*, pp. 18–54.

128 On the German frontier, see Bowlus, *Franks, Moravians and Magyars*, pp. 90–234; Bowlus, 'Die militarische Organisation des karolingischen Südostens', *FmS* 31 (1997), pp. 46–69.

129 Louis the Pious, Spanish Constitution, 1 January, 815 (Boretius 132), ch. 1; Charles the Bald, Precept for Spain, 11 June 844 (Boretius 256; Tessier 46), ch. 1.

130 Mühlbacher 179. On all this, see Collins, 'Charles the Bald and Wifrid the Hairy', pp. 185–7.

131 For *aprisiones*, see most recently, C.J. Chandler, 'Between court and counts: Carolingian Catalonia and the *aprisio* grant, 778–897', *EME* 11.1 (2002), pp. 19–44.

132 Capitulary to be dealt with by Bishops, 829 (Boretius 186), ch. 7; Capitulary for the *Missi*, 829 (Boretius 188), ch. 5; Capitulary issued at Worms, August 829 (Boretius 193), ch. 7; Capitulary for the *Missi*, 819 (Boretius 141), ch. 27.

133 Einhard, Letter 23.

134 Capitulary of Corteolona, May 825 (Azzara/Moro 28; Boretius 165), ch. 1, 3; Memoranda given to the Counts, Corteolona 822–23 (Azzara/Moro 21; Boretius 158), ch. 18.

135 General Letter of Louis and Lothar, December 828 (Boretius 185).

136 Admonition to all Orders within the Kingdom, 823–25 (Boretius 150), ch. 16. The precise campaign meant by the law is unknown.

137 Capitulary of Worms, August 829 (Boretius 192), ch. 13. This was called *scaftlegi*.

138 *First Annals of Fontanelle, s.a.* 841. The phrase *bellum plusquam civile* is from Isidore, *Etymologies*, 18.1 (repeated by Hrabanus Maurus in his *On the Nature of Things* 20.1) and meant a war fought not just between citizens but between members of the same family.

139 *Formulae Imperiales* 7.

140 R. Le Jan, 'Frankish giving of arms and rituals of power: continuity and change in the Carolingian period', in F. Theuws and J.L. Nelson (eds.), *Rituals of Power from Late Antiquity to the Early Middle Ages* (Leiden, 2000), pp. 281–309.

141 Fulda charter 471.

142 Some Bavarian examples: Freising charter 246 (806–11): armour; Freising charter 268a (807–8): a horse, a spear and a shield; Freising charter 399b (8 April 813): two good horses; Freising charter 284 (19 February, 815): a horse; Mondsee charter 57 (26 May 824): a horse.

143 See, e.g., Schieffer, Lothar II, 6 (12 November, 856), for a man called Winnibert and his sons.

144 Notker *Deeds of Charles*, 2.4.

145 F. Prinz, *Klerus und Krieg im früheren Mittelalter: Untersuchungen zur Rolle der Kirche beim Aufbau der Königsherrschaft* (Monographien zur Geschichte des Mittelalters; Stuttgart, 1971), pp. 73–146 remains fundamental. See also Nelson, 'The Church's military service in the ninth century'.

146 The privileges are collected in the Prüm cartulary, the 'Golden Book of Prüm', and also printed as, e.g., Schieffer, Lothar I, 56; Schieffer, Lothar II, 3; Kehr, Louis the German 134; Font-Réaulx 7; Kehr, Arnulf 29. Even Salomon, 'duke and prince of the Bretons' got in on the act: Prüm charter 70 (7 October 860). However, see also Tessier 73 for the fact that even here this state of affairs was not entirely guaranteed.

147 Others include St-Maixent in Poitou (Levillain 9, issued by Pippin I, and Levillain 61, issued by Pippin II), Hornbach (Schieffer, Lothar I, 15) and the royal chapel in Frankfurt (Kehr, Louis the Younger 18; Kehr, Charles III 65).

148 Kehr, Charles III 158 (the authenticity of which is apparently not beyond doubt, though a revocation of complete immunity seems an odd thing for a monastery to forge). See also Schieffer, Louis the Child 3.

149 Kehr, Charles III 47 (Reggio), though this is a confirmation; Kehr, Charles III 111 (Asti).

150 *Cartae Senonicae* 19.

151 *Formulae Salicae Merkelianae* 41; *Formulae Imperiales* 37 (exemption for *negotiatores* – traders), 43 (exemption for royal foresters); *Collectio Patavienses* 3.

152 Polytptych of St-Germain-des-Prés; K. Elmshäuser and A. Hedwig, *Studien zum Polyptychon von Saint-Germain-des-Prés* (Cologne, 1993), pp. 413, 415.

153 Mühlbacher 130 (a good horse); Kehr, Louis the German 70 (two horses with shields and spears); Schieffer, Zwentibold 18 (six horses); see below, p. 149.

154 Hincmar, *On the Governance of the Palace*, pp. 27–8; At p. 12, Hincmar claims to have based his work on a lost work of Adalard of Corbie. J.L. Nelson is now ('Aachen as a place of power' in M. De Jong and F. Theuws (eds.), *Topographies of Power in the Early Middle Ages* (Leiden, 2001), pp. 217–41, at pp. 226–8) content to believe that the work may indeed fundamentally relate to the situation of the early ninth century (specifically 812) but, given that we do not have even a fragment of Adalard's original, it seems safest to assume that the work is, at best, an idealised view of 'how things were in the good old days' written, around a core provided by Adalard, for a late ninth-century king. Nelson's earlier view that the situation described in the *De Ordine* is difficult to push further back than Charles the Bald's reign may be preferable (J.L. Nelson, 'Legislation and consensus under Charles the Bald', in her *Politics and Ritual in Early Medieval Europe*, pp. 91–111, at p. 109). The argument by B.S. Bachrach, 'Adalhard of Corbie's *De ordine palatii*: Some methodological observations regarding chapters 29–36', *Cithara* 41 (2001), pp. 3–34, that the information in the *De Ordine* may be taken without difficulty as a direct and accurate description of a late eighth-century state of affairs, seems to me to be going too far. Hincmar himself only appears to claim his document to describe a situation going back to the days of Louis the Pious; *On the Governance of the Palace* ch. 1, 37.

155 Concerning the Corsican Expedition, Feb. 825 (Azzara/Moro 25; Boretius 162).

156 Concerning the Expedition to be made against the Saracens, 847 (Azzara/Moro 33; Boretius 203).

157 Concerning the Beneventan Expedition, early 866 (Azzara/Moro 45; Boretius 218).

158 Wanner 20, 47 and 35. He also exempted the advocate of the Abbey of St-Michael, Diliano (Wanner 24). These constitute all the exemptions issued by the emperor. Louis' father Lothar I had also exempted Italian advocates and

freemen: Schieffer, *Lothar I*, 102. Tabacco reached a similar conclusion to this in the 1960s: Tabacco, 'Il regno Italico'.

159 See, above all, J.L. Nelson, *Charles the Bald* (London, 1992).

160 Tessier 21 (8 March, 843).

161 Tessier 73.

162 The latter, he said, was called *Lantweri* (a word later enshrined in the Landwehr or militia regiments of modern Germany). It seems that Charles meant that it was the circumstance in which the service was exacted, rather than the service itself, which was called *Lantweri*. First Treaty of Meersen, 847 (Boretius 204), ch. 3.5.

163 J.L. Nelson, 'Translating images of authority. The Christian Roman emperors in the Carolingian world', in her *The Frankish World, 750–900* (London, 1996), pp. 89–98, at p. 95.

164 Edict of Pîtres, 25 June, 864 (Boretius 273).

165 J. Hassall and D. Hill, 'Pont-de-l'Arche: Frankish influence on the West Saxon burh?' *Archaeological Journal* 197 (1970), pp. 188–95; B. Dearden, 'Charles the Bald's fortified bridge at Pîtres (Seine): recent archaeological investigations', *Anglo-Norman Studies* 11 (1989), pp. 107–12; S. Coupland, 'The fortified bridges of Charles the Bald', *JMH* 17 (1991), pp. 1–12.

166 Edict of Pîtres, ch. 33.

167 E.g., Edict of Pîtres, ch. 28.

168 *AB*, s.a. 859. The translation is Nelson's. Earlier editors assumed that the passage must have referred to Viking *potentiores* but Nelson's rendering seems more accurate.

169 Above, p. 43.

170 Notker, *Deeds of Charles* 2.2–4; above, pp. 96–7.

171 S. Coupland, 'The Frankish tribute payments to the Vikings and their consequences', *Francia* 26.1 (1999), pp. 57–75, at pp. 64–4, reaches the same conclusion.

172 *The Annals of St-Bertin. Ninth-Century Histories*, vol. 1, trans. J.L. Nelson (Manchester, 1991), p. 101, n. 20.

173 For a somewhat different reading, see C. Gillmor, 'Charles the Bald and the small free farmers, 862–69', *MASS*, pp. 38–47.

174 Charles' grandson Charles *Simplex* (whose sobriquet may mean 'the Simple' but may also mean 'the Straightforward' or 'the Plain-Speaking') eventually became ruler of the West Franks in 893.

175 On Brittany, see (in English) the two excellent works which survey the area from different social and political perspectives: W. Davies, *Small Worlds: The Village Community in Early Medieval Brittany* (London, 1988), with discussion of military matters at pp. 170–1, 182–4; J.M.H. Smith, *Province and Empire: Brittany and the Carolingians* (Cambridge, 1992), with military affairs at pp. 19–20, 29–30, 131–3; Both cite the relevant primary sources in detail.

176 Regino, *Chronicon*, s.a. 874 (discussing events of 868).

177 Smith, *Province and Empire*, p. 30, n. 87, citing the *Life of St Winwaloë*, 1.8.

178 *GSR* 1.7.

179 Smith, *Province and Empire*, p. 131.

180 Davies, *Small Worlds*, pp. 48–50.

181 See, e.g., Redon charter 78 (6 March 863).

182 E.g., Redon charters 126 (1 April 858), 242 (24 May 869).

183 *GSR* 1.7.

184 Redon charter 116.

185 See Redon charters 171 (26 March 840), 136 (9 April 842), 138 (2 March 846).

186 Davies, *Small Worlds*, pp. 164–75.

187 Birch 201, Sawyer 106, *EHD* doc. 73.

188 The classic, if doubtless overly systemic, formulation was C.W. Hollister, *Anglo-Saxon Military Institutions on the Eve of the Norman Conquest* (Oxford, 1962), pp. 38–58.

189 Abingdon charter 9; as it exists in a twelfth-century copy the charter is not above suspicion, though the passage on military service appears to have found general acceptance as being probably genuine: S.E. Kelly, *Charters of Abingdon Abbey, Part 1* (Anglo-Saxon Charters, vol. 7; Oxford, 2000), p. 44. I cannot see anything in the language which looks more at home in the ninth than the twelfth century or vice versa. I would see it as potentially suspect.

190 Abels, *Lordship and Military Obligation in Anglo-Saxon England*, pp. 97–115 is excellent, a clear and judicious discussion of a thorny problem with a long life in Anglo-Saxon military historiography. See also, for another splendid discussion, N.P. Brooks, 'England in the ninth century: the crucible of defeat', *TRHS* 5th ser. 29 (1979), pp. 1–20, reprinted with postscript in his *Communities and Warfare 700–1400* (London, 2000), pp. 48–68.

191 Sawyer 294, 302–5, 307–8, 314, 322; Birch 447, 468, 469–72, 474, 483.

192 Sawyer 315; *EHD* doc. 89.

193 See the concise and helpful discussion in S.D. Keynes and M. Lapidge (trans.), *Alfred the Great* (Harmondsworth, 1983), pp. 232–4. I am grateful to Charlie Insley for discussion of this topic.

194 *Life of Alfred*, 12.

195 Hincmar, *On Churches and Chapels*, pp. 119–20, discussed in J.L. Nelson, 'The Church's military service in the ninth century', pp. 15–30, reprinted in her *Politics and Ritual in Early Medieval Europe*, pp. 117–32 (I cite the reprint). Nelson translates the relevant portion of Hincmar's text at pp. 117–18. Nelson prefers to see Hincmar's view as stemming from his reading of Bede and Gregory the Great. That he had heard of Æthelwulf's decimation when the king passed through Francia on his way to Rome seems equally plausible.

196 R. Abels, 'English logistics and military administration, 871–1066: the impact of the Viking wars', *MASS*, pp. 256–65.

197 In a striking example of Anglo-Saxon history's reluctance to consider a broader European context, Keynes and Lapidge, after noting the continental parallels to Alfred's work in their excellent notes to their translation of Asser's *Life of Alfred*, remark, with something almost approaching petulance, that 'we may suppose that Alfred was intelligent enough to think of it for himself': Keynes and Lapidge (trans.), *Alfred the Great*, pp. 228, n. 23. Heaven forfend that England's Darling learn from the French! For a better critique of the notion, see Brooks, 'The development of military obligations in eighth and ninth century England', p. 35, and his 'European medieval bridges: a window onto changing concepts of state power', in his *Communities and Warfare 700–1400*, pp. 1–31, which puts Alfred's insistence on fortress and bridgework in a longer Anglo-Saxon tradition.

198 *Burghal Hidage*; D. Hill, 'The Burghal Hidage: the establishment of a text.' *Med. Arch.* 13 (1969), pp. 84–92; D. Hill and A. Rumble (ed.), *The Defence of Wessex: The Burghal Hidage and Anglo-Saxon Fortifications* (Manchester, 1996), esp. N.P. Brooks, 'The administrative background to the burghal hidage', at pp. 128–50 (reprinted in Brooks, *Communities and Warfare 700–1400*, pp. 114–37; I cite the reprint).

199 The territory around London is largely heavy soil, which was not good farmland at this period, and forested until later in the Middle Ages. Thus the region is generally devoid of Roman villas and of post-Roman cemeteries.

200 *ASC s.a.* 893, 895, 1016.

201 Brooks, 'The administrative background to the burghal hidage', pp. 123–9.

202 *ASC s.a.* 893.

203 Keynes and Lapidge (trans.), *Alfred the Great*, p. 286, point out that this parallels the tripartite division of Alfred's financial resources and court, mentioned by Asser, *Life of Alfred*, 100. This seems more likely than the other possible parallel cited by Keynes and Lapidge, the bipartite division of the Amazon army described in the Old English translation of Orosius' *History* made at Alfred's court. Brooks, 'The administrative background to the burghal hidage', p. 115, is of the opinion that the 'men who guarded the burhs' were a permanent garrison.

204 Cp. pp. 40–53 above.

205 On which see, e.g., J. Campbell, 'Observations on English government from the tenth to the twelfth century', in his *Essays in Anglo-Saxon History* (London, 1986), pp. 155–70; Campbell 'The late Anglo-Saxon state: a maximum view' and 'The united kingdom of England: the Anglo-Saxon achievement', both in his *The Anglo-Saxon State* (London, 2000), pp. 1–30 and 31–53 respectively.

206 Abels, *Lordship and Military Organisation in Anglo-Saxon England*, p. 64.

207 *ASC*[A] *s.a.* 878; For interesting discussion of the politics of this period, see J.L. Nelson, 'A king across the sea: Alfred in continental perspective', *TRHS* 5th series, 26 (1986), pp. 45–68.

208 R. Fleming, 'Monastic lands and England's defence in the Viking Age', *EHR* 100 (1985), pp. 247–65. For formidable critique, however, see D. Dumville, 'Ecclesiastical lands and the defence of Wessex in the first Viking-Age', in his *Wessex and England from Alfred to Edgar: Six Essays on Political, Cultural and Ecclesiastical Revival* (Woodbridge, 1992), pp. 29–54. Nevertheless the essential thrust of Fleming's argument remains suggestive.

209 N. Lund, 'Allies of God or man? The Viking expansion in a European perspective', *Viator* 20 (1989), pp. 45–59, at pp. 52–4; for more detail on Viking armies, see Gareth Williams' forthcoming volume in this series.

210 As argued by C.P. Wormald, 'Viking Studies: whence and whither?' in R.T. Farrell (ed.), *The Vikings* (Chichester, 1982), pp. 128–53.

211 The raid on northern Germany in 845 is one exception; *AB*. Another is Godfred's major attack on Frisia in 810; *ARF*.

212 *AB s.a.* 861.

213 *AB s.a.* 861, 862.

214 K.L. Maund, '"A turmoil of warring princes": political leadership in ninth-century Denmark', *Haskins Society Journal* 6 (1995), pp. 29–47. This is most clearly the case with various Viking leaders in Francia – see, for example, S. Coupland, 'From poachers to gamekeepers: Scandinavian warlords and Carolingian kings', *EME* 7.1 (1998), pp. 85–114; Lund, 'Allies of God or man?', pp. 50–2. Something similar may have governed the careers of the leaders of the Great Army in England, 865–78, as A.P. Smyth, *Scandinavian Kings in the British Isles, 850–880* (Oxford, 1977) suggests. Smyth drew many of the details of his reconstruction from late and questionable sources, but the outline is nevertheless suggestive.

215 Lund, 'Allies of God or man?', pp. 52–3.

216 *AB s.a.* 861, 862. Eventually the army 'separated into many fleets' (*per plures classes se dividunt*).

217 *AB s.a.* 853.

218 *ASC s.a.* 876.

219 Lund, 'Scandinavia, *c.*700–1066', pp. 213–14.

220 *Ohthere's Account*, p. 20.

221 *ASC s.a.* 838. See also below, p. 113.

222 Below, pp. 114–15.

223 See, e.g., D. Ó Cróinín, *Early Medieval Ireland 400–1200* (London, 1995), pp. 139–41, for the distinction of 'free' from 'base' clientship.

224 There are brief but very good comments on this in S. Foster, *Picts, Scots and Gaels* (London, 1996), pp. 104–7.

225 S. Foster (ed.), *The St Andrews Sarcophagus* (Dublin, 1998). Davidian imagery is also found on a sword chape in the St Ninian's Isle hoard. It is illustrated in Foster, *Picts, Scots and Gaels*, p. 103.

226 K. Forsyth, 'Evidence of a lost Pictish source in the *Historia Regum Anglorum* of Symeon of Durham', in S. Taylor (ed.), *Kings, Clerics and Chronicles in Scotland, 500–1297: Essays in Honour of Marjorie Ogilvie Anderson on the Occasion of her Ninetieth Birthday* (Dublin, 2000), pp. 19–34, at pp. 25–26. My thanks to Charlie Insley for drawing my attention to this reference.

227 'Continuation' of Bede, *s.a.* 750.

228 Foster, *Scots, Picts and Gaels*, p. 94.

229 Ibid., p. 105, with discussion at pp. 113–14.

230 C.P. Wormald, '*Engla Lond*: the making of an allegiance', in his *Legal Culture in the Early Medieval West: Law as Text, Image and Experience* (London, 1999), pp. 359–82.

5 RAISING AN ARMY (3): ALLIES, MERCENARIES AND TRAINING THE TROOPS

1 I have used foreign mercenaries as a separate category for reasons which will become clear below. Professional career soldiers from within the kingdom have been discussed above, subsumed in the categories of bodyguards and retinues. In the absence of professional standing armies, there was no other category into which they could fall in the early Middle Ages. I also distinguish mercenaries from contingents supplied by allied or subject peoples.

2 E. James, *Britain in the First Millennium* (London, 2000), p. 135.

3 *HL* 5.29; N. Christie, *The Lombards* (Oxford, 1995), pp. 98–100, for the possibility that some of their graves have been discovered.

4 Saxon *pueri LH* 7.46: Childeric the Saxon: *LH* 7.3, 8.18, 10.22.

5 *HW* 25.

6 J. Haldon, *Warfare, State, and Society in the Byzantine World, 565–1204* (London, 1999); H. Kennedy, *The Armies of the Caliphs: Military and Society in the Early Islamic State* (London, 2001).

7 For the early medieval economy, see R. Hodges, *Dark Age Economics. The Origins of Towns and Trade, AD 600–1000* (London, 1982); Hodges, *Towns and Trade in the Age of Charlemagne* (London, 2000); R. Hodges and D.B. Whitehouse, *Mohammed, Charlemagne and the Origins Europe* (London, 1983); R. Hodges and W. Bowden (eds.), *The Sixth Century. Production, Distribution and Demand* (Leiden, 1998); I.L. Hansen and C.J. Wickham (eds.), *The Long Eighth Century* (Leiden, 2000). Older but still of use are R. Doehaerdt, *The Early Middle Ages. Economy and Society* (Amsterdam, 1978); G. Duby, *Rural Economy and Country Life in the Medieval West* (London, 1968); Duby, *The Early Development of the European Economy: Warriors and Peasants from the Seventh to the Twelfth Century* (London, 1974).

8 See below, p. 174.

9 R. Hodges, *The Anglo-Saxon Achievement* (London, 1989), pp. 150–85; R.S. Lopez, *The Commercial Revolution of the Middle Ages* (Cambridge, 1976).

10 C. Scull, 'Urban structures in pre-Viking England?', in J. Hines (ed.), *The Anglo-Saxons from the Migration to the Eighth Century. An Ethnographic Perspective* (Woodbridge, 1997), pp. 269–98.

11 This fact is rejected in blanket fashion by B.S. Bachrach, 'Early medieval Europe', in K. Raaflaub and N. Rosenstein (eds.), *War and Society in the Ancient and Medieval Worlds. Asia, the Mediterranean, Europe, and Mesoamerica* (Cambridge, Mass.),

pp. 271–307, at p. 275, n. 8. Bachrach, however, cites no evidence in support of his argument (see further below, p. 125 n. 40). By contrast, for the voluminous data accumulated since the Second World War in support of drastic urban decline followed by slow recovery between c.400 and c.900, see, e.g., the essays in M.W. Barley (ed.), *European Towns. Their Archaeology and Early History* (London, 1977); R. Hodges and B. Hobley (eds.), *The Rebirth of Towns in the West, 700–1050*. C.B.A. (London, 1988); N. Christie and S.T. Loseby (eds.), *Towns in Transition. Urban Evolution in Late Antiquity and the Early Middle Ages* (Aldershot, 1996); G.P. Brogiolo and B. Ward Perkins (eds.), *The Idea and the Ideal of the Town Between Late Antiquity and the Early Middle Ages* (Leiden, 1999). See also M.O.H. Carver, *Arguments in Stone: Archaeological Research and the European Town in the First Millennium*, Oxbow Monographs 29 (Oxford, 1993); H. Clarke and B. Ambrosiani, *Towns in the Viking Age* (rev. edn; London, 1995).

12 M. Mallett, 'Mercenaries', in M. Keen (ed.), *Medieval Warfare. A History* (Oxford, 2000), pp. 209–29.

13 In 860, Weland's Vikings wanted the 3,000 lb in silver demanded from Charles the Bald to be weighed under inspection, presumably to ensure they were not paid in debased coin. Weland raised the price to 5,000 lb silver, plus food supplies, when he was not paid quickly enough and then compelled the band he had been paid to attack to pay his army 6,000 lb silver. In 877 the Vikings on the Seine also demanded to weigh out the 5,000 lb silver paid to them (*AB s.a.* 860, 861, 877).

14 *ASC s.a.* 838. I have treated this instance as fundamentally different in its mechanics from Carolingian attempts to settle Danish leaders on fiefs in return for defending key coastal areas against other Vikings.

15 D. Ó Corráin, 'Ireland, Wales, man and the Hebrides', in P.H. Sawyer, *Oxford Illustrated History of the Vikings* (Oxford, 1997), pp. 83–109, at p. 89.

16 J. Barrow, 'Survival and mutation: ecclesiastical institutions in the Danelaw in the ninth and tenth centuries', in D.M. Hadley and J.D. Richards (eds.), *Cultures in Contact: Scandinavian Settlement in England in the Ninth and Tenth Centuries* (Turnhout, 2001), pp. 155–76; D.M. Hadley, 'And they proceeded to plough and to support themselves: the Scandinavian settlement of England', *Anglo-Norman Studies* 19 (1996), pp. 69–96; Hadley, *The Northern Danelaw: Its Social Structure, c.800–1100* (London, 2000), pp. 5–17.

17 J.L. Nelson, 'The Frankish Empire', in Sawyer (ed.), *Oxford Illustrated History of the Vikings*, pp. 19–47, at p. 36; S. Coupland, 'The Frankish tribute payments to the Vikings and their consequences', *Francia* 26.1 (1999), pp. 57–75.

18 S. Coupland, 'From poachers to gamekeepers: Scandinavian warlords and Carolingian kings', *EME* 7.1 (1998), pp. 85–114.

19 See *AB s.a.* 862 for the hiring of Vikings by the Bretons, and by Robert the Strong. Bretons also allied with the Northmen in 866.

20 B. Kreutz, *Before the Normans. Southern Italy in the Ninth and Tenth Centuries* (Philadelphia, 1996), pp. 18–54.

21 Regino, *Chronicon s.a.* 860 (discussing events of 851).

22 M. Rouche, *L'Aquitaine des Wisigoths aux Arabes, 418–781: Naissance d'une région* (Toulouse, 1979).

23 R. Collins, 'The ethnogenesis of the Basques', in H. Wolfram and W. Pohl (eds.), *Typen der Ethnogenese unter besonderer Berücksichtigung der Bayern* (Vienna, 1990), pp. 35–44.

24 T. Reuter, 'The recruitment of armies in the Early Middle Ages: what can we know?' *MASS*, pp. 32–7.

25 W. Davies, *Patterns of Power in Early Wales* (Oxford, 1990), p. 77.

26 For Byzantine parallels, see Haldon, *Warfare, State, and Society in the Byzantine World, 565–1204*, pp. 92–3.

27 Fredegar, *Chronicle* 4.68.
28 Bede, *HE* 3.24.
29 *LH* 10.3; *Austrasian Letters* 40–1. The campaign is discussed by Christie, *The Lombards*, pp. 87–9.
30 P. Fouracre, *The Age of Charles Martel* (London, 2000), p. 168.
31 *LH* 4.21.
32 Nithard, *Histories*, 3.5–6.
33 Cassiodorus, *Variae*, 5.23.
34 *Ibid.* 1.40.
35 Hrabanus, *On the Training of the Roman Military*; M. Innes, *State and Society in the Early Middle Ages. The Middle Rhine Valley 400–1000* (Cambridge, 2000), p. 145. An interesting and useful survey of the differences between Vegetius' original (*On Matters Military*) and Hrabanus' epitome is presented by Bachrach, *Early Carolingian Warfare: Prelude to Empire*, pp. 84–131. Bachrach is, however, more than optimistic in assuming that these differences accurately and unproblematically reflect ninth-century military actuality, a conclusion which flatly contradicts not only the narrative sources' (by this date) increasingly detailed accounts of campaigns but also the material and pictorial evidence for military equipment. For the latter, see below ch. 8.
36 See above, p. 101 for the training of Breton *pueri*.
37 See above, pp. 49–50.
38 For a similar career path, see *Life of Arnulf* 3 and, albeit in this case not said to have involved military service, the *Life of Eligius* 1.3–7.
39 Innes, *State and Society in the Early Middle Ages*, pp. 145–6.
40 *AB* s.a. 859. See above, p. 100 for a possible context.
41 *AMP* s.a. 717.
42 *CFred* 39; *AV* s.a. 884; *CA3* 12.
43 *AB* s.a 864.
44 Above, pp. 101–2.
45 Nithard, *Histories*, 3.6.
46 *AB* s.a. 864. He died two years later, never really having recovered; *AB* s.a. 866. Charles was the uncle of the Carloman killed (similarly aged eighteen) by a wild boar in 884, and of Louis III who died in 882 (yet again between the ages of seventeen and nineteen) by riding into a door lintel whilst in hot pursuit of a girl, for a bit of a laugh say the *Annals of St-Vaast*.
47 Ado of Vienne, *Chronicon*, p. 323.
48 See further below, p. 189.

6 RAISING AN ARMY (4): THE SIZE OF ARMIES

1 H. Delbrück, *History of the Art of War, Volume II: The Barbarian Invasions* (trans. W.J. Renfroe, of German 3rd edition of 1909; Lincoln, Nebraska, 1980); B.S. Bachrach, 'Early medieval military demography: some observations on the methods of Hans Delbrück', in Donald J. Kagay and L.J. Andrew Villalon (eds.) *The Circle of War in the Middle Ages: Essays on Medieval Military and Naval History* (Woodbridge, 1999), pp. 3–20, unconvincingly attempts to reject Delbrück's methodology, which, ironically, in spite of its age remains far more solid than Bachrach's own.
2 J.F. Verbruggen, 'L'Armée et la stratégie de Charlemagne', in H. Beumann (ed.), *Karl der Grosse: Lebenswerk und Nachleben, Vol. 1, Persönlichkeit und Geschichte* (Düsseldorf, 1965), pp. 420–36; Verbruggen, *The Art of Warfare in Western Europe during the Middle Ages* (2nd rev. edn, trans. S. Willard and Mrs R.W. Southern;

Woodbridge 1997), pp. 5–9; F.-L. Ganshof, 'L'Armée sous les Carolingiens', *SdS*15, pp. 109–30.

3   K. F. Werner, 'Heeresorganisation und Kriegführung im deutschen Königreich des 10. und 11. Jahrhunderts', *SdS*15, pp. 791–843.

4   C. Sánchez-Albornoz, 'El ejército y la guerra en el reino Asturleones 718–1037', *SdS*15, pp. 293–428.

5   *Ibid.*, p. 351.

6   P.H. Sawyer, *The Age of the Vikings* (London, 1962), pp. 118–36.

7   F.M. Stenton, *Anglo-Saxon England* (posthumous 3rd edition; Oxford, 1971), p. 243 and n. 1.

8   *Ibid.*, p. 593.

9   E. John, 'English feudalism and the structure of Anglo-Saxon Society', in E. John, *Orbis Britanniae and Other Studies* (Leicester, 1966), pp. 128–53. See above, p. 57. John's work was summarily dismissed – and excluded from the bibliography! – by Dorothy Whitelock when she completed the third, posthumous edition of Stenton's classic history; Stenton, *Anglo-Saxon England*, p. 723. The absence of reference to Sawyer from p. 243, n. 1, clearly inspired by his work, suggests a like fate. Fortunately, the ideas of both survived this historiographical airbrushing and the debate continued into the early 1980s. P.H. Sawyer, *Kings and Vikings* (London, 1982), pp. 93–94, where Sawyer admits that when Viking armies combined they could make 'a formidable force'; C.P. Wormald, 'Viking Studies: whence and whither?' in R.T. Farrell (ed.), *The Vikings* (Chichester), pp. 128–53.

10 N.P. Brooks, 'England in the ninth century: the crucible of defeat', *TRHS* 5th ser. 29 (1979), pp. 1–20, reprinted with postscript in his *Communities and Warfare 700–1400* (London, 2000), pp. 48–68. Low numbers for Viking armies (at least in phases after the initial landfall) are suggested by the analyses of C. Gillmor, 'War on the rivers: Viking numbers and mobility on the Seine and Loire, 841–886', *Viator* 19 (1988), pp. 79–109. Though the methodology used by Gillmor might not convince everyone, the results are certainly suggestive.

11 B.S. Bachrach, 'Medieval military historiography', in M. Bentley (ed.) *The Routledge Companion to Historiography* (London, 1997), pp. 203–20; Bachrach, 'Early medieval military demography: some observations on the methods of Hans Delbrück'; Bachrach, *Early Carolingian Warfare: Prelude to Empire* (Philadelphia, 2000).

12 Bachrach, 'Medieval military historiography'.

13 J.L. Nelson, 'The Frankish Empire', in P. Sawyer (ed.), *The Oxford Illustrated History of the Vikings* (Oxford, 1997), pp. 19–47, at pp. 38–40; T. Reuter, 'The recruitment of armies in the early Middle Ages: what can we know?', *MASS*, pp. 32–7; Reuter, 'Carolingian and Ottonian warfare', in M. Keen (ed.), *Medieval Warfare. A History* (Oxford, 1999), pp. 13–35. On the occasion of the re-edition of his classic work, Verbruggen stayed with his initial estimates of medieval army sizes: Verbruggen, *The Art of Warfare in Western Europe during the Middle Ages*, pp. 5–9. Bachrach, 'Medieval military historiography', p. 215, n. 31, claims that Werner's estimates were accepted by P. Contamine. However, if one actually reads Contamine (P. Contamine, *War in the Middle Ages* (trans. M. Jones; Oxford, 1984), pp. 25–6), we see that though he sees Werner's calculations as reasoned, he also concedes that they might 'appear too optimistic'.

14 E.g., W. Goffart, *Barbarians and Romans AD 418–585: The Techniques of Accommodation* (Princeton, 1980), pp. 231–4.

15 K. Hannestad, 'Les forces militaires d'après la guerre gothique de Procope', *Classica et Medievalia* 21 (1961), pp. 136–83.

16 Strasbourg: *Res Gestae* Amm. Marc. 16.12.26; 600 Franks: *ibid.* 17.2; armies of 2,000 men (four units of about 500 men each): *ibid.* 27.8.8.

17 *LH* 2.31.

18 *Acts* 2.41: 'Then they that gladly received his word were baptized; and the same day there were added unto them about three thousand souls'; J.M. Wallace-Hadrill, *The Long-Haired Kings* (London, 1962), p. 170.

19 R. Collins, *Early Medieval Spain: Unity in Diversity, 400–1000* (2nd edn; London, 1995), pp. 151–7. Arab sources are also notoriously late and difficult to evaluate.

20 *LH* 9.31; Isidore of Seville, *History of the Goths* 54.

21 Technically of course, this meant 69, 79 and 89, but the point is the use of round numbers. *LH* 3.18, 4.51, 5.10, 6.15, 6.20, 9.19, 9.26, 10.12, 10.31 (Eufronius); *Life of the Fathers*. 8.5, 11.3, 12.3, 14.4, 15.4; in general, see M. Handley, 'The early medieval inscriptions of Britain, Gaul and Spain. Studies in function and culture' (Ph.D. thesis, University of Cambridge, 1998), 45–69.

22 *LH* 9.19. Study of Merovingian society, age of marriage and so on, suggests that Sichar, married and with children, may have been as much as ten years older than Gregory's estimate. See, e.g., G. Halsall, 'Female status and power in Merovingian central Austrasia: the burial evidence', *EME* 5.1 (1996), pp. 1–24.

23 I am grateful to Dr Mark Handley for this information. Handley, 'The early medieval inscriptions of Britain, Gaul and Spain'.

24 N. Lozovsky, 'Carolingian geographical tradition: was it geography?' *EME* 5.1 (1996), pp. 25–44.

25 I.N. Wood, 'The use and abuse of Latin hagiography in the early medieval west', in E. Chrysos and I.N. Wood (eds.), *East and West: Modes of Communication* (Leiden, 1999), pp. 93–109. The interesting case discussed by Wood is that of the Life of Gregory of Utrecht

26 Nelson, 'The Frankish Empire', p. 39, provides a helpful table.

27 J. Bill, 'Ships and seamanship', in P. Sawyer (ed.), *The Oxford Illustrated History of the Vikings*, pp. 182–201.

28 M.K. Lawson, 'The collection of Danegeld and Heregeld in the reigns of Æthelred and Cnut', *EHR* 99 (1984), pp. 721–38. For the debate on the matter between Lawson and J. Gillingham see *EHR* 104 (1989), pp. 373–406 and *EHR* 105 (1990), pp. 939–61; D.M. Metcalf, 'Large Danegelds in relation to war and kingship. Their implications for monetary history, and some numismatic evidence', in S. Chadwick Hawkes (ed.), *Weapons and Warfare in Anglo-Saxon England* (Oxford University Committee for Archaeology Monograph 21; Oxford, 1989), pp. 179–89.

29 *ASC* s.a. 757.

30 K. Leyser, 'The battle at the Lech, 955', in his *Medieval Germany and its Neighbours* (London, 1982), pp. 43–67, at p. 58.

31 *Ibid.*, pp. 58–9, for sober evaluation of the strength of Ottonian armies. For further discussion of Ottonian examples suggestive of small armies see also Reuter, 'The recruitment of armies in the Early Middle Ages'; Reuter, 'Carolingian and Ottonian warfare'.

32 Sidonius, *Letters* 3.3.

33 *LH* 2.24.

34 J. Morris, *The Age of Arthur: A History of the British Isles from 350 to 650* (Chichester, 1973), n. 96.3. Morris (pp. 96–7) thought that Ecdicius may been inspired by Ambrosius Aurelianus!

35 Werner, 'Heeresorganisation und Kriegführung im deutschen Königreich des 10. und 11. Jahrhunderts'.

36 *Ibid.*, 'discussione', pp. 855–6. Werner responded 'Oui' and 'C'est ça', though he wondered whether the early medieval discrepancy would have been that high.

37 A. Ryder, *The Kingdom of Naples under Alfonso the Magnanimous: The Making of Modern State* (Oxford, 1976), pp. 259–90.

38 *ASC* s.a. 893; Æthelweard, *Chronicle*, *s.a.* 893.

39 *ASC* s.a. 892–6. The Viking forces totalled, according to the Chronicle, 330 ships, so perhaps approaching 10,000 men in all. Nevertheless, even if we accept this figure, Alfred could have caused serious problems for the Vikings even with an initial force to hand of only 1,000 men, outnumbered 10:1. A force of 10,000 would have been, as we shall see, incredibly difficult to supply, the more so since the foodstuffs of the region will have been taken into fortified centres. The Danes could not sit down to besiege a *burh* without leaving themselves open to attack by Alfred's field army, doubtless growing as Alfred called up his reserves. By 896 the army had been driven out of Wessex without being able to make much of an inroad, and eventually broke up.

40 This has been Bachrach's approach. Bachrach simply rejects the masses of archaeological and other recent work on the early medieval economy, which he sees as somehow propagating a 'primitivist' view of the period. Instead, he bases his arguments on work on population and economy dating from the early decades of the twentieth, and sometimes from the nineteenth centuries. These works, often very good for their time, obviously predate the development of archaeology as a discipline, especially in the early medieval period, and of course frequently approach the written data in ways nowadays thought of as unsophisticated and uncritical. Bachrach, however, claims that these have retained their value, though since he ignores all subsequent work it is difficult to see how he can tell this.

41 The best study of the archaeological evidence for the fate of the infrastructure of Roman Britain remains A.S. Esmonde Cleary, *The Ending of Roman Britain* (London, 1989). For references to the fate of Roman towns across western Europe, see above, p. 113, n. 11.

42 This is the conclusion reached in G. Halsall, *Settlement and Social Organisation. The Merovingian Region of Metz* (Cambridge, 1995).

43 Southern Gaul: S.T. Loseby, 'Marseille: a late antique success story?', *JRS* 82 (1992), pp. 165–85; Loseby, 'Marseille and the Pirenne Thesis I: Gregory of Tours, the Merovingian kings and "Un Grand Port", in R. Hodges and W. Bowden (eds.), *The Sixth Century. Production, Distribution and Demand* (Leiden, 1998), pp. 203–29. Spain: P.C. Díaz, 'City and territory in Hispania in late antiquity', in G.P. Brogiolo, N. Gauthier and N. Christie (eds.), *Towns and their Territories Between Late Antiquity and the Early Middle Ages* (Leiden, 2000), pp. 3–35; S. Keay, *Roman Spain* (London, 1989), pp. 202–17; S. Gutiérrez Lloret, 'Eastern Spain in the sixth century in the light of archaeology', in Hodges and Bowden (eds.), *The Sixth Century*, pp. 161–84; Italy: T.W. Potter, *Roman Italy* (London, 1987), pp. 210–20 for convenient survey of post-Roman Italy; B. Ward-Perkins, 'The towns of northern Italy: rebirth or renewal?', in R. Hodges and B. Hobley (eds.), *The Rebirth of Towns in the West, 700–1050*. C.B.A. (London, 1988), pp. 16–27.

44 *LH* 6.45. He says that this procession totalled 4,000 people. The figure is probably not to be taken literally but the point may stand that Gregory thought that Rigunth's convoy was equivalent to a small army.

45 *LH* 10.3, where an army devastates the area of Metz on its way to Italy. See also *LH* 7.24.

46 E.g., *LH* 7.35, 8.30.

47 B.S. Bachrach, *The Anatomy of a Little War: A Military and Diplomatic History of the Gundovald Affair* (Boulder, 1994), pp. xviii–xx. This is another instance of Bachrach's attempts to sanitise warfare.

48 W. Goffart, *The Narrators of Barbarian History, AD 550–800: Jordanes, Gregory of Tours, Bede, Paul the Deacon* (Princeton, 1988), pp. 112–234, at p. 220.

49 Cassiodorus, *Variae* 2.8, 5.10–11; *LV* 8.1.8.

50 *Lex Ribv.* 68.3; and Burgundian Law 38. For discussion of tax obligations see W. Goffart, 'Old and New in Merovingian Taxation', *P&P* 96 (1982), pp. 3–21; LV 9.2.6

51 Childebert's Decrees, dated 1 March 594, 595 and 596, at Andernach, Maestricht and Cologne respectively.

52 See chapter 3.

53 The famous *emporia* are Hamwic ('Saxon Southampton') Ipswich, London and York in England, Dorestad and Quentovic, as well as some minor sites such as Domberg, in Francia, and Ribe, Hedeby, Helgö and Birka in Scandinavia. At this time, Mediterranean trade seems largely to have died out, though it was, of course, to revive dramatically in the tenth century. The best recent overview of English *emporia* is C. Scull, 'Urban structures in pre-Viking England?', in J. Hines (ed.), *The Anglo-Saxons from the Migration to the Eighth Century. An Ethnographic Perspective* (Woodbridge, 1997), pp. 269–98. See also M. Anderton (ed.), *Anglo-Saxon Trading Centres. Beyond the Emporia* (Glasgow, 1999).

54 For studies of urban development in the period see above, p. 113 n. 11.

55 H. Clarke and B. Ambrosiani, *Towns in the Viking Age* (rev. edn; Leicester, 1995), pp. 156–8.

56 The population of the great *emporium* at Dorestad has, for instance, been estimated at between 1,000 and 2,000 souls; Clarke and Ambrosiani, *Towns in the Viking Age*, p. 29. The population of Paris is estimated at 10,000–15,000 between the eighth and ninth centuries: P. Velay, *From Lutetia to Paris: The Island and the Two Banks* (Paris, 1992), p. 109. If anything, this seems generous.

57 Reuter, 'The recruitment of armies in the Early Middle Ages', p. 36.

58 E.g., *LH* 10.3.

59 Amm. Marc. 17.2.

60 F.L. Ganshof, 'Charlemagne's army', in his *Frankish Institutions under Charlemagne* (trans. B. Lyon; Providence, RI, 1968), pp. 59–68, at p. 66.

61 J. Haldon, *Warfare, State, and Society in the Byzantine World, 565–1204* (London, 1999), pp. 99–106.

62 Estimates of the total Roman army: A.H.M. Jones, *The Later Roman Empire 284–602* (Oxford, 1964), p. 683; A. Cameron, *The Later Roman Empire* (London, 1993), p. 35. The source is the *Notitia Dignitatum* of *c.*400. Estimates depend upon ideas of the strength of army units. The list is incomplete and does not include hired barbarian contingents. However, we have no idea of the relationship of actual to theoretical unit strengths. Contemporary references to corrupt practices amongst army officers suggest that this might be considerable. Jones, *The Later Roman Empire*, pp. 644–6; R. Macmullen, *Corruption and the Decline of Rome* (New Haven, 1988), pp. 171–7, and 122–70 *passim*. Strasbourg: Amm. Marc. 16.12; Adrianople: *ibid.* 31.12–13. Estimates: P. Heather, *The Goths* (London, 1996), pp. 134–5; T.S. Burns, 'The battle of Adrianople: a reconsideration', *Historia* 22 (1973), pp. 336–45; Persian campaign: Amm. Marc. 23.2–25.8. Small armies: Jones, *The Later Roman Empire*, p. 682; above, n. 16.

63 A.E. Prince, 'The strength of English armies in the reign of Edward III', *EHR* 46 (1931), pp. 353–71.

64 P. Fouracre, 'Frankish Gaul to 814', *NCMH*, pp. 85–109, at p. 106. This involved campaigns in southern Italy and in Bavaria. Frankish troops also attacked Brittany.

65 For the calculation, see J. France, *Western Warfare in the Age of the Crusades, 1000–1300* (London, 1999), p. 35.

66 The movements of Napoleonic armies are probably best followed in detail in V.J. Esposito and J.R. Elting, *A Military History and Atlas of the Napoleonic Wars* (revd. edn; London, 1999).

67 Memorandum on military affairs (King 27; Boretius 73), ch. 3.

68 Below, ch. 9.
69 The so-called 'doctrine of overwhelming force'.
70 Nithard, *Histories* 1.5.
71 *AMP s.a.* 717. The account dates to the early ninth century.
72 Regino, *Chronicon, s.a.* 882.
73 V. Hanson, *The Western Way of War. Infantry Battle in Classical Greece* (2nd edn; Berkeley, 2000), p. 104.
74 *CA3* 10.

7 CAMPAIGNING

1 A. Curry, reviewing M. Keen (ed.), *Medieval Warfare: A History* (Oxford, 2000), in *War in History* 9 (2001), p. 219.
2 For an English *précis* of the campaign, see E.A. Thompson, *The Goths in Spain* (Oxford, 1969), pp. 221–5. On the text, see R. Collins, 'Julian of Toledo and the royal succession in late seventh-century Spain', in P.H. Sawyer and I.N. Wood (ed.), *Early Medieval Kingship* (Leeds, 1977), pp. 30–49; M. de Jong, 'Adding insult to injury: Julian of Toledo and his *Historia Wambae*, in P. Heather (ed.), *The Visigoths: From the Migration Period to the Seventh Century* (Woodbridge, 1999), pp. 373–89.
3 This account is translated in S. Coupland, 'The Vikings in Francia and Anglo-Saxon England to 911', *NCMH*, pp. 190–201, at p. 193.
4 Above, p. 96.
5 See, e.g., *LH* 6.41.
6 As with the three decrees of Childebert II.
7 See, e.g., Mühlbacher 143; Tessier 237; Birch 389.
8 See above, ch. 2.
9 *LH* 2.27. See I.N. Wood, 'Gregory of Tours and Clovis', *Revue Belge de Philologie et d'Histoire* 63 (1985), pp. 249–72, for discussion of Gregory's source for the episode, which involved a certain grim humour: D. Shanzer, 'Laughter and humour in the early medieval Latin west', in G. Halsall (ed.), *Humour, History and Politics in Late Antiquity and the Early Middle Ages* (Cambridge, 2002), pp. 25–47, at p. 31.
10 J. Campbell, 'The sale of land and the economics of power in early England', in his *The Anglo-Saxon State* (London, 2000), pp. 227–45, at pp. 244–5.
11 Boretius 233–239; Kehr, Charles III 17.
12 See above, pp. 57–9. The association of these codes stems from the similarity of Ine's Laws, ch. 20, and Wihtred's laws, ch. 28, about strangers. S. Keynes, 'England, 700–900', *NCMH*, pp. 18–42, at pp. 25–6.
13 *CFred*, 45.
14 *CFred*, 45, very loosely translating '*dum his et aliis modis Franci et Wascones semper inter se altercarent*'.
15 Felix, *Life of Guthlac*, 17–19.
16 See above, ch. 2.
17 *LH* 4.14; 3.11. See I.N. Wood, 'Clermont and Burgundy 511–34', *Nottingham Medieval Studies* 32 (1988), pp. 119–25, for discussion of the dating and other significance of these events.
18 Although this is the first clearly described ritual of royal anointing, the ritual seems to have been an established part of Gothic king-making. His rival Paul had also had himself anointed (*Letter of Paul to Wamba*). Gildas says (*On the Ruin of Britain* 21) that post-Roman British kings were anointed in the fifth century, though that could result from the generally Old Testament tone of his sermon.
19 *HW* 10.

20 See, e.g., *ARF s.a.* 805, 806, *AF s.a.* 851, 856, 864, 892.

21 B.S. Bachrach, 'Military organisation in Aquitaine under the early Carolingians', *Speculum* 49 (1974), pp. 1–33 at pp. 9–13; M. Rouche, *L'Aquitaine des Wisigoths aux Arabes, 418–781: Naissance d'une Région* (Toulouse, 1979), pp. 354–8; G. Fournier, 'Les campagnes de Pépin le Bref en Auvergne et la question des fortifications rurales en VIIIe siècle', *Francia* 2 (1975), pp. 123–35.

22 See, e.g., the campaigns of 742 (*CFred*, 25 – this may have involved the storming of one stronghold), 760 (*CFred*, 41), 763, 766 and 767 (*CFred*, 47–49), 768 (*CFred*, 51–53; *ARF*) and 769 (*ARF*).

23 *CFred*, 42–43. *AMP* & *ARF s.a.* 767 record the capture of various strongholds including three *castra*, but this looks to me more like the receiving of surrender than formal siege warfare.

24 *CFred*, 46.

25 *CFred*, 35 (753: Grifo killed along with two opposing Frankish counts), 44 (762: Gascon Count Mantio killed by Frankish Counts Australd and Galeman), 45 (763: Count Chilping of the Auvergne killed by Counts Adelard and Australd; Count Ammanugus of Poitiers killed by the men of St-Martin, Tours), 47 (*c.*763: major battle between Franks and Gascons).

26 *CFred*, 37–38.

27 *HW* 10.

28 *ASC s.a.* 661. Wulfhere's harrying may have been preceded by victory over the West Saxons at *Posentesburh*. The foes of King Cenwalh of the West Saxons at that battle are not recorded, however.

29 The only recorded harrying by Offa is that of the Hastings region in 771, recorded by Simeon of Durham, *History of the Kings*.

30 *LH* 2.32.

31 B.S. Bachrach, *The Anatomy of a Little War: A Military and Diplomatic History of the Gundovald Affair* (Boulder, 1994), pp. xvii–xviii.

32 *LH* 5. Preface.

33 As, e.g., in the normalist analysis of N. Hooper, 'The Anglo-Saxons at war', in S. Chadwick Hawkes (ed.), *Weapons and Warfare in Anglo-Saxon England*, Oxford University Committee for Archaeology Monograph 21 (Oxford, 1989), pp. 191–202. This is a good article but suffers from the assumption that early medieval warfare was much the same as warfare after the tenth century. A key tenet of the present volume is that it was not.

34 Earlier writers thought that defeat in battle removed a king's prestige and throne-worthiness. Certainly the Irish law-tract *Crith Gablach* envisaged that defeat in battle might produce exceptional circumstances for a king. D. Ó Cróinín, *Early Medieval Ireland 400–1200* (London, 1995), p. 80, citing the text. As G. Mac Niocaill, *Ireland Before the Vikings* (Dublin, 1972), pp. 45–6 points out, defeat was a serious matter, but it is difficult to find instances of kings actually being deposed because of military failure. The situation does not seem radically different from that in most of the rest of western Europe

35 The war is described in *LH* 4.47–51.

36 Indeed Gregory seems to have been provoked into writing his *Histories* by the seriousness of this war.

37 See the Appendix, listing military affairs for the decade 581–90. Although there were thirty-seven incidents of large-scale violence or the summoning of armies there were only three pitched battles between Franks.

38 Fredegar, *Chronicle*, 4.38–42.

39 *Ibid.* 4.27.

40 *Ibid.* 4.37.

41 *Ibid.* 4.53.

42 See Appendix for an outline.

43 *LH* 9.11, 9.20.

44 These figures are arrived at by adding up all the references to warfare in all the available sources, and dividing 250 (years between 600 and 850) by this number.

45 For these events, see *ARF* and *Rev. Ann. s.a.* 782, and Charlemagne's First Saxon Capitulary (King 3; Boretius 26).

46 See, e.g., Fredegar, *Chronicle*, 4.42 for Chlothar II's sparing of his godson, Merovech.

47 *HE* 3.24.

48 G. Halsall, 'Playing by whose rules? A further look at Viking atrocity in the ninth century', *Medieval History* 2.2 (1992), pp. 3–12. This attempts to resolve the long-standing debate on the atrocity of the Vikings following Peter Sawyer's famous statement that Viking warfare was just an extension of 'normal Dark Age activity'; P.H. Sawyer, *The Age of the Vikings* (2nd edn; London, 1971), p. 205. For the counter to Sawyer's argument, see, e.g., C.P. Wormald, 'Viking Studies: whence and whither?' in R.T. Farrell (ed.), *The Vikings* (Chichester, 1982), pp. 128–53. Sawyer presents a strong case that Viking attacks were in aims, objectives and general conduct generally analogous to those waged by Christian rulers. Wormald, however, presents equally convincing evidence for the real terror that the Vikings produced. The way out of the impasse is surely by noting the absence of shared norms of conduct in the conflict. See also S. Coupland, 'The rod of God's wrath or the people of God's wrath? The Carolingians' theology of the Viking invasions', *Journal of Ecclesiastical History* 42.4 (1991), pp. 535–54.

49 *Order for the Coronation of Charles the Bald.*

50 For an excellent discussion, see M. McCormick, *Eternal Victory: Triumphal Rulership in Late Antiquity, Byzantium and the Early Medieval West* (paperback edn; Cambridge, 1990), pp. 306–14 (Visigoths), 344–52 (Franks), wth the literature cited there. The *Caroline Litany* includes invocation of life and victory to King Charles and to the whole army of the Franks. M. McCormick, 'The liturgy of war in the early middle ages: crisis, litanies, and the Carolingian monarchy', *Viator* 15 (1984), pp. 1–23. See also J. Flori, *L'Idéologie du Glaive: Préhistoire de la Chevalerie* (Geneva, 1983), pp. 84–7.

51 McCormick, *Eternal* Victory, p. 309; Nithard, *Histories* 2.6, following the interpretation of McCormick, *Eternal Victory*, p. 358, n. 132; E. Goldberg, '"More devoted to the equipment of battle than the splendor of banquets": frontier kingship, military ritual and early knighthood at the court of Louis the German', *Viator* 30 (1999), pp. 41–78, at pp. 61–7.

52 Capitulary to the Bishops (Boretius 21).

53 Concerning the Expedition to be made against the Saracens, 847 (Azzara/Moro 33; Boretius 203).

54 See, e.g., B. Kreutz, *Before the Normans: Southern Italy in the Ninth and Tenth Centuries* (Philadelphia, 1996), pp. 26–7.

55 See J.L. Nelson, 'The quest for peace in a time of war: the Carolingian Brüderkrieg, 840–43', in J. Fried (ed.), *Träger und Instrumentarien des Friedens im Hohen und späten Mittelalter* (Vorträge und Forschungen 43; Sigmaringen, 1996), pp. 87–114; Nelson, 'The ritualisation of Frankish warfare in the ninth century', in G. Halsall (ed.), *Violence and Society in the Early Medieval West* (Woodbridge, 1998), pp. 90–107.

56 G. Halsall, 'Violence and society in the early medieval west: an introductory survey', in Halsall (ed.), *Violence and Society in the Early Medieval West*, pp. 1–45, at p. 33; J.L. Nelson, 'The ritualisation of Frankish warfare in the ninth century', pp. 90–107.

57 *LH* 3.7.

58 *Beowulf*, ll.2379–2489.

59 *ARF s.a.* 787. For discussion, see S. Airlie, 'Narratives of triumph and submission: Charlemagne's mastering of Bavaria', *TRHS* 6th ser. 9 (1999), pp. 93–119. For the build-up of pro-Carolingan factions within Bavaria, see C.R. Bowlus, *Franks, Moravians and Magyars: The Struggle for the Middle Danube, 788–907* (Philadelphia, 1995), p. 38.

60 *ARF s.a.* 791; See also the Convent of Bishops on the Banks of the Danube, Summer 796.

61 McCormick, *Eternal Victory*, pp. 309–10.

62 The genre of military treatises continued in the Byzantine east but again the relationship between their prescriptions and actual practice is problematic. J. Haldon, *Warfare, State, and Society in the Byzantine World, 565–1204* (London, 1999); M. Whitby and M. Whitby, *The History of Theophylact Simocatta: An English Translation with Introduction and Notes* (Oxford, 1986), p. xxiv, point out convergences between the recommendations of the *Strategikon* and the conduct of Byzantine Balkan campaigns under Maurice. The similarities are nevertheless of a very general nature, and the precise direction of influence, whether from practice to treatise or from treatise to practice, is unclear.

63 Hrabanus Maurus, *On the Training of the Roman Military*. See above, p. 116, n. 35.

64 Above, p. 122.

65 *CFred* 48, for 766. Wallace-Hadrill's translation of Fredegar, *Chronicle* 4.90, which suggests a Mayfield held in the 640s, is misleading. The passage should read 'Flaochad, having collected together the dukes and bishops of the kingdom of Burgundy, held a *placitum* [a legal resolution of a dispute] at Chalon in the month of May'. *Placita* could be and were held at all times of year. P. Fouracre, 'Placita and the settlement of disputes in later Merovingian Francia', in W. Davies and P. Fouracre (eds.), *The Settlement of Disputes in Early Medieval Europe* (Cambridge, 1986), pp. 23–43.

66 *AB s.a.* 858, 859. J.L. Nelson, *The Annals of St-Bertin. Ninth-Century Histories*, vol. I, (Manchester, 1991), p. 89, n. 2, notes that Charles celebrated 15 January as the date of his recovery of the kingdom.

67 Astronomer, *Life of Louis*, 45.

68 Birch 389.

69 *ASC s.a.* 825.

70 Fredegar, *Chronicle*, 4.68.

71 For analysis of the Avar campaigns, see Bowlus, *Franks, Moravians and Magyars*, pp. 46–60; Pohl, *Die Awaren*, pp. 312–23.

72 On Liudewit's revolt, see C.R. Bowlus, *Franks, Moravians and Magyars*, pp. 60–71.

73 *Rev.Ann. s.a.* 778; Einhard, *Life of Charles* 9; *ARF s.a.* 824. It is worth noting that no source before the eleventh century locates the first defeat at Roncesvalles. That later epics did so may have resulted from an early confusion of the two engagements. R. Collins, 'Spain: The northern kingdoms and the Basques, 711–910', *NCMH*, pp. 272–89, at p. 285.

74 *HW* 10–12.

75 See above, nn. 68, 69.

76 *HL* 6.54.

77 *LHF* 52; *CFred* 9.

78 Astronomer, *Life of Louis*, 14–15.

79 Constantius of Lyon, *Life of Germanus of Auxerre*, 17.

80 *LH* 7.35.

81 *HW* 11–13.

82 Regino, *Chronicon s.a.* 891.

83 Boretius 132, 256 (=Tessier 46).

84 I can find no mention of it in documents relating to the other ninth-century

Marches, which is odd. In the Spanish documents (as previous note) it is coupled with *excubiae* (guard duty), in turn translated as *wactas* or *guaitas* (watch). This duty is to be found in other, especially frontier, areas. *Exploratores* are referred to in the kingdom of the Asturias from at least 878; C. Sánchez-Albornoz, 'El ejército y la guerra en el reino Asturleones 718–1037', *SdS*15, pp. 293–428, at p. 407–8.

85 *AMP s.a.* 690 [*recte* 687].
86 J.F. Verbruggen, *The Art of Warfare in Western Europe during the Middle Ages* (2nd rev. edn, trans. S. Willard and R.W. Southern; Woodbridge 1997), pp. 316, 320–1.
87 I owe this information to a paper given by Gabriel Pepper of University College London, based upon his doctoral research. I am also grateful to Andrew Reynolds for discussion of the topic. For *herepaths* in Alfred's reforms see R. Abels, *Alfred the Great: War, Kingship and Culture in Anglo-Saxon England* (London, 1998), p. 204.
88 N.P. Brooks, 'European medieval bridges: a window onto changing concepts of state power', in his *Communities and Warfare 700–1400* (London, 2000), pp. 1–31, is fundamental.
89 Nithard, *Histories*, 2.6, 3.7.
90 *Ibid.*, 3.3.
91 *LH* 6.19, 9.32.
92 *LH* 2.37.
93 For post-Roman British earthworks, see above, p. 51, n. 59; for the Danevirke, see above p. 89, n. 92; for Offa's Dyke, see C. Fox, *Offa's Dyke: A Field Survey of the Western Frontier-Works of Mercia in the Seventh and Eighth Centuries A.D.* (London, 1955).
94 For defences against the Vikings, see ch. 10.
95 *LH* 6.45.
96 *LV* 9.2.6. For a parallel from Ostrogothic territories, see Cassiodorus, *Variae* 3.41, 5.13; See above pp. 60, 128.
97 Capitulary concerning Estates, 800 (Boretius 32), ch. 30, 64 (carts), 68 (utensils).
98 Capitulary of Aachen, late 802, early 803 (King 14; Boretius 77), ch. 10.
99 Letter to Fulrad, mid-806 (King 22; Boretius 75).
100 Capitulary of Boulogne, October 811 (King 28; Boretius 74), ch. 8.
101 General Letter of Louis and Lothar, December 828 (Boretius 185).
102 *Formulae Imperiales* 7.
103 For the south-eastern frontiers of the Frankish world see Bowlus, *Franks, Moravians and Magyars*, building upon methodologies pioneered by the German historian W. Störmer.
104 See, e.g., the *hostilitium* levied in cash or kind from the estates of St-Germain-des-Prés, recorded in its *Polyptych*.
105 Astronomer, *Life of Louis*, 15.
106 K. Leyser, 'Early Medieval Warfare', in his *Communications and Power in Medieval Europe: The Carolingian and Ottonian Centuries* (ed. T. Reuter; London, 1994), pp. 29–50, at p. 45. For Byzantine logistics, see the excellent analysis by Haldon, *Warfare, State, and Society in the Byzantine World, 565–1204*, pp. 166–70, 287–92. The ground-breaking works were M. Van Creveld, *Supplying War: Logistics from Wallerstein to Patton* (Cambridge 1977), and D. Engels, *Alexander the Great and the Logistics of the Macedonian Army* (Berkeley, 1978).
107 *ARF s.a.* 810.
108 Above, p. 58.
109 *Formulae Imperiales* 7.
110 E.g., *LH* 7.35, 10.3; Gregory of Tours, *Life of the Fathers*, 17.1; Fredegar, *Chronicle*, 4.27; *HL* 5.5.
111 *LH* 7.35, a passage with several references to baggage trains.

112 *AB s.a.* 876.

113 Regino, *Chronicon*, s.a. 891.

114 Einhard, Letter 42. The client, Gunthard, offered to pay the *haribannus*, presumably in the sense of the fine for non-attendance, instead.

115 Edict of Pîtres (Boretius 273), ch. 26, and see above, p. 100, for possible context.

116 See, e.g., Bavarian Law, 2.4–6; Alemannic Law 26(27).

117 See, e.g., Rothari's Edict, 6; Alamannic Law 25.

118 Capitulary added to the laws (Boretius 39), ch. 6; Capitulary to be added to the laws, 818/9 Boretius 139), ch. 6.

119 Capitulary of Boulogne, October, 811 (King 28; Boretius 74), ch. 6.

120 Letter to the bishops of Aquitaine. The story of Clovis' attempts to restrict looting was known by Gregory of Tours, who tells of the punishment meted out to some soldiers who disobeyed the order; *LH* 2.37.

121 E.g., *LH* 6.31, 8.30, 10.3.

122 *LH* 4.49, 6.31.

123 Cassiodorus, *Variae* 2.8, 3.38, 5.10–11; L.A. García Moreno, 'Legitimate and illegitimate violence in Visigothic law', in Halsall (ed.), *Violence and Society in the Early Medieval West*, pp. 46–59, at p. 51, and refs. See also Bavarian Law, 2.5.

124 *HW* 10.

125 *AB s.a.* 868.

126 Boretius 70, ch. 4.

127 Capitulary of Aachen, late 802/early 803 (King 14; Boretius 77), ch. 10. Capitulary concerning Estates (Boretius 32), ch. 64 specifies that the carts sent from royal estates were to carry twelve measures of wine.

128 See, e.g., Ine's Laws, 70.1.

129 *AB s.a.* 865.

130 *LH* 3.32, 10.3; *ARF s.a.* 820; *AF s.a.* 877, 883(II), 882(II).

131 Charles Martel: *CFred*, 21–4; Pippin I: *CFred*, 53; Lothar II: *AB s.a.* 869; Charles the Bald: AB s.a. 877.

132 *Rev. Ann. s.a.* 791; *AF s.a.* 888, 896.

133 *LH* 10.3. See also *LH* 8.30.

134 *Rev.Ann. s.a.* 798.

135 E.g., Rothari's Edict, 8; Italian capitulary of 801, ch. 3; First Aachen Capitulary, 810 (Boretius 64), ch. 13; Lothar I's Capitulary of Corteolonna for the counts (Azzara/Moro21; Boretius 158), ch. 18.

136 Boretius 300 (14 June 859).

137 *ARF s.a.* 788. Tassilo was accused of *herisliz*.

138 See G. Williams' forthcoming volume in this series.

139 R. Abels, *Alfred the Great*, p. 126.

140 The basic sources for these events are the *ASC s.a.* 865–80 and Asser, *Life of Alfred*, 20–60. An excellent discussion may be found in Abels, *Alfred the Great*, pp. 112–19 and 124–68.

141 Asser, *Life of Alfred*, 35.

142 The *ASC, s.a.* 874, describes Ceolwulf as a 'foolish king's thegn' set up as a puppet ruler by the Danes, but this seems to be West Saxon propaganda. The next ruler of Mercia was Alfred's son-in-law Æthelræd, Ceolwulf having quietly disappeared from history. For plausible reconstruction of Mercian dynastic politics, see C. Hart, 'The Kingdom of Mercia', in A. Dornier (ed.), *Mercian Studies* (Leicester, 1977), pp. 43–61, at p. 57.

143 This attack seems to have been timed to arrive at Christmas. We know this because the battle of *Meretune* took place on 22 March (the date of death of Bishop Heahmund of Sherborne who was killed there) and, following the *Chronicle's* detailed account of the campaign, we can work back from that date.

144 The attack on St-Hilary, Poitiers, appears to have taken place around Christmas 863; *AB s.a.* 863. A winter campaign also took place in 852–3 and an attack was made on Tours in November 853.

145 E. Christiansen, *The Norsemen in the Viking Age* (Oxford, 2002), pp. 177–8.

146 Regino, *Chronicon, s.a.* 867.

147 H. Clarke and B. Ambrosiani, *Towns in the Viking Age* (rev. edn; Leicester, 1995), p. 104.

148 A.P. Smyth, *Scandinavian Kings in the British Isles, 850–880* (Oxford, 1977), p. 148.

149 Sedulius Scottus, *On Christian Rulers*, 3.

150 See below, ch. 9.

151 The 'monuments' include the towns of Chester, Cirencester and York, Hadrian's Wall, prehistoric hillforts and barrows, dykes and other earthworks. The battle of Degsastan ('Degsa's Stone') in 603 was probably also located by a pre-existing landmark, a cairn of some sort, and if the usual location of the battle, at Dawston Burn in Liddesdale, is correct it might have been at a river crossing too.

152 *ASC s.a.* 1006.

153 A. Reynolds, pers. comm.

154 See further below, pp. 220–1.

155 *HL* 5.40–41; *CA3* 23; other battles fought at rivers can be found in Fredegar, *Chronicle* 4.25–26 and *LHF* 41.

156 E.g., the stand-off at Brienne (858); Saucourt (881); Tertry (687). The *AMP* (*s.a.* 690) say that Tertry came about because Pippin of Herestal had heard that there was a Neustrian army within his territory.

157 *LH* 6.31.

158 The count of Paris and his brother found themselves on opposing sides in 840.

159 *AB s.a.* 833 (*Campus-Mentitus*, in a marginal comment); Thegan, *Life of Louis* 42 (*Campus-Mendacii*); Astronomer, *Life of Louis*, 48 (*Campus-Mentitus*). Though the sources use the Latin translation, the name presumably originates as a bitter German pun: Lügenfeld (Lies-field) for Rotfeld.

160 See above, p. 138, and for a possible change in the pattern of warfare.

161 *AB s.a.* 882; *AF s.a.* 882 (I) (for the rashness and the size of the army); Regino, *Chronicon, s.a.* 882 (for the participants). F. Prinz, *Klerus und Krieg im früheren Mittelalter: Untersuchungen zur Rolle der Kirche beim Aufbau der Königsherrschaft* (Monographien zur Geschichte des Mittelalters; Stuttgart, 1971), p. 126.

162 *Rev.Ann. s.a.* 782. See also below, p. 196.

163 *AF s.a.* 849.

164 *HL* 6.24.

165 *HL* 6.26.

166 *LH* 5.17.

167 As in some Carolingian civil wars. For a similar attitude in Visigothic Spain, see *HW* 10.

168 *ARF s.a.* 820.

169 *LH* 10.3.

170 *LH* 6.41.

171 See P. Bourdieu, *Outline of a Theory of Practice* (trans. R. Nice; Cambridge, 1977), pp. 11–12, for theory of the use of challenges.

172 *Letter of Paul to Wamba.*

173 See Christiansen, *The Norsemen in the Viking Age*, pp. 182–8 for excellent discussion, with examples. This inspired my own comments. A good example comes from *AF s.a.* 886(I) and Regino, *Chronicon, s.a.* 887. The Vikings were at first content to sit in their fortifications but when some leading Franks died they came out to fight, with success.

174 *ARF. s.a.* 822.

175 Simeon of Durham, *History of the Kings s.a.* 771. Note that if Simeon, writing in the twelfth century, had not found this in a lost set of Northumbrian annals even this information would be lost.

176 *AB s.a.* 865.

177 Regino, Chronicon, *s.a.* 860 (describing 851).

178 *AB s.a.* 876.

179 Mühlbacher 179.

180 See also Leyser, 'Early Medieval Warfare', pp. 34–5.

181 *CFred* 44.

8 WEAPONRY AND EQUIPMENT

1 For studies and especially illustration of armament in this period, see:

For the immediately post-Roman period in general: I. Lebedynsky, *Armes et Guerriers Barbares au Temps des Grandes Invasions, IVe au VIe Siècle après J.C.* (Paris, 2001).

For the Alamans: R. Christlein, *Die Alamannen: Archäologie eines lebendigen Volkes* (3rd edn; Stuttgart, 1991), pp. 63–76; M. Martin, 'Kleider machen Leute: Tracht und Bewaffnung in fränkischer Zeit', in K. Fuchs (ed.), *Die Alamannen* (Stuttgart, 1997), pp. 349–58, at pp. 356–7.

For Anglo-Saxon England: N.P. Brooks, 'Arms, status and warfare in late-Saxon England' and 'Weapons and armour in the *Battle of Maldon*', both in his *Communities and Warfare 700–1400* (London, 2000), pp. 138–61 and 162–74 respectively; L. Webster and J. Backhouse (eds.), *The Making of England* (London, 1991), pp. 59–62, 221–6, 276–9; D.M. Wilson, *The Anglo-Saxons* (3rd edn; Harmondsworth, 1981), pp. 114–35.

For the Bavarians: W. Menghin, *Frühgeschichte Bayerns* (Stuttgart, 1990), pp. 104–9.

For post-Roman Britain (including west and north Britain and Ireland): L. Alcock, *Arthur's Britain* (Harmondsworth, 1971), pp. 327–35, reprinted with some updated bibliography in Alcock, *Economy, Society and Warfare among the Britons and Saxons* (Cardiff, 1987), pp. 295–300; M. and L. De Paor, *Early Christian Ireland* (London, 1958), pp. 105–6, plates 34, 57; L. Laing and J. Laing, *The Picts and Scots* (Stroud, 1993), pp. 59–64; H. Mytum, *The Origins of Early Christian Ireland* (London, 1992), pp. 119–22; M. Redknap, *The Christian Celts: Treasures of Late Celtic Wales* (Cardiff, 1991), pp. 26–8; E. Rynne, 'The impact of the Vikings on Irish weapons', *Atti del Congresso Internazionale delle Scienze Preistoriche e Protohistoriche* 3 (Rome, 1962), pp. 181–4.

For Merovingian Gaul: M. Martin, 'Observations sur l'armament de l'époque mérovingienne précoce', in F. Vallet and M. Kazanski (eds.), *L'Armée Romaine et les Barbares du IIIe au VIIe Siècle* (Paris, 1993), pp. 395–409; F. Siegmund, 'Kleidung und Bewaffnung der Männer im östlichen Frankenreich', in A. Wieczorek, P. Périn, K. von Welck and W. Menghin (eds.), *Die Franken: Wegbereiter Europas 5. bis 8. Jahrhundert* (2nd edn; Mainz 1997), pp. 691–706; J. Werner, 'Bewaffnung und Waffenbeigabe in der Merowingerzeit', *SdS*15, pp. 95–108.

For Carolingian Francia: K.F. Werner, 'Armées et guerres en Neustrie', in P. Périn and L.C. Feffer (eds.), *La Neustrie: Les Pays au Nord de la Loire de Dagobert à Charles le Chauve (VIIe–IXe Siècles)* (Paris, 1985), pp. 49–55; S. Coupland, 'Carolingian arms and armour in the ninth century', *Viator* 21 (1990), pp. 29–50.

For Lombard Italy: N. Christie, 'Longobard weaponry and warfare, A.D.1–800', *Journal of Roman Military Equipment Studies* 2 (1991), pp. 1–26; G.C. Menis (ed.), *I Longobardi* (2nd edn; Milan 1992), pp. 96, 100–1,120–1, 184–97; W. Menghin, *Die Langobarden* (Stuttgart, n.d.), pp. 146–88 *passim*.

For Ostrogothic Italy: V. Bierbrauer, O. von Hessen and E.A. Arslan (eds.), *I Goti* (Milan, 1994), pp. 190–1.

For the Saxons: H. Steuer, 'Bewaffnung und Kriegsführung der Sachsen und Franken', in C. Stiegemann and M. Wemhoff (eds.), *799: Kunst und Kultur der Karolingerzeit: Beiträge zum Katalog der Ausstellung* (Mainz, 1999), pp. 310–22; H. Westphal, 'Zur Bewaffnung und Ausrüstung bei Sachsen und Franken: Gemeinsamkeiten und Unterschiede am Beispiel der Sachkultur', in Stiegemann and Wemhoff (eds.), *799: Kunst und Kultur* pp. 323–7.

For Scandinavia and the Vikings: P.G. Foot and D.M. Wilson, *The Viking Achievement* (London, 1970), pp. 272–82; J. Graham Campbell, *Viking Artefacts: A Select Catalogue* (London, 1980); E. Roesdahl, *Viking Age Denmark* (trans. S. Margeson and K. Williams; London, 1982), pp. 134–9; A. Nørgård Jørgensen, 'Weapon sets in Gotlandic grave finds from 530–800 AD', in L. Jørgensen (ed.), *Chronological Studies of Anglo-Saxon England, Lombard Italy and Vendel Period Sweden* (Arkaeologiske Skrifter 5; Copenhagen 1992).

2   H. Härke, 'Early Saxon weapon burials: frequencies, distributions and weapon combinations', in S. Chadwick-Hawkes (ed.), *Weapons and Warfare in Anglo-Saxon England* (Oxford, OUCA Monograph 21, 1989), pp. 49–61; Härke, '"Weapon graves"? The background of the Anglo-Saxon weapon burial rite', *P&P* 126 (1990), pp. 22–43; Härke, *Angelsächsische Waffengräber des 5. bis 7. Jahrhunderts* (Zeitschrift für Archäologie des Mittelalters, Beiheft 6; Cologne, 1992); Härke, 'Changing symbols in a changing society: the Anglo-Saxon weapon rite', in M. Carver (ed.), *The Age of Sutton Hoo* (Woodbridge, 1992), pp. 149–65.

3   See, e.g., G. Halsall, *Early Medieval Cemeteries: An Introduction to Burial archaeology in the Post-Roman West* (Glasgow, 1995), p. 11.

4   P. Bone, The development of Anglo-Saxon swords from the fifth to the eleventh century', in Chadwick-Hawkes (ed.), *Weapons and Warfare in Anglo-Saxon England*, pp. 63–70, is a very useful introduction to the early medieval sword. See also H.R. Ellis Davidson, *The Sword in Anglo-Saxon England: Its Archaeology and Literature* (Oxford, 1962); V.I. Evison, 'The Dover ring-sword and other sword-rings and beads', *Archaeologia* 101 (1967), pp. 63–118 and plates VIII–XV. J. Petersen, *De Norske Vikingesverd, en typologisk-kronologisk studie over Vikingetidens vaaben* (Videnskappselskapets Skrifter 2. Hist. Filos. Kl. 4; Kristiania, 1919) is still the key typological study for the later period. Some early medieval swords are illustrated in E. Oakeshott, *Records of the Medieval Sword* (Woodbridge, 1991); W. Menghin, 'Zur Tragweise frühmittelalterlicher Langschwerter', *Archäologische Korrespondenzblätte* 3 (1973), pp. 243–9.

5   Petersen's Type L. D.M. Wilson, 'Some neglected late Anglo-Saxon swords', *Medieval Archaeology* 9 (1965), pp. 32–54.

6   Ellis Davidson, *The Sword in Anglo-Saxon England*, pp. 217–24. For early medieval metalworking techniques, E. Salin, *La Civilisation Mérovingienne*, vol. III (Paris, 1957), retains its value and interest.

7   Especially in the sixth century, they were the items of male equipment in which most technological skill was invested.

8   Gregory of Tours, *LH* 5.17.

9   Bede, *Life of St. Cuthbert*, 6. The description of the male side of a family as 'the spear side' can be found in *King Alfred's Will*. The poem, *Brunanburh* describes the battle as a 'meeting of spears'.

10 See, e.g., M.J. Swanton, *The Spearheads of the Anglo-Saxon Settlements* (London, 1973).

11 Härke, *Angelsächsische Waffengräber des 5. bis 7. Jahrhunderts*, p. 115.

12 Swanton, *The Spearheads of the Anglo-Saxon Settlements*, pp. 115–38.

13 *Fragmentary Chronicle of Saragossa* s.a. 531.

14   *Histories* 5.2.4–8.
15   E. James, *The Franks* (Oxford, 1988), pp. 227–9; L.C. Feffer and P. Périn, *Les Francs, tome 2: À l'Origine de la France* (Paris, 1987), p. 108.
16   See, e.g., the 'St.-Gall Maccabees', illustrated in J. Hubert, J. Porcher and W.F. Volbach, *Carolingian Art* (trans. J. Emmons, S. Gilbert and R. Allen; London, 1970), p. 177.
17   Isidore, *Etymologies*, 18.6.9. The etymology was repeated by Hrabanus Maurus, *On the Nature of Things* 20.6.
18   U. Dahmlos, 'Francisca – bipennis – securis: Bemerkungen zu archäologischem Befund und schriftlicher Überlieferung', *Germania* 55 (1977), pp. 141–65.
19   *Ripuarian Law* 40.11.
20   Illustrated in E. Roesdahl (ed.), *The Vikings in England* (London, 1981), p. 14; Graham Campbell, *Viking Artefacts*, p. 185.
21   Roesdahl, *Viking Age in Denmark*, p. 136.
22   D.A. Gale, 'The seax', in S. Chadwick-Hawkes (ed.), *Weapons and Warfare in Anglo-Saxon England*, pp. 71–83 is a useful introduction. H. Dannheimer, 'Rekonstruktion der Saxscheide aus Grab 2 von St-Jakob bei Polling: Zur Tragweise des Saxes in der späten Merowingerzeit', *Germania* 52 (1974), pp. 131–40.
23   Gale, 'The seax', pp. 78–9.
24   Bows from Oberflacht: S. Schiek, *Das Gräberfeld der Merowingerzeit bei Oberflacht* (Forschungen und Berichte zur Vor- und Frühgeschichte in Baden-Württemberg 41/1; Stuttgart, 1992), pp. 26–8, 97–8; from Hedeby: Graham Campbell, *Viking Artefacts*, p. 74.
25   *LH* 5.48.
26   *Wars*, e.g., 5.27.27, 8.32.6.
27   *LV* 9.2.9; Laws of Aistulf 2–4; Capitulary Concerning Estates (Boretius 32), ch. 64; Letter to Fulrad (King 22; Boretius 75); Aachen Capitulary (King 15; Boretius 77), ch. 9, ch. 17.
28   J. Manley, 'The archer and the army in Late Saxon England', *Anglo-Saxon Studies in Archaeology and History* 4 (1985), pp. 223–35.
29   Härke, *Angelsächsische Waffengräber des 5. bis 7. Jahrhunderts*, pp. 87, 107–9.
30   T.M. Dickinson and H. Härke, *Early Anglo-Saxon Shields* (= *Archaeologia* 110; London, 1993) is an excellent discussion of this item of military hardware. For seventh and eighth-century shields, see V.I. Evison, 'Sugar-loaf shield bosses', *Antiquaries Journal* 43 (1963), pp. 38–96.
31   H. Paulsen, *Alamannischer Adelsgräber von Niederstotzingen* (Stuttgart, 1967); illustrated in Feffer and Périn, *Les Francs, tome 2: À l'Origine de la France*, p. 110.
32   See the Birsay stone, illustrated in L. Laing and J. Laing, *The Picts and Scots*, p. 137, fig. 107; the Eassie Priory stone, illustrated *ibid.* p. 133, fig. 103.
33   Dickinson and Härke, *Early Anglo-Saxon Shields*, p. 55.
34   *Ibid.*, pp. 44–6, 71.
35   E.g., *Gododdin* A.11, A.36.
36   Sutton Hoo: A.C. Evans, *The Sutton Hoo Ship Burial* (rev. edn; London, 1994), pp. 49–55. Continental examples: Lombard example from Stabio: Menis (ed.), *I Longobardi*, pp. 190–1; another fine Lombard example now in the Museo Nazionale di Villa Guinigi, Lucca: C. Bertelli and G.P. Brogiolo (eds.), *Il Futuro di Longobardi: L'Italia e la Costruzione dell'Europa di Carlo Magno* (Geneva/Milan, 2000), pp. 39, 45–6.
37   Paulinus, *On Duke Eric*, verse 10. The *Gododdin* repeatedly mentions shattered shields as the mark of a hard fighter.
38   *AB s.a.* 876.
39   Agathias, *Histories*, 2.8.3.
40   *LH* 10.3.

41 *LH* 2.37, 4.46, 6.26, 7.38. The last of these references, with its phrase *a circulis loricae* ('by the rings of his *lorica*'), certainly means mail; the second almost certainly also does, for here a crook puts a *lorica* in a chest to make it sound like, and feel as heavy as, a chest full of coins; the third probably does too, as a soldier is dragged under water by the weight of his *lorica*. The other reference is to King Clovis, and it seems likely that the king of the Franks would be wearing metallic body armour.

42 Made from long strips of metal laced together at the top and bottom.

43 See above, p. 61. The term used by the law is *zaba*.

44 E.g., *Gododdin* B².26, B².33, A.18, A.32.

45 *Thuringian Law* 31. The term used is *vestis bellica*, *id est lorica* ('the shirt of war, that is his *lorica*'). Although in classical Latin the term *lorica* was vague and need only mean a leather cuirass, unless qualified by terms like *squamata*, *hamata* or *segmentata* (for scale, mail and segmented armour respectively), in the early Middle Ages it usually meant mail (or at least metallic) armour. In the seventh century, Isidore thought that a *lorica* was a mail shirt, though he also defined *lorica squamata*: *Etymologies*, 18.13, copied as ever by Hrabanus Maurus, *On the Nature of Things*, 20.13.

46 J.F. Verbruggen, 'L'Armée et la stratégie de Charlemagne', in H. Beumann (ed.), *Karl der Grosse: Lebenswerk und Nachleben*, vol. 1, *Persönlichkeit und Geschichte* (Düsseldorf, 1965), pp. 420–36, at p. 424, made the interesting suggestion that Carolingian legislation penalising those who did not attend the muster with their armour was aimed at warriors hoping to be issued with a second, free suit.

47 Examples of lamellar armour include: Castel Trosino grave 58 (Lombard): Menis (ed.), *I Longobardi*, pp. 186–7; Niederstotzingen (Alamannic): Paulsen, *Alamannischer Adelsgräber von Niederstotzingen*; illustrated in Feffer and Périn, *Les Francs, tome 2: À l'Origine de la France*, p. 111; Krefeld Gellep (Frankish): James, *The Franks*, p. 228.

48 Clearly illustrated in E. James, *The Franks* (Oxford, 1988), p. 62, plate 13.

49 Helmets may be shown on the Dupplin Cross, illustrated S. Foster, *Picts, Scots and Gaels* (London, 1996), p. 99, and possibly the Aberlemno stone; for Hornhausen, see H. Roth, *Kunst der Völkerwanderungszeit* (Frankfurt-am-Main, 1979), pp. 311–12, plate 299.

50 Hornhausen: Roth, *Kunst der Völkerwanderungszeit*; Lindisfarne tombstone: see above, n. 20.

51 Webster and Backhouse (eds.), *The Making of England*, pp. 101–2. The Merovingian terracotta plaque from Grésin (Puy de Dôme) also possibly shows a helmet: E. Salin, *La Civilisation Mérovingienne* vol. IV (Paris, 1959), plate 11.1.

52 Leather strips protecting the midriff and sometimes the upper arms. As with the appearance of pteruges in Carolingian manuscripts, this may be the result of classical influence, as such armour was common in the Graeco-Roman world. None the less, such forms of armour were practical and inexpensive, and seem to be shown on the Hornhausen stone too, where classical influences may not have been as pre-eminent.

53 Ittenheim: J. Hubert, J. Porcher and W.F. Volbach, *Europe of the Invasions* (New York, 1969), p. 211; B. Schnitzler (ed.), *A l'Aube du Moyen Age: L'Alsace Mérovingienne* (Strasbourg, 1997), p. 54; Stabio: see above, n. 36; Val di Nievole: Menis (ed.), *I Longobardi* p. 96; Bertelli and Brogiolo (eds.), *Il Futuro di Longobardi*, pp. 97, 100–1.

54 *Ibid.* pp. 229–31.

55 For *Spangenhelme*, see K. Böhner, 'Die frühmittelalterlichen Spangenhelme und die nordischen Helme der Vendelzeit', *Jahrbuch des römisch-germanischen Zentralmuseums Mainz* 41.2 (1994), pp. 471–549, at pp. 471–533. A mail aventail was also found at Castel Trosino: Menis (ed.), *I Longobardi*, p. 184.

56 R. Underwood, *Anglo-Saxon Weapons and Warfare* (Stroud, 1999), pp. 104–5.

57 Coupland, 'Carolingian arms and armour in the ninth century', p. 33. The Corbie Psalter does show a helmet which looks very like a Spangenhelm; *NCMH*, plate 19.

58 E. Kramer, I. Stoumann and A. Gregg (eds.), *Kings of the North Sea, AD 250–850* (Newcastle, 2000), p. 148, no. 53.

59 Vendel-Valsgärde: Böhner, 'Die frühmittelalterlichen Spangenhelme und die nordischen Helme der Vendelzeit', pp. 534–47 and Abb. 38: Sutton Hoo: Evans, *The Sutton Hoo Ship Burial*, pp. 46–9.

60 Webster and Backhouse (eds.), *The Making of England*, pp. 59–60.

61 The Pioneer Helmet: Underwood, *Anglo-Saxon Weapons and Warfare*, pp. 103–4; J. Foster, 'A boar figurine from Guilden Morden, Cambridgeshire', *Medieval Archaeology* 21 (1977), pp. 166–7.

62 St Petersburg Public Library Ms.Q.v.XIV.1, illustrated in D. Nicolle, *Arthur and the Anglo-Saxon Wars* (Osprey Men at Arms series 154; London, 1984), p. 19.

63 Roth, *Kunst der Völkerwanderungszeit*, pp. 262–3 and plate 199a.

64 *Ibid.*, p. 296 and plate 267; Paulsen, *Alamannischer Adelsgräber von Niederstotzingen*.

65 D. Tweddle, *The Anglian Helmet from York* (London, 1992).

66 Graham Campbell, *Viking Artefacts*, p. 252.

67 See, e.g., 'St-Gall, Golden Psalter', 'St-Gall Book of Maccabees' and 'St-Amand Prudentius', illustrated in Hubert, Porcher and Volbach, *Carolingian Art*, pp. 172, 178, 189 respectively. The accuracy of these depictions is defended by Coupland, 'Carolingian arms and armour in the ninth century', p. 34.

68 Evidence of late Roman leather helmets with partial metal fittings has been found at Richborough; M. Lyne, 'Late Roman helmet fragments from Richborough', *Journal of Roman Military Equipment Studies* 5 (1994), pp. 97–105.

69 Late medieval and early modern border reiving may provide a parallel. Reivers usually restricted defensive armour to a helmet and a quilted jack, or a simple back- and breast-plate, even if they possessed more complete suits of armour for more formal warfare or ceremonial encounters.

70 See above, pp. 128–9, and below, pp. 207–9.

71 N.P. Brooks, 'Arms, status and warfare in late-Saxon England'; Brooks, 'Weapons and armour in the *Battle of Maldon*'.

72 Regino, *Chronicon s.a.* 867 [*recte* 866].

73 See below, pp. 185–6.

74 Gothic example from Ravenna: Bierbrauer, von Hessen and Arslan (eds.), *I Goti*, pp. 177, 193–4; Lombard example from Castel Trosino: Menis (ed.), *I Longobardi*, p. 180.

75 S. Gollub, 'Der fränkische Friedhof in Olk, Krs. Trier-Saarburg', *Trierer Zeitschrift* 36 (1973), pp. 223–75; S. Gollub, 'Das fränkisches Reitergrab von Olk', *Kurtrierisches Jahrbuch* 14 (1974), pp. 241–7; R. Wihr, 'Konservierung und Restaurierung des silbertauschierten Pferdegeschirrs von Olk, Krs. Trier-Saarburg', *Trierer Zeitschrift* 36 (1973), pp. 277–91.

76 Schnitzler (ed.), *À l'Aube du Moyen Age*, p. 55.

77 B.S. Bachrach, 'A picture of Avar-Frankish warfare from a Carolingian psalter of the early ninth century in the light of the *Strategikon*', *Archivum Eurasii Medii Aevi* 4 (1986), pp. 5–27. 'St-Gall Book of Maccabees', illustrated in Hubert, Porcher and Volbach, *Carolingian Art*, p. 178.

78 L.T. White, *Medieval Technology and Social Change* (Oxford, 1962), pp. 1–38.

79 Where the shaft of the lance is gripped under the armpit.

80 See, e.g., B.S. Bachrach, 'Charles Martel, mounted shock combat, the stirrup and feudalism', *Studies in Medieval and Renaissance History* 7 (1970), pp. 49–75.

81 I am very grateful to Dr Falko Daim for discussion of this topic.

82 B.S. Bachrach, 'The origin of Armorican chivalry', *Technology and Change* 10.2 (1969), pp. 166–71, at p. 168.

83 Ermold the Black: *In Honour of Emperor Louis*, Bk. 3, lines 1628–31. The point turns on Ermold's use of the verb *armare*. The Breton warrior *armat* his hands with weapons, and *armat* his horse. The sense is clearly that he equips his hands with weapons, and equips – saddles up, as we might say – his horse, not that he armours it. He is obviously not armouring his hands with weapons!

84 E. Knol, W. Prummel, H.T. Uyttershaut, M.L.P. Hoogland, W.A. Casparie, G.J. de Langen, E. Kramer and J. Schelvis, 'The early medieval cemetery of Oosterbeintum (Friesland)', *Palaeohistoria* 37/38 (1995/96), pp. 245–416.

85 *Lex Ribv.* 40.11: stallion – 7 *solidi*; sword and scabbard – 7 *solidi*; mail-coat – 12 *solidi*; helmet – 6 *solidi*; spear and shield – 2 *solidi*; 'leggings' – 6 *solidi*. The recent edition of the text does not tally with the calculations of R. Doehaerd, *The Early Middle Ages in the West: Economy and Society* (trans. W.G. Deakin; Amsterdam 1978), p. 240, or J.F. Verbruggen, *The Art of Warfare in Western Europe during the Middle Ages* (2nd rev. edn, trans. S. Willard and Mrs R.W. Southern; Woodbridge 1997), p. 23. These are based upon an older edition, where the stallion is valued at 12 *solidi* and cattle between 1–3 *solidi*.

86 J.L. Nelson, 'The Frankish Empire', in P. Sawyer (ed.), *The Oxford Illustrated History of the Vikings* (Oxford, 1997), pp. 19–47, at p. 37.

87 See also above, p. 163.

88 W. Davies, *Small Worlds: The Village Community in Early Medieval Brittany* (London, 1986), pp. 56–60 for the use of money in Breton transactions. A horse is worth 9 *solidi* in Redon charter 138; two horses and some cash added up to 20 *solidi* in Redon charter 136; a horse and a dog (called Couuiranus) together were worth 20 *solidi* in Redon charter 171. The monks of Redon offered Risweten 20 *solidi* with which to buy himself a horse and a mail shirt in *GSR* 1.7. In view of the charter evidence (and *Lex Ribvaria*) this looks like a fair price.

89 Freising charters 580 and 555.

90 Mühlbacher 130.

91 Burgundian Law 4.1 (*c*.500) also specifies that a horse of the best quality was worth 10 *solidi*. Schiaparelli 220 (Lucca, 2 July, 768) mentions a horse worth 13 *solidi*, whereas Schiaparelli 288 (January, 774) involves a sale of land for a horse worth 7 *solidi*. In CDL5 15 (Rieti, November 749), six horses are valued at 60 *solidi*. There are exceptions. CDL5 14 (Rieti, November 749) mentions two horses together worth 50 *solidi*!

92 For sales of land in return for horses, not valued in *solidi*, see, e.g., Fulda charter 18 (18 May 758), Lorsch charters 1895 (2–4 January 767), 247 (768–9) and 2522 (September 773), and CDL5 41 (Rieti, December 764).

93 Procopius, *Wars* 8.31.19–20; see below, p. 192. It may be that, as the context of the battle, and especially its sequel, showed, Totila realised the desperation of the Gothic army's situation and did not wish to be recognised on the battle-field.

9 BATTLE

1 Asser, *Life of King Alfred* 56.

2 See above, ch. 3, n. 26.

3 Huns called Scythians: Sidonius, *Poems* 2.239, 7.246; Avars called Huns: *LH* 4.23, 4.29; Magyars called Avars: *AF s.a.* 894, 900.

4 See G. Halsall, '"Funny Foreigners": laughing with the barbarians in Late Antiquity', in G. Halsall (ed.), *Humour, History and Politics in Late Antiquity and the Early Middle Ages* (Cambridge 2002), pp. 89–113, at pp. 109–13, for the

suggestion that Procopius used his account of the siege of Rome as an opportunity for extended ridicule of the Goths and their attempts at Romanizing.

5 Nithard, *Histories* 2.10 (Scholz's translation).

6 Asser, *Life of King Alfred*, *c.*37–39. The translation that of Keynes and Lapidge but I have retained Asser's classical terms, including *comes* (in spite of its rather odd ring), to show how classicism could affect early medieval accounts.

7 See *The Battle of Brunanburh* (*ASC s.a.* 937), and compare it with Anglo-Saxon descriptions of 'biblical' battles in *Genesis* and *Judith* and the statement of 'how things are' in *Maxims I*. These poems, standardised though they are, nevertheless provide interesting snippets of information, too often ignored, which allow us to modify the accepted images of pre-Conquest English warfare. See further below, pp. 183–4.

8 L. Lönnroth, 'The Vikings in history and legend', in P.H. Sawyer (ed.), *The Oxford Illustrated History of the Vikings* (Oxford, 1997), pp. 225–49, at p. 226.

9 Above, pp. 71–4 and refs.

10 R. Glover, 'English warfare in 1066', *EHR* 262 (1952), pp. 1–18; R. Allen Brown, *The Origins of English Feudalism* (London, 1973); R.A. Brown, 'The battle of Hastings', *Proceedings of the Battle Conference on Anglo-Norman Studies* 3 (1981), pp. 1–21.

11 N. Higham, 'Cavalry in early Bernicia', *Northern History* 27 (1991), pp. 236–41; C. Cessford, 'Cavalry in early Bernicia: a reply', *Northern History* 29 (1993), pp. 185–7; N. Hooper, 'The Aberlemno stone and cavalry in Anglo-Saxon England', *Northern History* 29 (1993), pp. 188–96.

12 Brown, 'The battle of Hastings', pp. 7–8. See also Brown, *The Origins of English Feudalism*, p. 38.

13 *ASC s.a.* 1055; John of Worcester, *s.a.* 1055.

14 *Encomium* 2.10: *comisum est ergo prelium pedestre*. Compare Suetonius *Lives of the Twelve Caesars. Domitian*, 4: *proelium duplex equestre ac pedestre comisit.*

15 *The Battle of Maldon*, ll.1–25. For the battle, see J. Cooper (ed.), *The Battle of Maldon: Fiction and Fact* (London, 1993); D.G. Scragg (ed.), *Battle of Maldon A.D. 991* (Oxford, 1991).

16 Amm. Marc., 16.12.34–35.

17 *Wars* 5.28.25.

18 *Wars* 5.28.21.

19 *Wars*, 8.35.19.

20 Asser, *Life of King Alfred*, 37–39, 56. See above, pp. 178–9.

21 Illustrated in R. Abels, *Lordship and Military Obligation in Anglo-Saxon England* (London, 1988), figure 2.

22 *Elene*, ll.41ff. and 99–147.

23 L. Alcock, 'Graves and status in Bernicia', in his *Economy, Society and Warfare among the Britons and Saxons* (Cardiff, 1987), pp. 235–66; H. Härke, *Angelsächsische Waffengräber des 5. bis 7. Jahrhunderts*, Zeitschrift für Archäologie des Mittelalters, Beiheft 6 (Cologne, 1992), pp. 94, 121–3; Sutton Hoo mound 17: M.O.H. Carver, 'The Anglo-Saxon cemetery at Sutton Hoo: an interim report', in M.O.H. Carver (ed.), *The Age of Sutton Hoo. The Seventh Century in North-Western Europe* (Woodbridge, 1992), pp. 343–71, at pp. 362–3, 368–9.

24 Bede, *Life of Cuthbert*, 5–6; above, p. 164.

25 *HE* 3.14 (where St Aidan is given a fine horse by King Oswine); For the saints' ownership of horses during the early secular phases of their lives, see, e.g.: Eddius, *Life of Wilfrid*, 2, where Wilfrid, on coming of age, obtains weapons, horses and clothes (*arma et equos vestimentaque*) for his *pueri*. In legal material, for the king's Welsh horsemen, see Ine 33.

26 Eddius, *Life of Wilfrid*, 19. The term is *equitatus exercitus.*

27 *Gododdin* B^1.46, A.35: Here the date of the poetry is not significant. It could date from any time between the seventh century and the eleventh and still support the argument made here.

28 *Maxims I*, ll.58ff.

29 *The Battle of Brunanburh*. The traditional argument has been forced to see this as sequential: as a hard-fought battle followed by lengthy mounted pursuit. This is not crystal clear from the poem's actual text, which talks about a day-long battle as well as this day-long pursuit, and follows the reference to West Saxon mounted companies with a discussion of Mercians not refusing combat to the Vikings.

30 For discussion, see N.P. Brooks, 'Arms, status and warfare in late-Saxon England', in his *Communities and Warfare 700–1400* (London, 2000), pp. 138–61.

31 N. Hooper, 'The Aberlemno stone and cavalry in Anglo-Saxon England', *Northern History* 29 (1993), pp. 188–96; G.D.R. Cruickshank, 'The battle of Dunnichen and the Aberlemno battle-scene', in E.J. Cowan and B.A. McDonald (ed.), *Alba: Celtic Scotland in the Medieval Era* (East Linton, 2000), pp. 69–87.

32 M. Biddle and B. Kjølbye-Biddle, 'The Repton Stone', *ASE* 14 (1985), pp. 233–92.

33 See, e.g., the late tenth-century manuscript of Prudentius' *Psychomachia* illustrated in C.R. Dodwell, *Pictorial Arts of the West, 800–1200* (New Haven, 1993), p. 104, fig. 89; Canterbury Hexateuch illustrated in Abels, *Lordship and Military Obligation in Anglo-Saxon England*, fig. 2.

34 As just one example we can cite the second panel of the illustration from the Canterbury Hexateuch mentioned above. As another, see the depiction of a king fighting on foot reproduced in N.P. Brooks, 'Arms, status and warfare in late-Saxon England', in his *Communities and Warfare 700–1400* pp. 138–61, plate D.

35 *Wars* 5.27.27, 8.29.16–21, 8.32, 6–10 (Goths); 3.8.27 (Vandals); 8.31.5 (Lombards).

36 *Wars* 6.25.2; Agathias, *Histories* 2.8.4 for the Franks lack of cavalry, but 1.21.6, 1.22.3, 1.22.6 for their appearance in battle; *LH* 2.37, 3.7, 9.31.

37 Fredegar, 4.90 might imply mounted combat, as horses were among the booty, though it could equally imply that the two sides dismounted to fight.

38 J. Oexle, 'Merowingerzeitliche Pferdebestattungen – Opfer oder Beigaben?', *FmS* 18 (1984), pp. 122–72.

39 R. Brulet, 'La tombe de Childéric et la topographie funéraire de Tournai à la fin du Ve siècle', in M. Rouche (ed.), *Clovis: Histoire et Mémoire, vol. 1: Clovis et son temps, l'évènement* (Paris, 1997), pp. 59–78.

40 See also above, pp. 82–3, 93, and refs.

41 *ARF s.a.* 804.

42 *Strategikon* 11.3.

43 Lupus of Ferrières, Letter 9.

44 Aistulf's Laws, chs. 2–3; above, pp. 82–3.

45 *Wars* 5.27.27. Halsall, 'Funny Foreigners': p. 112, for the suggestion that Procopius' reference to Gothic *hoplitoi* is deliberately ironic.

46 Ratchis' Laws, 4; above, p. 82.

47 Poor soldiers to have a bow at least: Capitulary of Aachen, 802/3 (King 14; Boretius 77), ch. 17; all soldiers to have bows: Capitulary of Aachen, 802/3 (King 14; Boretius 77), ch. 9; Letter to Fulrad (King 22; Boretius 75).

48 Regino, *Chronicon, s.a.* 891.

49 B.S. Bachrach, 'Charles Martel, mounted shock combat, the stirrup and feudalism', *Studies in Medieval and Renaissance History* 7 (1970), pp. 49–75, at pp. 51–3.

50 Regino, *Chronicon, s.a.* 860, describing events of 851.

51 Regino, *Chronicon s.a.*, 891. The *AF* completely omit this engagement.
52 As, fifteen years previously, it had prevented the flight of Charles the Bald's army at Andernach.
53 See below, p. 190.
54 Sedulius Scottus, *On Christian Rulers*, 3; above, p. 156.
55 *HE* 3.2; Adomnán, *Life of St Columba*, 1.1.
56 *AMP s.a.* 690 (recte 687).
57 *AF s.a.* 876; *AB s.a.* 876.
58 J.L. Nelson (trans.), *The Annals of St-Bertin. Ninth-Century Histories*, vol. I (Manchester, 1991), p. 197, n. 30, suggests that Charles' the Bald's position in the battle was 'weak from the start'. This seems unlikely.
59 *Strategikon* 11.3.
60 *HL* 5.5.
61 Regino, *Chronicon s.a.* 891.
62 Clearly another Frankish commander had forgotten to pack his copy of Vegetius!
63 *AF s.a.* 893
64 *Rev. Ann. s.a.* 778; Einhard *Life of Charles*, 9.
65 *LH* 4.42.
66 *HL* 6.56.
67 See below, p. 221. F.T. Wainwright, 'Nechtansmere', *Antiquity* 22 (1948), pp. 82–97, for plausible conjecture.
68 Roncesvalles: above, n. 64; Robert the Strong: *AB s.a.* 862; Sueves: Hydatius, *Chronicle* 81[91]; Simeon of Durham, *Historia Regum, s.a.* 756, seems to suggest that the Northumbrian army was likewise attacked on the way back from an attack on the Strathclyde Welsh
69 Astronomer, *Life of Louis*, 47.
70 *AF s.a.* 882 (II).
71 *AF s.a.* 882 (I).
72 *HL* 5.7.
73 *HL* 5.36.
74 *AB s.a.* 841; Nithard, *Histories* 2.6 claims that Lothar's men fled before battle. Given that Charles was only seventeen or eighteen at the time, the skill and invention may rather have been that of the senior warriors in his army. In later life, Charles was a skilful and cunning though somewhat unlucky commander; he may here have been learning his trade, though it is possible that he displayed his ability at cunning stratagems at this early age.
75 Regino, *Chronicon, s.a.* 891. For the 'useless' Alamannic army, see *AF s.a.* 891. See also, above, p. 151.
76 *Wars* 8.31.19–20 (Dewing's translation).
77 E.A. Thompson, *Romans and Barbarians. The Decline of the Western Empire* (Madison, WI, 1982), pp. 108–9.
78 *HL* 5.40–41.
79 For these events, see Nithard, *Histories* II.10; for discussion see J.L. Nelson, 'The ritualisation of Frankish warfare in the ninth century', in G. Halsall (ed.), *Violence and Society in the Early Medieval West*, pp. 90–107, at pp. 98–100.
80 *AB s.a.* 876; For discussion, Nelson, 'The ritualisation of Frankish warfare in the ninth century', pp. 101–3.
81 Asser, *Life of Alfred*, 38.
82 For examples, mostly from late Anglo-Saxon England, see N. Hooper, 'The Anglo-Saxons at war', in S. Chadwick Hawkes (ed.), *Weapons and Warfare in Anglo-Saxon England*, Oxford University Committee for Archaeology Monograph 21 (Oxford, 1989), pp. 191–202, at p. 197. See also K. Leyser, 'The battle at the Lech, 955', in his *Medieval Germany and its Neighbours* (London, 1982), pp. 43–67,

at p. 61, for a similar speech by Henry the Fowler to his troops before battle against the Magyars.

83 P.G. Foot and D.M. Wilson, *The Viking Achievement* (London, 1970), p. 285.

84 *HE* 3.18.

85 Regino, *Chronicon*, *s.a.* 874; K. Leyser, 'Early medieval warfare', in his *Communications and Power in Medieval Europe. The Carolingian and Ottonian Centuries* (ed. T. Reuter; London, 1994), pp. 29–50, at p. 39.

86 Fredegar, 4.38.

87 *Chronicle of 754*, 80.

88 *LH* 3.6, 4.42, 6.4. At *LH* 2.37, 10.5, Gregory uses the term in a disparaging sense, to mean 'gang'.

89 Agathias, *History* 2.7.8–9.

90 *Ibid.*, 1.21.6.

91 *HE* 3.24.

92 Snorri, *Saga of Hakon the Broadshouldered*, 16.

93 *ASC*[E] *s.a.* 603; *HE* 1.34.

94 Leyser, 'The battle at the Lech, 955'; Leyser, 'Early medieval warfare', p. 36.

95 *Rev. Ann. s.a.* 782.

96 *Waltharius* lines 179ff. One should not overburden this evidence, as the poem originated in a monastic milieu and may have been, to some extent, a satire on secular life, but it is certainly very suggestive.

97 For trumpets at the start of battle, see, e.g., *HL* 5.10, 5.41; *HW* 13, 17.

98 Snorri, *St Olaf's Saga*, 223.

99 Fredegar, 4.90.

100 *LH* 8.45.

101 *LH* 3.6; *HW* 18.

102 *LH* 2.37.

103 *Wars* 8.32.6.

104 Regino, *Chronicon*, *s.a.* 867.

105 Illustrated in J. Hubert, J. Porcher and W.F. Volbach, *Carolingian Art* (trans. J. Emmons, S. Gilbert and R. Allen; London, 1970), p. 173.

106 The reference to mead-filled warriors in *Gododdin* (e.g., A.21) is vague in that it may be a reference to the feasting hall rather than the battlefield.

107 S.L.A. Marshall, *Men against Fire: The Problem of Battle Command in Future War* (New York, 1947).

108 For an excellent evocation of such battle, in the classical Greek context, see V. Hanson, *The Western Way of War. Infantry Battle in Classical Greece* (2nd edn; Berkeley, 2000). There has been extensive debate upon whether Hanson is correct in reading the hoplite battle as a simple shoving match, but his is certainly a very plausible interpretation. For the debate see V. Hanson (ed.), *Hoplites: The Ancient Greek Battle Experience* (London, 1991).

109 See, the Anglo-Saxon poem *The Battle of Maldon* and discussion in N.P. Brooks, 'Weapons and armour in the *Battle of Maldon*', in his *Communities and Warfare 700–1400*, pp. 162–74.

110 E.g., *Wars* 5.29.21. Three East Roman bodyguards distinguish themselves by going out from the 'phalanx' and killing enemy warriors with their spears. Byzantine bodyguards (Procopius uses the archaic term *doryphoroi*, though they were probably called *bucellarii* in reality) seem to have been used much like western 'guards', *gasindii*, *gardingi* and *antrustiones* (see above, ch. 3) and given independent commands, as well as being deployed as units. Procopius uses two old Attic words for bodyguards: *hypaspistai* and *doryphoroi*. Only the latter group seem to be sent out individually. Perhaps we have here a similar two-tiered bodyguard such as we have encountered in Merovingian Gaul and Anglo-Saxon England (above,

pp. 48–9), and thus, as with their blurred distinction between infantry and cavalry, Belisarius' Byzantine army in Italy was rather less different from its western contemporaries than is often supposed.

111 Most famously Marshall, *Men against Fire*; see A.K. Goldsworthy, *The Roman Army at War 100BC–AD200* (Oxford, 1996), p. 222, for an interesting attempt to apply this to Roman hand-to-hand combat.

112 The early eleventh-century Old English poem *The Battle of Maldon* is, although later than our period, probably the best example of this poetic 'atomisation' of early medieval battle.

113 *Wars* 5.29.16.

114 *AF s.a.* 894.

115 *Ibid. s.a.* 876.

116 See above, p. 143. I think, given the ubiquity and tactical importance of banners and of the importance of the office of standard-bearer, that J.L. Nelson, 'The Church's military service in the ninth century: a contemporary comparative view?' in Nelson, *Politics and Ritual in Early Medieval Europe*, pp. 117–32, at p. 123, n. 25, possibly reads too much into the association of a banner-bearer (*guntfanonarius*) with ecclesiastical contingents in Boretius 274, ch. 13.

117 *ASC* [all versions except A], *s.a.* 878.

118 Most famously in *Njal's Saga*, 157 and *Orkneyinga Saga*, 11–12.

119 *AF s.a.* 891.

120 Lothar I, *Capitulary concerning the Expedition to be made against the Saracens* (Azzara/Moro 33; Boretius 203), ch. 13. See also Astronomer, *Life of Louis*, ch. 13, describing the 804 Frankish campaign in Spain: 'William commanded, Ademar bore the standard, and they had a powerful force with them' (P.D. King's translation); it might just, as in Trempe's recent German translation, also read 'William was the leading standard bearer and Ademar was also there . . .' but King's translation seems preferable.

121 Henry of Huntingdon, *History of the English*, 4.19. The term he uses for standard bearer is *vexillifer*. This is probably to be seen in conjunction with the fact that earlier in the chapter he describes the approaching armies as *legiones* with *vexilla*.

122 Venantius, *Miracles of Hilary* 21.

123 *Notae Historicae Sangallenses*, p. 70.

124 *AB s.a.* 844.

125 Engelbert, *Poem on the Battle of Fontenoy*, verses 4–5 (betrayal), 9 (early success of Lothar).

126 E.g., *Rev. Ann. s.a.* 775; *AB s.a.* 866 (Franks 'put to flight even without a battle'); *AV s.a.* 882 suggests precipitate flight by Bishop Wala's army at the battle of Remich.

127 *Rev. Ann. s.a.* 794.

128 *Wars* 5.29.25–34.

129 See above, pp. 189–90.

130 *Strategikon* 3.5.

131 *Rev. Ann. s.a.* 775. *ARF, s.a.* 775 simply reports a Frankish victory.

132 *AB s.a.* 866.

133 *AV s.a.* 881; *AB s.a.* 881.

134 Note, too, how the fragmentary nature of our sources might give a misleading impression. Taken in isolation and amidst a general shortage of data such as exists for Anglo-Saxon warfare, the statement that Louis dismounted might lead to the supposition that Frankish armies always dismounted to fight.

135 Asser, *Life of Alfred* 36.

136 *ASC, s.a.* 840; 871 (the battles of *Meretun* and Wilton).

137 *HL* 6.35.

138 *LH* 10.9.
139 *GSR* 1.7 implies a stand-off for three or four days before the battle was started by a Frankish night attack; Regino, *Chronicon*, *s.a.* 860 (referring to events of 851) describes a two-day battle.
140 *HL* 5.19.
141 *Wars* 8.35.15–33.
142 *GSR* 1.7.
143 Simeon of Durham, *History of the Kings s.a.* 759.
144 For other three-day battles, see *AB s.a.* 844 (Anglo-Saxons against Danes), 854 (Danish civil war).
145 See also Goldsworthy, *The Roman Army at War 100BC–AD200*, pp. 224–6, who reaches a similar conclusion about imperial Roman battle. Goldsworthy's conclusion seems preferable to that of P. Sabin, 'The face of Roman battle', *JRS* 90 (2000), pp. 1–17, who sees the length of Roman battles resulting from prolonged missile exchanges.
146 *Rev. Ann. s.a.* 778; Einhard, *Life of Charles* 9.
147 *CFred* 44.
148 *Rev. Ann. S.a.* 778; Einhard, *Life of Charles*, 9.
149 *LH* 4.29
150 J. Engström, 'The Vendel chieftains – a study of military tactics', *MASS*, pp. 248–55.
151 Agathias, *Histories* 1.22.
152 *AMP s.a.* 716.
153 Snorri, *St Olaf's Saga*, 205.
154 C. Sánchez-Albornoz, 'El ejército y la guerra en el reino Asturleones 718–1037', *SdS*15, pp. 293–428, p. 344, n. 198.
155 F.T. Wainwright, 'The battles at Corbridge', in his *Scandinavian England* (Chichester, 1975), pp. 163–79, at p. 168.
156 See above for their use of a position behind a marsh at the Dyle; earlier in the campaign they had raided Frankish supply trains from marshes and woods; in 882, according to the *AV*, they managed to elude a Frankish pursuit by dispersing into the woods of Vicogne, near Condé.
157 *LH* 3.7.
158 *HL* 4.44.
159 Regino, *Chronicon*, *s.a.* 887, *AV s.a.* 886.
160 Sánchez-Albornoz, 'El ejército y la guerra en el reino Asturleones 718–1037', p. 344, n. 198, and p. 414, and refs.
161 For brief survey, see G. Halsall, *Early Medieval Cemeteries: An Introduction to Burial Archaeology in the Post-Roman West* (Glasgow, 1995), esp. pp. 5–13, 45–51.
162 R. Woolf, 'The ideal of men dying with their lord in the *Germania* and in *The Battle of Maldon*', *ASE* 5 (1976), pp. 63–81; the issue is put beyond doubt by S. Fanning, 'Tacitus, "Beowulf" and the comitatus', *Haskins Society Journal* 9 (2001), pp. 17–38.
163 J. Keegan, *The Face of Battle* (Harmondsworth, 1976), pp. 47–9.
164 *HE* 4.22; see above, p. 58.
165 S.J. Wenham, 'Anatomical interpretations of Anglo-Saxon weapon injuries', in Chadwick Hawkes (ed.), *Weapons and Warfare in Anglo-Saxon England*, pp. 123–39.
166 See above, pp. 120–3.
167 Nithard, *Histories* 3.1.
168 *AB s.a.* 841.
169 *ASC, s.a.* 827.
170 *Annals of Ulster s.a.* 721 [*recte* 722].

171 *AB s.a.* 844.

172 The *AF* say that 'no one can recall a greater loss among the Franks in the present age', whereas Regino, in the early tenth century, says that Fontenoy killed so many Franks that they were unable to defend their lands properly thereafter (*Chronicon, s.a.* 841). Agnellus of Ravenna, *Book of the Bishops of the Church of Ravenna*, 174, claims that 40,000 men died there. Clearly this was a major battle. Yet we should not be too misled by these statements. The three royal brothers and their nephew Pippin were able to continue raising armies and fighting battles against each other for the next few years. J.L. Nelson, 'The ritualisation of Frankish warfare in the ninth century', claims that the trauma of Fontenoy was such that a *damnatio memoriae* was declared on those who fell there. This seems unlikely because other Frankish aristocrats who fell in battle in this civil war, before and after Fontenoy, *were* named.

173 Leyser, 'Early medieval warfare', pp. 34–5.

174 This is hushed up by the narrative sources, but there are clear hints that Alfred's succession was not as smooth and 'natural' as he would wish us to believe: J.L. Nelson, 'A king across the sea: Alfred in continental perspective', *TRHS* 5th series, 26 (1986), pp. 45–68.

175 Saucourt is celebrated in the Old High German eulogy the *Ludwigslied*. For the Dyle, see above, pp. 186–8.

176 *LH* 9.31.

177 *LH* 4.23, 50.

178 *AB s.a.* 844.

179 Regino, *Chronicon, s.a.* 891.

180 Carver, 'The Anglo-Saxon cemetery at Sutton Hoo: An interim report', pp. 357, 368, 370.

181 *CA3* 16.

182 *CA3* 26, 27.

10 FORTIFICATION AND SIEGE WARFARE

1 R. Samson, 'The Merovingian nobleman's home: castle or villa?' *JMH* 13 (1987), pp. 287–315; Samson, 'Knowledge, constraint and power in inaction: the defenseless medieval wall', *Historical Archaeology* 26 (1992), pp. 26–44.

2 This was the case with cities under Lombard law; Rothari's Edict, 37–38.

3 As, for instance, in the case of trading privileges. There might well be legal differences between the inhabitants of a town and those of the countryside.

4 Sidonius, *Poems* 22.

5 Samson 'The Merovingian nobleman's home'. Samson also points out that archaeological verification of reports like Sidonius' is difficult to find.

6 In Spain, the evidence is far from clear and as in Gaul comes most often from written sources. L.A. García Moreno, 'El habitat rural disperso en la peninsula Iberica durante la antigüedad tardia (siglos V–VII)', *Antiguidad Cristiana* 8 (1991), pp. 265–73, provides a survey. For Italy, see, e.g., the curious site at Anguillara: T.W. Potter, *Roman Italy* (London, 1987), p. 217. Potter discusses other evidence for the fortification of sites in this period. For a recent survey of the fate of villas of western Europe, see G. Ripoll and J. Arce, 'The transformation and end of Roman *villae* in the west (fourth–seventh centuries): problems and perspectives', in G.P. Brogiolo, N. Gauthier and N. Christie (eds.), *Towns and their Territories Between Late Antiquity and the Early Middle Ages* (Leiden, 2000), pp. 63–114, with bibliography cited there.

7 Yeavering: B. Hope-Taylor, *Yeavering – An Anglo-British centre of early Northumbria* (London, 1977); C. Scull, 'Post-Roman phase I at Yeavering: a reconsideration',

Medieval Archaeology 35 (1991), pp. 51–63. Carolingian palaces: A. Renoux, 'Karolingische Pfalzen in Nordfrankreich (751–987)', H. Grewe, 'Die Königspfalz zu Ingelheim am Rhein', M. Untermann, '"*Opere mirabili constructa*": Die Aachener "Residenz" Karls des Grossen' and S. Gai, 'Die Pfalz, Karls des Grossen in Paderborn: Ihre Entwicklung von 777 bis zum Ende des 10. Jahrhunderts', all in C. Stiegemann and M. Wemhoff (eds.), *799: Kunst und Kultur der Karolingerzeit: Beiträge zum Katalog der Ausstellung* (Mainz, 1999), pp. 130–7, 142–51, 152–64, 183–96 respectively; Cynewulf & Cyneheard: ASC s.a. 757.

8 P. Velay, *From Lutetia to Paris: The Island and the Two Banks* (Paris, 1992).

9 Collapsing walls: Angoulême: *LH* 2.37; Metz: Fredegar, *Chronicle* 2.60.

10 M. Innes, *State and Society in the Early Middle Ages: The Middle Rhine Valley 400–1000* (Cambridge 2000), p. 97.

11 Flodoard, *History of the Church of Rheims*, 2.19; cp. Tessier 130. See also E. James, *The Origins of France: From Clovis to the Capetians, 500–1000* (London, 1982), p. 63; A. Renoux, 'Les manifestations de la puissance publique: enceintes, palais et châteaux', in P. Demolon, H. Galinié and F. Verhaeghe (eds.), *Archéologie des Villes dans le Nord-Ouest de l'Europe (VIIe–XIIIe siècle): Actes du IVe Congrès Internationale d'Archéologie Médiévale (Douai, 1991)* (Douai, 1994), pp. 61–82 at p. 65.

12 H. Galinié, 'Reflections on early medieval Tours', in R. Hodges and B. Hobley (eds.), *The Rebirth of Towns in the West, 700–1050* (London, 1988), pp. 57–62; Galinié, 'Tours from an archaeological standpoint', in C.E. Karkhov, K.M. Wickham-Crowley and B.K. Young (eds.), *Spaces of the Living and the Dead: An Archaeological Dialogue* (Oxford and Oakville, CT, 1999), pp. 87–105.

13 V. Notin and J.-M. Desbordes (eds.), *Augustoritum. Aux Origines de Limoges* (Limoges, 1990).

14 H.H. Anton, *Trier im frühen Mittelalter* (Paderborn, 1987).

15 G. Halsall, *Settlement and Social Organisation: The Merovingian Region of Metz* (Cambridge, 1995), pp. 228–36 for Metz itself and pp. 202–8 for the *castra* in Lorraine.

16 Hamwic: M. Brisbane, 'Hamwic (Saxon Southampton): an 8th century port and production centre', in Hodges and Hobley (eds.), *The Rebirth of Towns in the West, 700–1050*, pp. 101–8; A. Morton, 'Hamwic in its context', in M. Anderton (ed.), *Anglo-Saxon Trading Centres. Beyond the Emporia* (Glasgow, 1999), pp. 48–62; Ipswich: K. Wade, 'Ipswich', in Hodges and Hobley (eds.), *The Rebirth of Towns in the West, 700–1050*, pp. 93–100.

17 Anglian York: R.A. Hall, 'York 700–1050', in Hodges and Hobley (eds.), *The Rebirth of Towns in the West, 700–1050*, pp. 125–32; E. James, 'Alcuin and York in the eighth century', in P.L. Butzer and D. Lohrmann (eds.), *Science in Western and Eastern Civilization in Carolingian Times* (Basel, 1993), pp. 23–39; Middle Saxon London: B. Hobley, 'Saxon London: Lundenwic and Lundenburh: two cities rediscovered', in Hodges and Hobley (eds.), *The Rebirth of Towns in the West, 700–1050*, pp. 69–82; A. Vince, *Saxon London. An Archaeological Investigation* (London, 1990).

18 For brief descriptions of these sites, see R. Hodges, *Dark Age Economics: The Origins of Towns and Trade 600–1000* (London, 1982), pp. 74–86; For Dorestad, see W.J.H. Verwers, 'Dorestad: a Carolingian town?' in Hodges and Hobley (eds.), *The Rebirth of Towns in the West, 700–1050*, pp. 52–6.

19 *LH* 2.37.

20 *Wars* 6.21.39 (Milan), 5.10.29 (Naples).

21 *LH* 2.33.

22 *LH* 7.38.

23 J.A. Trimpe Burger, 'The geometrical fortress of Oost-Souburg (Zealand)', *Château Gaillard* 7 (Caen, 1975), pp. 215–19.

24 S. Coupland, 'From poachers to gamekeepers: Scandinavian warlords and Carolingian kings', *EME* 7.1 (1998), pp. 85–114.

25 J. Hassall and D. Hill, 'Pont-de-l'Arche: Frankish influence on the West Saxon burh?', *Archaeological Journal* 197 (1970), pp. 188–95; B. Dearden, 'Charles the Bald's fortified bridge at Pîtres (Seine): recent archaeological investigations', *Anglo-Norman Studies* 11 (1989), pp. 107–12; S. Coupland, 'The fortified bridges of Charles the Bald', *JMH* 17 (1991), pp. 1–12.

26 E.g., Gregory of Tours, *Miracles of Martin* 2.17 (a pontoon bridge across the Loire at Amboise); Gregory of Tours, *Glory of the Martyrs*, 68 (a pontoon bridge across the Rhone at Arles).

27 D. Hill, 'The Burghal Hidage: the establishment of a text', *Medieval Archaeology* 13 (1969), pp. 84–92; D. Hill and A. Rumble (eds.), *The Defence of Wessex: The Burghal Hidage and Anglo-Saxon Fortifications* (Manchester, 1996).

28 Wareham, e.g., was used as a base by the Danes in 875, which must mean that it was already a significant site, probably because of its Minster church. Royal Commission on Historical Monuments, 'Wareham West Walls', *Medieval Archaeology* 3 (1959), pp. 120–38, only concludes that the walls were post-Roman, possibly after *c*.700.

29 Above, chapter 4.

30 R.A. Hall, *The English Heritage Book of Viking York* (London, 1994).

31 Danelaw: R.A. Hall, 1989. 'The five boroughs of the Danelaw: a review of present knowledge', *ASE* 18 (1989), pp. 149–206; Birka and Hedeby: H. Clarke and B. Ambrosiani, *Towns in the Viking Age* (Leicester, 1991). Significantly the Scandinavian settlement at Dublin, refounded in 910, was defended by a D-shaped work reminiscent of those at Hedeby and Birka. P. Wallace, 'The archaeology of Viking Dublin', in H.B. Clarke and A. Simms (eds.), *The Comparative History of Urban Origins in Non-Roman Europe*. BAR(S)255 (Oxford, 1985), pp. 103–46.

32 R.W. Feachem, 'Fortifications', in F.T. Wainwright (ed.), *The Problem of the Picts* (Edinburgh, 1955), pp. 66–86. See above, p. 51, n. 62.

33 L. Alcock, *Economy, Society and Warfare among the Britons and Saxons* (Cardiff, 1987), pp. 151–219.

34 L. Alcock, *Cadbury Castle, Somerset: The Early Medieval Archaeology* (Cardiff, 1995).

35 Examples of this can be found at Carew (K.R. Dark, *Britain and the End of the Roman Empire* (Stroud, 2000), pp. 184–5) and at Dinas Powys (Alcock, *Economy, Society and Warfare among the Britons and Saxons*, pp. 5–150).

36 To take a small sample, the *Annals of Ulster* record six burnings or sieges between 672 and 685: a Scottish stronghold in 672/3, the siege of 'Baitte' (apparently somewhere in Scotland) in 679/80, the siege of Dunottar in 680/1, the destruction of Dunadd and Dun Duirn in 682/3, and the burning of Dunolly in 685/6.

37 This was the interpretation of F.T. Wainwright, 'Nechtansmere', *Antiquity* 22 (1948), pp. 82–97.

38 See above, p. 52, n. 64.

39 See A. Stoclet, *Autour de Fulrad de Saint-Denis (v.710–784)* (Geneva, 1993), pp. 60–75.

40 See P. Fouracre, *The Age of Charles Martel* (London, 2000).

41 W. Best, R. Gensen and P.R. Hömberg, 'Burgenbau in einer Grenzregion', in C. Stiegemann and M. Wemhoff (eds.), *799: Kunst und Kultur der Karolingerzeit: Beiträge zum Katalog der Ausstellung* (Mainz, 1999), pp. 328–45; M. Hardt, 'Linien und Säume, Zonen und Räume an der Ostgrenze des Reiches im frühen und hohen Mittelalter', and M. Schmauder, 'Überlegungen zur östlichen Grenze des karolingischen Reiches unter Karl dem Grossen', both in W. Pohl and H. Reimitz (eds.), *Grenze und Differenz im früheren Mittelaltern*, (Österreichische Akademie der

Wissenschaften: Vienna, 2000), pp. 39–56 and 57–97 respectively. M. Hardt, 'Elbe, Saale and the frontiers of the Carolingian Empire', and H. Wolfram, 'The creation of the Carolingian frontier system, *c*.800', both in W. Pohl, I.N. Wood and H. Reimitz (ed.), *The Transformation of Frontiers: From Late Antiquity to the Carolingians* (Leiden, 2001), pp. 219–32 and 233–45 respectively.

42 Above, p. 148. The precise nature of the *herepaths* is unknown; were they routes for armies, routes constructed by armies, or routes taken to military musters? Given the use of the word *here*, the first of these options seems preferable. It seems fairly clear, however, that they have some administrative function within the Anglo-Saxon kingdoms.

43 For a useful survey, see N. Christie, *The Lombards* (Oxford, 1995), pp. 170–82; G. Schmiedt, 'Le fortificazioni altomedievali in Italia viste dal'aero', *SdS*15, pp. 800–927; G.P. Brogiolo, 'Towns, forts and countryside: archaeological models for northern Italy in the early Lombard period (AD 568–650)', in Brogiolo, Gauthier and Christie (eds.), *Towns and their Territories Between Late Antiquity and the Early Middle Ages*, pp. 299–324.

44 R. Francovich, 'Changing structures of settlements', in C. La Rocca (ed.), *Italy in the Early Middle Ages, 476–1000* (Oxford, 2002), pp. 144–67, at pp. 151–67.

45 For a brief introduction to British crannogs, see L. Alcock, *Arthur's Britain* (Harmondsworth, 1971), pp. 227–8. For the probably royal site at Llangorse crannog in Wales, see M. Redknap, *The Christian Celts: Treasures of Late Celtic Wales* (Cardiff, 1991), pp. 16–25. For Irish crannogs, see B. Proudfoot, 'Economy and settlement in rural Ireland', in L. Laing (ed.), *Studies in Celtic Survival* (BAR(B) 37; Oxford, 1977), pp. 83–106, at pp. 90–1.

46 M. Stout, *The Irish Ringfort* (Irish Settlement Studies 5; Dublin, 1997). For brief description, see Proudfoot, 'Economy and settlement in rural Ireland', pp. 85–9 and 90–3. For fuller discussion see H. Mytum, *The Origins of Early Christian Ireland* (London, 1992) *passim*.

47 Asser, *Life of Alfred*, 30.

48 *Ibid.*, 35.

49 M. Biddle and B. Kjølbye-Biddle, 'Repton and the "great heathen army", 873–4', in J. Graham-Campbell, R. Hall, J. Jesch and D.N. Parsons (eds.), *Vikings and the Danelaw: Select Papers from the Proceedings of the Thirteenth Viking Congress* (Oxford, 2001), pp. 45–96.

50 *ASC s.a.* 893.

51 *Wars* 7.8.10; 7.22.7; 7.24.3, 9.

52 G. Ripoll López, 'On the supposed frontier between the *Regnum Visigothorum* and Byzantine *Hispania*', in Pohl, Wood and Reimitz (eds.), *The Transformation of Frontiers*, pp. 95–115.

53 J.N. Hillgarth, 'Coins and chronicles: propaganda in sixth-century Spain and the Byzantine background', *Historia* 15 (1966), pp. 483–508.

54 *AB s.a.* 873; Regino, *Chronicon, s.a.* 873.

55 *Wars* 5.16–6.10.

56 See, e.g., Tacitus' strikingly similar account of the Batavians and their inability to use siege engines: *Histories* 4.23.

57 *Wars* 6.12.1–22.

58 *Wars* 5.23.9–12.

59 *Wars* 5.22.22.

60 *HL* 6.20.

61 *HL* 5.8.

62 *ARF s.a.* 776. Given the triumphalist, propagandist nature of the *Royal Frankish Annals*, the comment on the inefficiency of the Saxon catapults may be unreliable.

63 Venantius, *Poems* 3.12.

64 *CFred* 20.

65 *CFred* 43.

66 *LH* 7.37–38.

67 *LH* 3.13 for the sieges of Chastel-Marlhac and Vollore.

68 *HW* 12, 18.

69 *CFred* 20.

70 *HW* 12–15, 17–19.

71 *AF s.a.* 894. For the significance of the storming of Bergamo, see J. Jarnut, 'Die Eroberung Bergamos (894): Eine Entscheidungsschlacht zwischen Kaiser Wido und König Arnulf', *Deutsches Archiv für Erforschung des Mittelalters* 30 (1974), pp. 208–15.

72 See p. 199.

73 Asser, *Life of Alfred*, 30.

EPILOGUE

1 R. Lavelle, 'Towards a political contextualization of peacemaking and peace agreements in Anglo-Saxon England', in D. Wolfthal, *Peace and Negotiation: Strategies for Coexistence in the Middle Ages and the Renaissance* (Arizona Studies in the Middle Ages and the Renaissance 4; Turnhout, 2000), pp. 41–55.

2 R. Abels, *Alfred the Great: War, Kingship and Culture in Anglo-Saxon England* (London, 1998), pp. 149–50; Abels, 'King Alfred's peace-making strategies with the Vikings', *Haskins Society Journal* 3 (1991), pp. 23–34. The same point had been made at about the same time by G. Halsall, 'Playing by whose rules? A further look at Viking atrocity in the ninth century', *Medieval History* 2, 2 (1992), pp. 3–12.

3 *HW* 29–30; M. McCormick, *Eternal Victory: Triumphal Rulership in Late Antiquity, Byzantium and the Early Medieval West* (paperback edition; Cambridge, 1990), pp. 303–4, 313–14, citing various earlier instances.

4 Nithard, *Histories* 4.3–6; *AB s.a.* 843.

5 See above, p. 58, n. 95.

6 Abels, 'King Alfred's peace-making strategies with the Vikings'; D. Dumville, 'The treaty of Alfred and Guthrum', in his *Wessex and England from Alfred to Edgar: Six Essays on Political, Cultural and Ecclesiastical Revival* (Woodbridge, 1992), pp. 1–23; P. Kershaw, 'The Alfred-Guthrum Treaty: scripting accommodation and interaction in Viking Age England', D.M. Hadley and J.D. Richards (eds.), *Cultures in Contact: Scandinavian Settlement in England in the Ninth and Tenth Centuries* (Turnhout, 2001), pp. 43–64.

7 Boretius 233–4 (840); 235 (856), 236 (880), 237 (883), 238 (888), 239 (891).

8 *LH* 6.31, 7.2. The war between Kent and Wessex in 694 was ended partly by the payment of compensation for the killing of the West Saxon king's brother (*ASC s.a.* 694). Similarly, the peace process between Northumbria and Mercia in 679 included compensation for the death of the brother of the king of Northumbria. *HE* 4.21.

9 See, e.g., *LH* 4.47, 4.51; Fredegar, *Chronicle* 4.53. Bishops were prominently involved in the negotiations between the sons of Louis the Pious: Nithard, *Histories* 4.3, 5.

10 *LH* 9.20.

SELECT BIBLIOGRAPHY

For a thorough bibliography of medieval military history, the reader is referred to E.U. Crosbie, *Medieval Warfare: A Bibliographical Guide* (New York, 2000). The bibliography below does not include all works cited in the notes but is mainly limited to the more commonly cited works and volumes of collected essays by more frequently cited authors, and to specifically military studies.

Note on abbreviations

Non-specialists might be slightly bemused by one or two of these abbreviations of primary sources, which seem to bear scant relation to the full title. This is simply because although I have rendered most source titles into English I have used the accepted abbreviations, which usually derive from the Latin title. Because of the wide readership at which this volume is aimed, where I am aware of a translation of the complete work (or most of it) into a modern language I have only cited that translation. Again, in order to increase accessibility I have wherever possible used English translations of the titles of primary sources, and (for similar reasons) sometimes used the numbering of sources given in translations rather than that of the accepted scholarly edition, though I have made it clear where this is done. Purists will have to grin and bear it. Royal or imperial charters are usually cited by the name of their editor or the title of the collection where they are to be found, followed by their number in the edition/collection, according to the abbreviations below. Charters from the cartularies of individual monasteries are, however, usually listed under the name of the monastery.

AB = *Annals of St-Bertin*: J.L. Nelson (trans.), *The Annals of St-Bertin. Ninth-Century Histories, Vol. I* (Manchester, 1991).

AF = *Annals of Fulda*: T. Reuter (trans.), *The Annals of Fulda. Ninth-Century Histories Vol. II* (Manchester, 1992).

Amm. Marc. = Ammianus Marcellinus, *Res Gestae*: J.C. Rolfe (trans.), *Ammianus Marcellinus* (3 vols.; London, 1935–39).

AMP = *Earlier Annals of Metz*: B. von Simson (ed.), *MGH SRG* 10 (Hanover–Leipzig, 1905); Years 688–725 in Fouracre-Gerberding, pp. 350–70.

ARF = *Royal Frankish Annals*: B.W. Scholz (trans.), *Carolingian Chronicles* (Ann Arbor, 1972), pp. 35–125.

ASC = *Anglo-Saxon Chronicle* (occasionally, where the variant manuscript traditions differ, the relevant version is given in square brackets): *EHD*, doc. 1.

ASE = *Anglo-Saxon England*.

Asser, *Life of Alfred*: S.D. Keynes and M. Lapidge (trans.), *Alfred the Great* (Harmondsworth, 1983), pp. 65–110.

AV = *Annals of St-Vaast*: B. de Simson (ed.), *MGH SRG* 12 (Hanover, 1909), pp. 40–82.

Azzara/Moro = C. Azzara and P. Moro (ed. and trans.), *I Capitolare Italici. Storia e diritto della dominazione carolingia in Italia* (Rome, 1998).

BAR(B) = British Archaeological Reports (British Series).

BAR(S) = British Archaeological Reports (Supplementary Series).

Birch = W. de G. Birch (ed.), *Cartularium Saxonicum* (3 vols.; 1885–93).

Boretius = A. Boretius (ed.), *MGH Legum Sectio 2: Capitularia Regum Francorum 1* (Hanover, 1883); A. Boretius and V. Krause (ed.), *MGH Legum Sectio 2: Capitularia Regum Francorum 2* (2 parts; Hanover, 1895–97). Capitularies are numbered sequentially across the two volumes.

Bradley = S.A.J. Bradley (trans.), *Anglo-Saxon Poetry* (London, 1982).

CA3 = *Chronicle of Alfonso III*: K. Baxter Wolf (trans.), *Conquerors and Chroniclers of Early Medieval Spain* (Liverpool, 1990), pp. 159–77.

Callander Murray = A. Callander Murray (trans.) *From Roman to Merovingian Gaul: A Reader* (Peterborough, Ont., 2000).

CDL4 = C.R. Brühl (ed.), *Codice Diplomatico Longobardo* vol. 4 (Fonti per la Storia d'Italia 65; Rome, 1981).

CDL5 = H. Zielinski (ed.), *Codice Diplomatico Longobardo* vol. 5 (Fonti per la Storia d'Italia 66; Rome, 1986).

CFred = Continuation of Fredegar: J.M. Wallace-Hadrill (ed. and trans.), *The Fourth Book of the Chronicle of Fredegar and its Continuations* (Oxford, 1960), pp. 80–121.

Dutton = P.E. Dutton, *Carolingian Civilization: A Reader* (Peterborough, Ont., 1996).

EHD = D.M. Whitelock (ed. and trans.), *English Historical Documents vol. 1, c.550–1042* (2nd edition; London 1979).

EHR = *English Historical Review*.

EME = *Early Medieval Europe*.

Fear = A.T. Fear (trans.), *Lives of the Visigothic Fathers* (Liverpool, 1997).

FmS = *Frühmittelalterliche Studien*.

Font-Réaulx = J. de Font-Réaulx (ed.), *Recueil des Actes de Louis II le Bègue, Louis III et Caroloman II, Rois de France (877–884)* (Paris, 1978).

Formulae = K. Zeumer (ed.), *MGH Leges Sectio 5. Formulae Merovingici et Karolini Aevi* (Hanover, 1886).

Fouracre-Gerberding = P. Fouracre and R. Gerberding (trans.), *Later Merovingian France: History and Hagiography, 640–720* (Manchester, 1996).

Gaudemet/Basdevant: J. Gaudemet and B. Basdevant (ed. and trans.), *Les Canons des Conciles Mérovingiens (VIe–VIIe Siècles)* (2 vols; Paris 1989).

GSR = *Acts of the Saints of Redon*: C. Brett (ed. and trans.), *The Monks of Redon. Gesta Sanctorum Rotonensium and Vita Conuuoionis* (Woodbridge, 1989), pp. 101–224.

Handbooks = *Medieval Handbooks of Penance. A translation of the Principal Libri Poenitentiales*, trans. J.T. McNeill and H.M. Gamer (New York 1990; originally 1938).

HE = Bede, *Ecclesiastical History*: B. Colgrave and R.A.B. Mynors (ed. and trans.), *Bede's Ecclesiastical History of the English People* (Oxford 1969).

HL = Paul the Deacon, *History of the Lombards*: W. Dudley Foulke (trans.), *Paul the Deacon. History of the Lombards* (Philadelphia 1974; originally 1907).

HW = Julian of Toledo, *History of King Wamba*: W. Levison (ed.), *MGH SRM* 5 (Hanover, 1910), pp. 501–26.

ICERV = J. Vives (ed.), *Inscripciones Cristianas de España Romana y Visigoda* (2nd edition; Barcelona and Madrid, 1969).

JMH = *Journal of Medieval History*.

JRS = *Journal of Roman Studies*.

Kehr (followed by name of the king in question) = P. Kehr (ed.), *MGH Diplomata Regum Germaniae ex Stirpe Karolinorum I: Ludowici Germanici, Karlomanni, Ludowici Iunioris Diplomata* (Berlin, 1934); *MGH Diplomata Regum Germaniae ex Stirpe Karolinorum II: Karoli III Diplomata* (Berlin, 1937); *MGH Diplomata Regum Germaniae ex Stirpe Karolinorum III: Arnolfi Diplomata* (Berlin, 1955).

King = P.D. King (trans.), *Charlemagne: Translated Sources* (Lancaster, 1986). Where followed by a number (rather than a page number), this refers to the selection of capitularies in the volume.

Kölzer = T. Kölzer (ed.), *MGH Diplomata Regum Francorum e Stirpe Merovingica* (2 vols.; Hanover, 2001).

Levillain = L. Levillain (ed.), *Recueil des Actes de Pépin Ier et de Pépin II Rois d'Aquitaine (814–48)* (Paris, 1926).

Lex Ribv. = *Ripuarian Law*: T.J. Rivers (trans.), *The Laws of the Salian and Ripuarian Franks* (New York 1986), pp. 167–214.

LH = Gregory of Tours, *Histories*: L. Thorpe (trans.), *Gregory of Tours: The History of the Franks* (Penguin 1974).

LHF = *Liber Historiae Francorum* (*Book of the History of the Franks*): B.S. Bachrach (trans.), *The Liber Historiae Francorum* (Laurence, KS 1973). More reliable translations of chapters 1–4 and 43–53 can be found in Fouracre-Gerberding, pp. 87–96, and of chapters 1–5, 11–14, 17, 31, 35–41, 43–53 in Callander Murray, pp. 492–98, 621–31.

Lombard Laws = K. Fischer Drew (trans.), *The Lombard Laws* (Philadelphia, PA, 1973).

LV = *Visigothic Law*: K. Zeumer (ed.), *MGH Legum Sectio I*, vol. 1, *Leges Visigothorum* (Hanover, 1902). S.P. Scott's early twentieth-century translation is available Online at http://libro.uca.edu/vcode/visigoths.htm. Note, however, that the numbering of clauses sometimes differs from that in the *MGH* edition. I have used the more accurate *MGH* numbering.

Manaresi = C. Manaresi (ed.), *I Placiti del "Regnum Italiae"* (Fonti per la Storia d'Italia 92; Rome, 1955).

MASS = A. Nørgård Jørgensen and B.L. Claussen (eds.), *Military Aspects of Scandinavian Society in a European Perspective AD 1–1300*, National Museum Studies in Archaeology and History 2 (Copenhagen, 1997).

MGH = *Monumenta Germaniae Historica*.

Mühlbacher = *MGH Diplomata Karolinorum I. Pippini, Carlomanni, Caroli Magni Diplomata*, ed. E. Mühlbacher (Hanover, 1906).

NCMH = R. McKitterick (ed.), *The New Cambridge Medieval History Vol. 2, c.700–c.900* (Cambridge, 1995).

NPNF = *Nicene and Post-Nicene Fathers*.

P&P = *Past & Present*.

PL = J.-P. Migne (ed.), *Patrologiae Cursus Completus. Series Latina* (221 vols.; Paris, 1844–63).

PLS = Salic Law: K.F. Drew (trans.), *The Laws of the Salian Franks* (Philadelphia, 1991); T.J. Rivers (trans.), *The Laws of the Salian and Ripuarian Franks* (New York 1987), pp. 39–144; but see C.P. Wormald's critical review of Drew's translation in *Early Medieval Europe* 2.1 (1993), pp. 77–9.

Rev. Ann. = *Revised Annals of the Frankish Kingdom*: King, pp. 108–31.

s.a. = *sub anno* ('under the year' – for annals or chronicle references).

Sawyer = P.H. Sawyer, *Anglo-Saxon Charters: An Annotated List and Bibliography* (London, 1968).

SCH = *Studies in Church History*.

Schiaparelli = L. Schiaparelli (ed.), *Codice Diplomatico Longobardo*, vol. I (Fonti per la Storia d'Italia 62; Rome, 1929); L. Schiaparelli (ed.), *Codice Diplomatico Longobardo*, vol. II (Fonti per la Storia d'Italia 63; Rome, 1933). Documents are numbered consecutively across the two volumes.

Schieffer (followed by name of the king in question) = T. Schieffer (ed.), *MGH Diplomata Karolinorum III: Lotharii I et Lotharii II Diplomata* (Berlin, 1966); T. Schieffer (ed.), *MGH Diplomata Regum Germaniae ex Stirpe Karolinorum IV: Zwentiboldi et Ludowici Infantis Diplomata* (Berlin, 1960).

SdS15 = *Ordinamenti Militari in Occidente Nell'Alto Medioevo (Settimane di Studio 15)* (Spoleto, 1968).

Spec. = *Speculum*.

SRM = *Scriptores Rerum Merovingicarum*.

SRG = *Scriptores Rerum Germanicarum in usum Scholarum*.

SS = *Scriptores*.

Tessier = G. Tessier (ed.), *Recueil des Actes de Charles II le Chauve* (3 vols; Paris 1953–55).

TRHS = *Transactions of the Royal Historical Society*

Visigothic Councils: J. Vives (ed.), *Concilios Visigóticos e Hispano-Romanos* (Barcelona, 1963).

Wanner = K. Wanner (ed.), *Ludovici II Diplomata* (Rome, 1994).

Wars = Procopius, *History of the Wars*: H.B. Dewing (ed. and trans.), *Procopius* (7 vols.; London 1914–40). The *History of the Wars* is to be found in vols. 1–5.

Primary sources (in addition to those listed under abbreviations)

Abbo, *Siege of Paris*: H. Waquet (ed. and trans.), *Abbon, Le Siège de Paris par les Normands: Poème de IXe Siècle* (Paris, 1942).

Abingdon Charters: S.E. Kelley (ed.), *Charters of Abingdon Abbey* (2 vols.; Anglo-Saxon Charters vols. 7 and 8; Oxford, 2000–1).

Ado of Vienne, *Chronicon*: *MGH SS* 2, ed. G.H. Pertz (Hanover, 1829), pp. 315–23.

Adomnán, *Life of St Columba*: R. Sharpe (trans.), *Adomnán of Iona: Life of St Columba* (Harmondsworth, 1995).

Æthelweard, *Chronicle*: A. Campbell (ed. and trans.), *Chronicon Æthelweard: The Chronicle of Æthelweard* (London, 1962).

Agathias, *The Histories*: J.D. Frendo (trans.), *Agathias: The Histories* (Berlin, 1975).

Agnellus of Ravenna, *History of the Bishops of the Church of Ravenna*: O. Holder-Egger (ed.), *MGH Scriptores rerum Langobardicarum et Italicarum saec. VI–IX* (Hanover, 1878), pp. 265–391.

Aistulf's Laws: *Lombard Laws*, pp. 227–38.

Alamannic Law: K. Lehmann (ed.), *MGH Legum Sectio* 1, vol. 5.1 (Hanover, 1888).

Alcuin, *Letters*: S. Allott (trans.), *Alcuin of York* (York, 1974); briefer selections: *EHD*, docs. 192–5, 198–203, 206–8; Dutton, pp. 106–19. I have used Allott's numbering.

Ambrose, *On the Christian Faith*: H. de Romestin (trans.), *Ambrose: Select Works and Letters*, NPNF, 2nd series vol. 10 (reprint: Grand Rapids, MI, 1989), pp. 199–314.

—— *On the Duties of the Clergy*: de Romestin (trans.), *Ambrose: Select Works and Letters*, pp. 1–89.

Angilbert, *On the Conversion of the Saxons*: E. Duemmler (ed.), *MGH Poetae Latini Aevi Carolini* 1 (Berlin, 1881), pp. 380–1.

Annals of Fontanelle: J. Laporte (ed. and trans.), *Mélanges de la Société de l'Histoire de Normandie* 15th series (Rouen & Paris, 1951).

Annals of Ulster. S. Mac Airt and G. Mac Niocaill (ed. and trans.), *The Annals of Ulster (to A.D. 1131)* (Dublin, 1983).

Astronomer, *Life of Louis*: A. Cabaniss (trans.), *Son of Charlemagne: A Contemporary Life of Louis the Pious* (Syracuse, NY, 1961); extract: King, pp. 167–80; Dutton, pp. 267–75.

Augustine, *The City of God*: W.M. Green *et al.* (ed. & trans.), *Augustine: The City of God against the Pagans* (7 vols.; London 1957–72).

—— *On the Correction of the Donatists* (= Letter 185): R. Stothert and A.H. Newman (trans.), *Augustine: Writings against Manichaeans and Donatists NPNF* 1st series, vol. 4 (reprint, Grand Rapids, MI, 1989), pp. 633–51.

—— *Against Faustus the Manichaean*: Stothert and Newman (trans.), *Writings against Manichaeans and Donatists*, pp. 155–345.

Austrasian Council of 742: *MGH Legum Sectio 3: Concilia* 2.1, *Concilia Aevi Karolini* 1 (Hanover, 1906), pp. 1–4.

Austrasian Letters (Epistulae Austrasiacae): W. Gundlach (ed.), *Corpus Christianorum Series Latina* 117 (Turnhout, 1957), pp. 403–70.

Battle of Brunanburh (= *ASC*[A–D] *s.a.* 936): Bradley, pp. 515–18.

Battle of Maldon: Bradley, pp. 518–28.

Bavarian Law: E. de Schwind (ed.), *MGH Legum Sectio* I, vol. 5.2 (Hanover, 1926).

Bede, *Letter to Ecgbert*: *Letter to Ecgbert*: *EHD*, doc.170.

—— *Life of Saint Cuthbert*: B. Colgrave (trans.), *Two Lives of Saint Cuthbert* (Cambridge 1940), pp. 141–307.

Beowulf: Bradley, pp. 408–94.

Braulio of Saragossa, *Letters*: C.W. Barlow (trans.), *The Iberian Fathers. Vol. 2. Braulio of Saragossa, Fructuosus of Braga* (Washington, 1969).

—— *Life of Aemilian*: Fear, pp. 15–43.

Burghal Hidage: S.D. Keynes and M. Lapidge (trans.), *Alfred the Great* (Harmondsworth, 1983), pp. 193–4.

Burgundian Law (Book of Constitutions): K.F. Drew (trans.), *The Burgundian Code* (Philadelphia, 1972).

Cartae Senonicae: *Formulae*, pp. 182–211.

Cassiodorus, *Variae*: T. Mommsen (ed.), *MGH Auctores Antiquissimi* 12 (Berlin, 1894). Extracts: S.J. Barnish (trans.), *Cassiodorus: Variae* (Liverpool, 1992).

Childebert II's Decrees: K.F. Drew (trans.), *The Laws of the Salian Franks* (Philadelphia, 1991), pp. 156–9.

Chronicle of 754: K. Baxter Wolf (trans.), *Conquerors and Chroniclers of Early Medieval Spain* (Liverpool 1990), pp. 111–58.

Clovis, Letter to the Bishops of Aquitaine: Callander Murray, pp. 267–8.

Collectio Pataviensis: Formulae, pp. 456–60.

Constantius of Lyon, *Life of Germanus of Auxerre*: F.R. Hoare (trans.), *The Western Fathers* (London, 1954), pp. 283–320, reprinted in T.F.X. Noble and T. Head (eds.), *Soldiers of Christ: Saints and Saints' Lives from Late Antiquity and the Early Middle Ages* (Philadelphia, 1995), pp. 75–106.

'Continuation' of Bede: *EHD* doc. 5, pp. 285–6.

Convent of Bishops on the Banks of the Danube, Summer 796. *MGH Legum Sectio 3: Concilia* 2.1, *Concilia Aevi Karolini* 1 (Hanover, 1906), pp. 172–6.

Council of Losne (673): Gaudemet/Basdevant, pp. 575–83.

Council of Mâcon I (581–3): Gaudemet/Basdevant, pp. 426–43.

Council of Orléans I (511): Gaudemet/Basdevant, pp. 70–91.

Council of Reisbach, 798: *MGH Legum Sectio 3: Concilia* 2.1, *Concilia Aevi Karolini* 1 (Hanover, 1906), pp. 196–201.

—— 799–800: *MGH Legum Sectio 3: Concilia* 2.1, *Concilia Aevi Karolini* 1 (Hanover, 1906), pp. 213–14.

Council of Toledo IV: Visigothic Councils, no. 21.

Desiderius of Cahors, *Letters*: W. Arndt (ed.), *MGH Epistolae Merowingici et Karolini* 1 (Berlin, 1892), pp. 191–214.

Eddius Stephanus, *Life of Wilfrid*: B. Colgrave (ed. and trans.), *The Life of Bishop Wilfrid by Eddius Stephanus* (Cambridge 1927).

Einhard, *Life of Charles*: Dutton, pp. 24–42.

—— *Letters*: Dutton, pp. 283–310.

Elene: Bradley, pp. 164–97.

Engilbert, *Poem on the Battle of Fontenoy*: Dutton, pp. 363–5.

Ermold the Black: *In Honour of Emperor Louis*: E. Duemmler (ed.), *MGH Poetae Latini Aevi Carolini* 2 (Berlin, 1884), pp. 5–79; extract: Dutton, pp. 265–7.

—— *Poem in Praise of King Pippin*: Duemmler (ed.), *MGH Poetae Latini Aevi Carolini* 2, pp. 79–91.

Eugippius, *Life of Severinus*: L. Bieler (trans.), *Eugippius: The Life of Saint Severin* (Fathers of the Church 55; Washington, 1965).

Felix, *Life of Guthlac*: B. Colgrave (ed. and trans.), *Felix's Life of Guthlac* (Cambridge 1956).

Flodoard, *History of the Church of Rheims*: J. Heller and G. Waitz (eds.), *MGH SS* 13 (Hanover, 1881), pp. 405–599.

Formulae Imperiales: Formulae, pp. 285–378.

Formulae Salicae Merkelianae: Formulae, pp. 239–63.

Fortunes of Men: Bradley pp. 341–3.

Fragmentary Chronicle of Saragossa: T. Mommsen (ed.), *MGH Auctores Antiquissimi* 9 *Chronica Minora saec. IV, V, VI, VII* vol. 2 (Berlin, 1894), pp. 221–3.

Fredegar, *Chronicle*: B. Krusch (ed.), *MGH SRM* 2 (Hanover, 1888), pp. 1–193. Extracts from Books 1–3 in Callander Murray, pp. 591–4; 597–621; Book 4 in J.M. Wallace-Hadrill (ed. and trans.), *The Fourth Book of the Chronicle of Fredegar and its Continuations* (Oxford, 1960), pp. 2–79, and Callander Murray, pp. 448–90.

Freising charters: T. Bitterauf (ed.), *Die Traditionen des Hochstifts Freising* (Quellen und Erörterungen zur bayerischen und deutschen Geschichte n.F. 4) (2 vols; reprint of original 1905–09 edition; Aalen, 1969).

Fulda Charters: E. Dronke (ed.), *Codex Diplomaticus Fuldensis* (reprint of original 1850 edition; Aalen, 1962).

Gildas, *On the Ruin of Britain*: M. Winterbottom (ed. and trans.), *Gildas: The Ruin of Britain and other Documents* (Chichester 1978).

Gododdin: J.T. Koch (ed. and trans.), *The Gododdin: Text and Context from Dark-Age North Britain* (Cardiff, 1997).

Gregory of Tours, *Glory of the Martyrs*: R. Van Dam (trans.), *Gregory of Tours: Glory of the Martyrs* (Liverpool 1988).

—— *Life of the Fathers*: E. James (trans.), *Gregory of Tours: The Life of the Fathers* (2nd edition; Liverpool 1991).

—— *Miracles of Martin*: R. Van Dam, *Saints and their Miracles in Late Antique Gaul* (Princeton 1993), pp. 199–303.

Grimoald's Laws: *Lombard Laws*, pp. 131–5.

Halitgar, *Roman Penitential*: Handbooks, pp. 295–314.

Henry of Huntingdon, *History of the English*: D. Greenway (ed. and trans.), *Henry Archdeacon of Huntingdon: Historia Anglorum: The History of the English People* (Oxford, 1996).

Hildebrandslied: P.J. Geary (ed.), *Readings in Medieval History* (rev. edition; Peterborough, Ont., 1991), pp. 138–9.

Hincmar of Rheims, *On Churches and Chapels*: M. Stratmann (ed.), *MGH Fontes Iuris Germanici Antiqui* 14 (Hanover, 1990).

—— *On the Governance of the Palace*: Dutton, pp. 485–99.

Hrabanus Maurus, *On the Nature of Things*: *PL* 111, cols.9–614; I used the transcription of Karlsruhe, Badische Landesbibliothek, Ms Augiensis 96 & 68 available Online at http://www.mun.ca/rabanus.

—— *On the Training of the Roman Military*: E. Dümmler (ed.), *Zeitschrift für deutsches Alterthum* 15 (1872), pp. 413–51.

Hydatius, *Chronicle*: R. Burgess (ed. and trans.), *The Chronicle of Hydatius and the Consularia Constantinopolitana* (Oxford, 1993).

Ine's Laws: *EHD*, doc. 32.

Isidore of Seville, *Etymologies*: W.M. Lindsay (ed.), *Isidori Hispalensis episcopi Etymologiarum sive Originum Libri XX* (2 vols.; Oxford, 1911).

—— *History of the Goths*: K. Baxter Wolf (trans.), *Conquerors and Chroniclers of Early Medieval Spain* (Liverpool 1990), pp. 81–110.

—— *Rule for Monks*: *PL* 83, cols. 867–94.

John of Biclaro, *Chronicle*: K. Baxter Wolf (trans.), *Conquerors and Chroniclers of Early Medieval Spain*, (Liverpool 1990), pp. 61–80.

John of Worcester: R.R. Darlington and P. McGurk (eds.), and J. Bray and P. McGurk (trans.), *The Chronicle of John of Worcester, Volume 2: The Annals from 450 to 1066* (Oxford, 1995).

Judith: Bradley, pp. 495–504.

King Alfred's Will: S.D. Keynes and M. Lapidge (trans.), *Alfred the Great* (Harmondsworth, 1983), pp. 173–8.

Laws of Hywel Dda: D. Jenkins (ed. and trans.), *The Law of Hywel Dda: Law Texts from Medieval Wales Edited and Translated* (Llandysul, 1986).

Letter of Paul to Wamba: W. Levison (ed.), *MGH SRM* 5 (Hanover, 1910), p. 500.

Life of Arnulf: B. Krusch (ed.), *MGH SRM* 2 (Hanover, 1888), pp. 426–46.

Life of Audoin: W. Levison (ed.), *MGH SRM* 5 (1910), pp. 536–67.

Life of Desiderius of Cahors: B. Krusch (ed.), *MGH SRM* (Hanover, 1902), pp. 547–602.

Life of Eligius: B. Krusch (ed.), *MGH SRM* 4 (Hanover, 1902), pp. 634–761; a translation by J.-A. McNamara is available Online at http://www.fordham.edu/halsall/basis/eligius.html.

Life of Fructuosus of Braga: Fear, pp. 123–44.

Life of Menelaus: W. Levison (ed.), *MGH SRM* 5 (1910), pp. 129–57.

Liutprand's Laws: *Lombard Laws*, pp. 137–214.

Lives of the Fathers of Mérida: Fear, pp. 45–105.

Lorsch Annals: King, pp. 137–45.

Lorsch charters: K. Glöckner (ed.), *Codex Laureshamensis* (3 vols.; Darmstadt, 1929–36).

Ludwigslied: Dutton, pp. 482–3.

Lupus of Ferrières, *Letters*: Dutton, pp. 425–33.

Maxims I: Bradley, pp. 344–50.

Mondsee charters: G. Rath and E. Reiter (eds.), *Das älteste Traditionsbuch des Klosters Mondsee* (Forschungen zur Geschichte Oberösterreichs 16; Linz, 1989).

Nithard, *Histories*: B.W. Scholz (trans.), *Carolingian Chronicles* (Ann Arbor, 1972), pp. 127–74.

Njal's Saga: Magnus Magnusson and Hermann Pálsson (trans.), *Njal's Saga* (Harmondsworth, 1960).

Notker, *Deeds of Charlemagne*: L. Thorpe (trans.), *Einhard and Notker the Stammerer, Two Lives of Charlemagne* (Harmondsworth, 1969).

Ohthere's Account: N. Lund (ed.) and C. Fell (trans.), *Two Voyagers at the Court of King Alfred: The Ventures of Ohthere and Wulfstan together with the Description of Northern Europe from the Old English Orosius* (York, 1984), pp. 18–22.

'Old Irish Penitential': Handbooks, pp. 155–68.

On King Pippin's Avar Victory: O. Holder-Egger (ed.), *MGH SRG* 7 (Hanover 1911), pp. 42–3.

Order for the Coronation of Charles the Bald: Dutton, pp. 443–5; Boretius 302.

Orkneyinga Saga: Hermann Pálsson and P. Edwards (trans.), *Orkneyinga Saga: The History of the Earls of Orkney* (Harmondsworth, 1981).

Passion of Leudegar: Fouracre-Gerberding, pp. 215–53.

Patrick, *Letter to Coroticus*: A.B.E. Hood (ed. and trans.), *St. Patrick: His Writings and Muirchu's Life* (Chichester 1978), pp. 35–8, 55–9.

Paulinus of Aquileia, *On Duke Eric*: O. Holder-Egger (ed.), *MGH SRG* 7 (Hanover 1911), pp. 44–6.

Paulinus of Pella, *Thanksgiving*: H. Ibsell (trans.), *The Last Poets of Imperial Rome* (Harmondsworth, 1971), pp. 242–62.

Penitential of Theodore: Handbooks, pp. 179–215.

Polyptych of St-Germain-des-Prés: D. Hägermann (ed.), *Das Polyptychon von St-Germain-des-Prés* (Cologne, 1993).

Prudentius: *Prudentius* ed. and trans. H.J. Thompson (2 vols.; London 1949–53).

Prüm charters (the Golden Book of Prüm): R. Nolden (ed.), *Das "Goldene Buch" von Prüm (Liber Aureus Prumiensis): Faksimile, Übersetzung der Urkunden, Einband* (Prüm, 1997).

'Pseudo-Bede I': Handbooks, pp. 217–33.

Ratchis' Laws: *Lombard Laws*, pp. 215–25.

Redon charters: A. de Courson (ed.), *Cartulaire de l'Abbaye de Redon en Bretagne* (Paris, 1863).

Regino of Prüm, *Chronicon*: F. Kurze (ed.), *MGH SRG* 50 (Hanover, 1890, repr. 1978).

Regino of Prüm, *On Ecclesiastical Discipline and Christian Religion*: (Extract) Handbooks, pp. 314–21.

Rothari's Edict: *Lombard Laws*, pp. 39–130.

Sacramentary of Gellone: A. Dumas (ed.), *Corpus Christianorum Series Latina* 159 (Turnhout, 1981).

Sedulius Scottus, *On Christian Rulers*: Dutton, pp. 402–11.

Sidonius Apollinaris, *Letters*: W.B. Anderson (ed. and trans.), *Sidonius: Poems and Letters*, (vol. 1; London, 1936), pp. 329–483; W.B. Anderson and E.H. Warmington (eds. and trans.), *Sidonius: Poems and Letters* (vol. 2; London, 1965).

Sidonius Apollinaris, *Poems*: W.B. Anderson (ed. and trans.), *Sidonius: Poems and Letters* (vol. 1; London, 1936).

Simeon of Durham, *History of the Kings*: J. Stephenson (trans.), *Simeon of Durham, A History of the Kings of England* (facsimile reprint of 1858 edition, Felinfach, 1987); important extracts: *EHD* doc. 3.

Snorri Sturluson, *St. Olaf's Saga*: L.M. Hollander (trans.), *Snorri Sturluson: Heimskringla: History of the Kings of Norway* (Austin, 1964), pp. 245–537.

Snorri Sturluson, *Saga of Hakon the Broadshouldered*: L.M. Hollander (trans.), *Snorri Sturluson: Heimskringla: History of the Kings of Norway* (Austin, 1964), pp. 768–88.

Strategikon: G.T. Denis (trans.), *Maurice's Strategikon: Handbook of Byzantine Military Strategy* (Philadelphia, 1984).

Tacitus, *Histories*: C.H. Moore and J. Jackson (trans.), *Tacitus: Histories and Annals* (4 vols.; London 1925–37).

Taio of Saragossa, *Letter to Bishop Quiricus of Barcelona*: PL 80, cols. 727–30.

Thegan, *Life of Louis*: Dutton, pp. 141–55. E. Tremp (ed. and trans.), *MGH SRG* 64 (Hanover, 1995).

Theodosian Code: C. Pharr (trans.), *The Theodosian Code and Novels and the Sirmondian Constitutions* (Princeton, 1952).

Thuringian Law: K.F. von Richthofen (ed.), *MGH Legum* 5 (folio; Hanover, 1875–89), pp. 103–42.

Venantius Fortunatus, *Poems*: C. Nisard and E. Rittier (eds. and trans.), *Venance Fortunat: Poésies Mêlées Traduites en Français* (Paris, 1887). Selection in J. George (trans.), *Venantius Fortunatus: Personal and Political Poems* (Liverpool, 1995).

Venantius Fortunatus, *Miracles of Hilary*: R. Van Dam, *Saints and their Miracles in Late Antique Gaul* (Princeton, 1993), pp. 155–61.

Waltharius: B. Murdoch (trans.), *Walthari: A Verse Translation of the Medieval Latin Waltharius* (Glasgow, 1989).

Wissembourg charters: K. Glöckner and A. Doll (eds.), *Traditiones Wizenburgenses: Die Urkunden des Klosters Weissenburg, 661–864* (Darmstadt, 1979).

Secondary sources

R. Abels, *Lordship and Military Obligation in Anglo-Saxon England* (London, 1988).

—— 'English logistics and military administration, 871–1066: the impact of the Viking wars', *MASS*, pp. 256–65.

—— *Alfred the Great: War, Kingship and Culture in Anglo-Saxon England* (London, 1998).

Airlie, S., 'The aristocracy', *NCMH*, pp. 431–50.

Alcock, L., *Arthur's Britain* (Harmondsworth, 1971).

—— *Economy, Society and Warfare among the Britons and Saxons* (Cardiff, 1987).

—— 'The activities of potentates in Celtic Britain, AD 500–800', in S. Driscoll and M. Nieke (eds.), *Power and Politics in Early Medieval Britain and Ireland* (Edinburgh, 1988), pp. 22–46.

—— 'Message from the dark side of the moon: western and northern Britain in the age of Sutton Hoo', in M.O.H. Carver (ed.), *The Age of Sutton Hoo: The Seventh Century in North-western Europe* (Woodbridge, 1992), pp. 205–15.

—— *Cadbury Castle, Somerset: The Early Medieval Archaeology* (Cardiff, 1995).

Bachrach, B.S., *Merovingian Military Organization, 481–751* (Minneapolis, 1972).

—— *Armies and Politics in the Early Medieval West* (Aldershot, 1993).

—— *The Anatomy of a Little War: A Military and Diplomatic History of the Gundovald Affair* (Boulder, 1994).

—— *Early Carolingian Warfare: Prelude to Empire* (Philadelphia, 2000).

Beeler, J., *Warfare in Feudal Europe, 730–1200* (Ithaca, 1971).

Bennett, M., 'Violence in eleventh-century Normandy: feud, warfare and politics', in Halsall (ed.), *Violence and Society in the Early Medieval West*, pp. 126–40.

Bertolini, O., 'Ordinamenti militari e strutture sociali dei Longobardi in Italia', *SdS*15, pp. 429–607.

Best, W., R. Gensen and P.R. Hömberg, 'Burgenbau in einer Grenzregion', in C. Stiegemann and M. Wemhoff (eds.), *799: Kunst und Kultur der Karolingerzeit: Beiträge zum Katalog der Ausstellung* (Mainz, 1999), pp. 328–45.

Biddle, M. and B. Kjølbye-Biddle, 'The Repton Stone', *ASE* 14 (1985), pp. 233–92.

—— 'Repton and the "great heathen army", 873–4', in J. Graham-Campbell, R. Hall, J. Jesch and D.N. Parsons (eds.), *Vikings and the Danelaw: Select Papers from the Proceedings of the Thirteenth Viking Congress* (Oxford, 2001), pp. 45–96.

Bierbrauer, V., O. von Hessen and E.A. Arslan (eds.), *I Goti* (Milan, 1994).

Böhner, K., 'Die frühmittelalterlichen Spangenhelme und die nordischen Helme der Vendelzeit', *Jahrbuch des römisch-germanischen Zentralmuseums Mainz* 41.2 (1994), pp. 471–549.

Bone, P., The development of Anglo-Saxon swords from the fifth to the eleventh century', in S. Chadwick-Hawkes (ed.), *Weapons and Warfare in Anglo-Saxon England* (Oxford University Committee for Archaeology Monograph 21; Oxford 1989), pp. 63–70.

Bouzy, O., 'Les armes symboles d'un pouvoir politique: l'épée du sacre, la Sainte Lance, l'Oriflamme, aux VIIIe–XIIe siècles', *Francia* 22/1 (1995), pp. 45–57.

Bowlus, C.R., *Franks, Moravians and Magyars: The Struggle for the Middle Danube, 788–907* (Philadelphia, 1995).

Brogiolo, G.P., 'Towns, forts and countryside: archaeological models for northern Italy in the early Lombard period (AD 568–650)', in G.P. Brogiolo, N. Gauthier and N. Christie (eds.), *Towns and their Territories between Late Antiquity and the Early Middle Ages* (Leiden, 2001), pp. 299–324.

Brooks, N.P., *Communities and Warfare 700–1400* (London, 2000).

Brown, R.A., *The Origins of English Feudalism* (London, 1973).

—— 'The battle of Hastings', *Proceedings of the Battle Conference on Anglo-Norman Studies* 3 (1981), pp. 1–21.

Burns, T.S., *Barbarians within the Gates of Rome: A Study of Roman Military Policy and the Barbarians, ca.375–425* (Bloomington, IN, 1994).

Campbell, J., *Essays in Anglo-Saxon History* (London, 1986).

—— *The Anglo-Saxon State* (London, 2000).

Cessford, C., 'Cavalry in early Bernicia: a reply', *Northern History* 29 (1993), pp. 185–7.

Chadwick Hawkes, S., (ed.), *Weapons and Warfare in Anglo-Saxon England* (Oxford University Committee for Archaeology Monograph 21; Oxford, 1989).

Christiansen, E., *The Norsemen in the Viking Age* (Oxford, 2002).

Christie, N., 'Longobard weaponry and warfare, A.D.1–800', *Journal of Roman Military Equipment Studies* 2 (1991), pp. 1–26.

—— *The Lombards* (Oxford, 1995).

Christlein, R., *Die Alamannen: Archäologie eines lebendigen Volkes* (3rd edition; Stuttgart, 1991).

Clausewitz, C. von, *On War* (ed. and trans. M. Howard and P. Paret; Princeton 1984).

Collins, R., *The Basques* (Oxford, 1986).

—— *Law, Culture and Regionalism in Early Medieval Spain* (Aldershot, 1992).

—— *Early Medieval Spain: Unity in Diversity, 400–1000* (2nd edition; London, 1995).

Contamine, P., *War in the Middle Ages* (trans. M. Jones; Oxford, 1984).

Coupland, S., 'Carolingian arms and armour in the ninth century', *Viator* 21 (1990), pp. 29–50.

—— 'The fortified bridges of Charles the Bald', *JMH* 17 (1991), pp. 1–12.

—— 'The rod of God's wrath or the people of God's wrath? The Carolingians' theology of the Viking invasions', *Journal of Ecclesiastical History* 42.4 (1991), pp. 535–54.

—— 'The Vikings in Francia and Anglo-Saxon England to 911', *NCMH*, pp. 190–201.

—— 'From poachers to gamekeepers: Scandinavian warlords and Carolingian kings', *EME* 7.1 (1998), pp. 85–114.

—— 'The Frankish tribute payments to the Vikings and their consequences', *Francia* 26/1 (1999), pp. 57–75.

Cross, J.E., 'The ethic of war in Old English', in P. Clemoes and K. Hughes (eds.), *England Before the Conquest. Studies in Primary Sources Presented to Dorothy Whitelock* (Cambridge, 1971), pp. 269–82.

Cruickshank, G.D.R., 'The battle of Dunnichen and the Aberlemno battle-scene', in E.J. Cowan and B.A. McDonald (eds.), *Alba: Celtic Scotland in the Medieval Era* (East Linton, 2000), pp. 69–87.

Dahmlos, U., 'Francisca – bipennis – securis': Bemerkungen zu archäologischem Befund und schriftlicher Überlieferung', *Germania* 55 (1977), pp. 141–65.

Dannheimer, H., 'Rekonstruktion der Saxscheide aus Grab 2 von St-Jakob bei Polling: Zur Tragweise des Saxes in der späten Merowingerzeit', *Germania* 52 (1974), pp. 131–40.

Dearden, B., 'Charles the Bald's fortified bridge at Pîtres (Seine): recent archaeological investigations', *Anglo-Norman Studies* 11 (1989), pp. 107–12.

Delbrück, H., *History of the Art of War, Volume II: The Barbarian Invasions* (trans. W.J. Renfroe, of German 3rd edition of 1909; Lincoln, NE, 1980).

Dickinson T.M. and H. Härke, *Early Anglo-Saxon Shields* (= *Archaeologia* 110; London, 1993).

Dominguez Monedero, A., 'Los ejércitos regulares tardorromanos en la Península Ibérica y el problema del pretendido "limes hispanus"', *Revista de Guimaraes* 93 (1983), pp. 101–32.

Duby, G., 'Les origines de la chevalerie', *SdS*15, pp. 739–61.

Dumville, D., 'The treaty of Alfred and Guthrum', in his *Wessex and England from Alfred to Edgar: Six Essays on Political, Cultural and Ecclesiastical Revival* (Woodbridge, 1992), pp. 1–23.

—— 'Ecclesiastical lands and the defence of Wessex in the first Viking-Age', in his *Wessex and England from Alfred to Edgar: Six Essays on Political, Cultural and Ecclesiastical Revival* (Woodbridge, 1992), pp. 29–54.

Ellis Davidson, H.R., *The Sword in Anglo-Saxon England: Its Archaeology and Literature* (Oxford, 1962).

Elton, H., *Warfare in Roman Europe, 350–425* (Oxford, 1996).

Engels, D., *Alexander the Great and the Logistics of the Macedonian Army* (Berkeley, CA, 1978).

Engström, J., 'The Vendel chieftains – a study of military tactics', *MASS*, pp. 248–55.

Escalona Monge, J., 'Las prestaciones de servicios militares y la organización de la sociedad feudal castellana: los infanzones de Espeja', *Castillos de España* 94 (1987), pp. 55–60.

Evans, S.S., *Lords of Battle: Image and Reality of the* Comitatus *in Dark-Age Britain* (Woodbridge, 1997).

Evison, V.I., 'Sugar-loaf shield bosses', *Antiquaries Journal* 43 (1963), pp. 38–96.

—— 'The Dover ring-sword and other sword-rings and beads', *Archaeologia* 101 (1967), pp. 63–118 and plates VIII–XV.

Fanning, S., 'Tacitus, 'Beowulf' and the comitatus', *Haskins Society Journal* 9 (2001), pp. 17–38.

Fasoli, G., 'Pace e guerra nell'alto medioevo', *SdS*15, pp. 15–47.

Flori, J., *L'Idéologie du Glaive: Préhistoire de la Chevalerie* (Geneva, 1983).

—— *La Guerre Sainte* (Paris, 2001).

Foot, P.G. and D.M. Wilson, *The Viking Achievement* (London, 1970).

Foster, J., 'A boar figurine from Guilden Morden, Cambridgeshire', *Medieval Archaeology* 21 (1977), pp. 166–7.

Foster, S., *Picts, Scots and Gaels* (London, 1996).

Fouracre, P., 'Attitudes towards violence in seventh- and eighth-century Francia', in Halsall (ed.), *Violence and Society in the Early Medieval West*, pp. 60–75.

—— *The Age of Charles Martel* (London, 2000).

Fournier, G., 'Les campagnes de Pépin le Bref en Auvergne et la question des fortifications rurales en VIIIe siècle', *Francia* 2 (1975), pp. 123–35.

Fox, C., *Offa's Dyke: A Field Survey of the Western Frontier-Works of Mercia in the Seventh and Eighth Centuries A.D.* (London, 1955).

France, J., *Western Warfare in the Age of the Crusades, 1000–1300* (London, 1999).

Fuller, J.F.C., *The Decisive Battles of the Western World and their Influence upon History* (2 vols., abridged and revised edition, ed. J. Terraine; London 1954–56).

Gale, D.A., 'The seax', in Chadwick-Hawkes (ed.), *Weapons and Warfare in Anglo-Saxon England*, pp. 71–83.

Ganshof, F.L., *Feudalism* (3rd edition; London, 1964).

—— 'L'Armée sous les Carolingiens', *SdS*15, pp. 109–30.

—— 'Charlemagne's army', in his *Frankish Institutions under Charlemagne* (trans. B. Lyon; Providence, RI, 1968), pp. 59–68.

García Moreno, L.A., 'Zamora del dominio imperial romano al visigodo. Cuestiones de Historia militar y geopolítica', *I. Congresso de Historia de Zamora* (1990), pp. 455–66.

—— 'Legitimate and illegitimate violence in Visigothic law', in Halsall (ed.), *Violence and Society in the Early Medieval West*, pp. 46–59.

Gasparri, S., 'Strutture militari e legami i dipendenza in età longobarda e carolingia', *Rivista Storica Italiana* 98 (1986), pp. 664–726.

Gibson M.T and J.L. Nelson (eds.), *Charles the Bald. Court and Kingdom* (2nd edition; Aldershot, 1990).

Gillmor, C., 'War on the rivers: Viking numbers and mobility on the Seine and Loire, 841–886', *Viator* 19 (1988), pp. 79–109.

—— 'Charles the Bald and the small free farmers, 862–69', *MASS*, pp. 38–47.

Glete, J., *Warfare at Sea, 1500–1650. Maritime Conflicts and the Transformation of Europe* (London, 2000).

—— *War and the State in Early Modern Europe: Spain, the Dutch Republic and Sweden as Fiscal-Military States, 1500–1650* (London, 2002).

Glover, R., 'English warfare in 1066', *EHR* 262 (1952), pp. 1–18.

Goetz, H.-W., 'Social and military institutions', *NCMH*, pp. 451–80.

Goffart, W., *Barbarians and Romans AD 418–585: The Techniques of Accommodation* (Princeton, 1980).

Goldberg, E., '"More devoted to the equipment of battle than the splendor of banquets": Frontier kingship, military ritual and early knighthood at the court of Louis the German', *Viator* 30 (1999), pp. 41–78.

Goldsworthy, A.K., *The Roman Army at War 100BC–AD200* (Oxford, 1996).

Graham Campbell, J., *Viking Artefacts: A Select Catalogue* (London, 1980).

Haldon, J., *The State and the Tributary Mode of Production* (London, 1993).

—— *Warfare, State, and Society in the Byzantine World, 565–1204* (London, 1999).

Halsall, G., 'Playing by whose rules? A further look at Viking atrocity in the ninth century', *Medieval History* 2/2 (1992), pp. 3–12.

—— 'Violence and Society in the early medieval west: an introductory survey', in Halsall (ed.), *Violence and Society in the Early Medieval West*, pp. 1–45.

—— 'Reflections on early medieval violence: the example of the "Blood Feud"', *Memoria y Civilización* 2 (1999), pp. 7–29.

Halsall, G., (ed.), *Violence and Society in the Early Medieval West* (Woodbridge, 1998).

Hammer, C.I., 'Land sales in eighth- and ninth-century Bavaria: legal, social and economic aspects', *EME* 6.1 (1996), pp. 47–76.

Hannestad, K., 'Les forces militaires d'après la guerre gothique de Procope', *Classica et Medievalia* 21 (1961), pp. 136–83.

Hanson, V., *The Western Way of War: Infantry Battle in Classical Greece* (2nd edition; Berkeley, CA, 2000).

Hardt, M., 'Linien und Säume, Zonen und Räume an der Ostgrenze des Reiches im frühen und hohen Mittelalter', in Pohl and Reimitz (eds.), *Grenze und Differenz im früheren Mittelalter*, pp. 39–56.

—— 'Elbe, Saale and the frontiers of the Carolingian Empire', in W. Pohl, I.N. Wood and H. Reimitz (eds.), *The Transformation of Frontiers: From Late Antiquity to the Carolingians* (Leiden, 2001), pp. 219–32.

Härke, H., 'Early Saxon weapon burials: frequencies, distributions and weapon combinations', in S. Chadwick Hawkes (ed.), *Weapons and Warfare in Anglo-Saxon England* (Oxford, OUCA Monograph 21, 1989), pp. 49–61.

—— '"Weapon graves"? The background of the Anglo-Saxon weapon burial rite', *P&P* 126 (1990), pp. 22–43.

—— *Angelsächsische Waffengräber des 5. bis 7. Jahrhunderts* (Zeitschrift für Archäologie des Mittelalters, Beiheft 6; Cologne, 1992).

—— 'Changing symbols in a changing society: the Anglo-Saxon weapon rite', in M. Carver (ed.), *The Age of Sutton Hoo: The Seventh Century in North-western Europe* (Woodbridge, 1992), pp. 149–65.

—— 'Early Anglo-Saxon military organisation: an archaeological perspective', *MASS*, pp. 93–101.

Haslam, J., 'Market and fortress in England in the reign of Offa', *World Archaeology* 19.3 (1987), pp. 76–93.

Hassall, J. and D. Hill, 'Pont-de-l'Arche: Frankish influence on the West Saxon burh?' *Archaeological Journal* 197 (1970), pp. 188–95.

Higham, N., 'Cavalry in early Bernicia', *Northern History* 27 (1991), pp. 236–41.

Hill, D., 'The Burghal Hidage: the establishment of a text', *Medieval Archaeology* 13 (1969), pp. 84–92.

Hill, D. and A. Rumble (eds.), *The Defence of Wessex: The Burghal Hidage and Anglo-Saxon Fortifications* (Manchester, 1996).

Hines, J., 'The military context of the *adventus saxonum*: some continental evidence', in S. Chadwick Hawkes (ed.), *Weapons and Warfare in Anglo-Saxon England*, OUCA, pp. 25–48.

Hollister, C.W., *Anglo-Saxon Military Institutions on the Eve of the Norman Conquest* (Oxford, 1962).

Hooper, N., 'The Anglo-Saxons at war', in Chadwick Hawkes (ed.), *Weapons and Warfare in Anglo-Saxon England*, pp. 191–202.

—— 'The Aberlemno stone and cavalry in Anglo-Saxon England', *Northern History* 29 (1993), pp. 188–96.

Hubert, J., J. Porcher and W.F. Volbach, *Europe in the Dark Ages* (London, 1969).

—— *Carolingian Art* (trans. J. Emmons, S. Gilbert and R. Allen; London, 1970).

Innes, M., *State and Society in the Early Middle Ages: The Middle Rhine Valley 400–1000* (Cambridge 2000).

James, E., 'The militarisation of Roman society, 400–700', *MASS*, pp. 19–24.

Jarnut, J., 'Die Eroberung Bergamos (894): Eine Entscheidungsschlacht zwischen Kaiser Wido und König Arnulf', *Deutsches Archiv für Erforschung des Mittelalters* 30 (1974), pp. 208–15.

John, E., 'English feudalism and the structure of Anglo-Saxon society', in E. John, *Orbis Britanniae and Other Studies* (Leicester, 1966), pp. 128–53.

—— 'War and society in the tenth century: the Maldon campaign', *TRHS*, 5th series, 27 (1977), pp. 173–91.

Keegan, J., *The Face of Battle* (London, 1976).

—— *A History of Warfare* (London, 1993).

Keen, M., (ed.), *Medieval Warfare: A History* (Oxford, 2000).

Kennedy, H., *The Armies of the Caliphs Military and Society in the Early Islamic State* (London, 2001).

Kershaw, P., '*Rex Pacificus*: studies in royal peacemaking and the image of the peace-making king in the early medieval west', Ph.D. Thesis, University of London (1999).

—— 'The Alfred-Guthrum Treaty: scripting accommodation and interaction in Viking Age England', D.M. Hadley and J.D. Richards (eds.), *Cultures in Contact: Scandinavian Settlement in England in the Ninth and Tenth Centuries* (Turnhout, 2001), pp. 43–64.

Laing, L. and J. Laing, *The Picts and Scots* (Stroud, 1993).

Lamm, J.P. and H. Nordstrom (eds.), *Statens Historiska Museum, Studies 2: Vendel Period* (Stockholm, 1983).

Lavelle, R., 'Towards a political contextualization of peacemaking and peace agreements in Anglo-Saxon England', in D. Wolfthal, *Peace and Negotiation: Strategies for Coexistence in the Middle Ages and the Renaissance* (Arizona Studies in the Middle Ages and the Renaissance 4; Turnhout, 2000), pp. 41–55.

Lawson, M.K., 'The collection of Danegeld and Heregeld in the reigns of Æthelred and Cnut', *EHR* 99 (1984), pp. 721–38.

Lebedynsky, I., *Armes et Guerriers Barbares au Temps des Grandes Invasions, IVe au VIe Siècle après J.C.* (Paris, 2001).

Le Jan, R., *Famille et Pouvoir dans le Monde Franc (VIIe–Xe siècles): Essai d'anthropologie sociale* (Paris, 1995).

—— 'Frankish giving of arms and rituals of power: continuity and change in the Carolingian period', in F. Theuws and J.L. Nelson (eds.), *Rituals of Power from Late Antiquity to the Early Middle Ages* (Leiden, 2000), pp. 281–309.

Leyser, K., 'The battle at the Lech, 955', in his *Medieval Germany and its Neighbours* (London, 1982), pp. 43–67.

—— *Communications and Power in Medieval Europe: The Carolingian and Ottonian Centuries* (ed. T. Reuter; London, 1994).

Liebeschuetz, J.H.W.G., 'The end of the Roman army in the western Empire', in J. Rich and G. Shipley (eds.), *War and Society in the Roman World* (London, 1993), pp. 265–76.

Lot, F., 'Études sur la bataille de Poitiers de 732', *Revue Belge de Philologie et d'Histoire* 26 (1948), pp. 33–59

Lund, N., 'Allies of God or man? The Viking expansion in a European perspective', *Viator* 20 (1989), pp. 45–59.

—— 'If the Vikings knew a *Leding* – What was it like?', in B. Ambrosiani and H. Clarke (eds.), *Developments around the Baltic and the North Sea in the Viking Age* (Birka Studies 3; Stockholm, 1994), pp. 98–105.

MacLean, S., 'Charles the Fat and the Viking Great Army: The military explanation for the end of the Carolingian empire (876–88)', *War Studies Journal* 3.2 (1998), pp. 74–95.

Mallett, M., 'Mercenaries', in M. Keen (ed.), *Medieval Warfare: A History* (Oxford, 2000), pp. 209–29.

Manley, J., 'The archer and the army in Late Saxon England', *Anglo-Saxon Studies in Archaeology and History* 4 (1985), pp. 223–35.

Markus, R., 'Saint Augustine's views on the "Just War"', *SCH* 20 (1983), pp. 1–14.

Martin, M., 'Observations sur l'armament de l'époque mérovingienne précoce', in F. Vallet and M. Kazanski (eds.), *L'Armée Romaine et les Barbares du IIIe au VIIe Siècle* (Paris, 1993), pp. 395–409.

—— 'Kleider machen Leute: Tracht und Bewaffnung in fränkischer Zeit', in K. Fuchs (ed.), *Die Alamannen* (Stuttgart, 1997), pp. 349–58.

McCormick, M., *Eternal Victory: Triumphal Rulership in Late Antiquity, Byzantium and the Early Medieval West* (paperback edition; Cambridge, 1990).

Menghin, W., 'Zur Tragweise frühmittelalterlicher Langschwerter', *Archäologische Korrespondenzblätte* 3 (1973), pp. 243–9.

Menis, G.C., (ed.), *I Longobardi* (2nd edition; Milan 1992).

Metcalf, D.M., 'Large Danegelds in relation to war and kingship. Their implications for monetary history, and some numismatic evidence', in S. Chadwick Hawkes (ed.), *Weapons and Warfare in Anglo-Saxon England*, pp. 179–89.

Muhlberger, S., 'War, warlords, and Christian historians from the fifth to the seventh century', in A. Callander Murray (ed.), *After Rome's Fall: Narrators and Sources of Early Medieval History: Essays presented to Walter Goffart* (Toronto, 1998), pp. 83–98.

Myrhe, B., 'Boathouses and military organization', *MASS*, pp. 169–83.

Nelson, J.L., *Politics and Ritual in Early Medieval Europe* (London, 1986).

—— *Charles the Bald* (London, 1992).

—— 'The quest for peace in a time of war: the Carolingian Brüderkrieg, 840–43', in J. Fried (ed.) *Träger und Instrumentarien des Friedens im hohen und späten Mittelalter* (Vorträge und Forschungen 43; Sigmaringen, 1996), pp. 87–114.

—— *The Frankish World, 750–900* (London, 1996).

—— 'The Frankish Empire', in P. Sawyer (ed.), *The Oxford Illustrated History of the Vikings* (Oxford, 1997), pp. 19–47.

—— 'The ritualisation of Frankish warfare in the ninth century', in G. Halsall (ed.), *Violence and Society in the Early Medieval West*, pp. 90–107.

Nørgård Jørgensen, A., 'Sea defence in Denmark AD 200–1300', *MASS*, pp. 200–9.

—— 'Weapon sets in Gotlandic grave finds from 530–800 AD', in *Chronological Studies of Anglo-Saxon England, Lombard Italy and Vendel Period Sweden*, ed. L. Jørgensen (Arkaeologiske Skrifter 5; Copenhagen 1992).

Oakeshott, E., *Records of the Medieval Sword* (Woodbridge, 1991).

Oexle, J., 'Merowingerzeitliche Pferdebestattungen – Opfer oder Beigaben?' *FmS* 18 (1984), pp. 122–72.

Oman, C.W.C., *A History of the Art of War in the Middle Ages, vol. 1: 378–1278AD* (London, 1924; reprinted 1991).

Pérez Sánchez, D., *El Ejército en la Sociedad Visigoda* (Salamanca, 1989).

Petersen, J., *De Norske Vikingesverd, en typologisk-kronologisk studie over Vikingetidens vaaben* (Videnskappselskapets Skrifter 2. Hist. Filos. Kl. 4; Kristiania, 1919).

Pohl, W., 'Konfliktverlauf und Konfliktbewältigung: Römer und Barbaren im früheren Mittelalter', *FmS* 26 (1992), pp. 165–207.

Pohl, W. and H. Reimitz (eds), *Grenze und Differenz im früheren Mittelalter*, (Österreichische Akadamie der Wissenschaften: Vienna, 2000).

Prinz, F., *Klerus und Krieg im früheren Mittelalter: Untersuchungen zur Rolle der Kirche beim Aufbau der Königsherrschaft* (Monographien zur Geschichte des Mittelalters; Stuttgart, 1971).

Renna, T., 'The idea of peace in the West, c.500–1150', *Journal of Medieval History* 6 (1980), pp. 143–67.

Reuter, T., 'Plunder and tribute in the Carolingian empire', *TRHS*, 5th series, 35 (1985), pp. 75–94.

—— 'The end of Carolingian military expansion', in P. Godman and R. Collins (eds.), *Charlemagne's Heir. New Perspectives on the Reign of Louis the Pious* (Oxford, 1990), pp. 391–405.

—— 'The recruitment of armies in the Early Middle Ages: what can we know?' *MASS*, pp. 32–37.

—— 'The medieval nobility in twentieth-century historiography', in Bentley (ed.), *The Routledge Companion to Historiography*, pp. 177–202.

—— 'Carolingian and Ottonian warfare', in Keen (ed.), *Medieval Warfare: A History*, pp. 13–35.

Reuter T. (ed. and trans.), *The Medieval Nobility* (Amsterdam, 1979).

Reynolds, S., *Fiefs and Vassals: The Medieval Evidence Reinterpreted* (Oxford, 1994).

Roth, H., *Kunst der Völkerwanderungszeit* (Frankfurt-am-Main, 1979).

Rynne, E., 'The impact of the Vikings on Irish weapons', *Atti del Congresso Internazionale delle Scienze Preistoriche e Protohistoriche* 3 (Rome, 1962), pp. 181–4.

Sabin, P., 'The face of Roman battle', *JRS* 90 (2000), pp. 1–17.

Samson, R., 'The Merovingian nobleman's home: castle or villa?' *JMH* 13 (1987), pp. 287–315.

—— 'Knowledge, constraint and power in inaction: the defenseless medieval wall', *Historical Archaeology* 26 (1992), pp. 26–44.

Sánchez-Albornoz, C., 'El ejército y la guerra en el reino Asturleones 718–1037', *SdS*15, pp. 293–428.

Scheibelreiter, G., *Die barbarische Gesellschaft, Mentalitätsgeschichte der europäischen Achsenzeit 5.–8. Jahrhundert* (Darmstadt, 1999).

Schmauder, M., 'Überlegungen zur östlichen Grenze des karolingischen Reiches unter Karl dem Grossen', in Pohl and Reimitz (eds.), *Grenze und Differenz im früheren Mittelalter*, pp. 57–97.

Schmiedt, G., 'Le fortificazioni altomedievali in Italia viste dal'aero', *SdS*15, pp. 800–927.

Shaw, B.D., 'War and violence', in G. Bowersock, P.R.L. Brown and O. Grabar (ed.), *Late Antiquity. A Guide to the Postclassical World* (Cambridge, MA, and London, 1999), pp. 130–69.

Siegmund, F., 'Kleidung und Bewaffnung der Männer im östlichen Frankenreich', in A. Wieczorek, P. Périn, K. von Welck and W. Menghin (ed.), *Die Franken: Wegbereiter Europas 5. bis 8. Jahrhundert* (2nd edition; Mainz 1997), pp. 691–706.

Smyth, A.P., *Scandinavian Kings in the British Isles, 850–880* (Oxford, 1977).

Southern, P. and K. Dixon, *The Late Roman Army* (London, 1996).

Steuer, H., 'Bewaffnung und Kriegsführung der Sachsen und Franken', in C. Stiegemann and M. Wemhoff (eds.), *799: Kunst und Kultur der Karolingerzeit: Beiträge zum Katalog der Ausstellung* (Mainz, 1999), pp. 310–22.

Stout, M., *The Irish Ringfort* (Irish Settlement Studies 5; Dublin, 1997).

Swanton, M.J., *The Spearheads of the Anglo-Saxon Settlements* (London, 1973).

Tabacco, G., 'Il regno Italico nei secoli IX–XI', *SdS*15, pp. 763–90.

Thompson, E.A., *The Goths in Spain* (Oxford, 1969).

—— *Romans and Barbarians. The Decline of the Western Empire* (Madison, WI, 1982).

Tomlin, R.S.O., 'The army of the late empire', in J.S. Wacher (ed.), *The Roman World* (London, 1987), pp. 107–23.

Trimpe Burger, J.A., 'The geometrical fortress of Oost-Souburg (Zealand)', *Château Gaillard* 7 (Caen, 1975), pp. 215–9.

Underwood, R., *Anglo-Saxon Weapons and Warfare* (Stroud, 1999).

Van Creveld, M., *Supplying War: Logistics from Wallerstein to Patton* (Cambridge 1977).

Verbruggen, J.F., 'L'Armée et la stratégie de Charlemagne', in H. Beumann (ed.), *Karl der Grosse: Lebenswerk und Nachleben, vol. 1, Persönlichkeit und Geschichte* (Düsseldorf, 1965), pp. 420–36.

—— *The Art of Warfare in Western Europe during the Middle Ages* (2nd rev. edition, trans. S. Willard and Mrs R.W. Southern; Woodbridge 1997).

Wainwright, F.T., 'Nechtansmere', *Antiquity* 22 (1948), pp. 82–97.

—— 'The battles at Corbridge', in his *Scandinavian England* (Chichester, 1975), pp. 163–79.

Wallace Hadrill, J.M., 'War and peace in the early Middle Ages', in his *Early Medieval History* (Oxford, 1975), pp. 19–38.

Wenham, S.J., 'Anatomical interpretations of Anglo-Saxon weapon injuries', in Chadwick Hawkes (ed.), *Weapons and Warfare in Anglo-Saxon England*, pp. 123–39.

Werner, J., 'Bewaffnung und Waffenbeigabe in der Merowingerzeit', *SdS*15, pp. 95–108.

Werner, K.F., 'Heeresorganisation und Kriegführung im deutschen Königreich des 10. und 11. Jahrhunderts', *SdS*15, pp. 791–843.

—— 'Armées et guerres en Neustrie', in P. Périn and L.C. Feffer (eds.), *La Neustrie: Les Pays au Nord de la Loire de Dagobert à Charles le Chauve (VIIe–IXe Siècles)* (Paris, 1985), pp. 49–55.

Westphal, H., 'Zur Bewaffnung und Ausrüstung bei Sachsen und Franken: Gemeinsamkeiten und Unterschiede am Beispiel der Sachkultur', in C. Stiegemann and M. Wemhoff (eds.), *799: Kunst und Kultur der Karolingerzeit: Beiträge zum Katalog der Ausstellung* (Mainz, 1999), pp. 323–7.

Whitby, M., 'The army, c.402–602', in A. Cameron, B. Ward-Perkins an M. Whitby (eds.), *The Cambridge Ancient History vol. 14: Late Antiquity: Empire and Successors, A.D. 425–600* (Cambridge, 2000), pp. 288–314.

White, L.T., *Medieval Technology and Social Change* (Oxford, 1962).

Wickham, C.J., 'The other transition: from the ancient world to feudalism', *P&P* 103 (1984), pp. 3–36.

Williams, G., 'Military institutions and royal power', in M.P. Brown and C.A. Farr (eds.), *Mercia. An Anglo-Saxon Kingdom in Europe* (London, 2001), pp. 295–309.

Wilson, D.M., 'Some neglected late Anglo-Saxon swords', *Medieval Archaeology* 9 (1965), pp. 32–54.

Wolfram, H., The creation of the Carolingian frontier system, c.800', in W. Pohl, I.N. Wood and H. Reimitz (eds.), *The Transformation of Frontiers: From Late Antiquity to the Carolingians* (Leiden, 2001), pp. 233–45.

Wood, I.N., 'The barbarian invasions and first settlements', in A. Cameron and P. Garnsey (eds.) *Cambridge Ancient History, Vol. 13: The Late Empire, A.D.337–425* (Cambridge, 1998), pp. 516–37.

Woolf, R., 'The ideal of men dying with their lord in the *Germania* and in *The Battle of Maldon*', *ASE* 5 (1976), pp. 63–81.

Wormald, C.P., 'Viking Studies: whence and whither?' in R.T. Farrell (ed.), *The Vikings* (Chichester, 1982), pp. 128–53.

INDEX

Lightning Source UK Ltd.
Milton Keynes UK
UKOW01f0414111017

310780UK00003B/16/P